Shojo Beat

VAMPIRE KNIGHT

Story & Art by
Matsuri
Hino

Vol. 7

VAMPIRE KNIGHT

Contents

The Story of VAMPIRE KNIGHT

1 Cross Academy, a private boarding school, is where the Day Class and the Night Class coexist. The Night Class—a group of beautiful elite students—are all vampires!

2 Four years ago, the pureblood Shizuka Hio bit Zero and robbed him of his family. Yuki has vowed to protect him. Shizuka's blood is necessary to save Zero from madness. Yuki tries to offer herself to Shizuka to save him, but Kaname secretly kills Shizuka.

3 Yuki tries to regain her forgotten memories, but mysterious powers prevent her from doing so. Yuki panics, and Zero holds her. What happened to Yuki in the past? Meanwhile, Kaname senses the resurrection of someone. Shiki is taken to meet a blood-covered man lying in a coffin who says he's in need of Shiki's body!

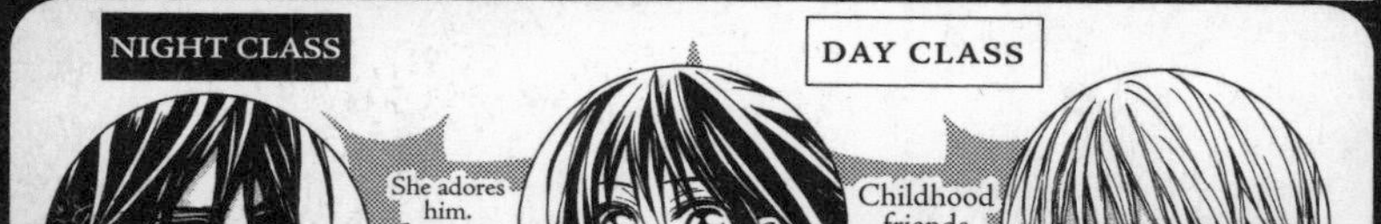

NIGHT CLASS
DAY CLASS
She adores him.
He saved her 10 years ago.
Childhood friends
Foster Father
KANAME KURAN
Night Class President and pureblood vampire. Yuki adores him.
TAKUMA ICHIJO
Night Class Vice President. He and Kaname are old friends.
YUKI CROSS
The heroine. The adopted daughter of the Headmaster, and a Guardian who protects Cross Academy.
HEADMASTER CROSS
ZERO KIRYU
Yuki's childhood friend, and a Guardian.Shizuka turned him into a vampire. He will eventually lose his sanity, falling to Level E.
※Purebloods are vampires who do not have a single drop of human blood in their lineage. They are very powerful, and they can turn humans into vampires by drinking their blood.
NIGHT CLASS STUDENTS
COUSINS
HANABUSA AIDO
Nickname: Idol
AKATSUKI KAIN
Nickname: Wild
SENRI SHIKI
He does things at his own pace.
ICHIRU
Zero's younger twin brother. He betrayed his family and served Shizuka.

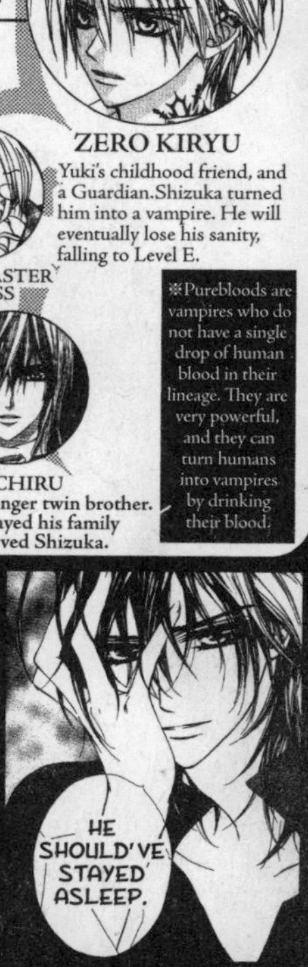

HE SHOULD'VE STAYED ASLEEP.

The one who rises from the darkness... What is his relationship to Kaname? He attacks Shiki?!

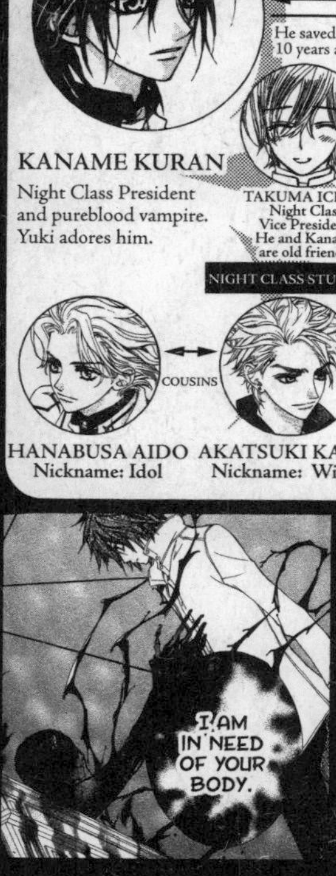

I AM IN NEED OF YOUR BODY.

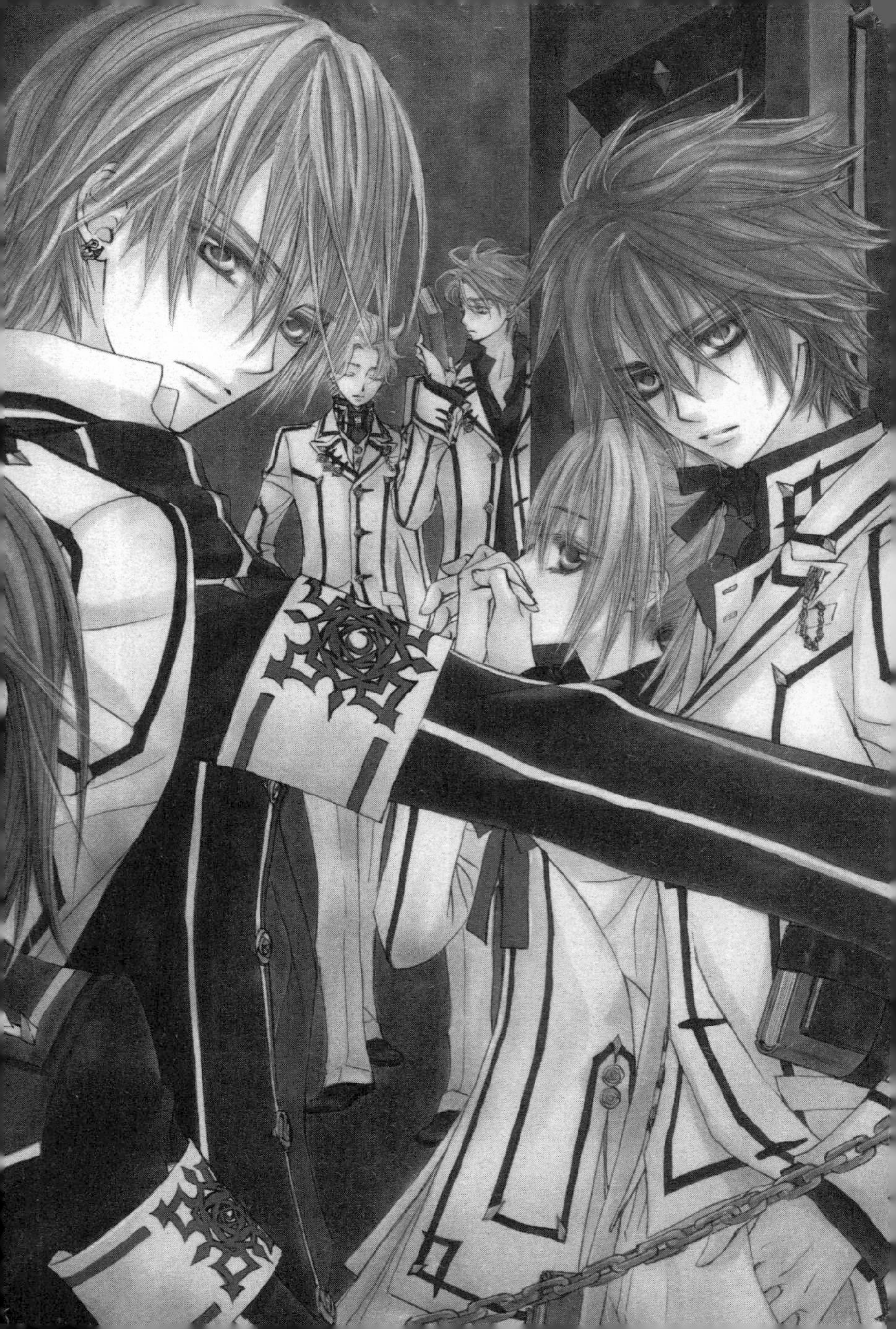

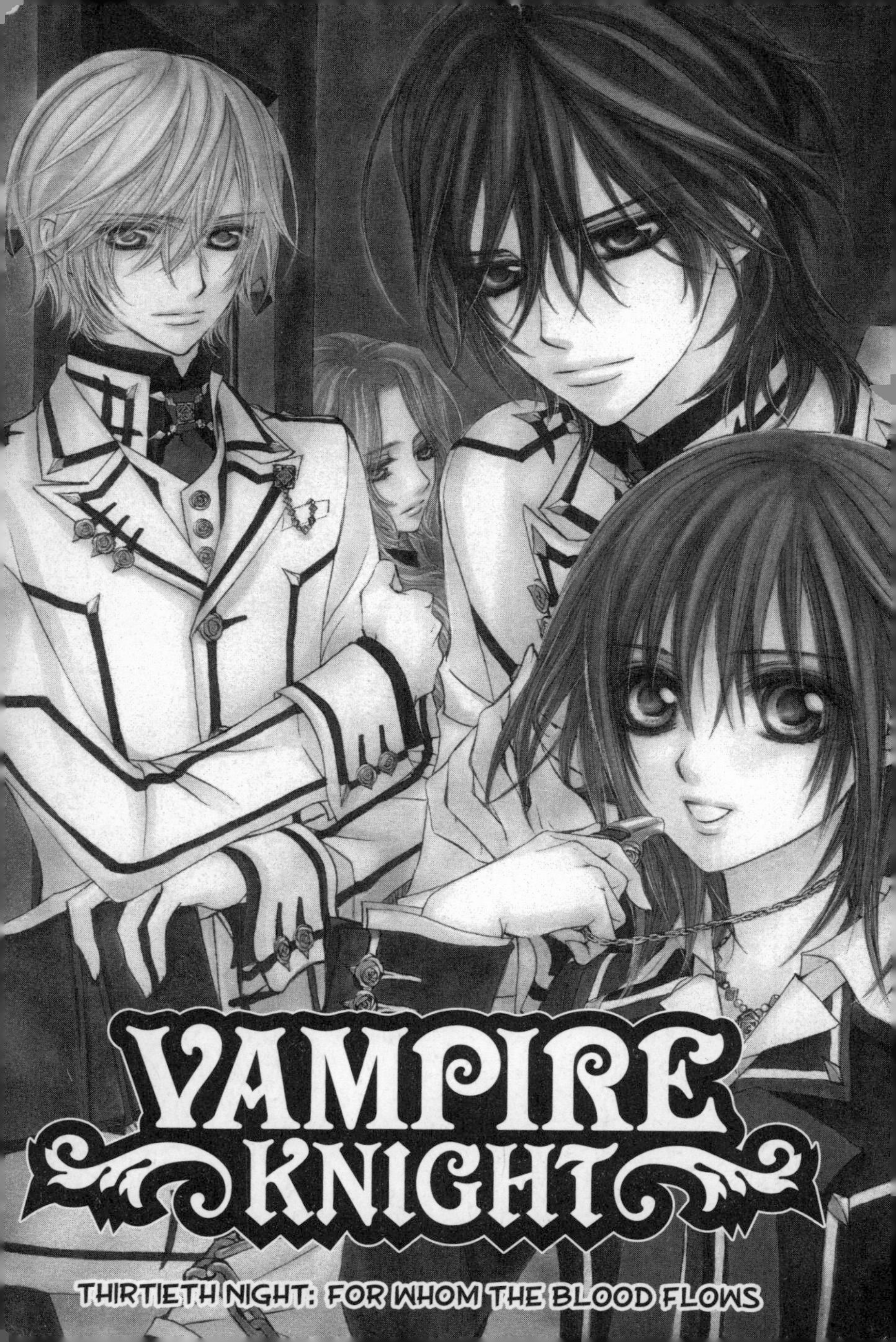
VAMPIRE KNIGHT
THIRTIETH NIGHT: FOR WHOM THE BLOOD FLOWS

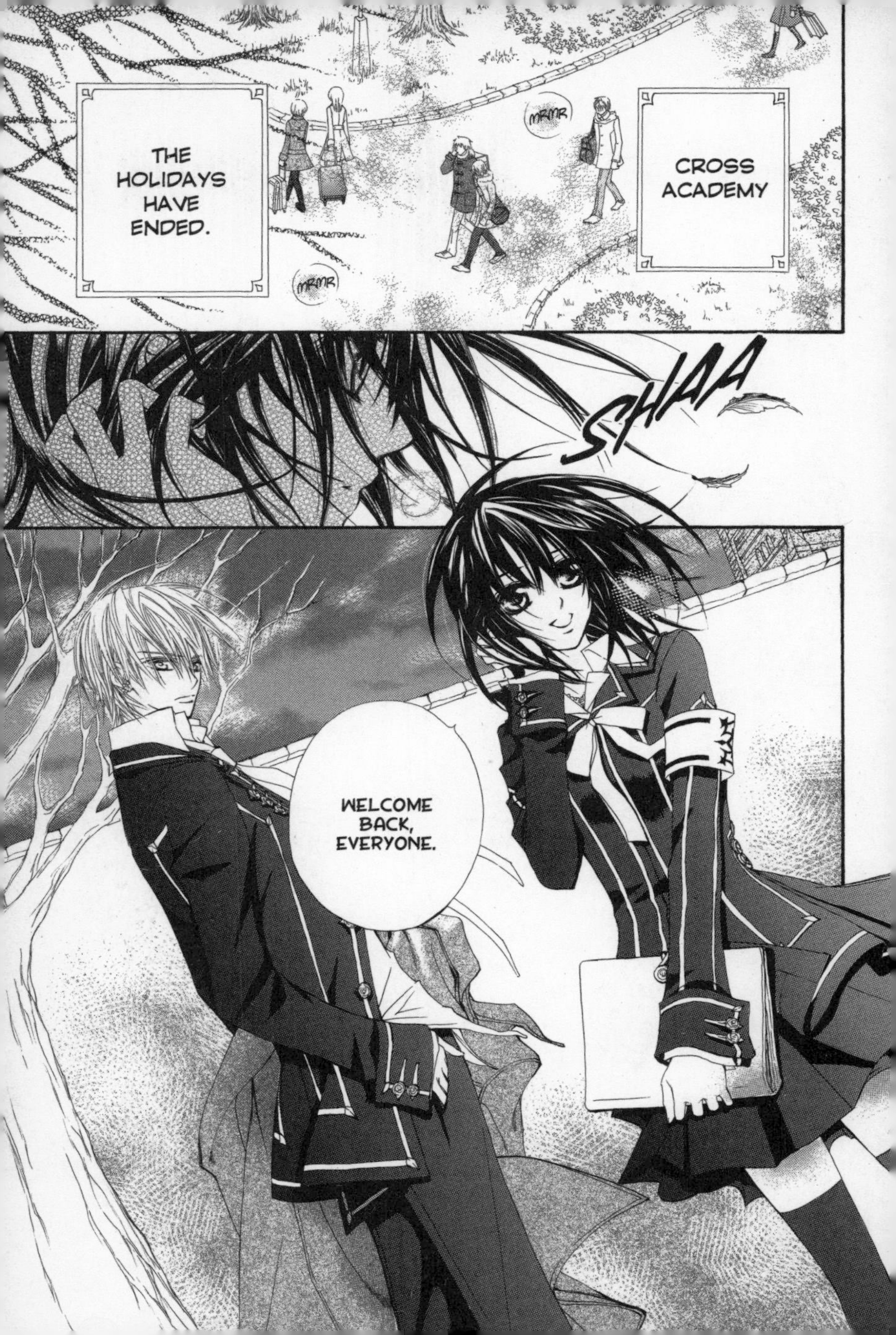
CROSS ACADEMY
MRMR
THE HOLIDAYS HAVE ENDED.
MRMR
SHAA
WELCOME BACK, EVERYONE.

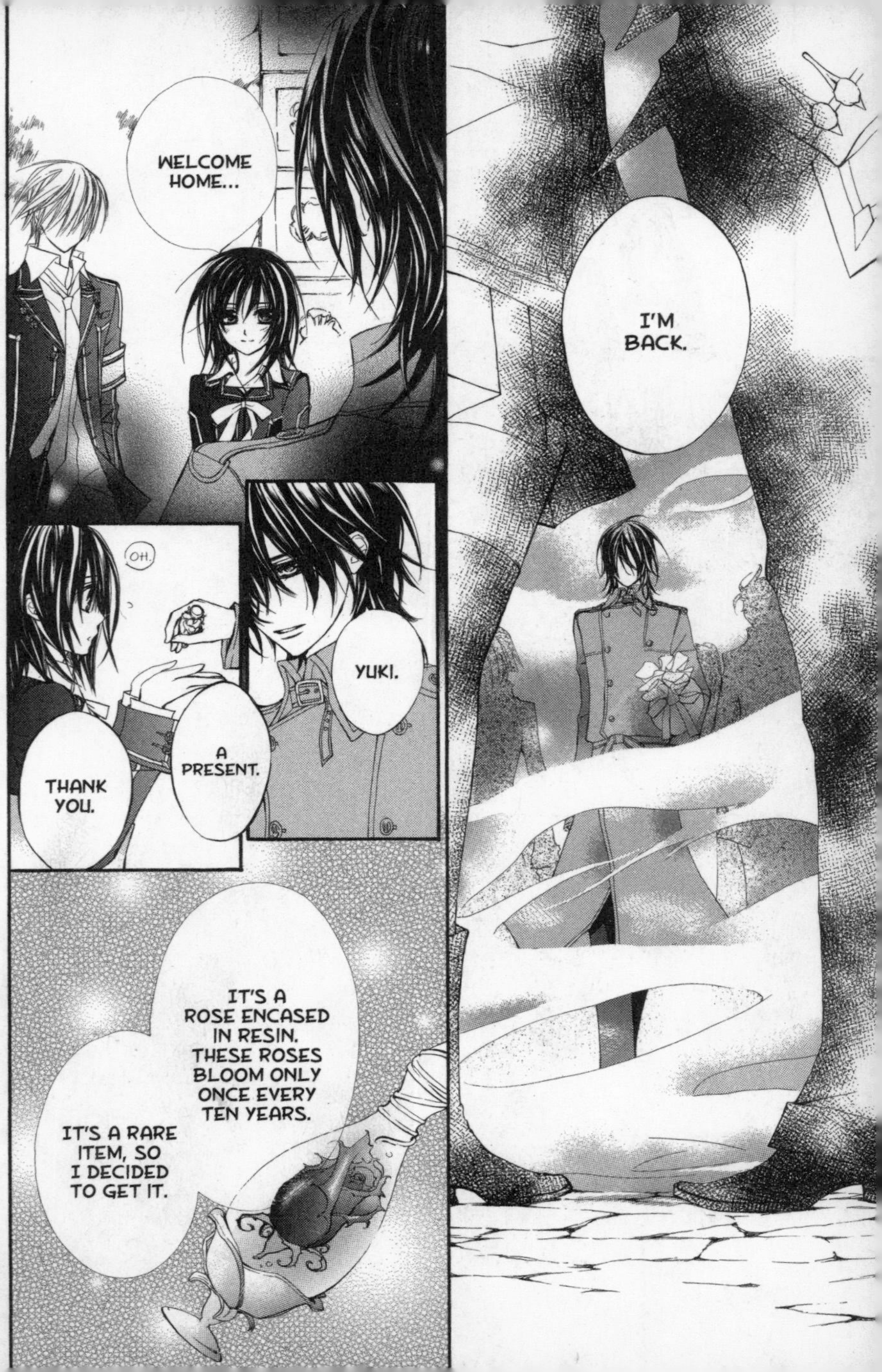
I'M BACK.
WELCOME HOME...
YUKI.
A PRESENT.
OH.
THANK YOU.
IT'S A ROSE ENCASED IN RESIN. THESE ROSES BLOOM ONLY ONCE EVERY TEN YEARS.
IT'S A RARE ITEM, SO I DECIDED TO GET IT.

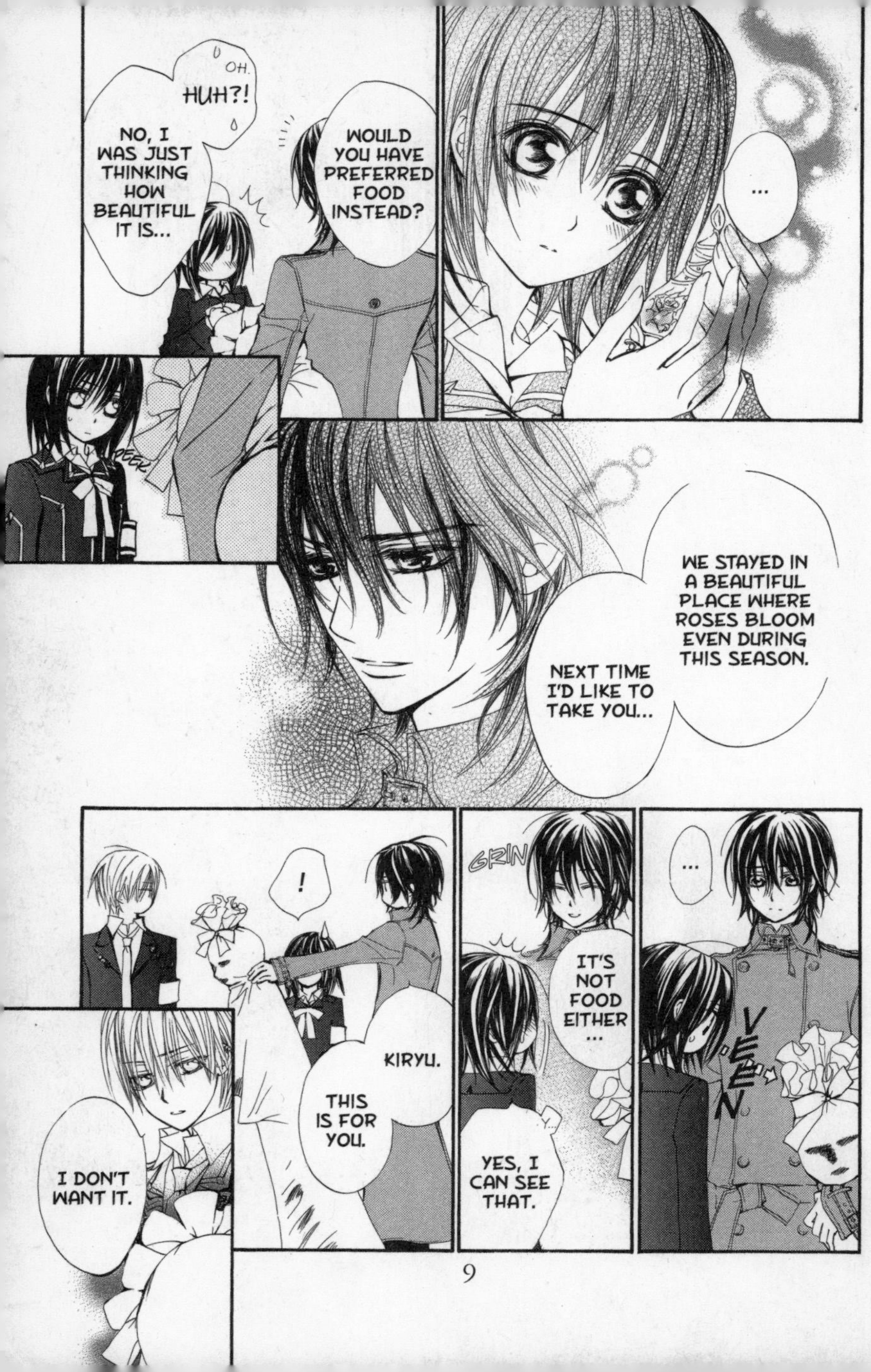
...
WOULD YOU HAVE PREFERRED FOOD INSTEAD?
HUH?!
OH.
NO, I WAS JUST THINKING HOW BEAUTIFUL IT IS...
PEEK
WE STAYED IN A BEAUTIFUL PLACE WHERE ROSES BLOOM EVEN DURING THIS SEASON.
NEXT TIME I'D LIKE TO TAKE YOU...
...
VEEN
GRIN
IT'S NOT FOOD EITHER ...
YES, I CAN SEE THAT.
!
KIRYU.
THIS IS FOR YOU.
I DON'T WANT IT.

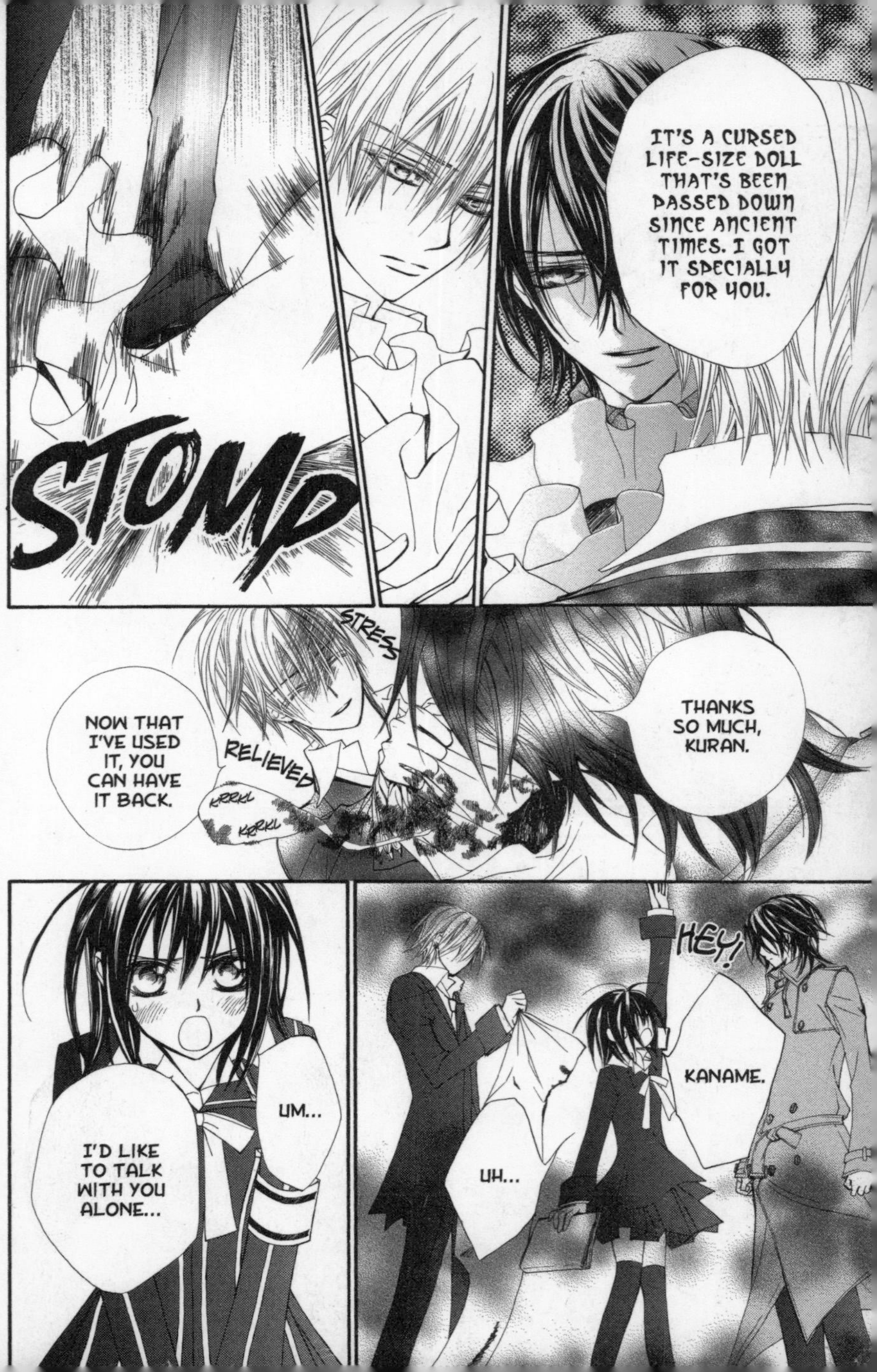
IT'S A CURSED LIFE-SIZE DOLL THAT'S BEEN PASSED DOWN SINCE ANCIENT TIMES. I GOT IT SPECIALLY FOR YOU.
STOMP
STRESS
THANKS SO MUCH, KURAN.
NOW THAT I'VE USED IT, YOU CAN HAVE IT BACK.
RELIEVED
KRRKL
KRRKL
HEY!
KANAME.
UH...
UM...
I'D LIKE TO TALK WITH YOU ALONE...

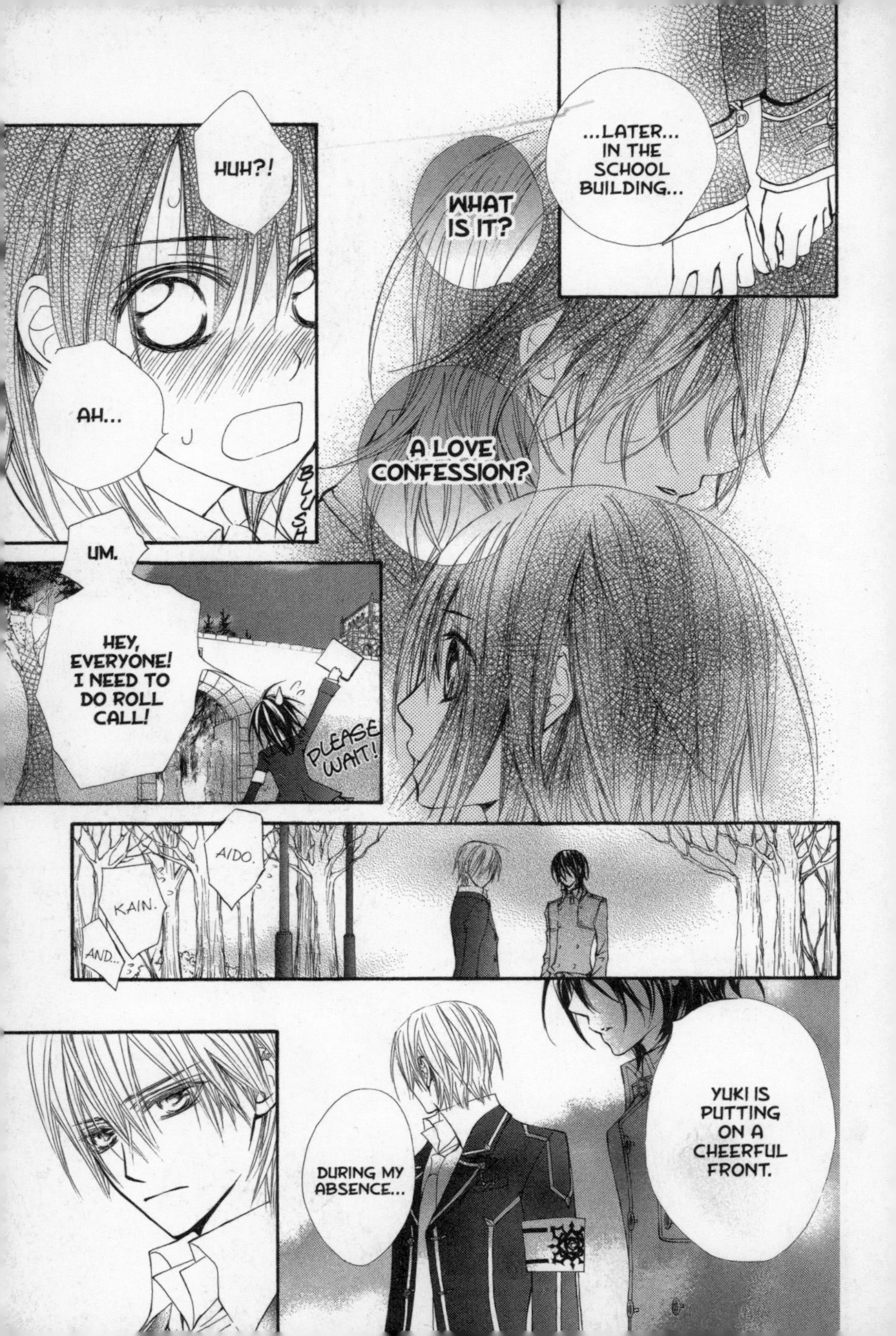
...LATER... IN THE SCHOOL BUILDING...
WHAT IS IT?
A LOVE CONFESSION?
HUH?!
AH...
BLUSH
UM.
HEY, EVERYONE! I NEED TO DO ROLL CALL!
PLEASE WAIT!
AIDO.
KAIN.
AND...
YUKI IS PUTTING ON A CHEERFUL FRONT.
DURING MY ABSENCE...

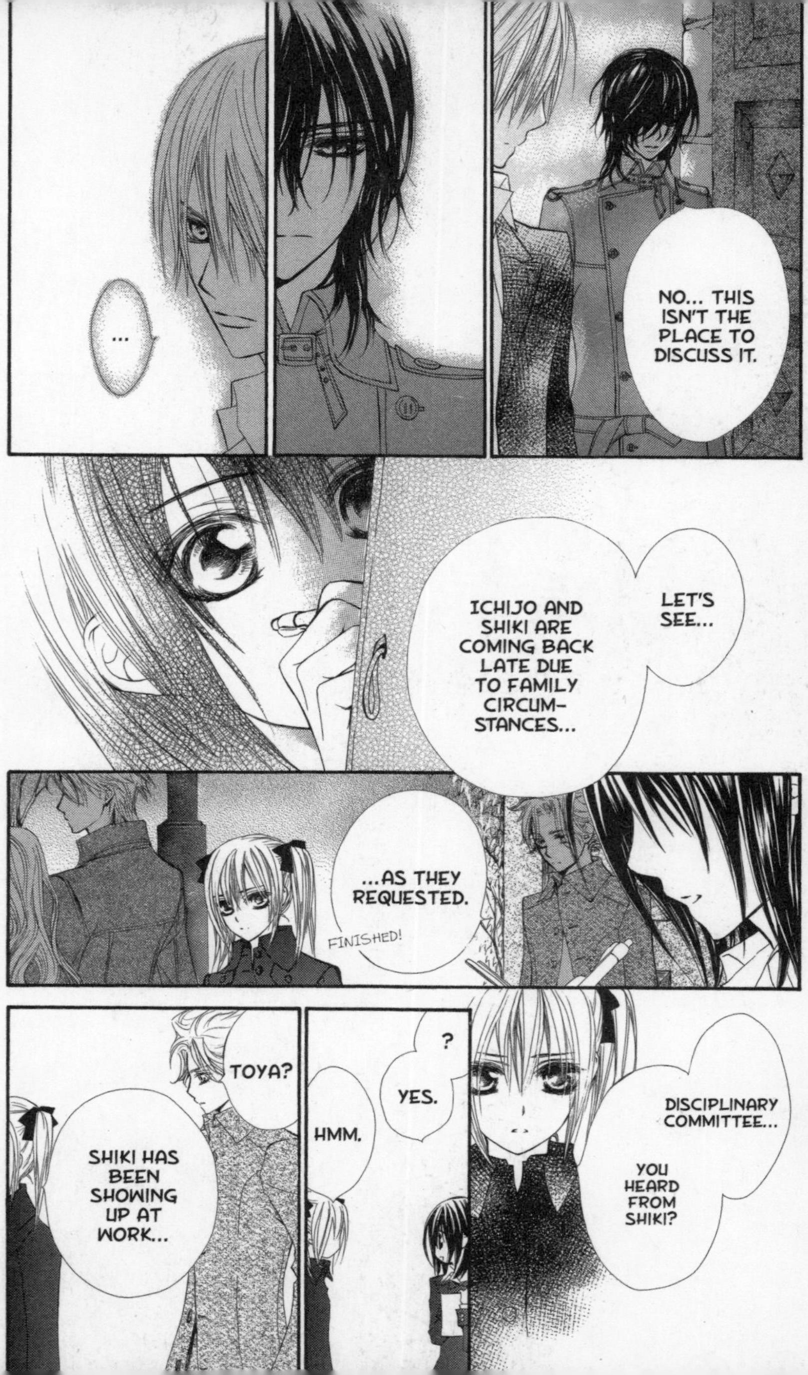
NO... THIS ISN'T THE PLACE TO DISCUSS IT.
...
LET'S SEE...
ICHIJO AND SHIKI ARE COMING BACK LATE DUE TO FAMILY CIRCUMSTANCES...
...AS THEY REQUESTED.
FINISHED!
DISCIPLINARY COMMITTEE...
YOU HEARD FROM SHIKI?
?
YES.
HMM.
TOYA?
SHIKI HAS BEEN SHOWING UP AT WORK...

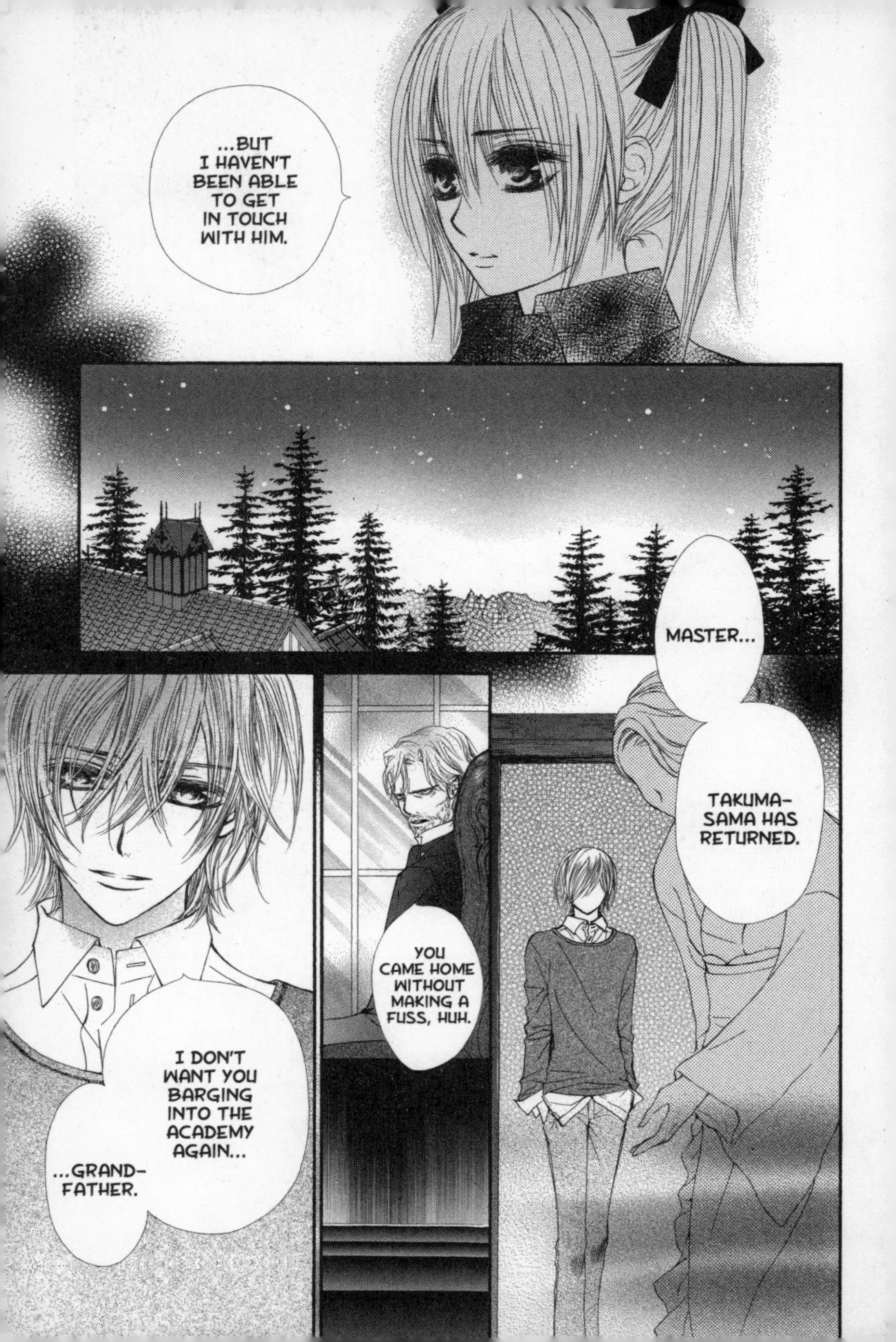
...BUT I HAVEN'T BEEN ABLE TO GET IN TOUCH WITH HIM.
MASTER...
TAKUMA-SAMA HAS RETURNED.
YOU CAME HOME WITHOUT MAKING A FUSS, HUH.
I DON'T WANT YOU BARGING INTO THE ACADEMY AGAIN...
...GRAND-FATHER.

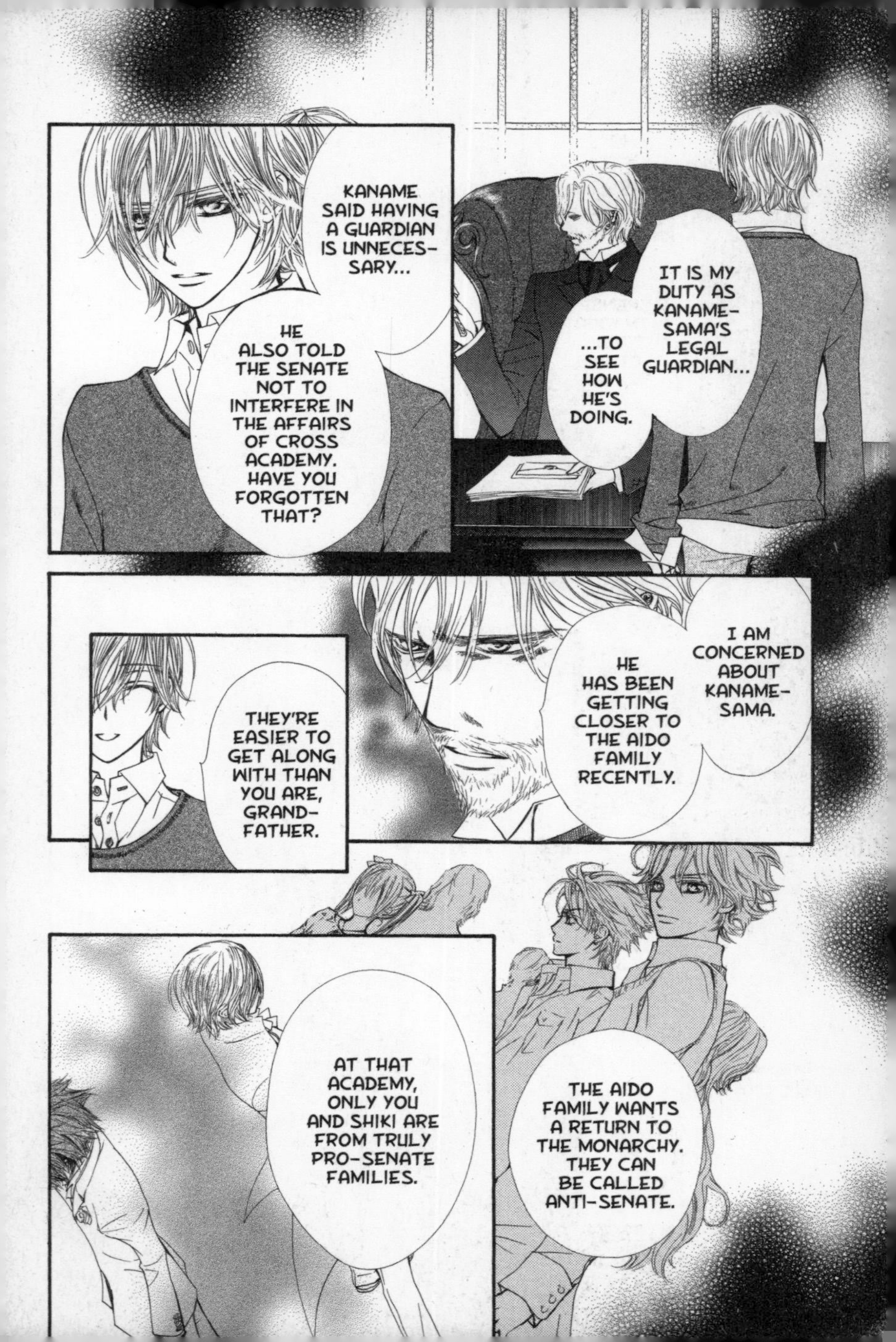
IT IS MY DUTY AS KANAME-SAMA'S LEGAL GUARDIAN...
...TO SEE HOW HE'S DOING.
KANAME SAID HAVING A GUARDIAN IS UNNECES-SARY...
HE ALSO TOLD THE SENATE NOT TO INTERFERE IN THE AFFAIRS OF CROSS ACADEMY. HAVE YOU FORGOTTEN THAT?
I AM CONCERNED ABOUT KANAME-SAMA.
HE HAS BEEN GETTING CLOSER TO THE AIDO FAMILY RECENTLY.
THEY'RE EASIER TO GET ALONG WITH THAN YOU ARE, GRAND-FATHER.
THE AIDO FAMILY WANTS A RETURN TO THE MONARCHY. THEY CAN BE CALLED ANTI-SENATE.
AT THAT ACADEMY, ONLY YOU AND SHIKI ARE FROM TRULY PRO-SENATE FAMILIES.

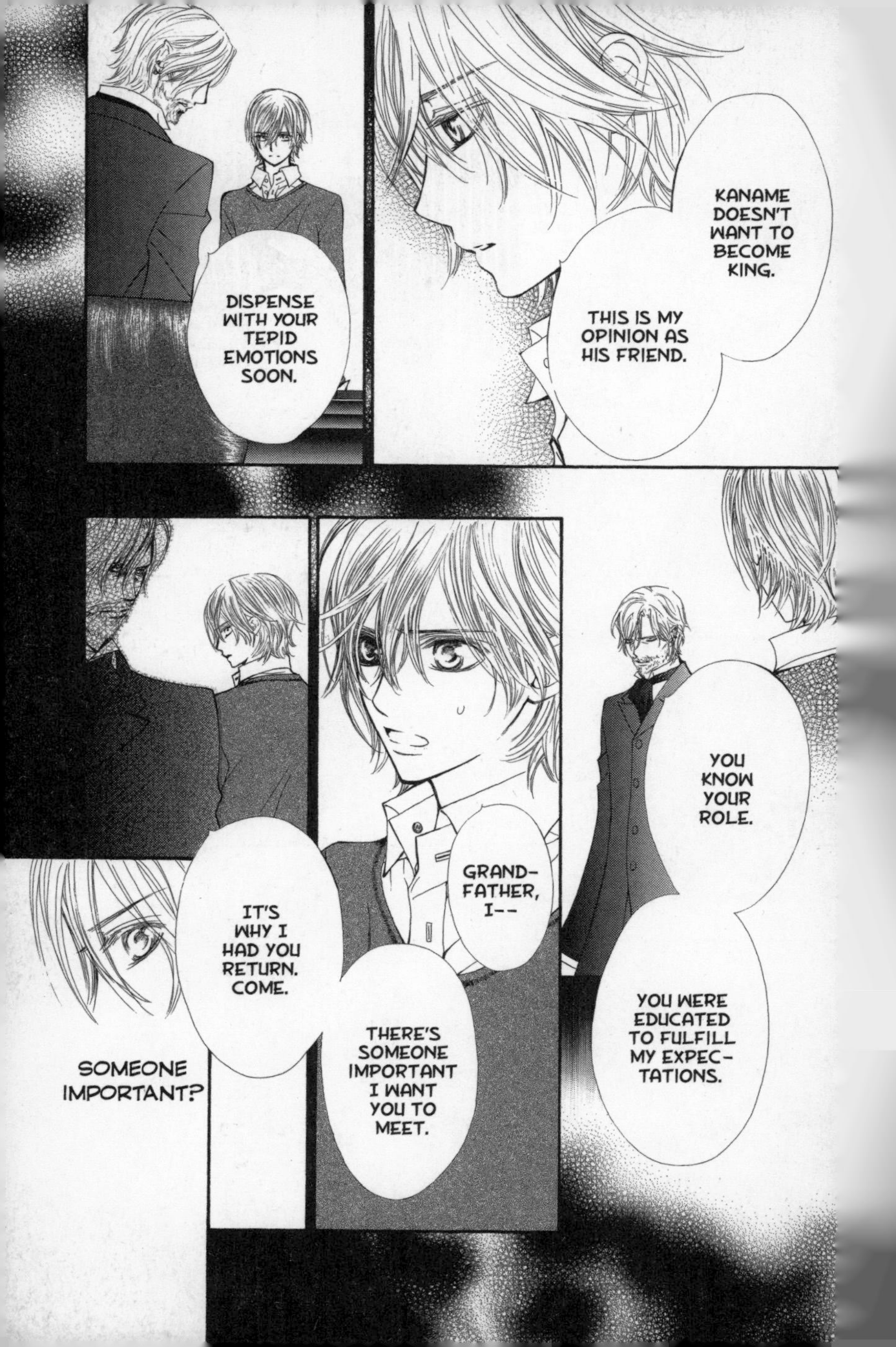
KANAME DOESN'T WANT TO BECOME KING.
THIS IS MY OPINION AS HIS FRIEND.
DISPENSE WITH YOUR TEPID EMOTIONS SOON.
YOU KNOW YOUR ROLE.
YOU WERE EDUCATED TO FULFILL MY EXPECTATIONS.
GRAND-FATHER, I--
IT'S WHY I HAD YOU RETURN. COME.
THERE'S SOMEONE IMPORTANT I WANT YOU TO MEET.
SOMEONE IMPORTANT?

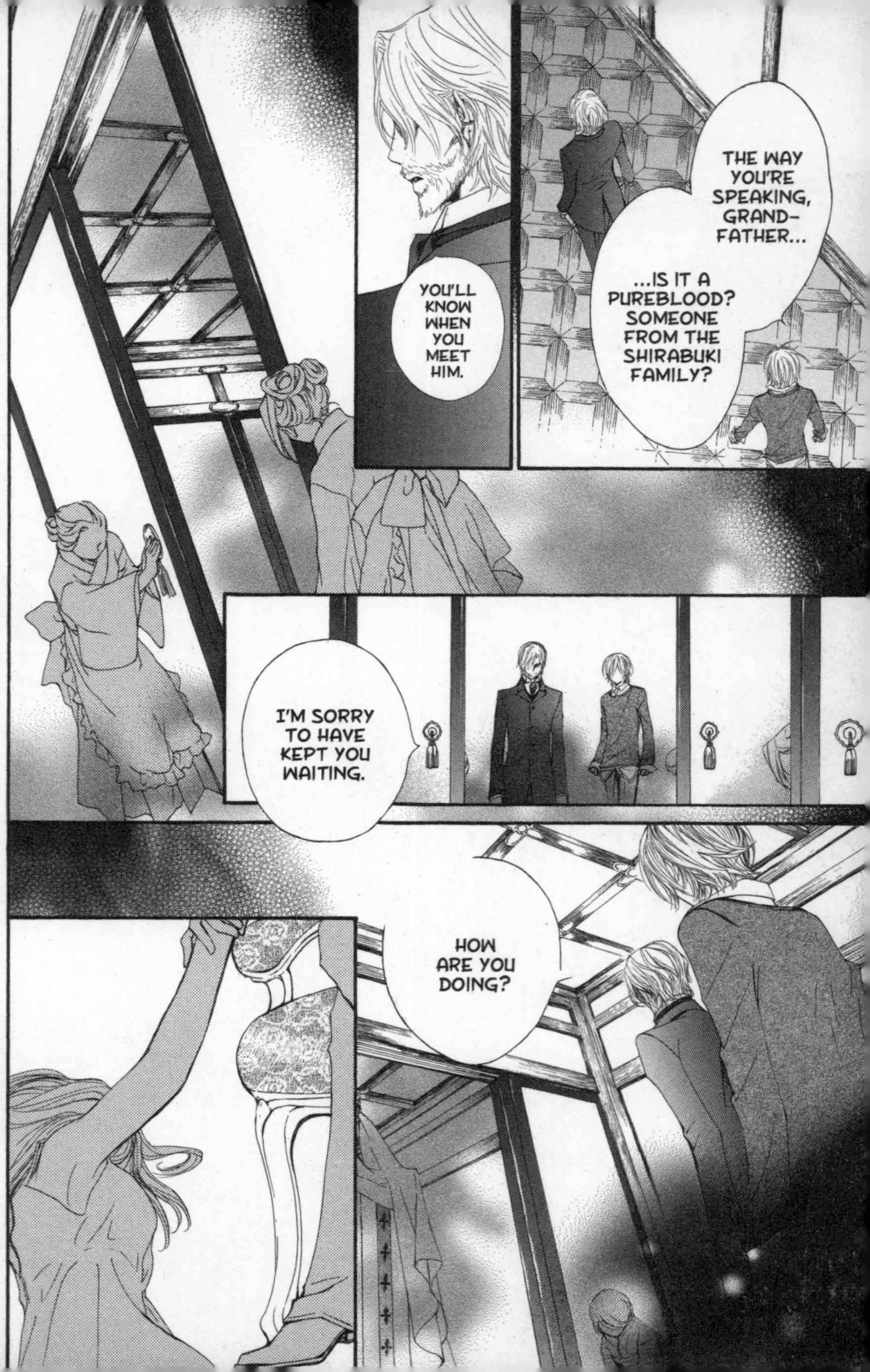
THE WAY YOU'RE SPEAKING, GRAND-FATHER...
...IS IT A PUREBLOOD? SOMEONE FROM THE SHIRABUKI FAMILY?
YOU'LL KNOW WHEN YOU MEET HIM.
I'M SORRY TO HAVE KEPT YOU WAITING.
HOW ARE YOU DOING?

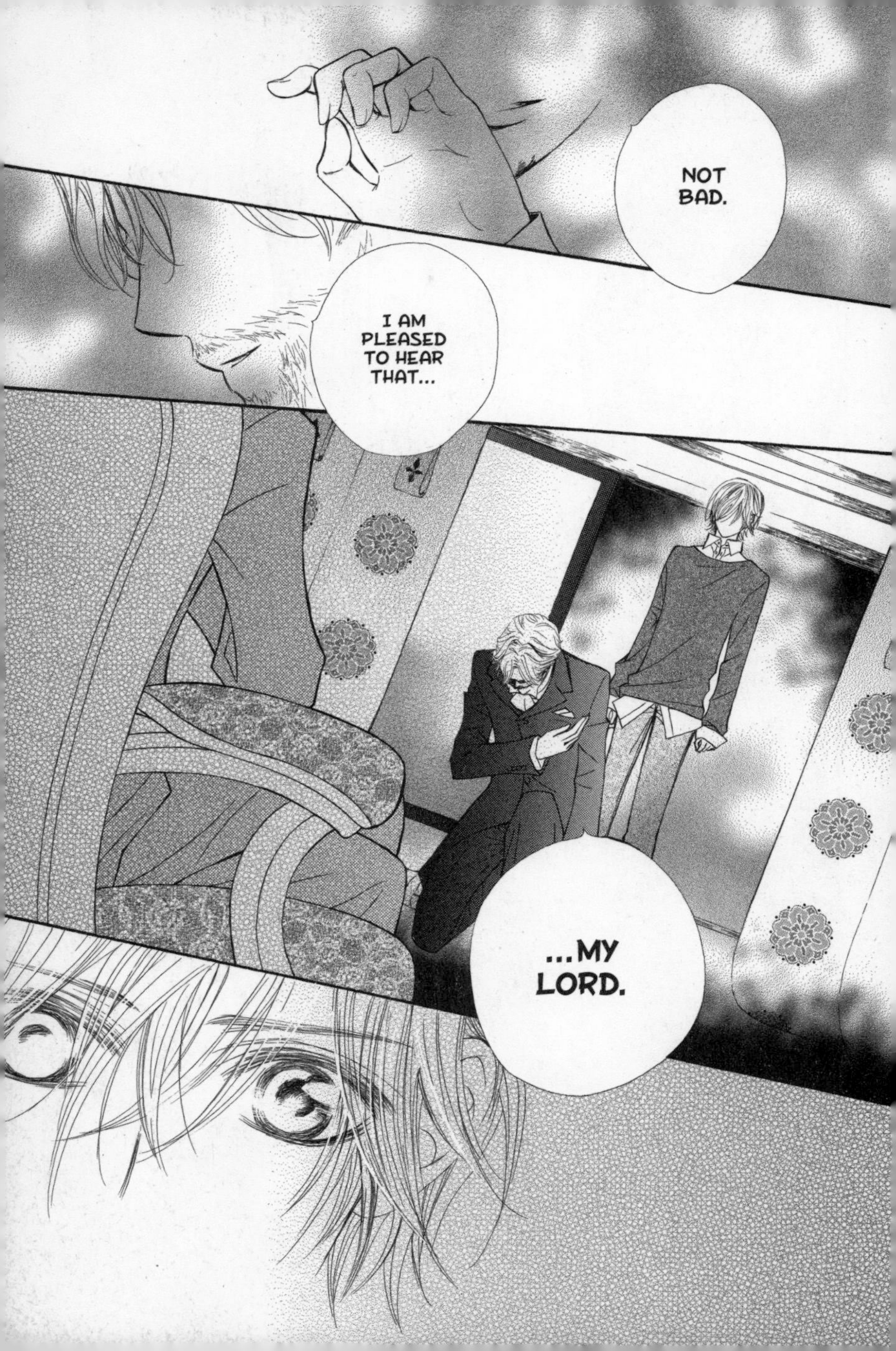
NOT BAD.
I AM PLEASED TO HEAR THAT...
...MY LORD.

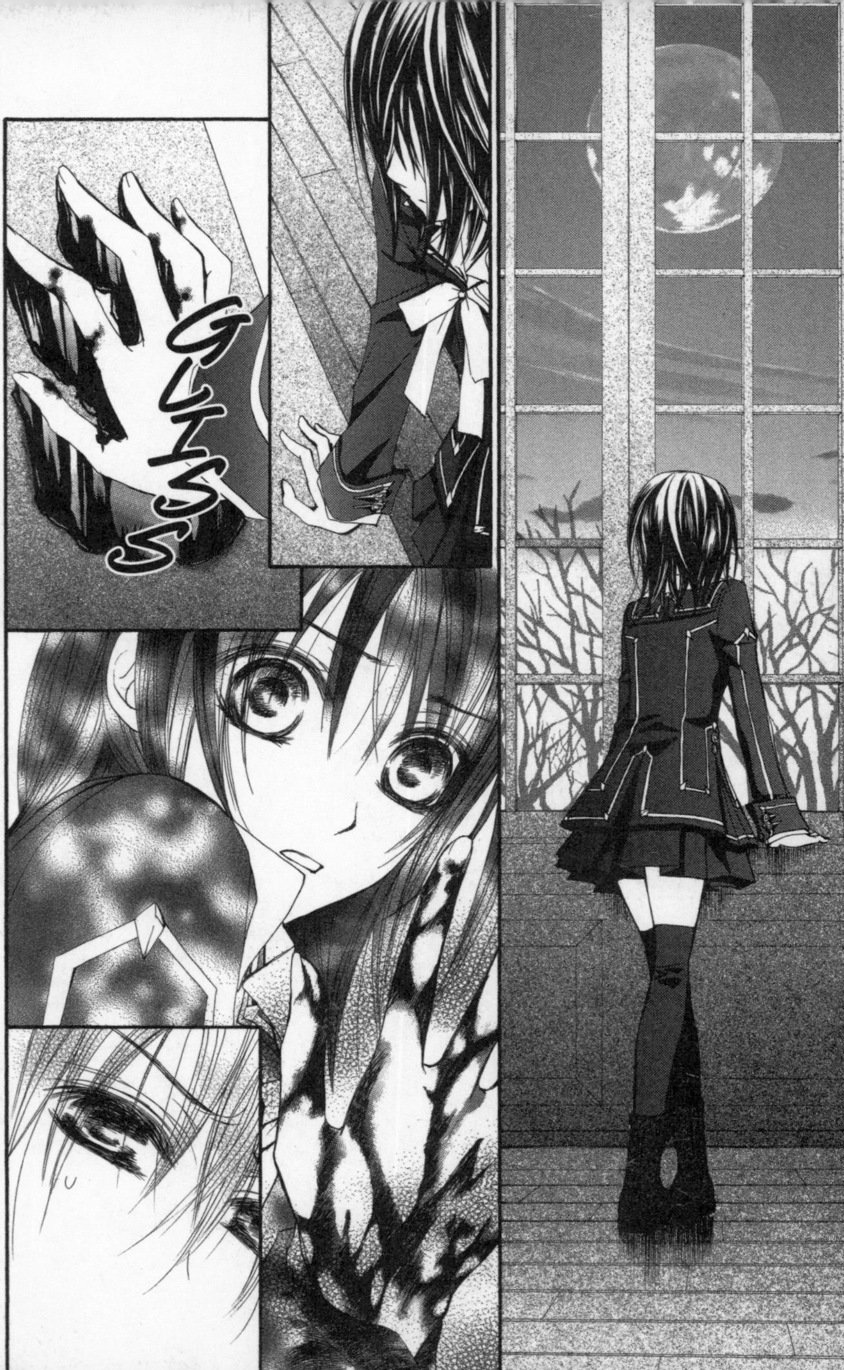
GLISSS

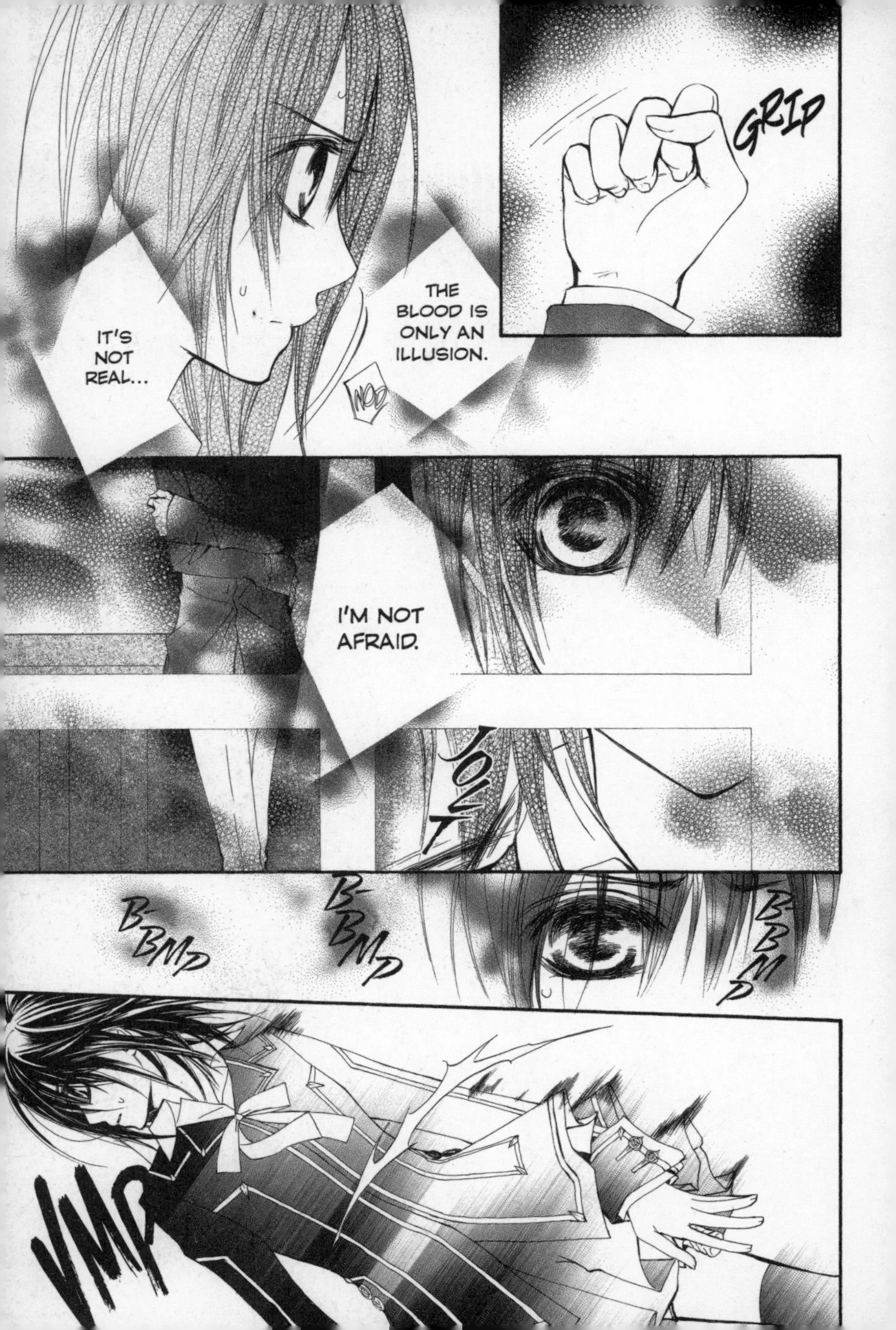
GRIP
THE BLOOD IS ONLY AN ILLUSION.
NOD
IT'S NOT REAL...
I'M NOT AFRAID.
JOLT
B-BMP
B-BMP
B-BMP
VMP

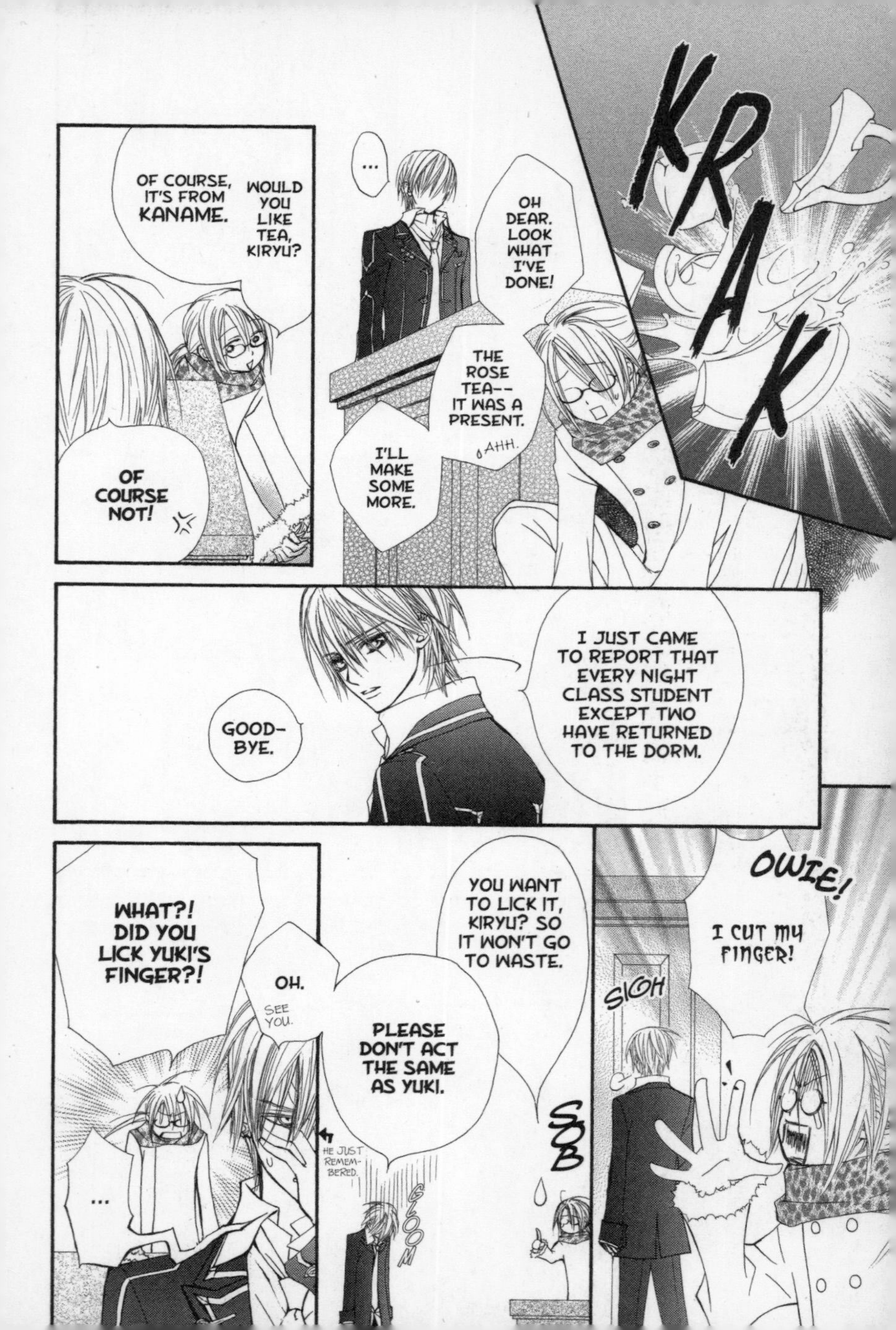
KRAK
OH DEAR. LOOK WHAT I'VE DONE!
...
THE ROSE TEA-- IT WAS A PRESENT.
AHH.
I'LL MAKE SOME MORE.
OF COURSE, IT'S FROM KANAME.
WOULD YOU LIKE TEA, KIRYU?
OF COURSE NOT!
I JUST CAME TO REPORT THAT EVERY NIGHT CLASS STUDENT EXCEPT TWO HAVE RETURNED TO THE DORM.
GOOD-BYE.
OWIE!
I CUT MY FINGER!
SIGH
YOU WANT TO LICK IT, KIRYU? SO IT WON'T GO TO WASTE.
SOB
PLEASE DON'T ACT THE SAME AS YUKI.
GLOOM
HE JUST REMEMBERED.
WHAT?! DID YOU LICK YUKI'S FINGER?!
OH.
SEE YOU.
...

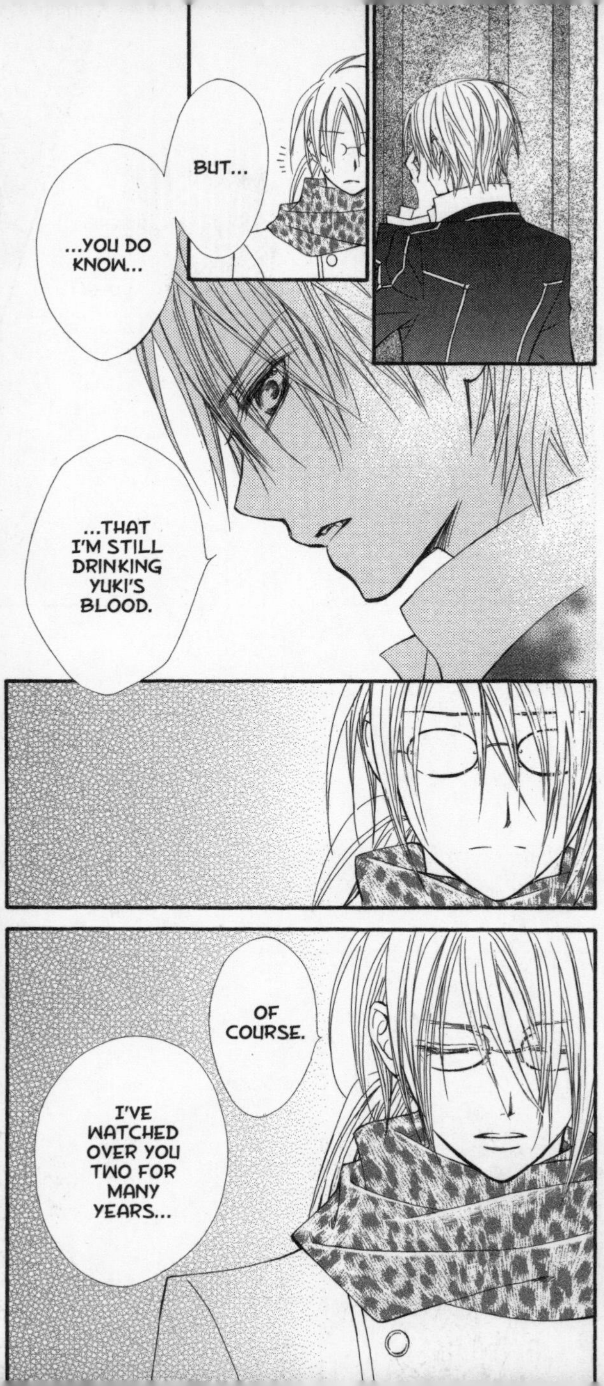
BUT...
...YOU DO KNOW...
...THAT I'M STILL DRINKING YUKI'S BLOOD.
OF COURSE.
I'VE WATCHED OVER YOU TWO FOR MANY YEARS...

I

This is *Vampire Knight*, vol. 7!!! Douhaa!! (↑ I have no idea what this is, but it's my soul shouting.)

Thank you, everyone... I'm able to continue because there are people who read my manga.

Thank you for your letters too... I read them as rewards when I feel "I did my best!!" or for some pep when I'm feeling low. (I feel bad about not being able to reply. But instead I'll do my best so I can draw interesting manga.)

◆

This volume contains a bonus manga. I didn't feel it was appropriate to insert bonus funnies in between the chapters. I'll do my best in the next volume!! So please excuse me... (I have lots of material. As always, it's silly...)

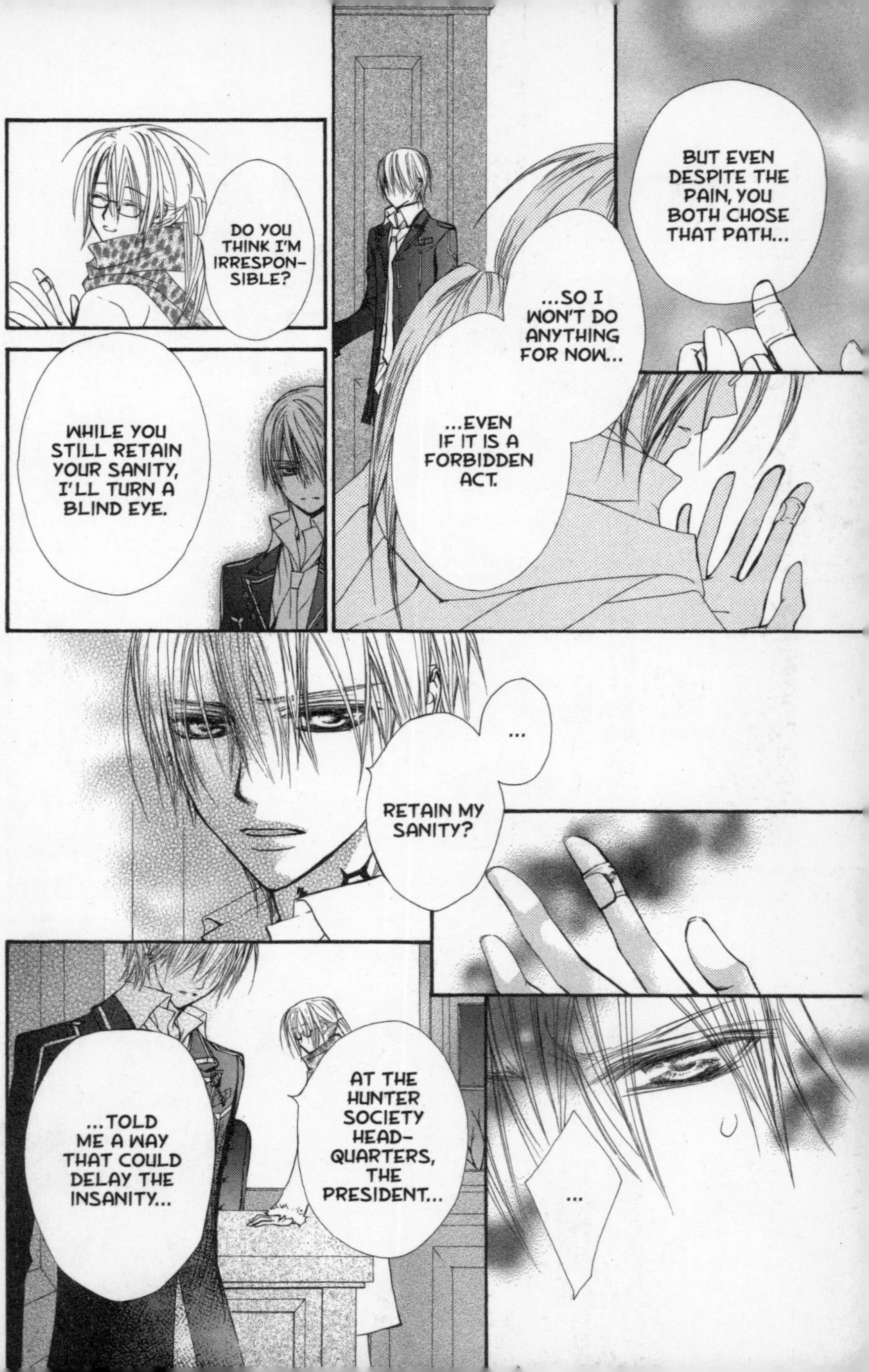
BUT EVEN DESPITE THE PAIN, YOU BOTH CHOSE THAT PATH...
...SO I WON'T DO ANYTHING FOR NOW...
...EVEN IF IT IS A FORBIDDEN ACT.
DO YOU THINK I'M IRRESPONSIBLE?
WHILE YOU STILL RETAIN YOUR SANITY, I'LL TURN A BLIND EYE.
...
RETAIN MY SANITY?
...
AT THE HUNTER SOCIETY HEAD-QUARTERS, THE PRESIDENT...
...TOLD ME A WAY THAT COULD DELAY THE INSANITY...

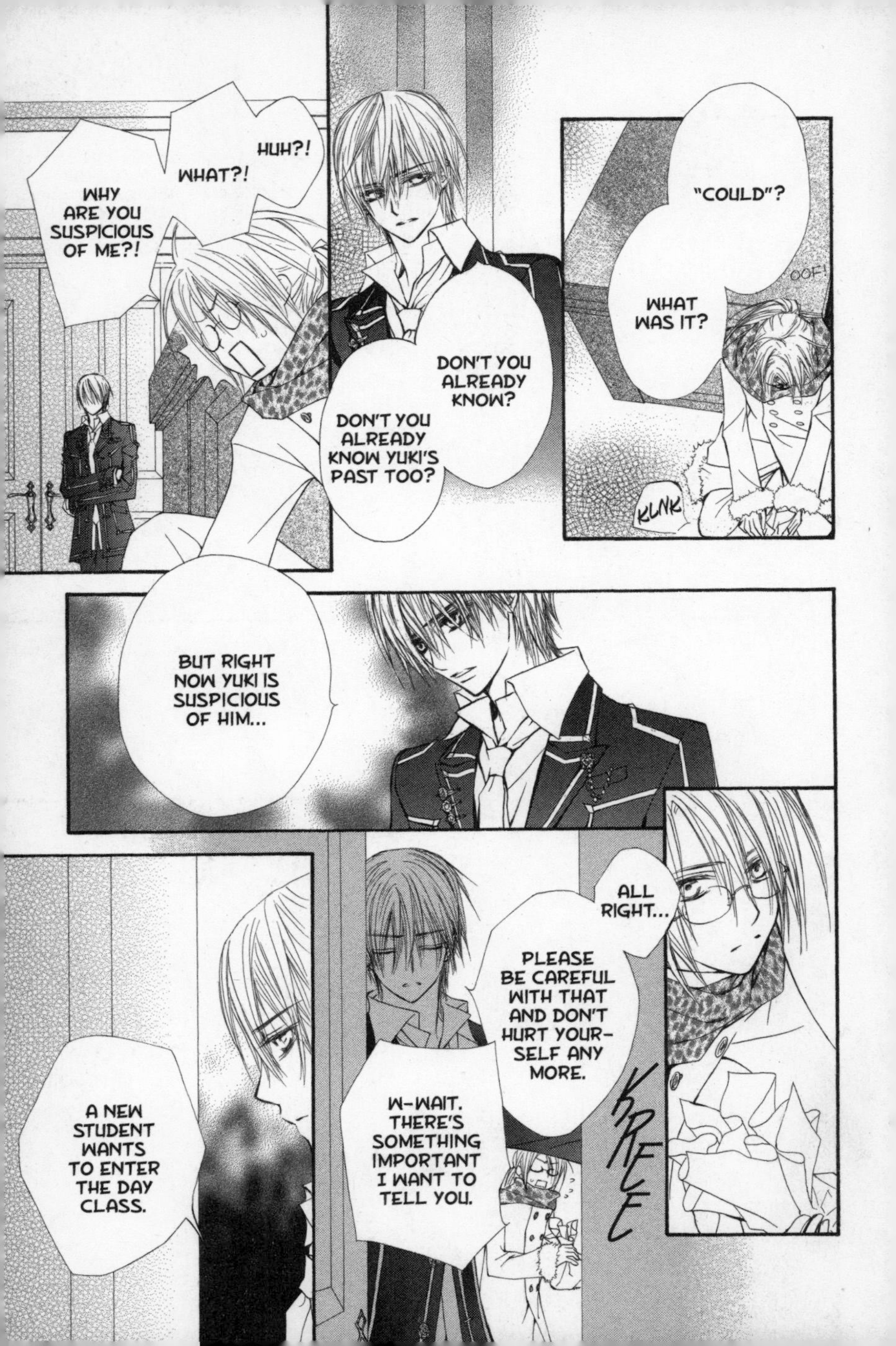
"COULD"?
WHAT WAS IT?
OOF!
KLNK
DON'T YOU ALREADY KNOW?
DON'T YOU ALREADY KNOW YUKI'S PAST TOO?
HUH?!
WHAT?!
WHY ARE YOU SUSPICIOUS OF ME?!
BUT RIGHT NOW YUKI IS SUSPICIOUS OF HIM...
ALL RIGHT...
PLEASE BE CAREFUL WITH THAT AND DON'T HURT YOUR-SELF ANY MORE.
KREEE
W-WAIT. THERE'S SOMETHING IMPORTANT I WANT TO TELL YOU.
A NEW STUDENT WANTS TO ENTER THE DAY CLASS.

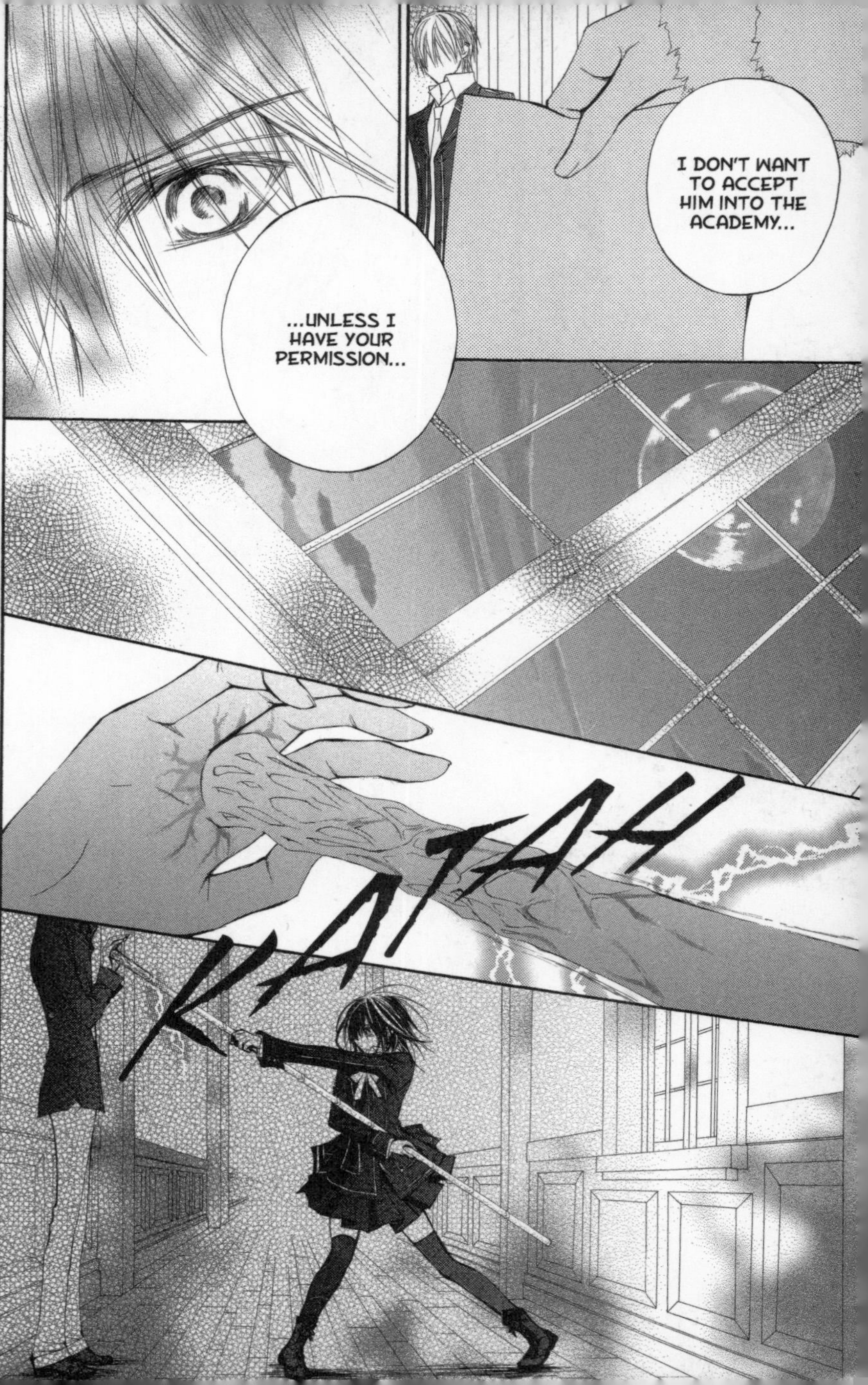
I DON'T WANT TO ACCEPT HIM INTO THE ACADEMY...
...UNLESS I HAVE YOUR PERMISSION...
KATAH

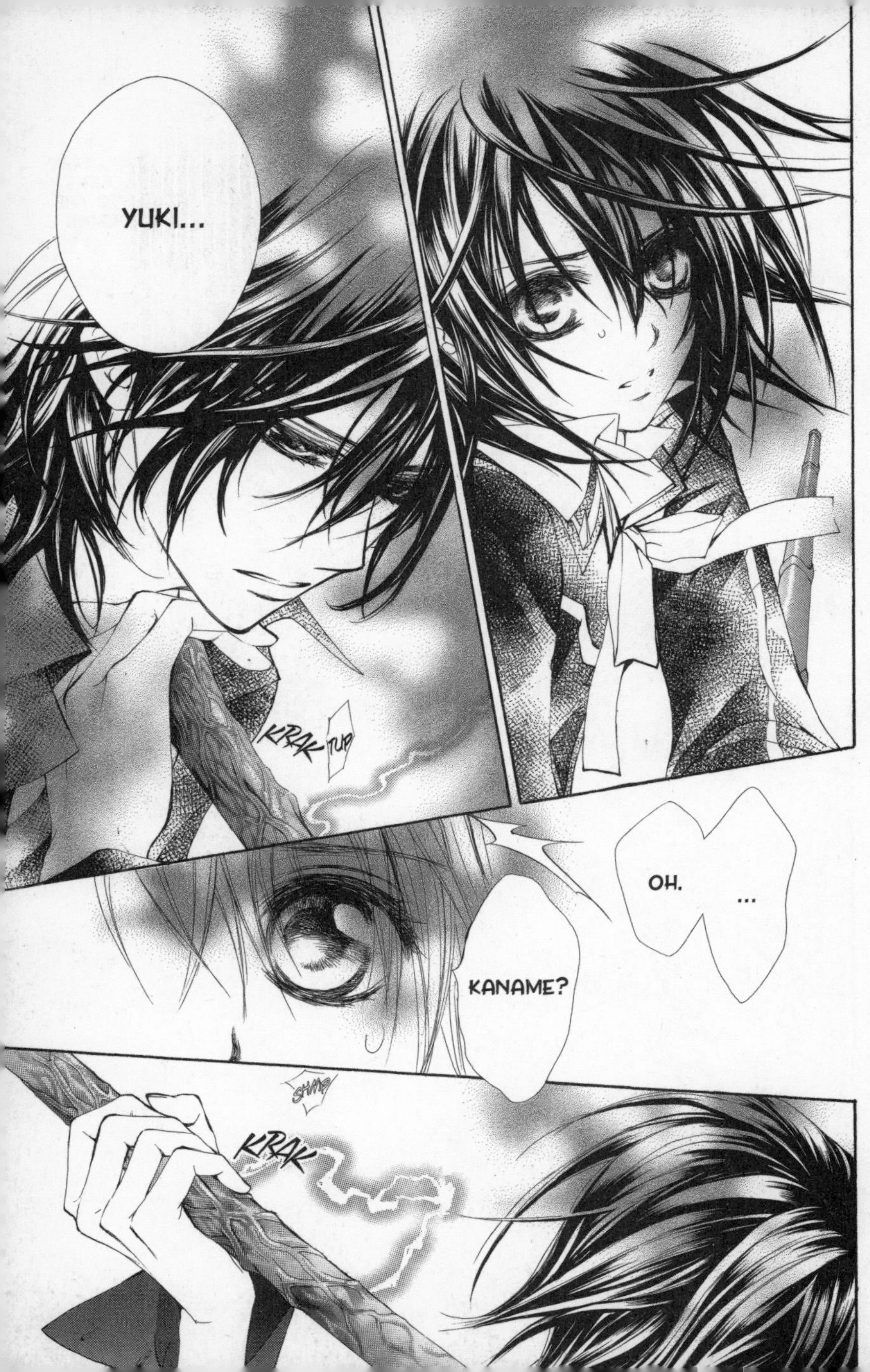
YUKI...
KRAK
TUP
...
OH.
KANAME?
SHMP
KRAK

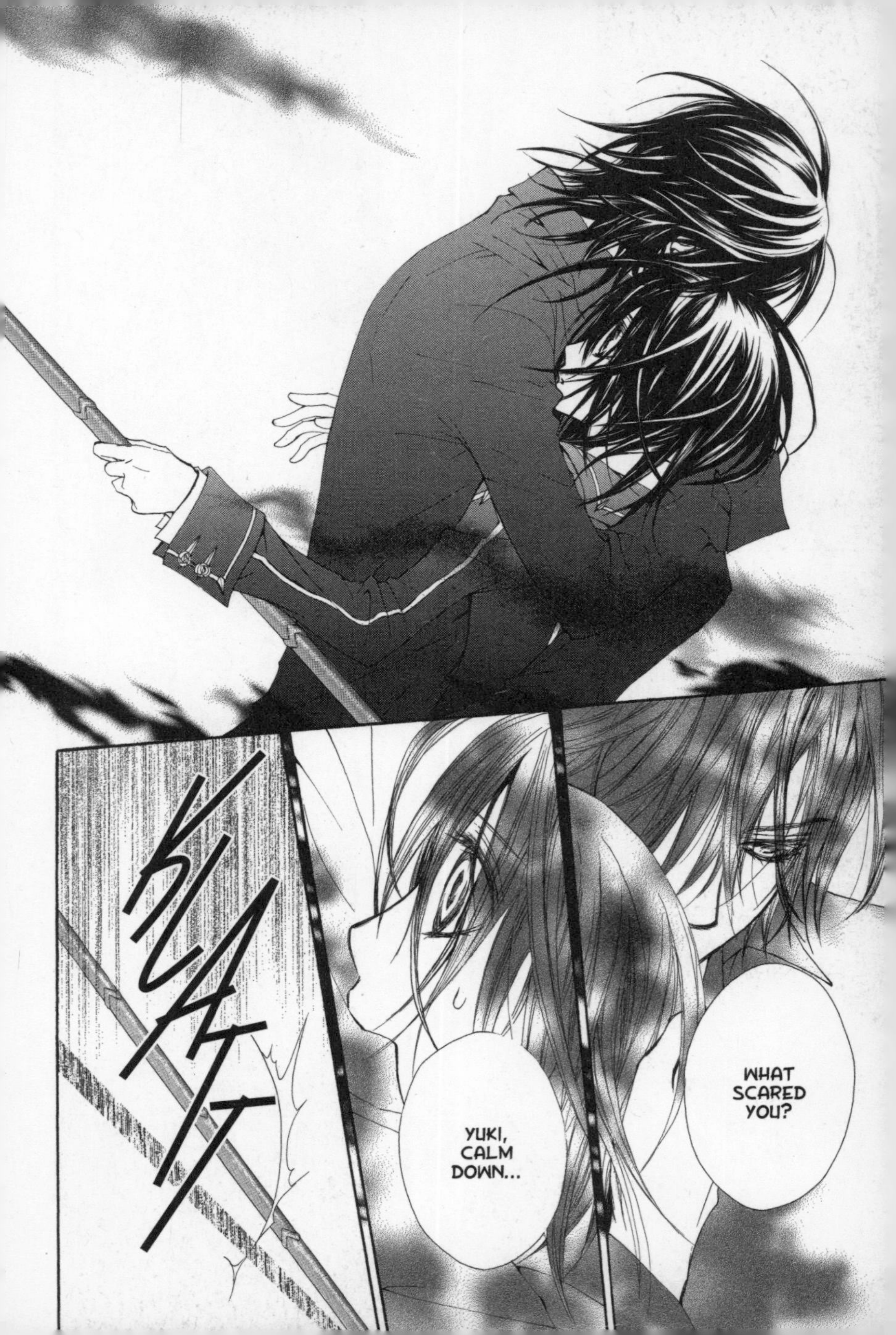
WHAT SCARED YOU?
YUKI, CALM DOWN...

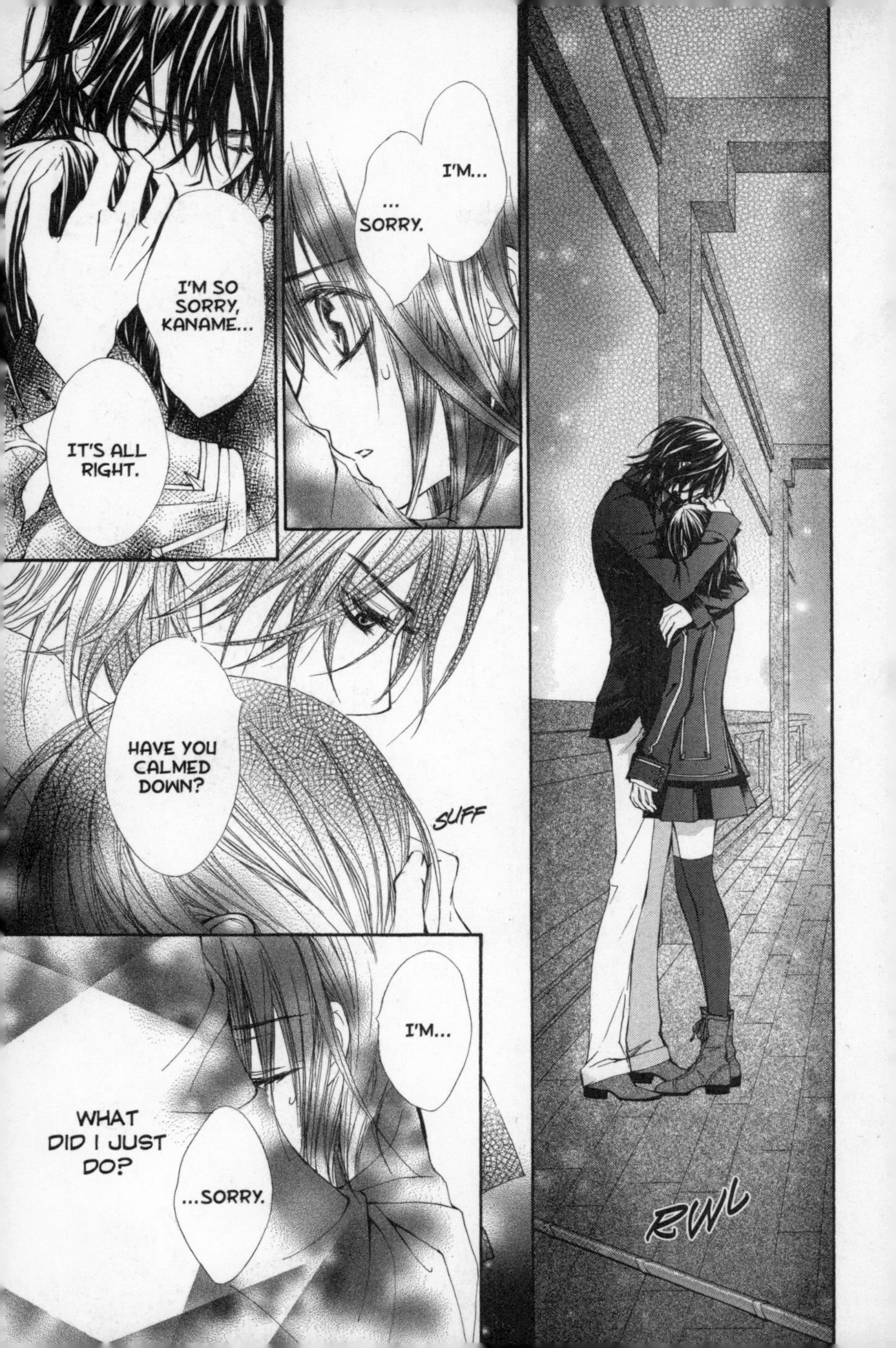
RWL
I'M...
... SORRY.
I'M SO SORRY, KANAME...
IT'S ALL RIGHT.
HAVE YOU CALMED DOWN?
SUFF
I'M...
...SORRY.
WHAT DID I JUST DO?

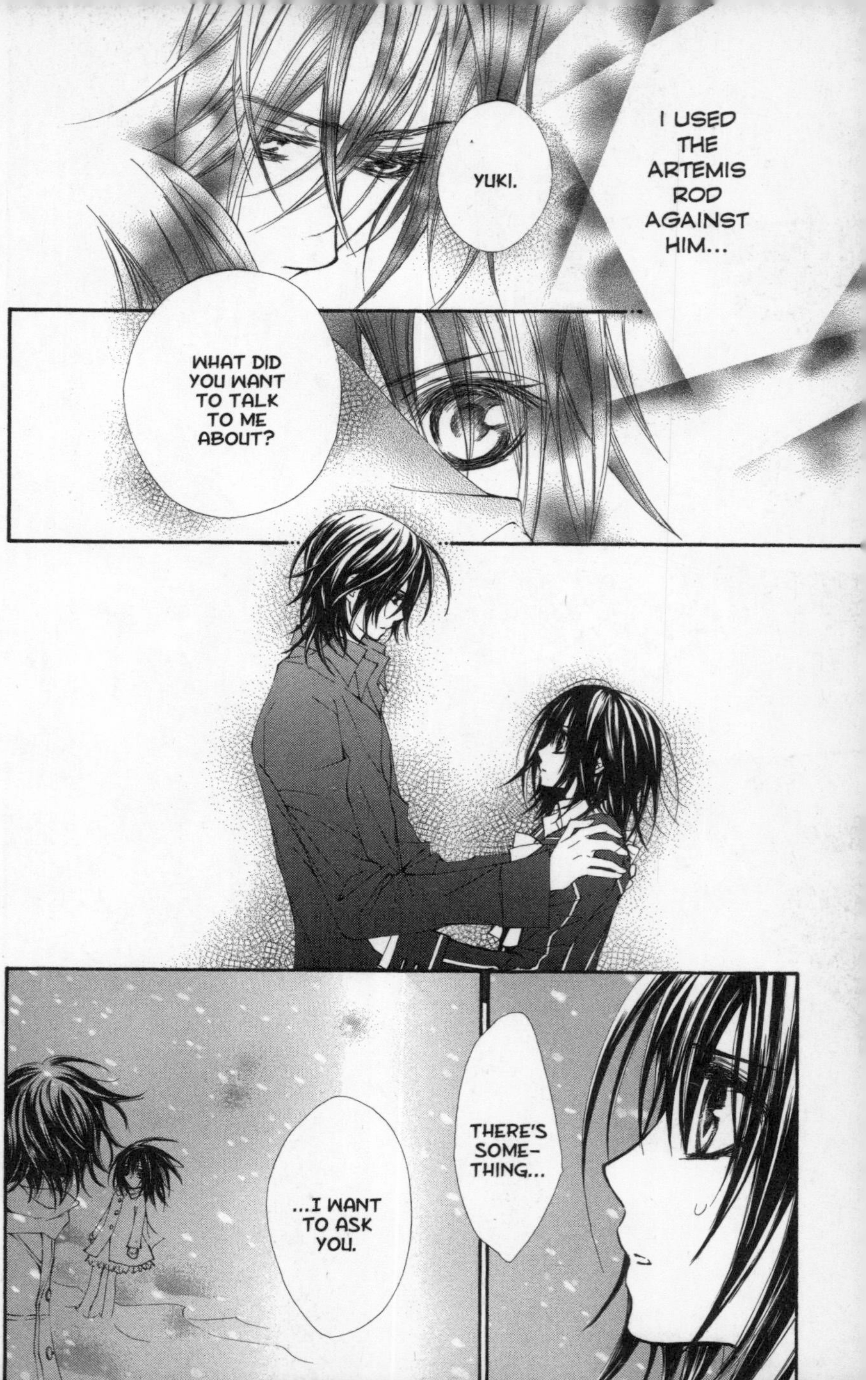
I USED THE ARTEMIS ROD AGAINST HIM...
YUKI.
WHAT DID YOU WANT TO TALK TO ME ABOUT?
THERE'S SOME-THING...
...I WANT TO ASK YOU.

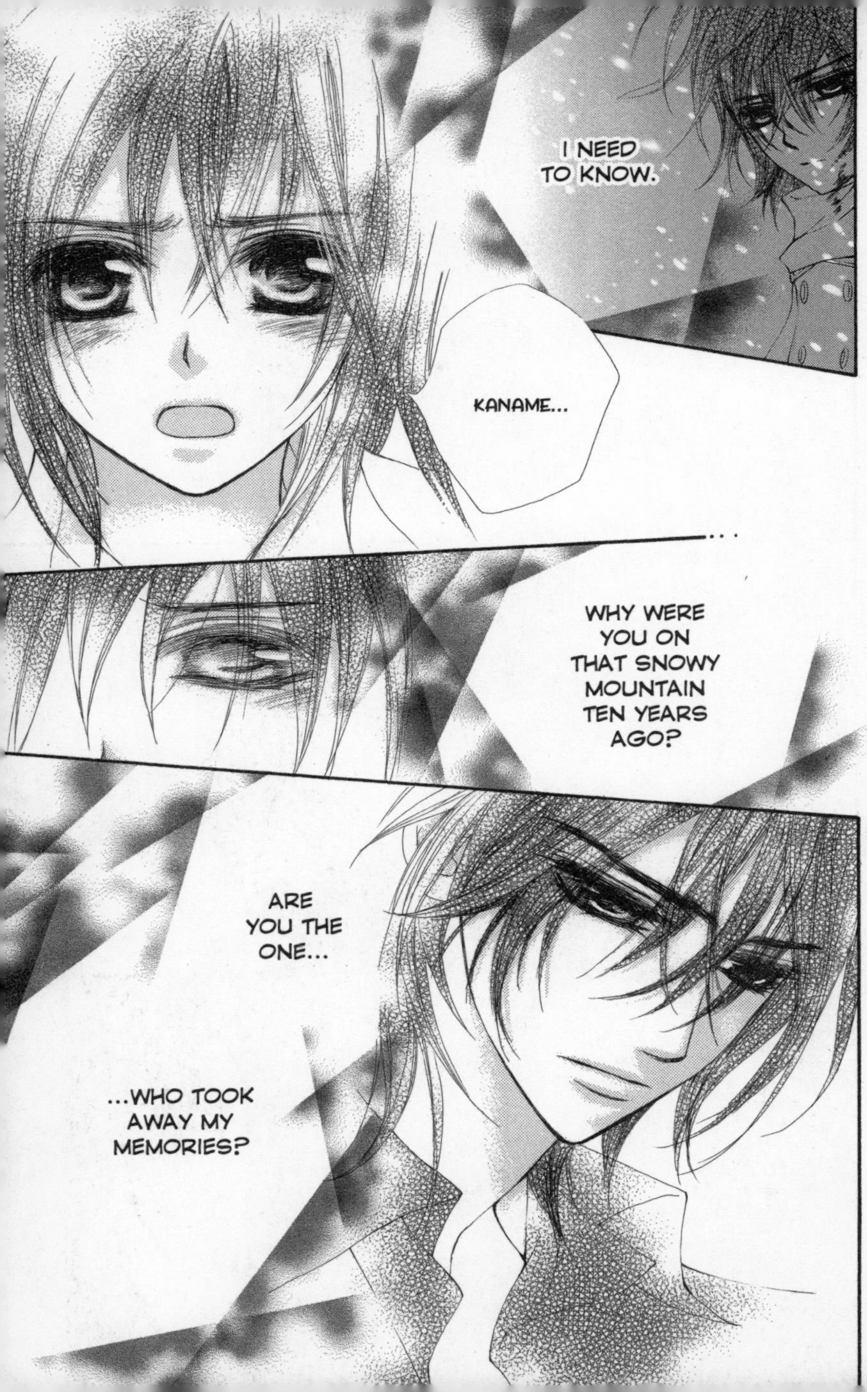
I NEED TO KNOW.
KANAME...
...
WHY WERE YOU ON THAT SNOWY MOUNTAIN TEN YEARS AGO?
ARE YOU THE ONE...
...WHO TOOK AWAY MY MEMORIES?

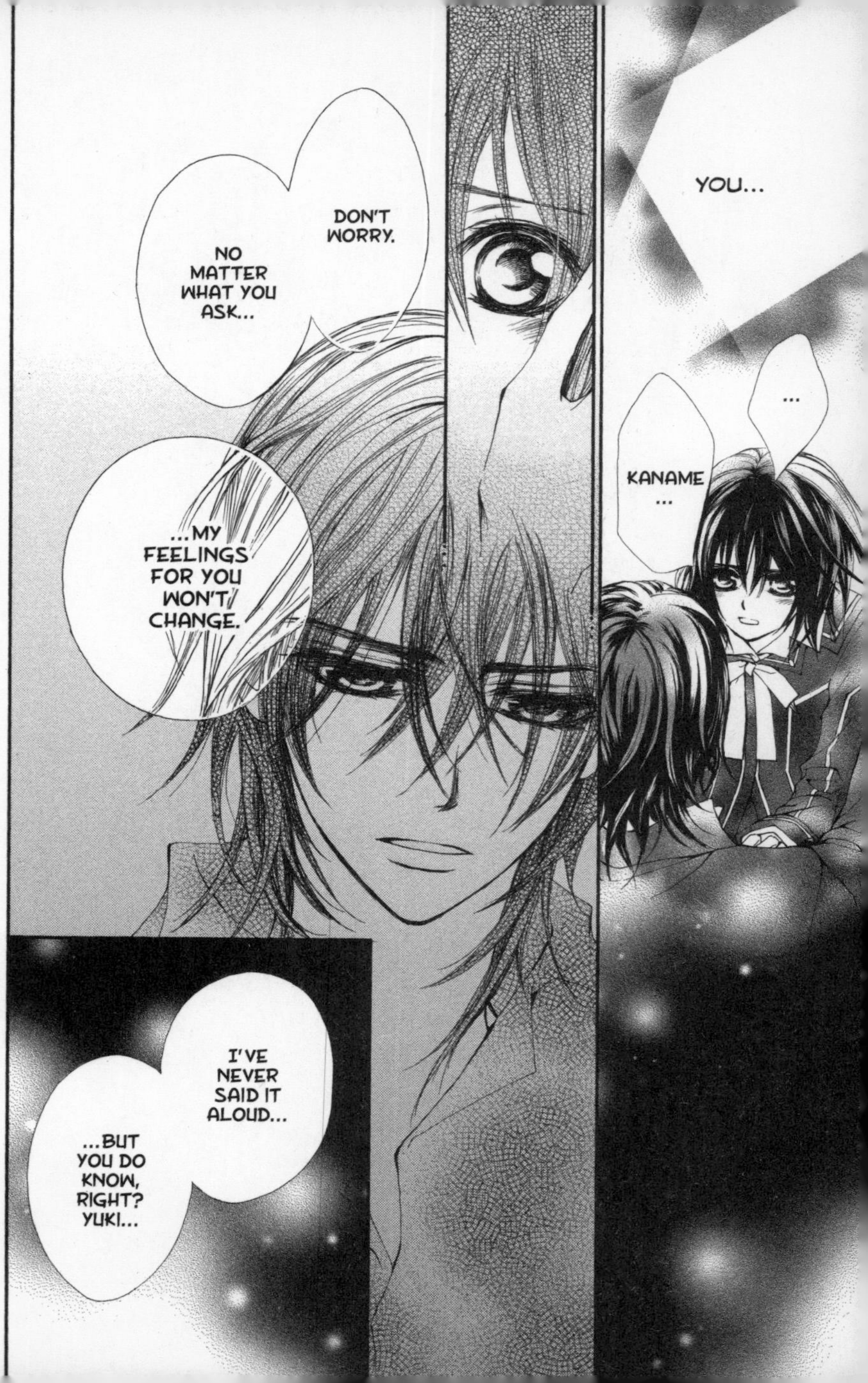
YOU...
...
KANAME ...
DON'T WORRY.
NO MATTER WHAT YOU ASK...
...MY FEELINGS FOR YOU WON'T CHANGE.
I'VE NEVER SAID IT ALOUD...
...BUT YOU DO KNOW, RIGHT? YUKI...

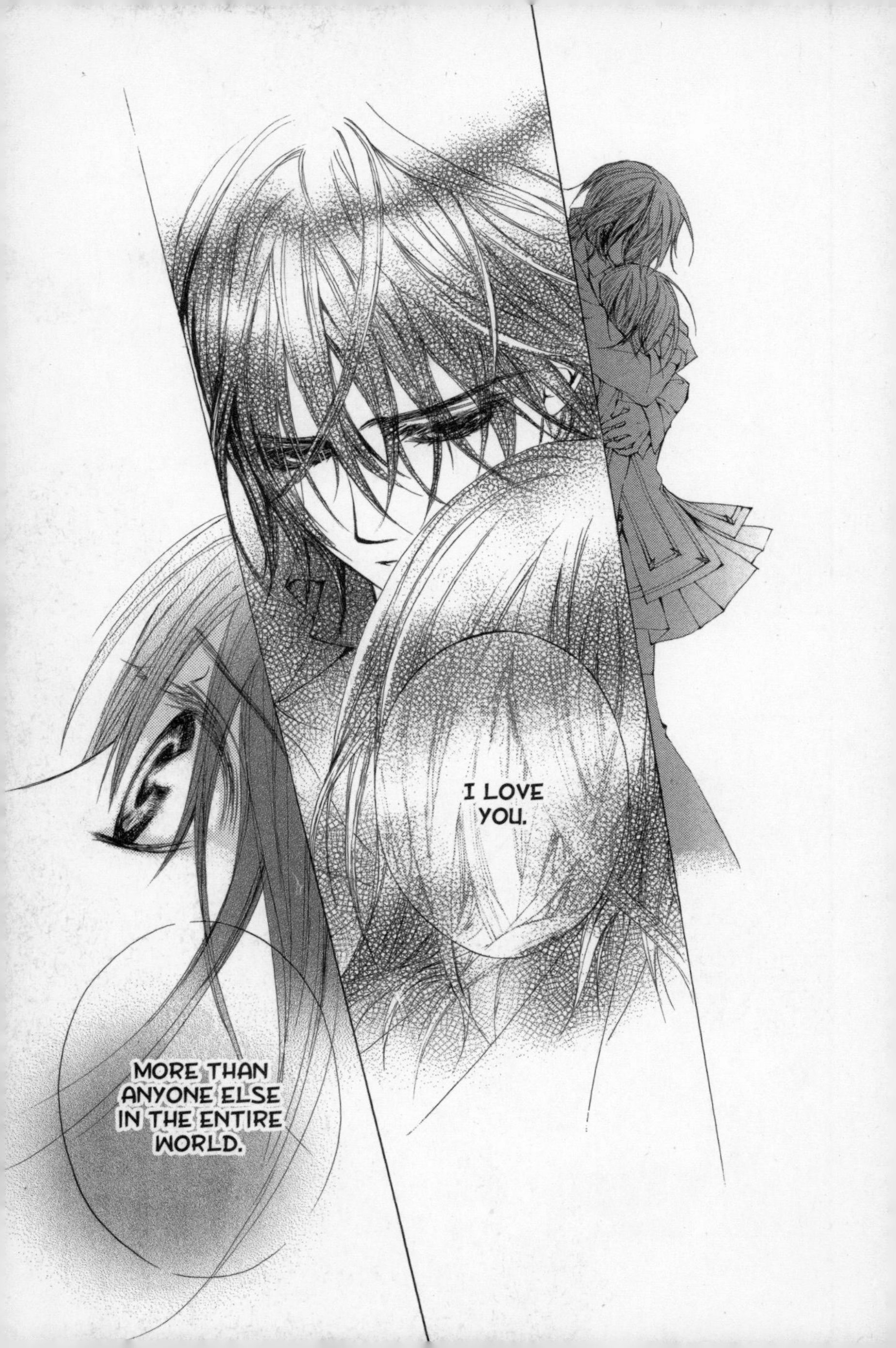
I LOVE YOU.
MORE THAN ANYONE ELSE IN THE ENTIRE WORLD.

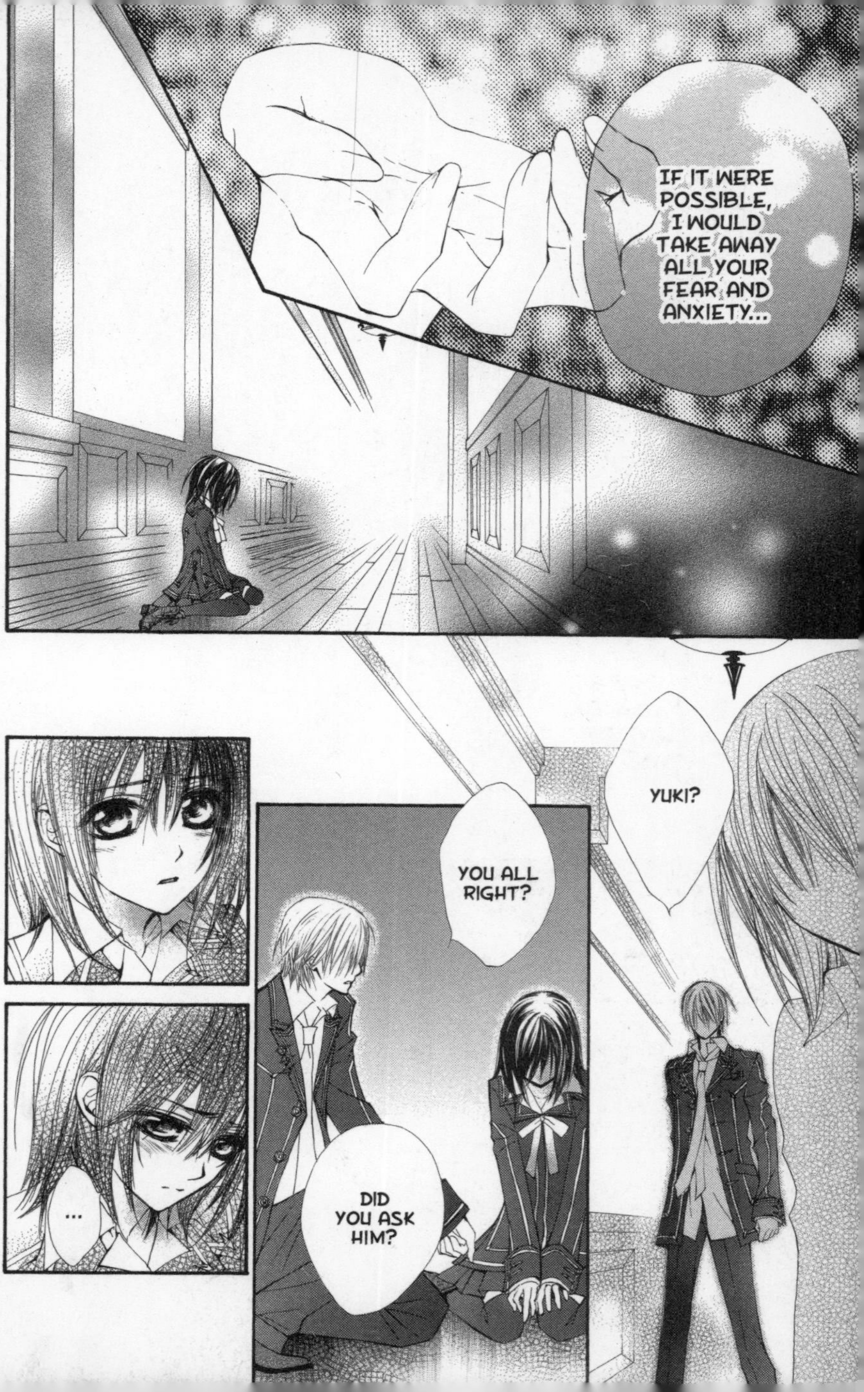
IF IT WERE POSSIBLE, I WOULD TAKE AWAY ALL YOUR FEAR AND ANXIETY...
YUKI?
YOU ALL RIGHT?
DID YOU ASK HIM?
...

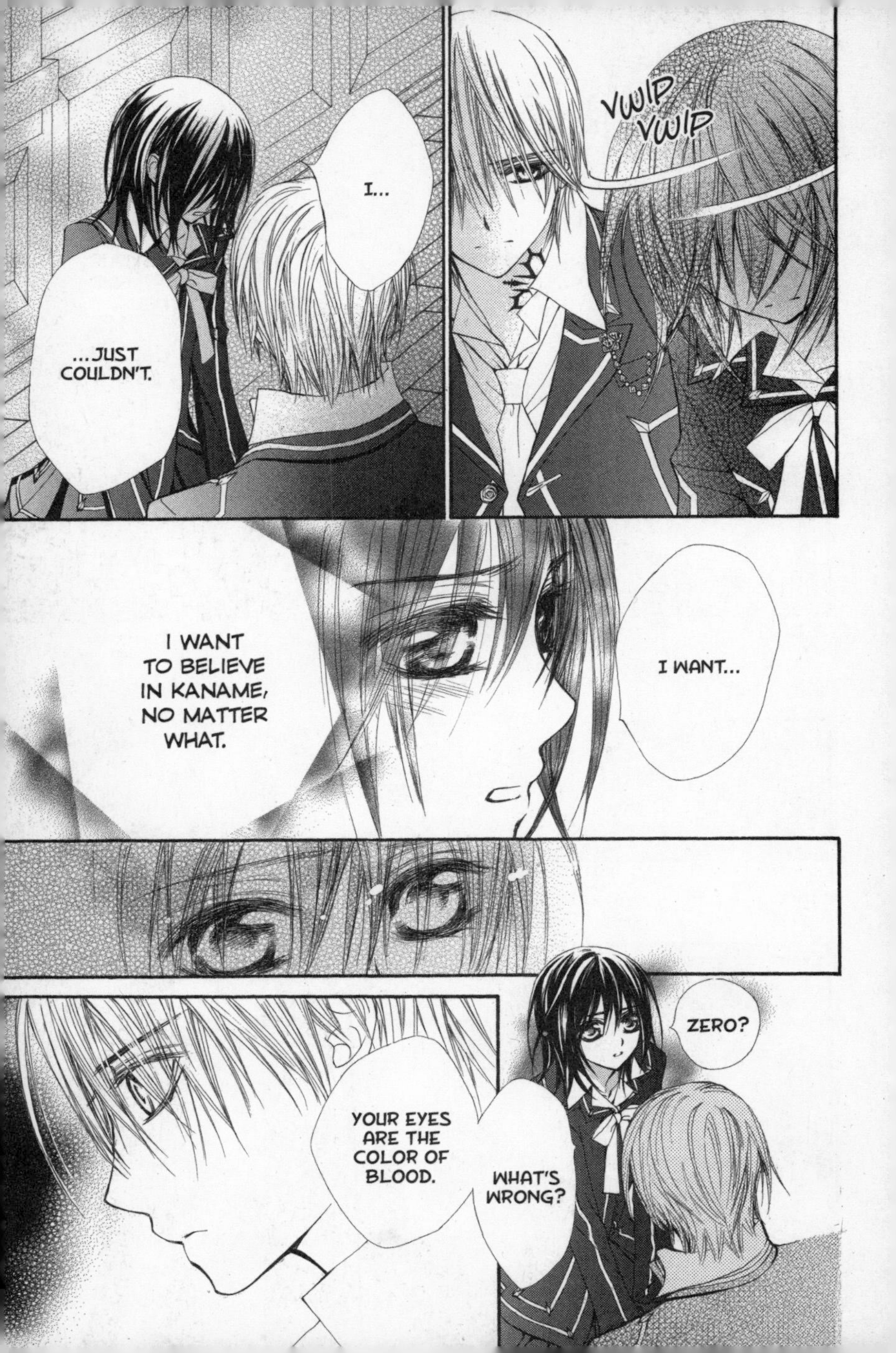
VWIP VWIP
I...
...JUST COULDN'T.
I WANT...
I WANT TO BELIEVE IN KANAME, NO MATTER WHAT.
ZERO?
WHAT'S WRONG?
YOUR EYES ARE THE COLOR OF BLOOD.

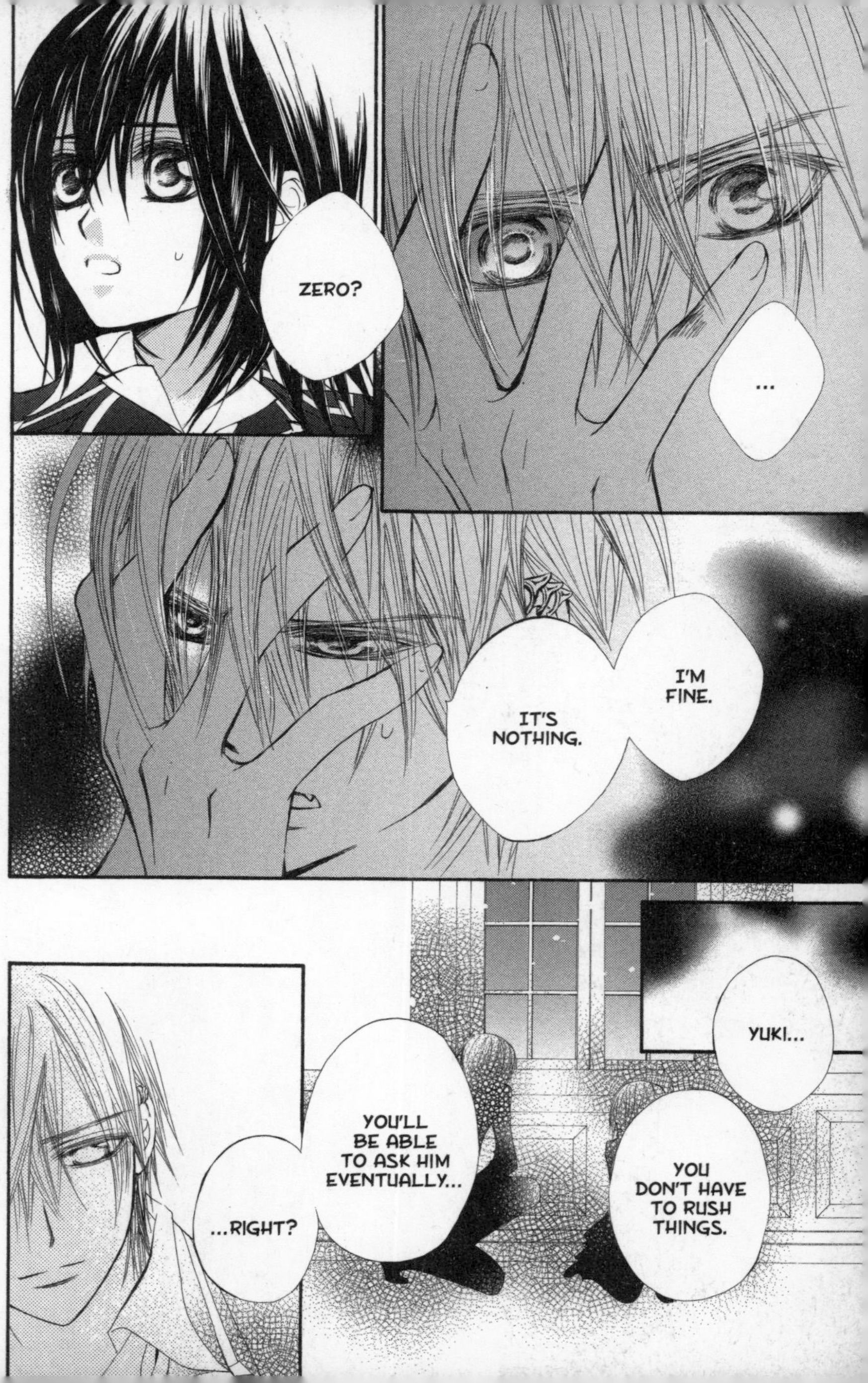
...
ZERO?
I'M FINE.
IT'S NOTHING.
YUKI...
YOU DON'T HAVE TO RUSH THINGS.
YOU'LL BE ABLE TO ASK HIM EVENTUALLY...
...RIGHT?

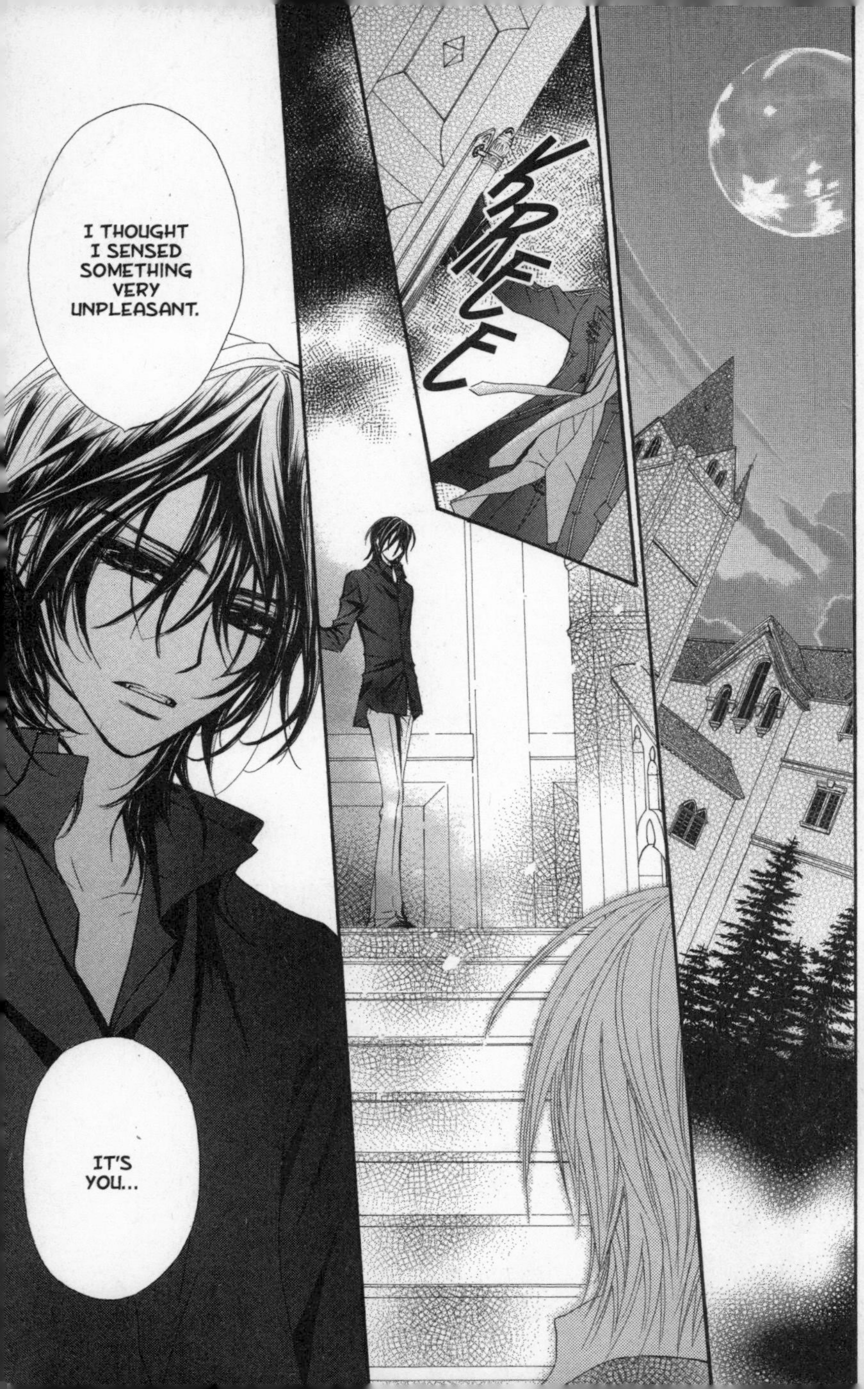
I THOUGHT I SENSED SOMETHING VERY UNPLEASANT.
IT'S YOU...

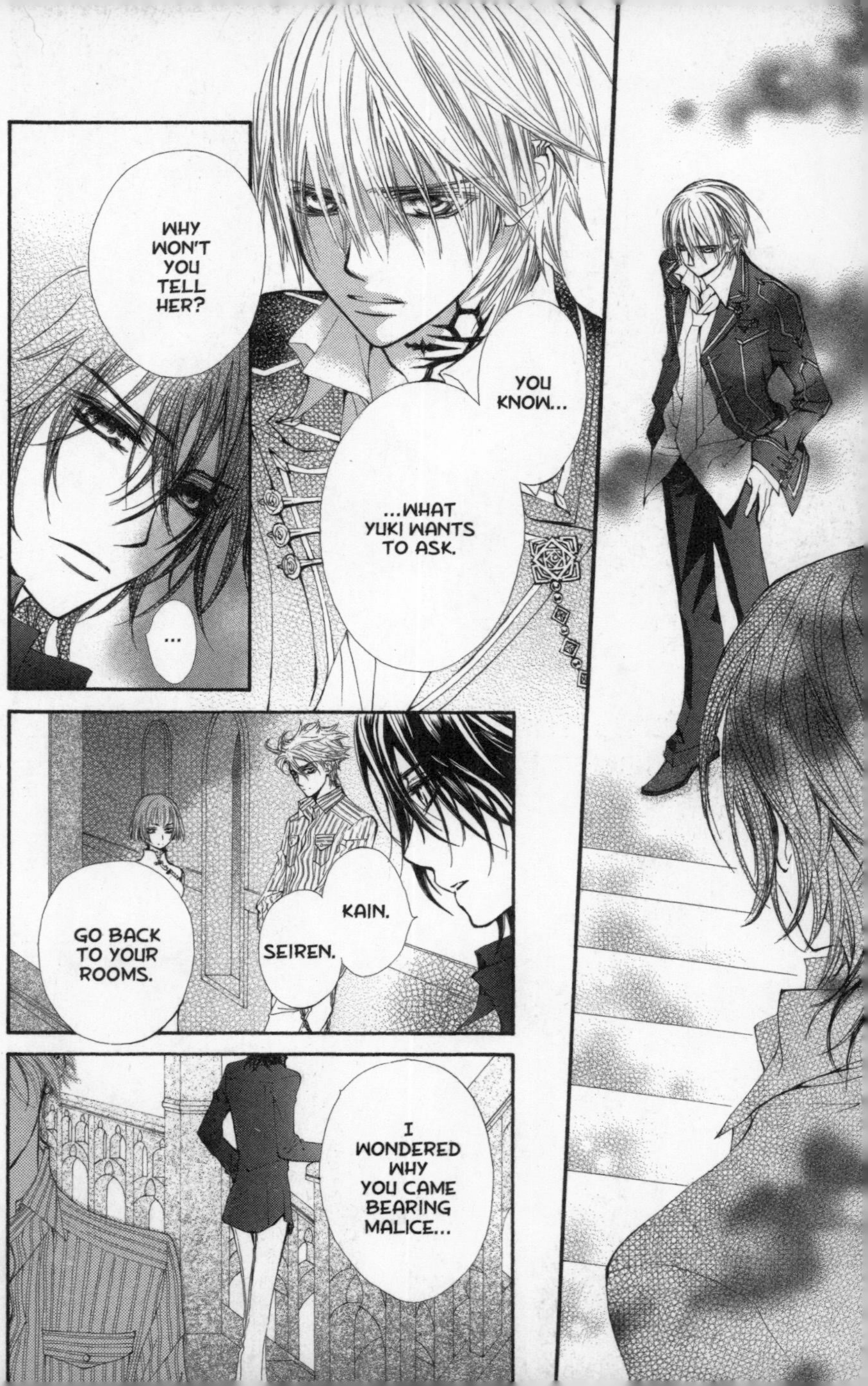
YOU KNOW...
...WHAT YUKI WANTS TO ASK.
WHY WON'T YOU TELL HER?
...
KAIN.
SEIREN.
GO BACK TO YOUR ROOMS.
I WONDERED WHY YOU CAME BEARING MALICE...

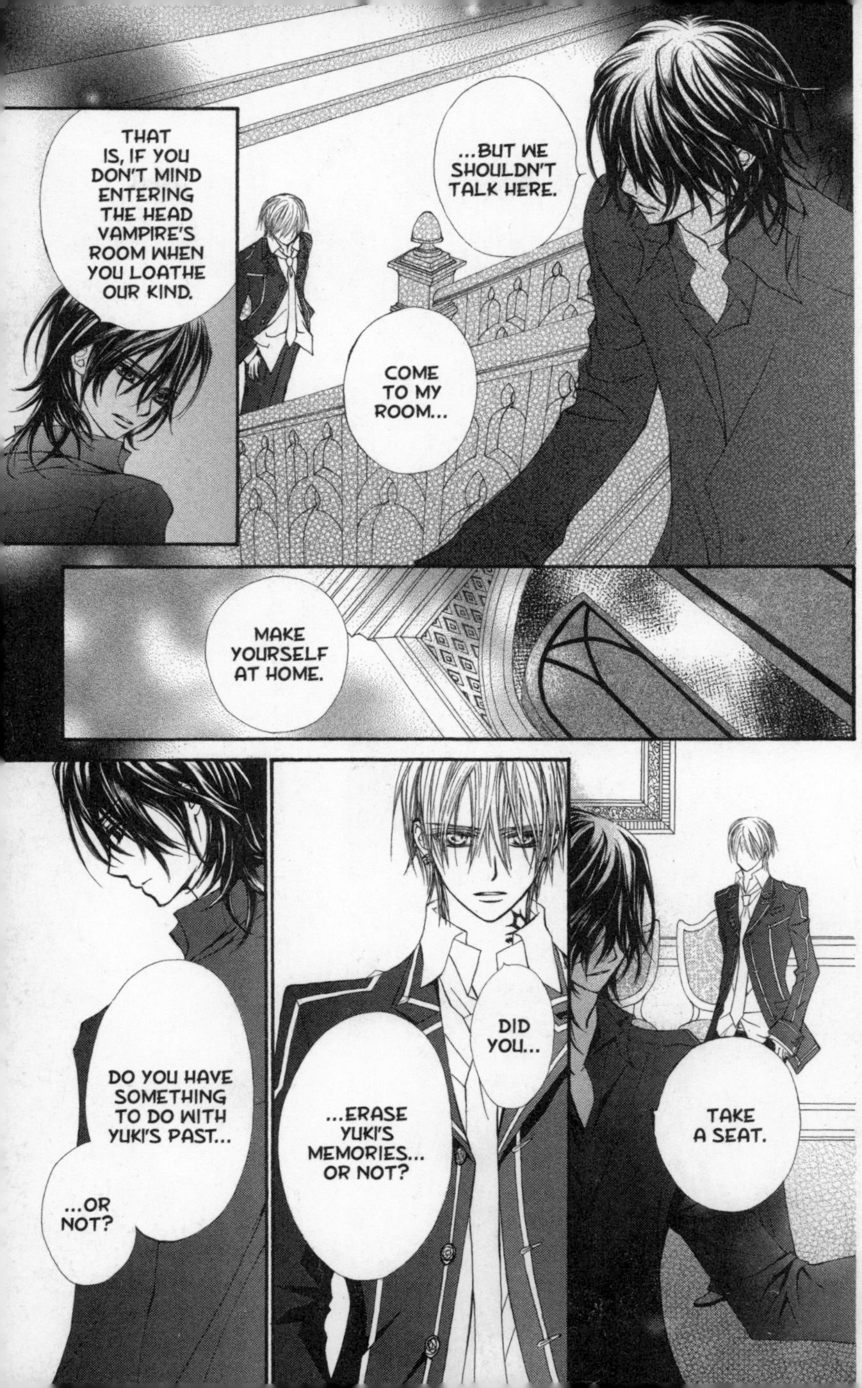
...BUT WE SHOULDN'T TALK HERE.
COME TO MY ROOM...
THAT IS, IF YOU DON'T MIND ENTERING THE HEAD VAMPIRE'S ROOM WHEN YOU LOATHE OUR KIND.
MAKE YOURSELF AT HOME.
TAKE A SEAT.
DID YOU...
...ERASE YUKI'S MEMORIES... OR NOT?
DO YOU HAVE SOMETHING TO DO WITH YUKI'S PAST...
...OR NOT?

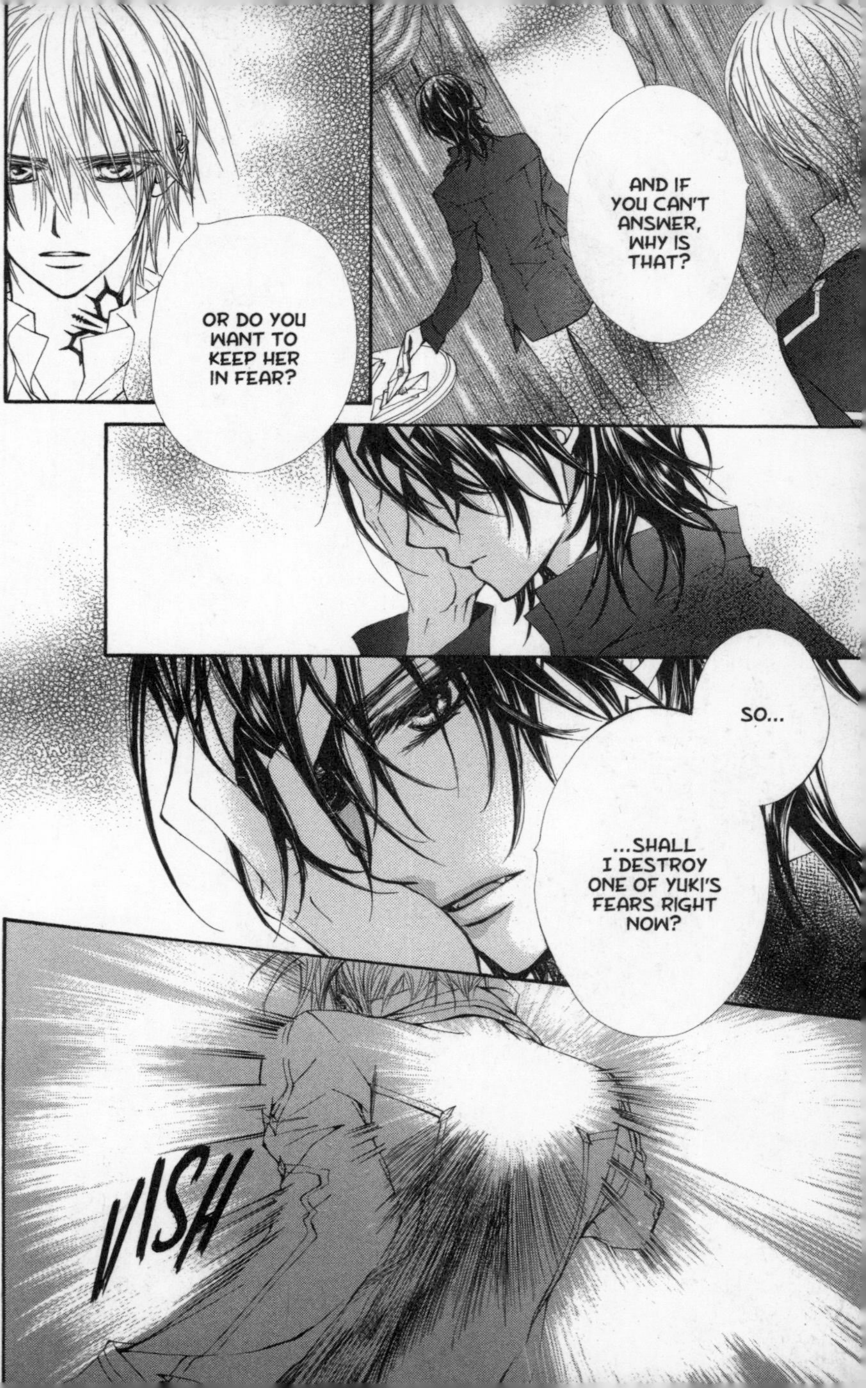
AND IF YOU CAN'T ANSWER, WHY IS THAT?
OR DO YOU WANT TO KEEP HER IN FEAR?
SO...
...SHALL I DESTROY ONE OF YUKI'S FEARS RIGHT NOW?
VISH

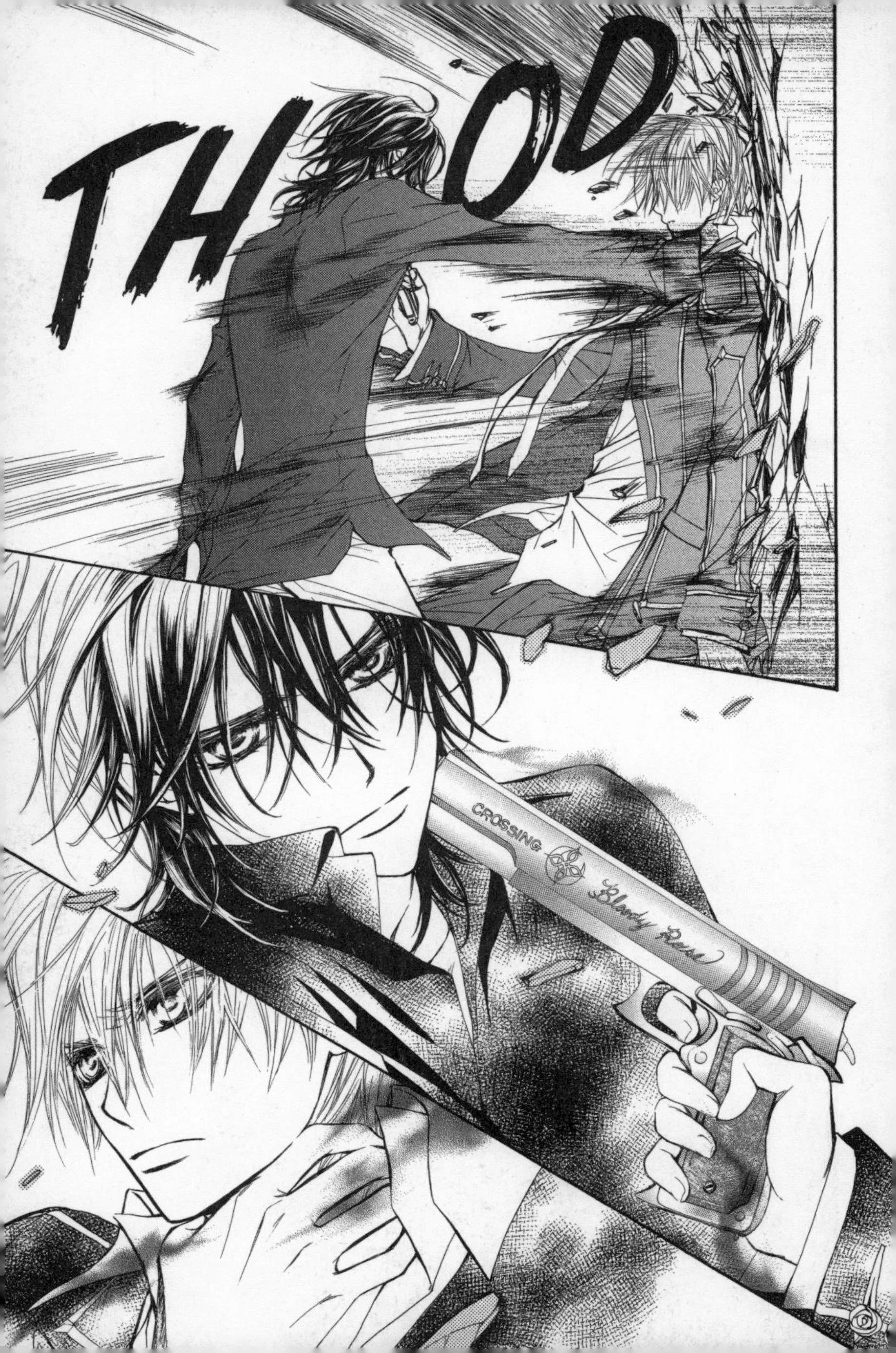
TH OD
CROSSING
Bloody Rose

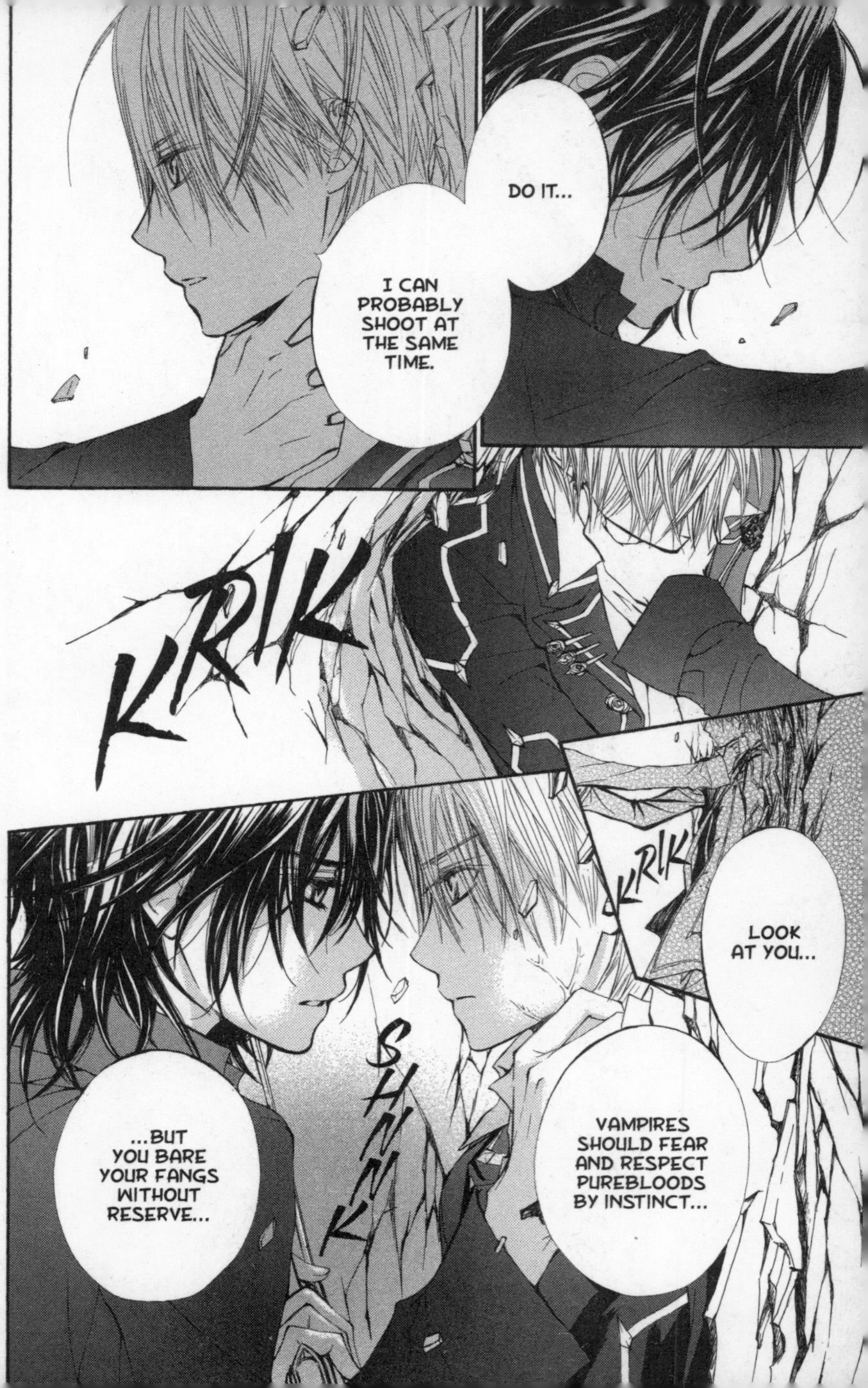
DO IT...
I CAN PROBABLY SHOOT AT THE SAME TIME.
KRIK
KRIK
LOOK AT YOU...
VAMPIRES SHOULD FEAR AND RESPECT PUREBLOODS BY INSTINCT...
...BUT YOU BARE YOUR FANGS WITHOUT RESERVE...

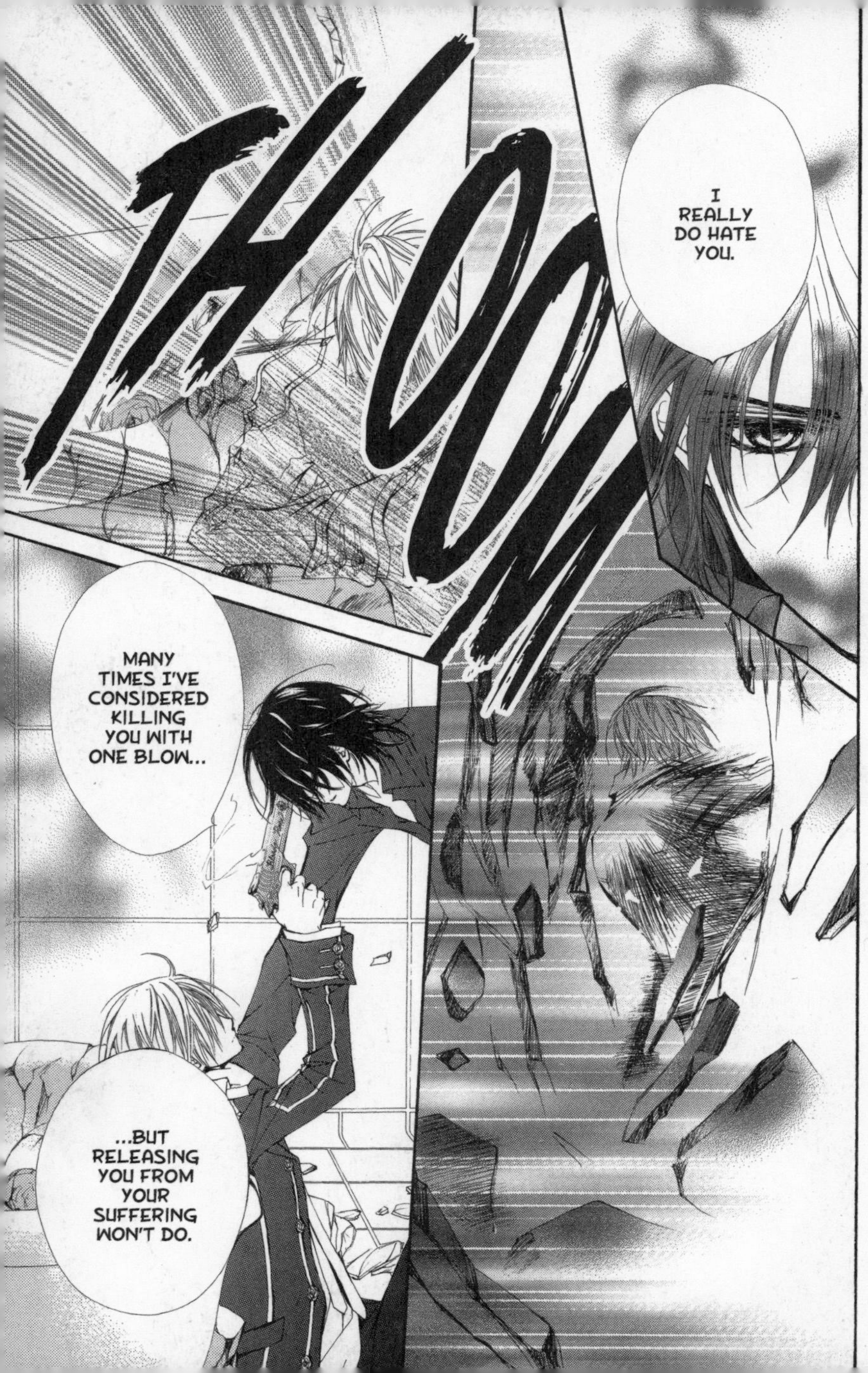
I REALLY DO HATE YOU.
THOOM
MANY TIMES I'VE CONSIDERED KILLING YOU WITH ONE BLOW...
...BUT RELEASING YOU FROM YOUR SUFFERING WON'T DO.

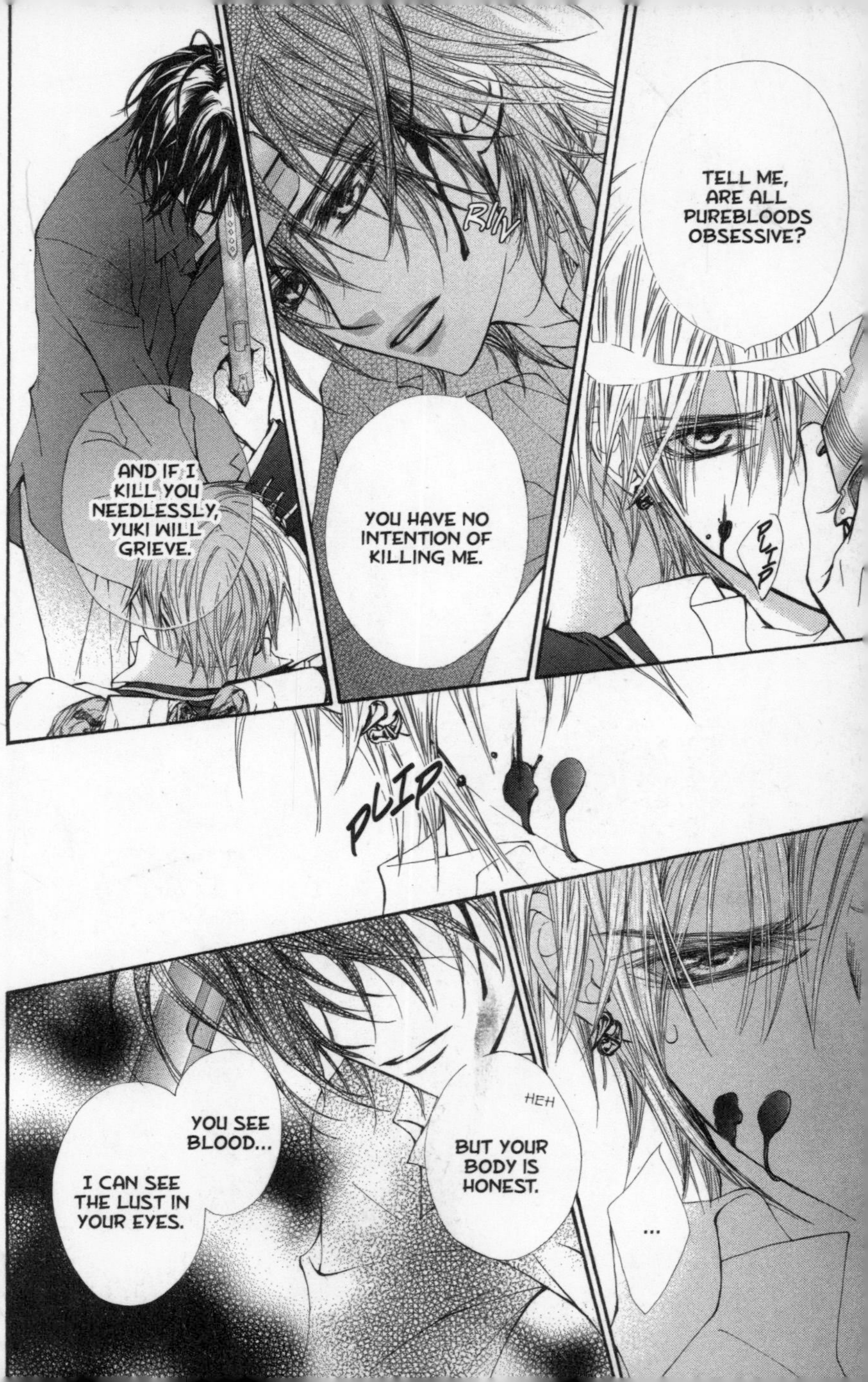
TELL ME, ARE ALL PUREBLOODS OBSESSIVE?
PLIP
RIIV
YOU HAVE NO INTENTION OF KILLING ME.
AND IF I KILL YOU NEEDLESSLY, YUKI WILL GRIEVE.
PLIP
...
HEH
BUT YOUR BODY IS HONEST.
YOU SEE BLOOD...
I CAN SEE THE LUST IN YOUR EYES.

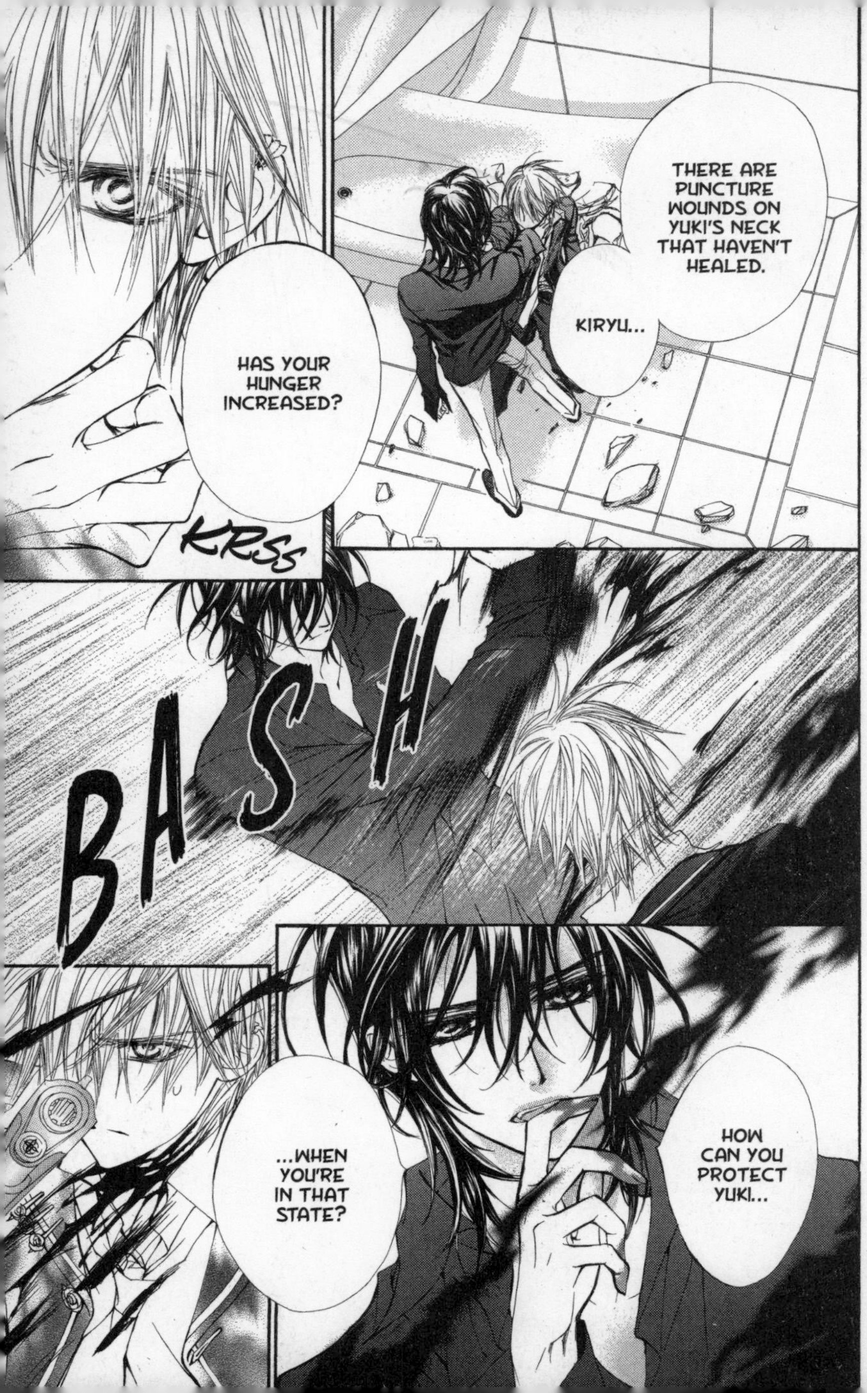
THERE ARE PUNCTURE WOUNDS ON YUKI'S NECK THAT HAVEN'T HEALED.
KIRYU...
HAS YOUR HUNGER INCREASED?
KRSS
BASH
HOW CAN YOU PROTECT YUKI...
...WHEN YOU'RE IN THAT STATE?

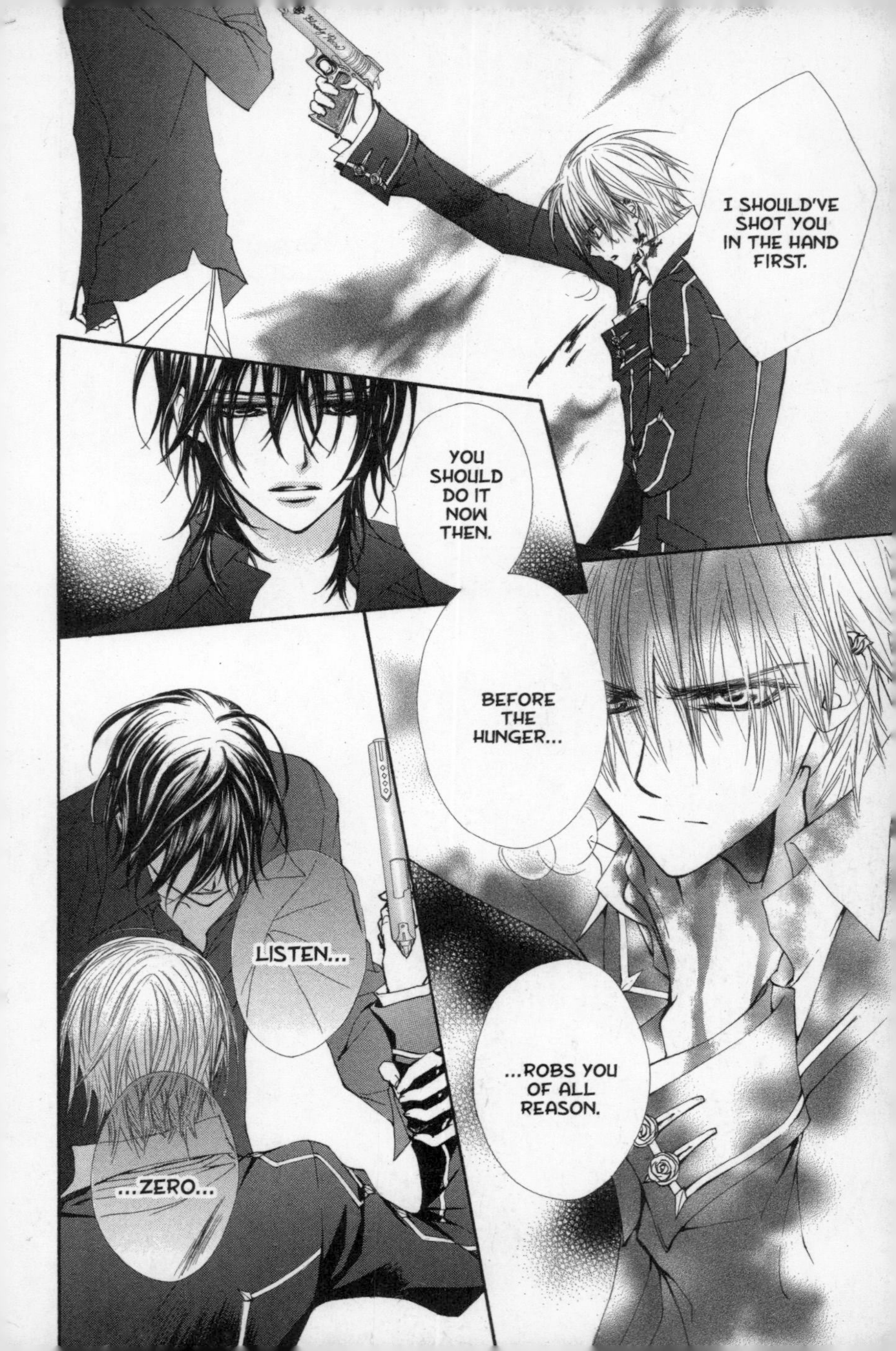
I SHOULD'VE SHOT YOU IN THE HAND FIRST.
YOU SHOULD DO IT NOW THEN.
BEFORE THE HUNGER...
...ROBS YOU OF ALL REASON.
LISTEN...
...ZERO...

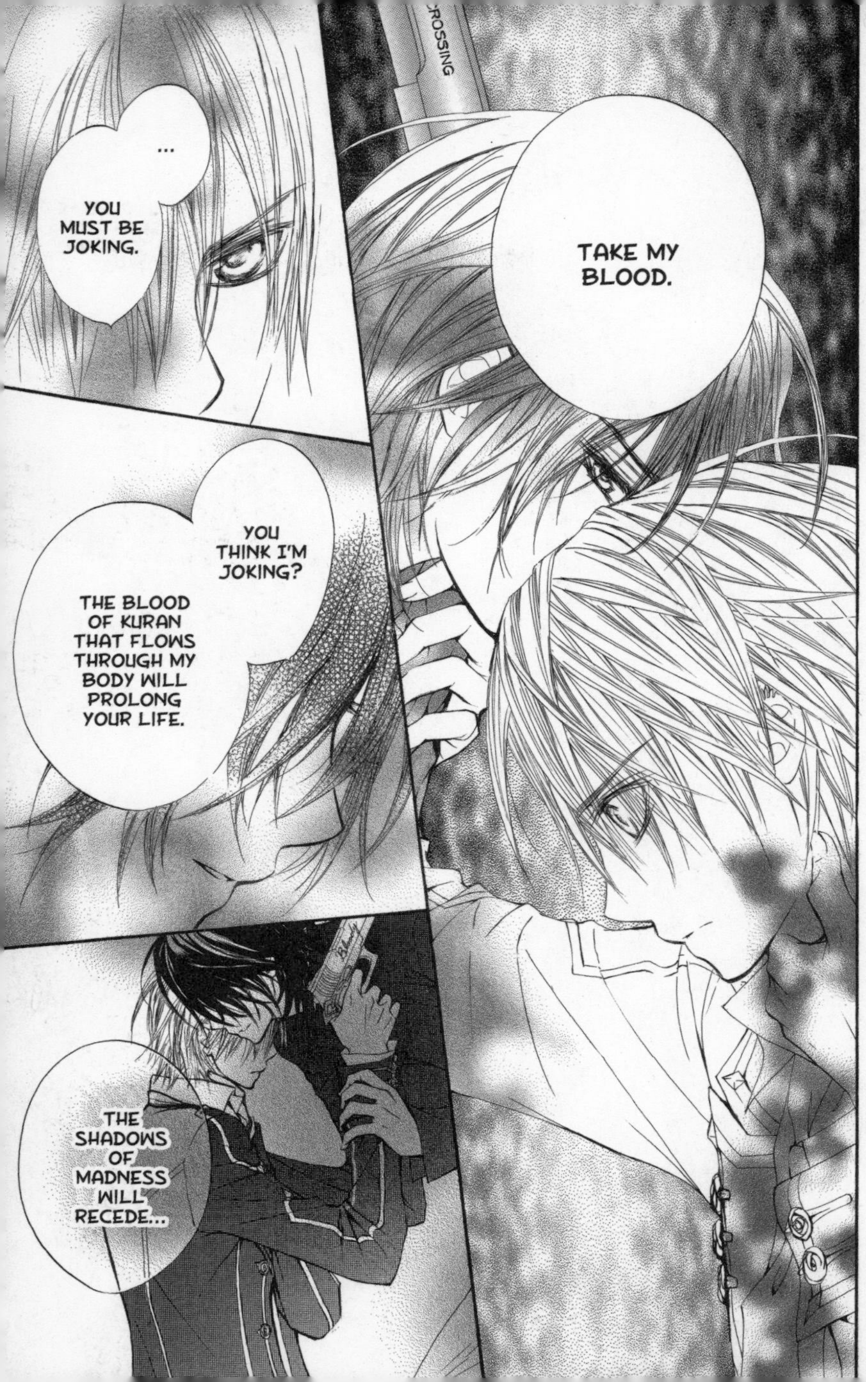
CROSSING
TAKE MY BLOOD.
...
YOU MUST BE JOKING.
YOU THINK I'M JOKING?
THE BLOOD OF KURAN THAT FLOWS THROUGH MY BODY WILL PROLONG YOUR LIFE.
THE SHADOWS OF MADNESS WILL RECEDE...

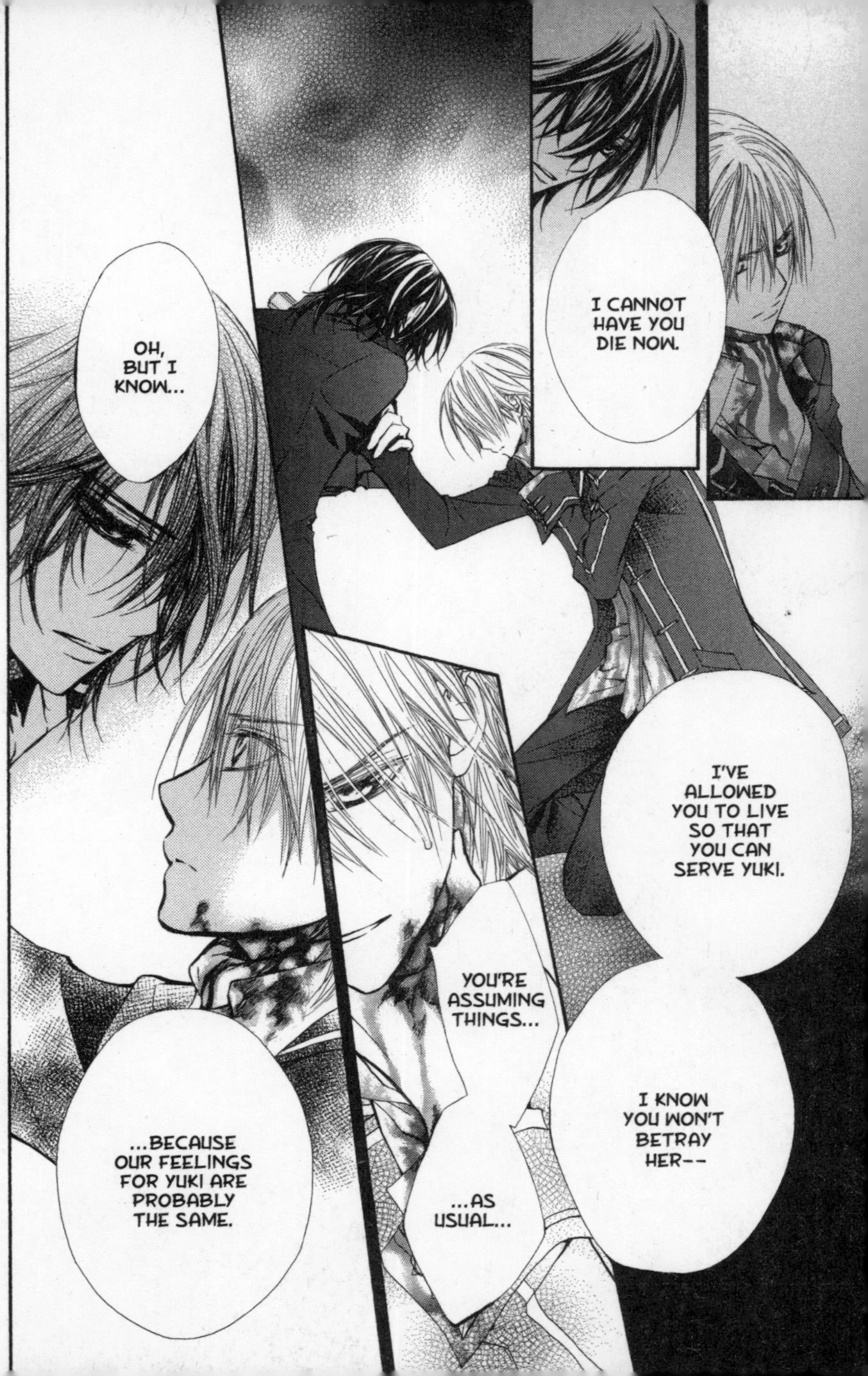
I CANNOT HAVE YOU DIE NOW.
I'VE ALLOWED YOU TO LIVE SO THAT YOU CAN SERVE YUKI.
I KNOW YOU WON'T BETRAY HER--
YOU'RE ASSUMING THINGS...
...AS USUAL...
OH, BUT I KNOW...
...BECAUSE OUR FEELINGS FOR YUKI ARE PROBABLY THE SAME.

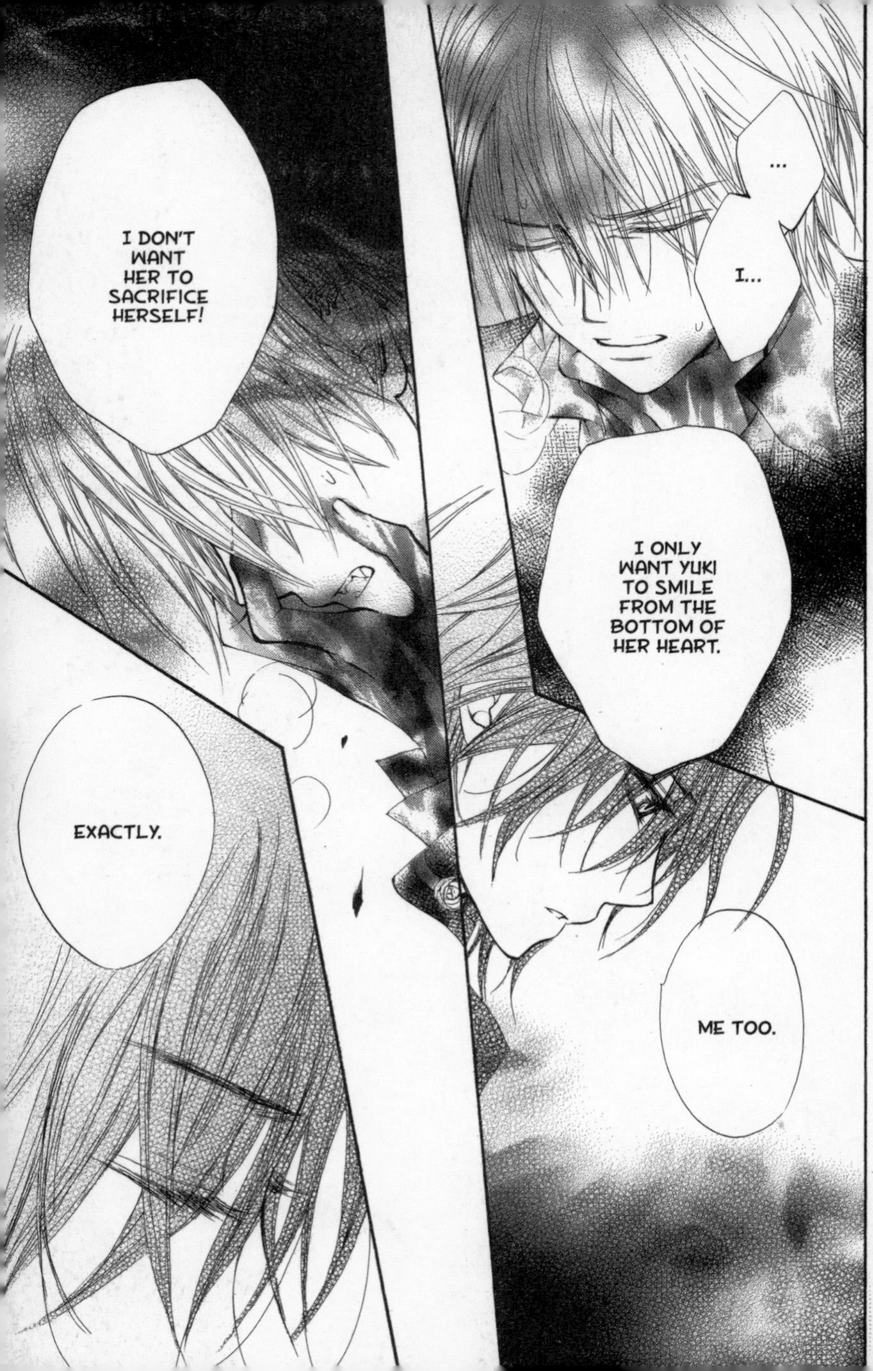
...
I...
I ONLY WANT YUKI TO SMILE FROM THE BOTTOM OF HER HEART.
I DON'T WANT HER TO SACRIFICE HERSELF!
ME TOO.
EXACTLY.

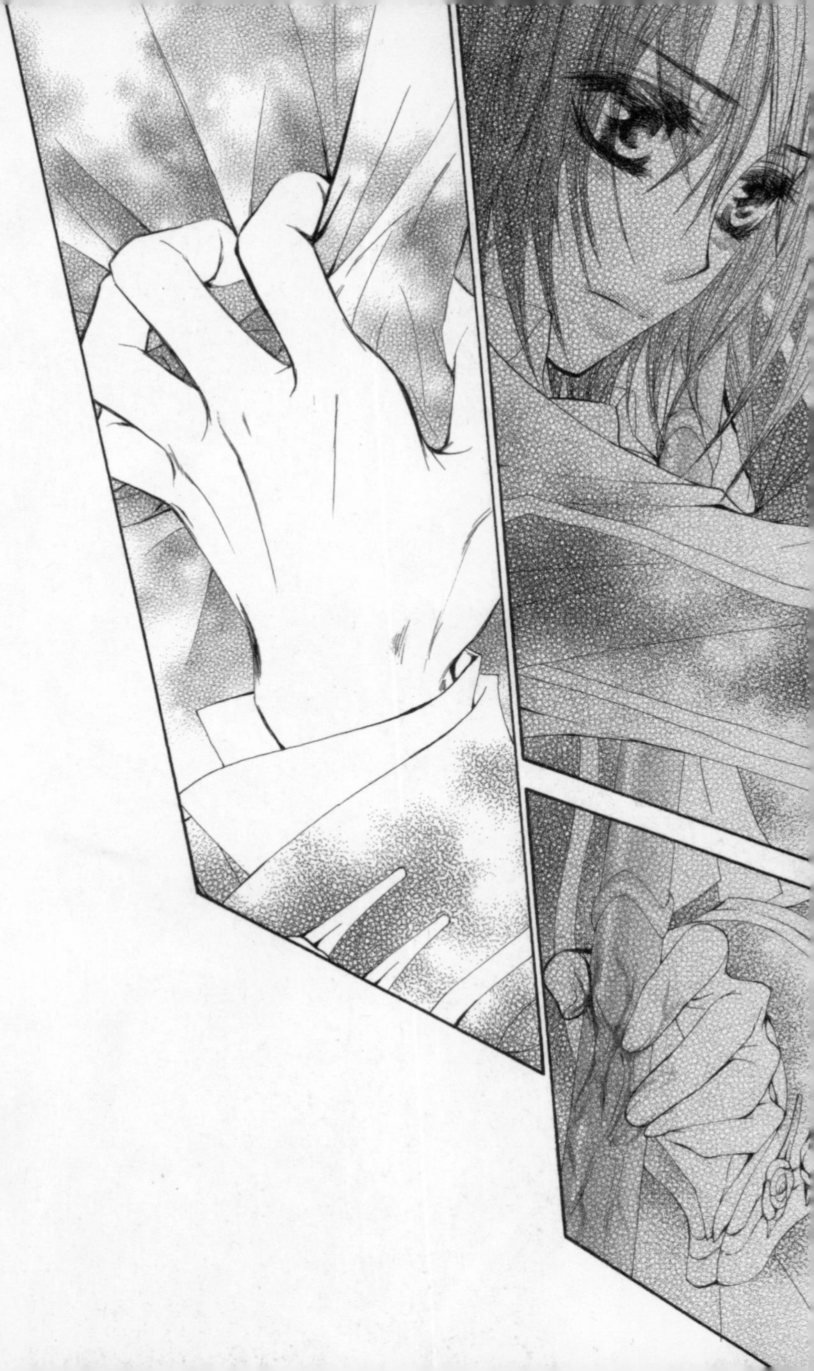

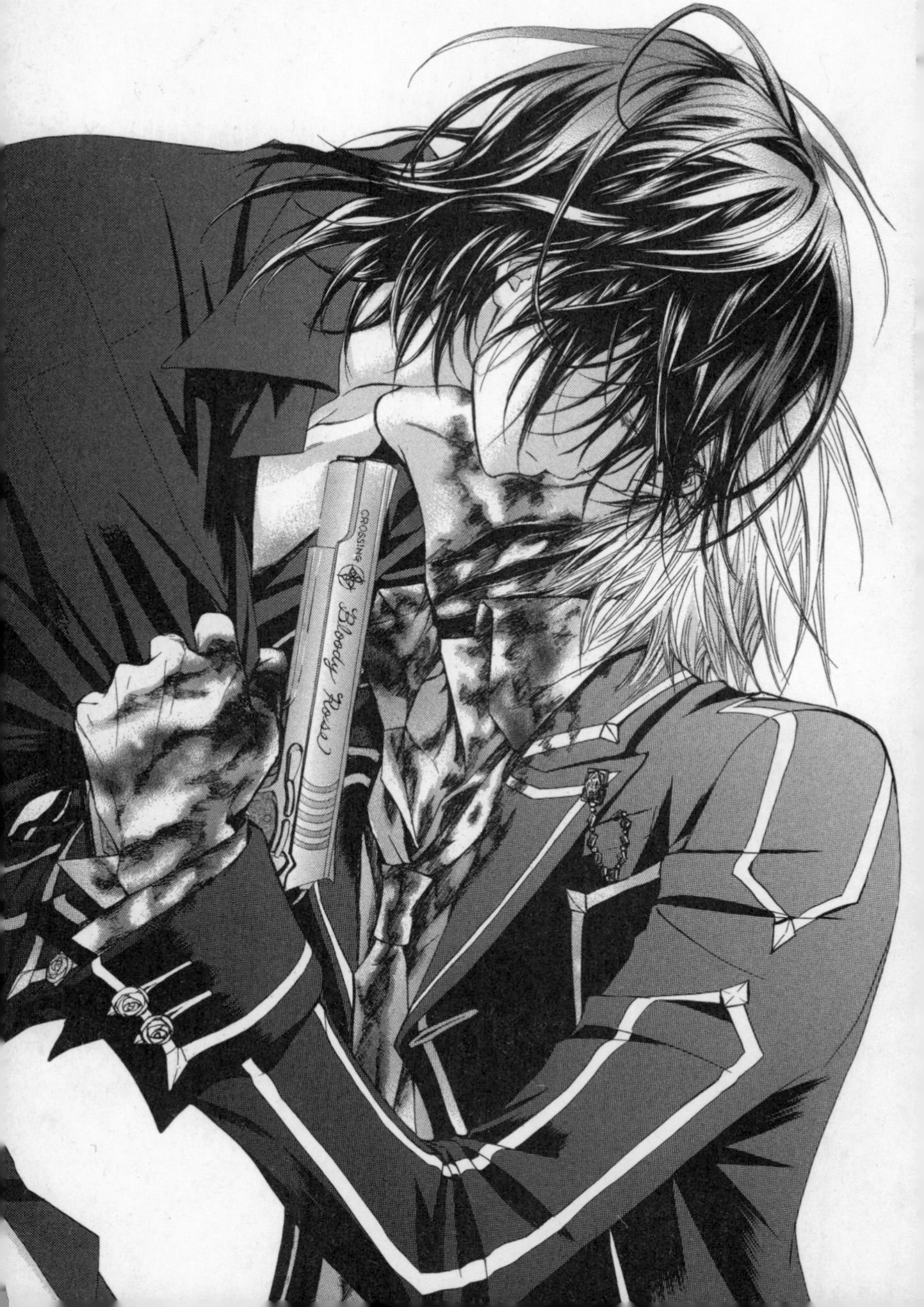
CROSSING
Bloody Rose

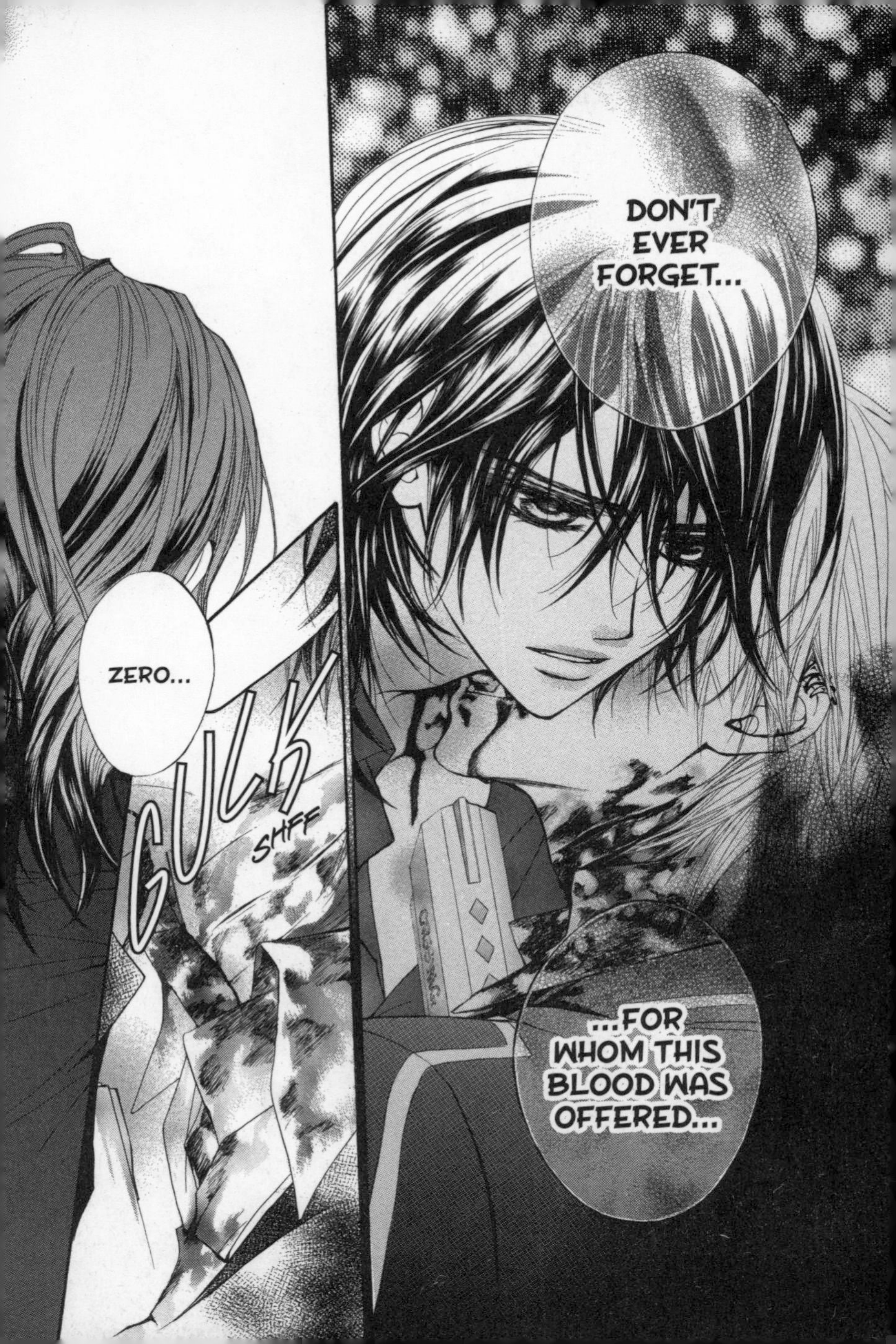
DON'T EVER FORGET...
...FOR WHOM THIS BLOOD WAS OFFERED...
ZERO...
GULK
SHFF

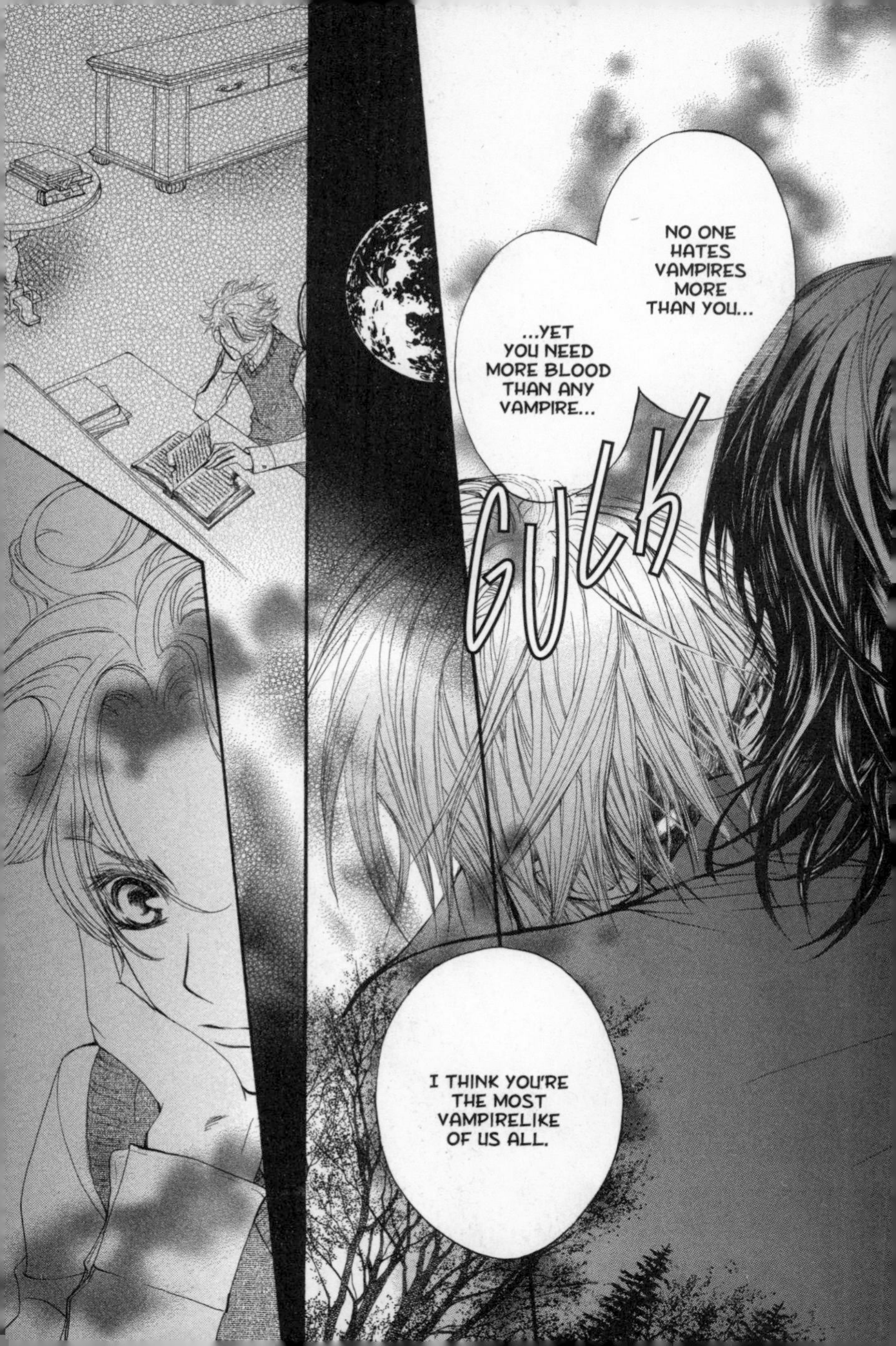
NO ONE HATES VAMPIRES MORE THAN YOU...
...YET YOU NEED MORE BLOOD THAN ANY VAMPIRE...
GULK
I THINK YOU'RE THE MOST VAMPIRELIKE OF US ALL.

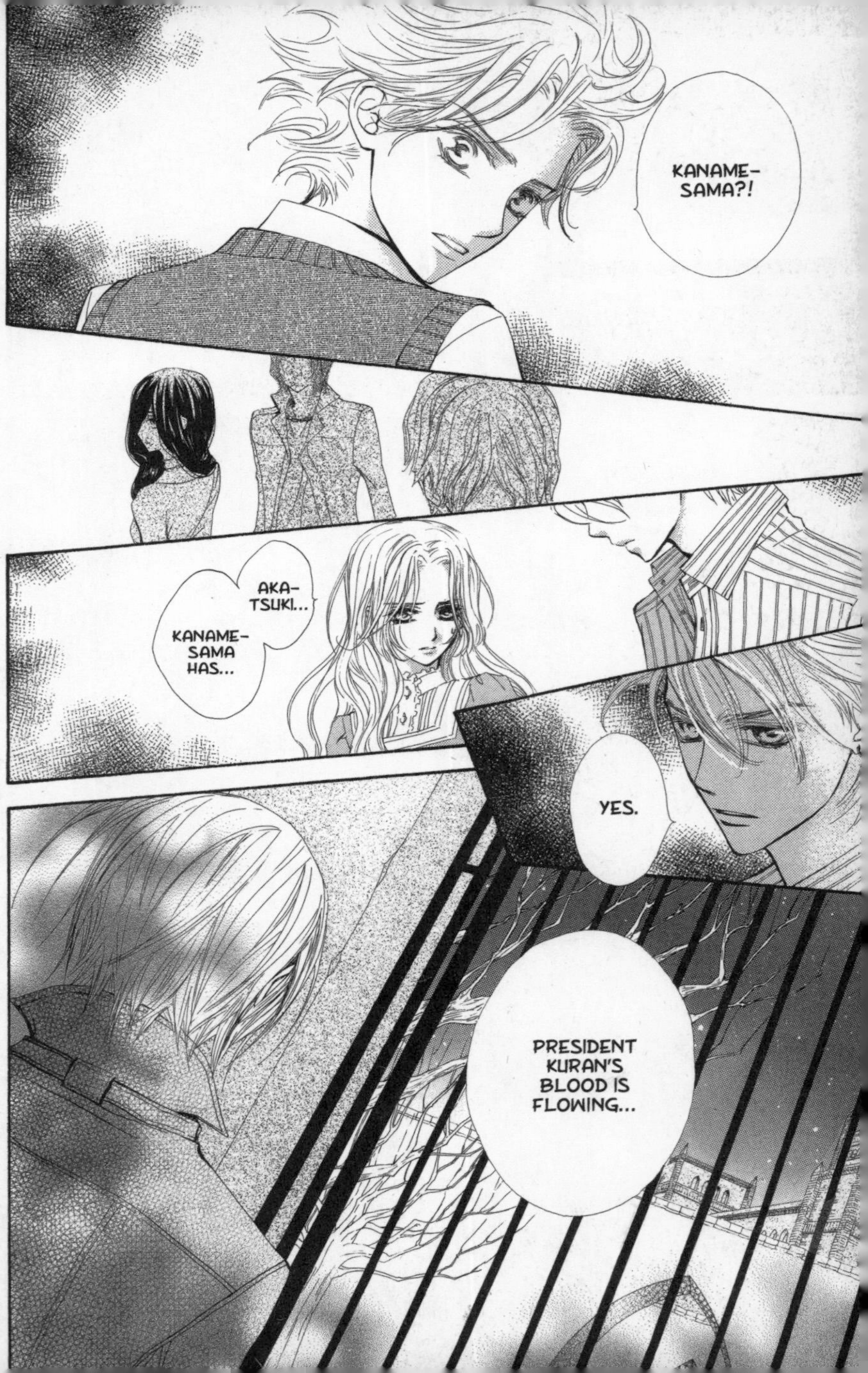
KANAME-SAMA?!
AKA-TSUKI...
KANAME-SAMA HAS...
YES.
PRESIDENT KURAN'S BLOOD IS FLOWING...

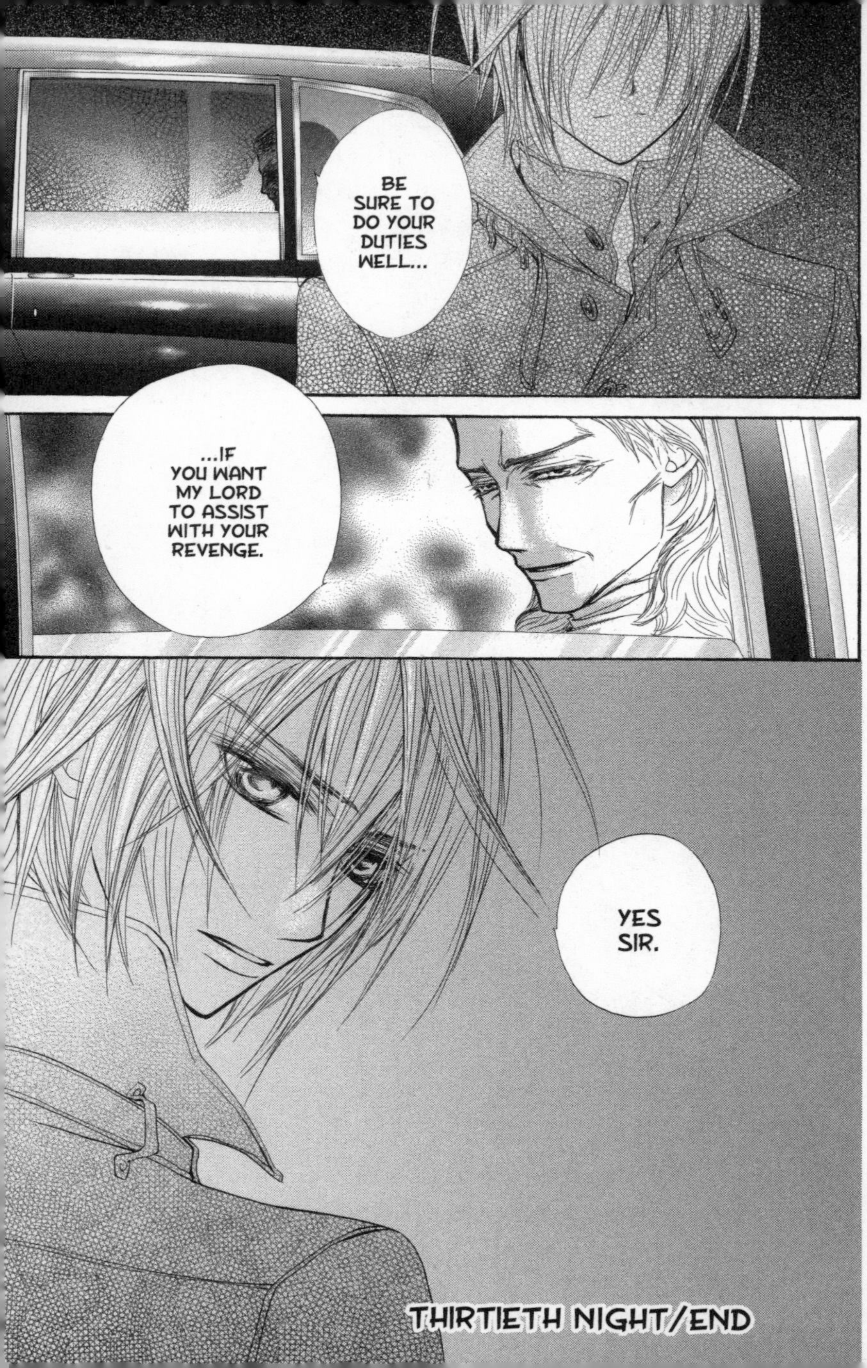
BE SURE TO DO YOUR DUTIES WELL...
...IF YOU WANT MY LORD TO ASSIST WITH YOUR REVENGE.
YES SIR.
THIRTIETH NIGHT/END

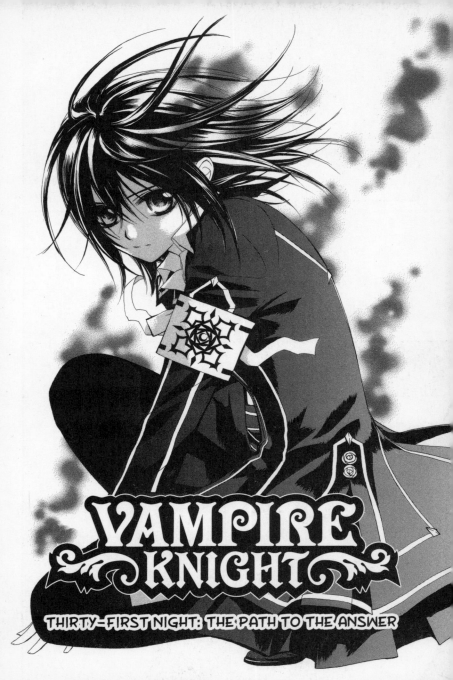

VAMPIRE KNIGHT

THIRTY-FIRST NIGHT: THE PATH TO THE ANSWER

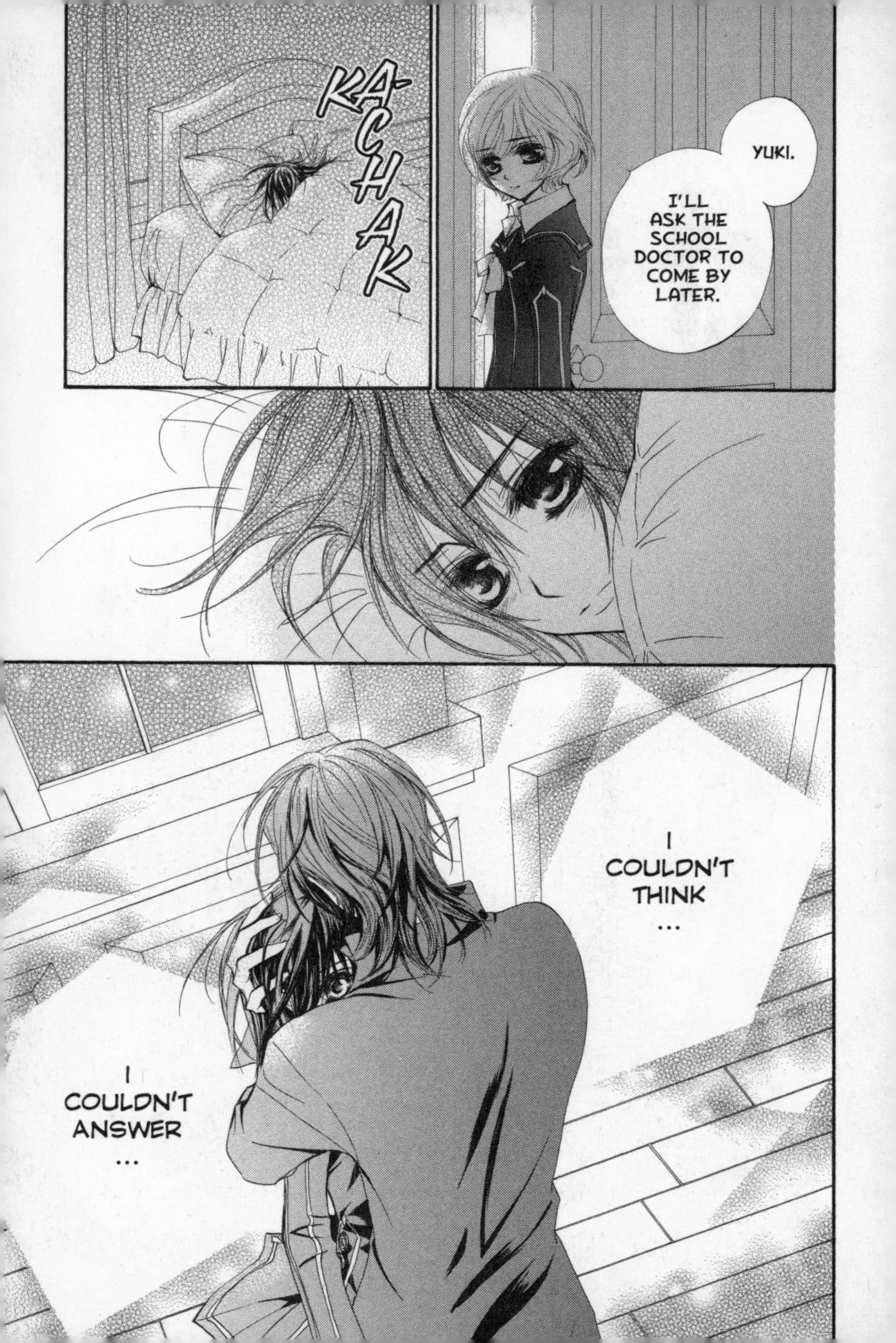
YUKI.
I'LL ASK THE SCHOOL DOCTOR TO COME BY LATER.
KA-CHAK
I COULDN'T THINK ...
I COULDN'T ANSWER ...

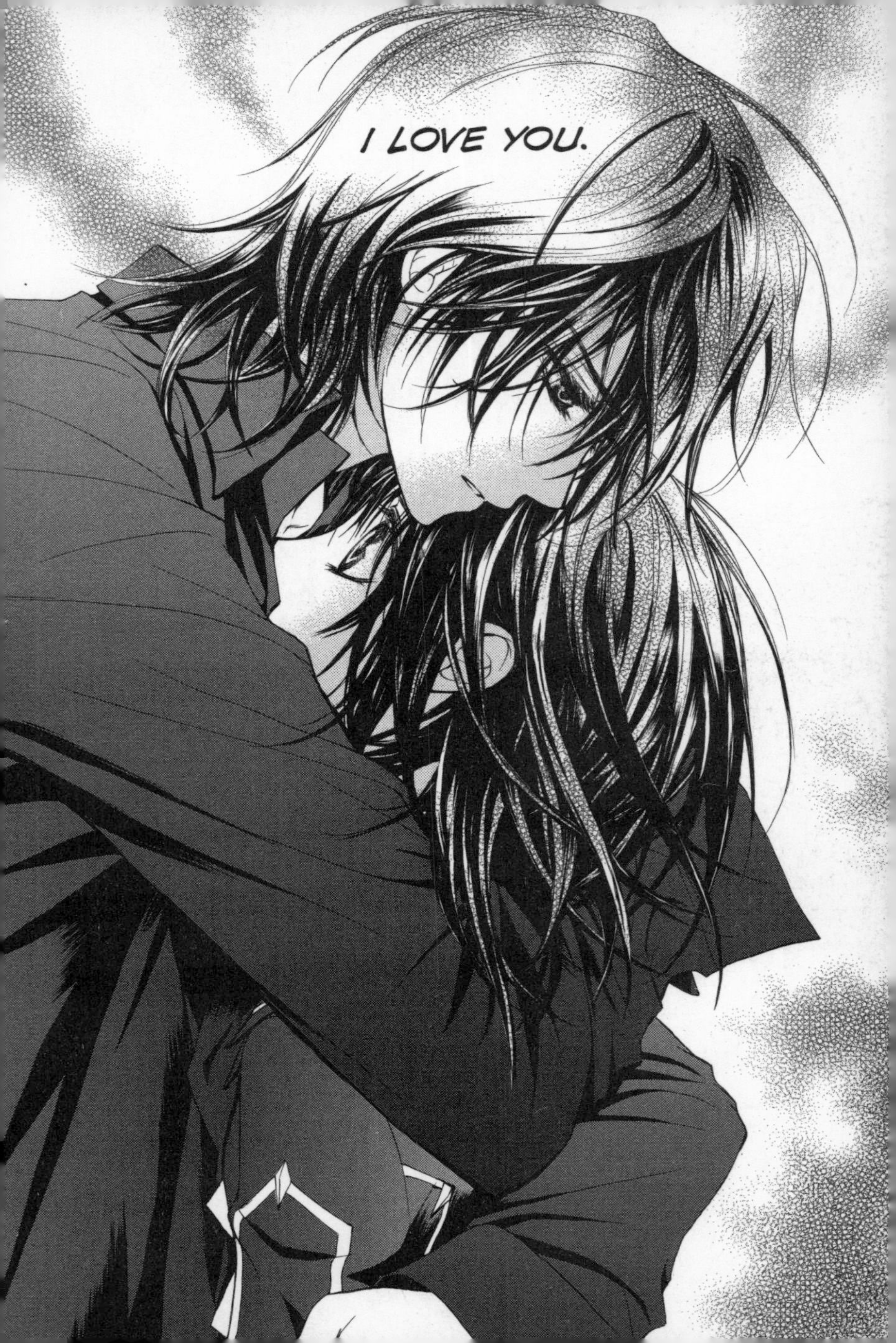
I LOVE YOU.

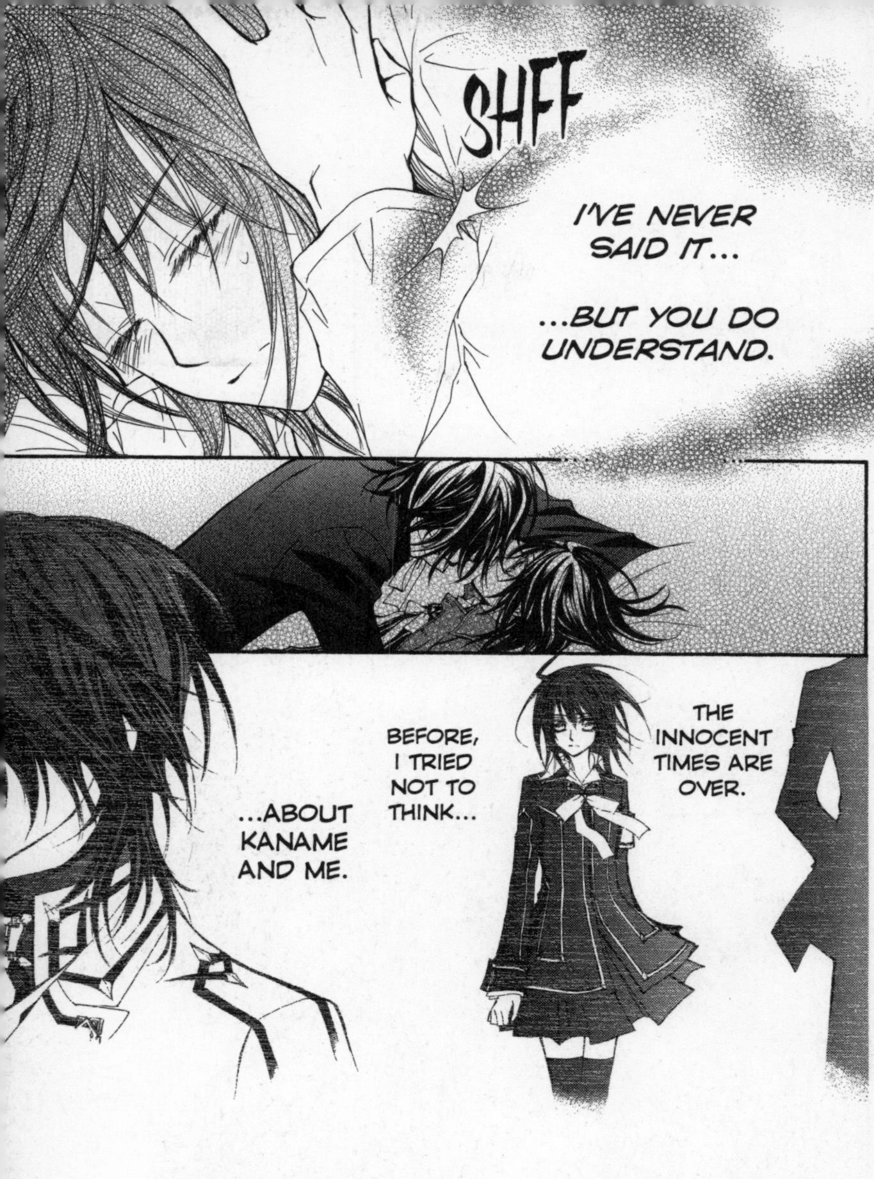
SHFF
I'VE NEVER SAID IT...
...BUT YOU DO UNDERSTAND.
THE INNOCENT TIMES ARE OVER.
BEFORE, I TRIED NOT TO THINK...
...ABOUT KANAME AND ME.

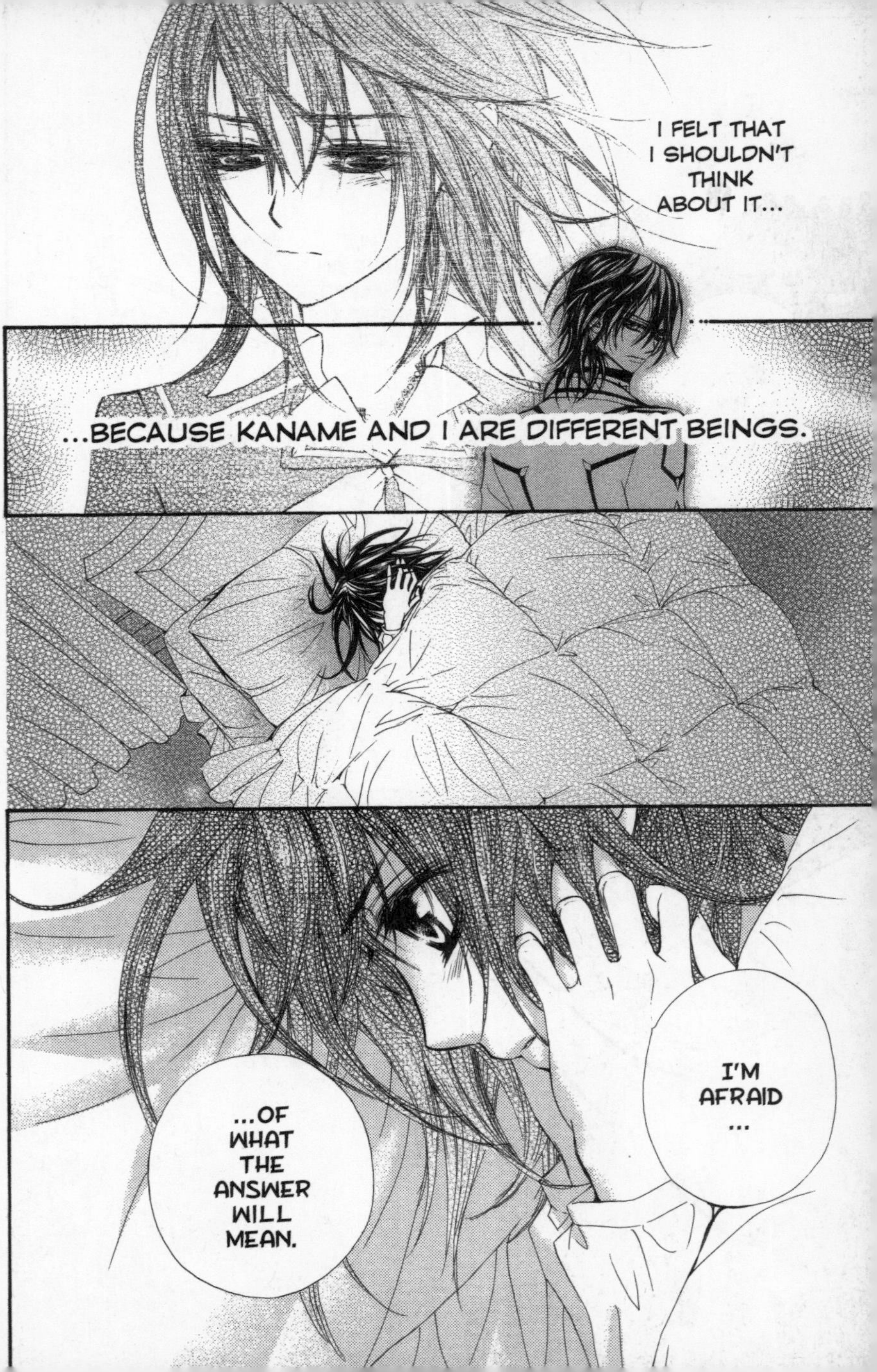
I FELT THAT I SHOULDN'T THINK ABOUT IT...
...BECAUSE KANAME AND I ARE DIFFERENT BEINGS.
I'M AFRAID ...
...OF WHAT THE ANSWER WILL MEAN.

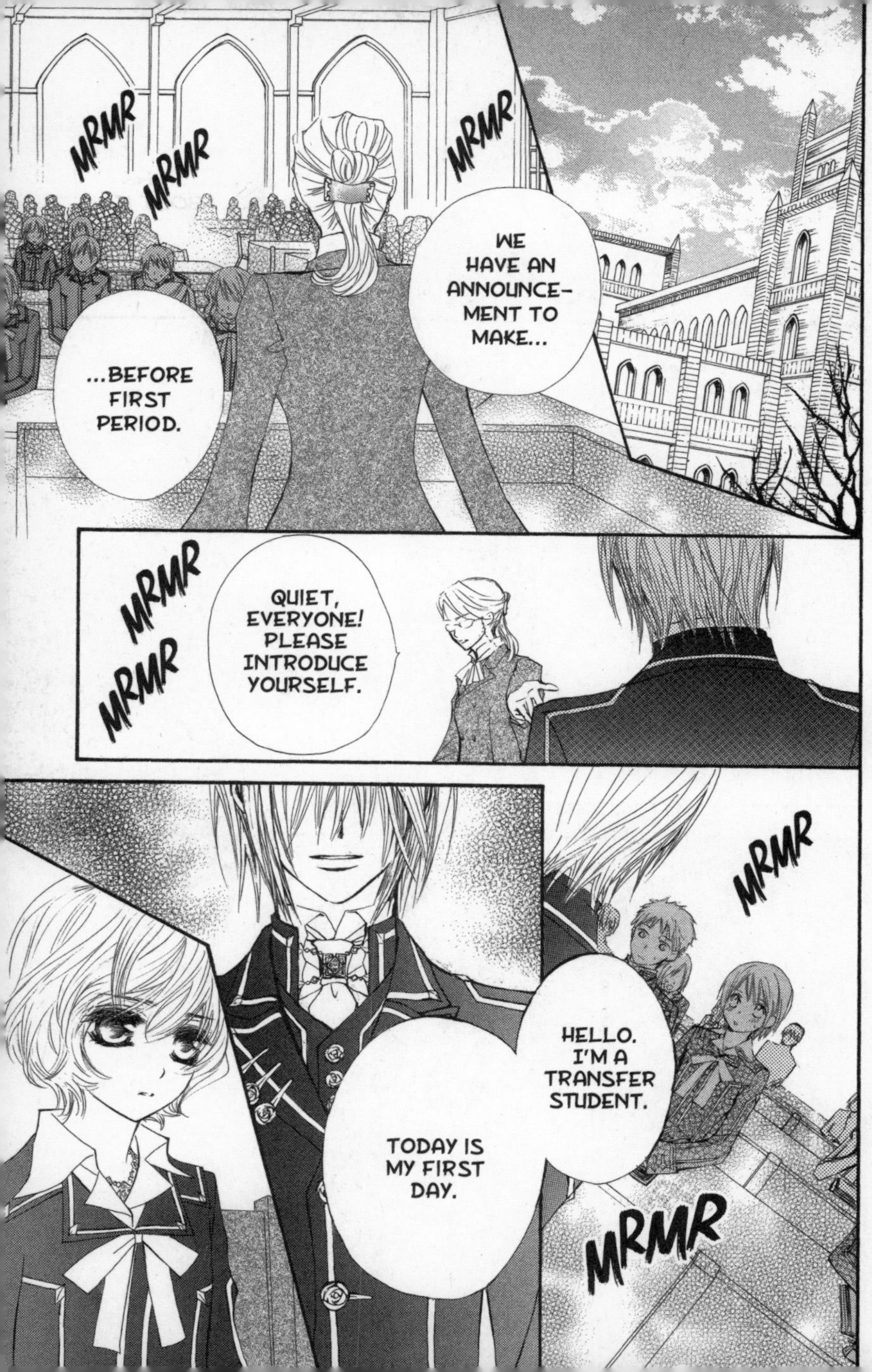
MRMR
WE HAVE AN ANNOUNCE-MENT TO MAKE...
...BEFORE FIRST PERIOD.
MRMR
MRMR
QUIET, EVERYONE! PLEASE INTRODUCE YOURSELF.
MRMR
MRMR
MRMR
HELLO. I'M A TRANSFER STUDENT.
TODAY IS MY FIRST DAY.
MRMR

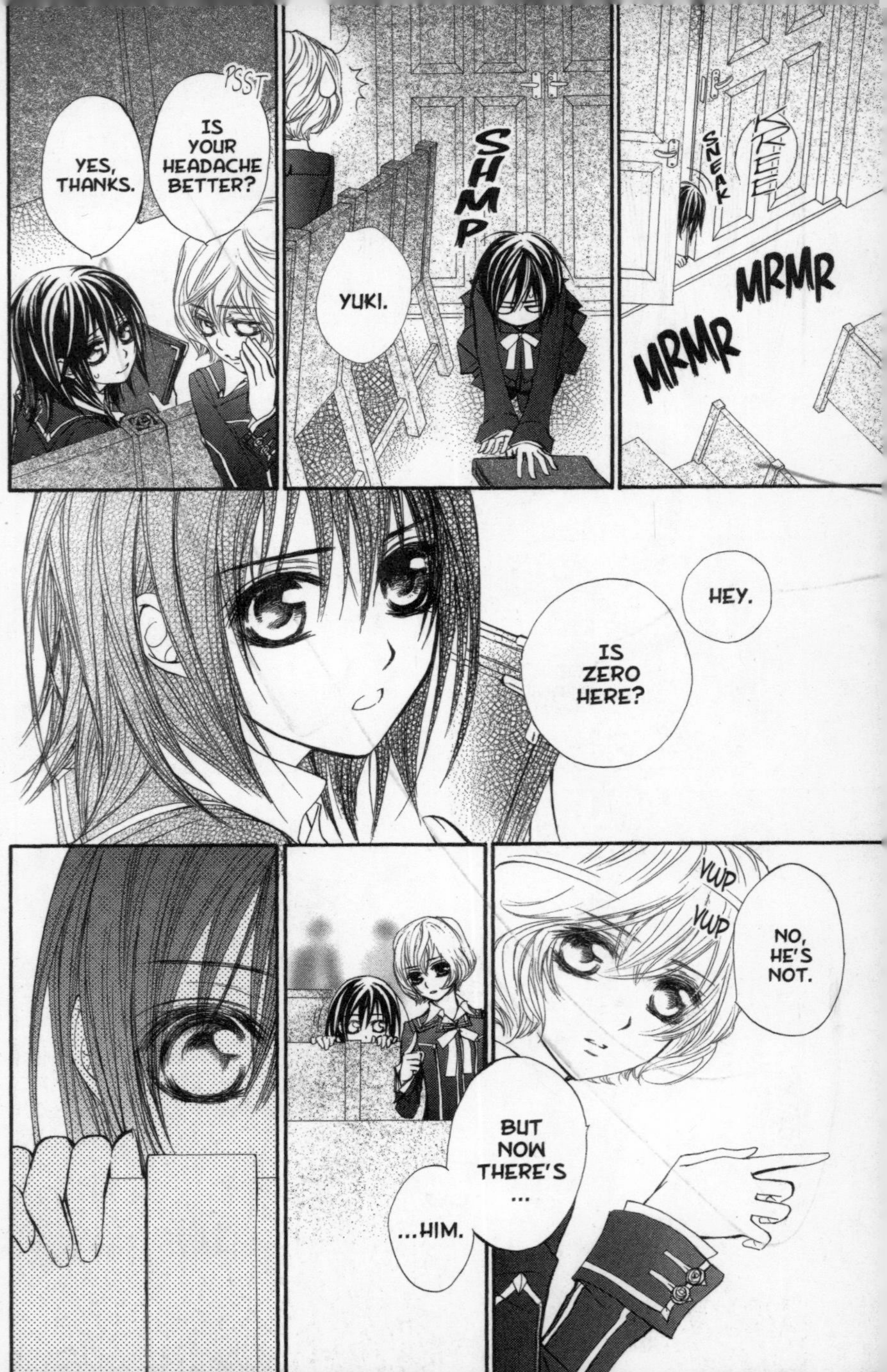
KREEE
SNEAK
MRMR
MRMR
SHMP
YUKI.
PSST
IS YOUR HEADACHE BETTER?
YES, THANKS.
HEY.
IS ZERO HERE?
VUP
VUP
NO, HE'S NOT.
BUT NOW THERE'S ...
...HIM.

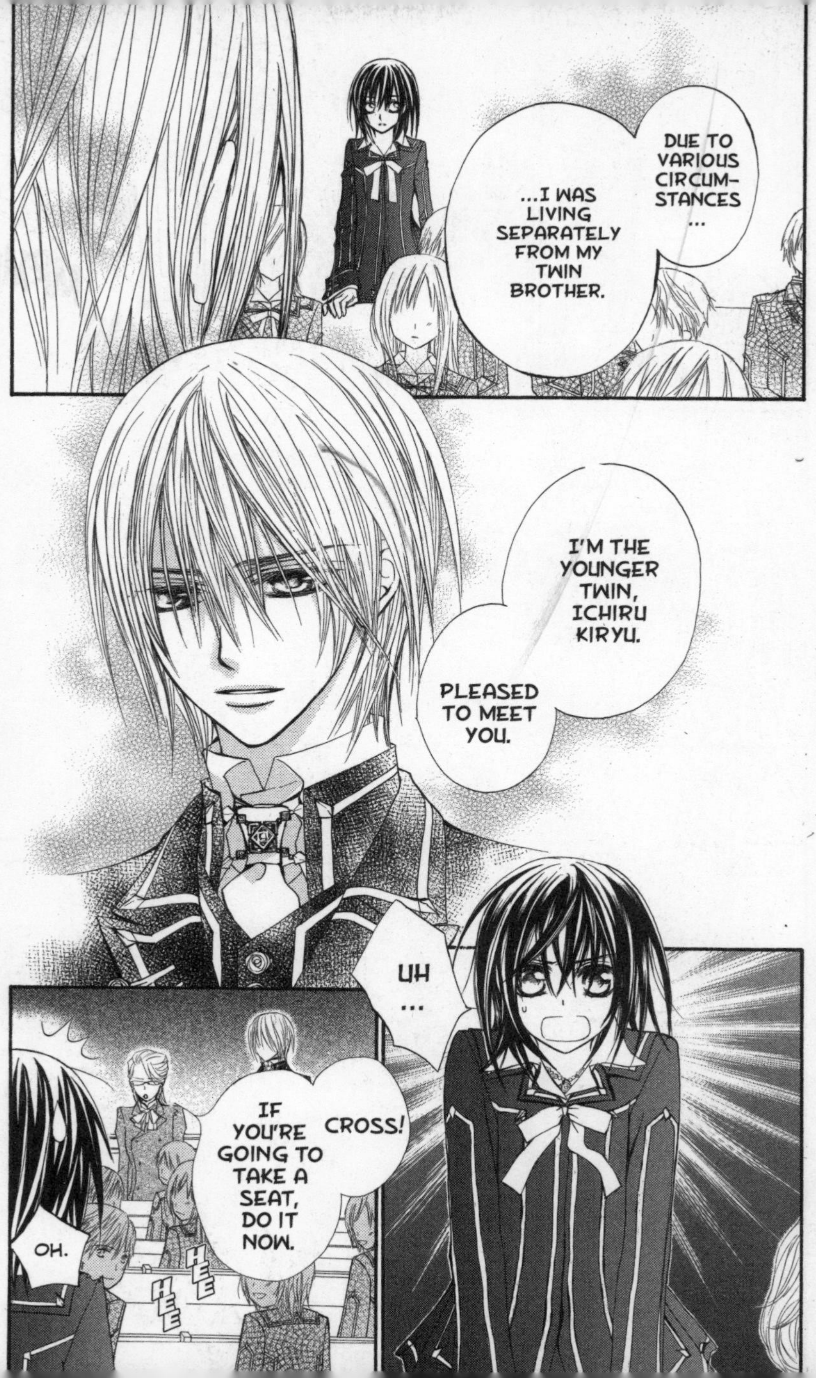
DUE TO VARIOUS CIRCUM-STANCES...
...I WAS LIVING SEPARATELY FROM MY TWIN BROTHER.
I'M THE YOUNGER TWIN, ICHIRU KIRYU.
PLEASED TO MEET YOU.
UH...
CROSS!
IF YOU'RE GOING TO TAKE A SEAT, DO IT NOW.
HEE HEE
OH.

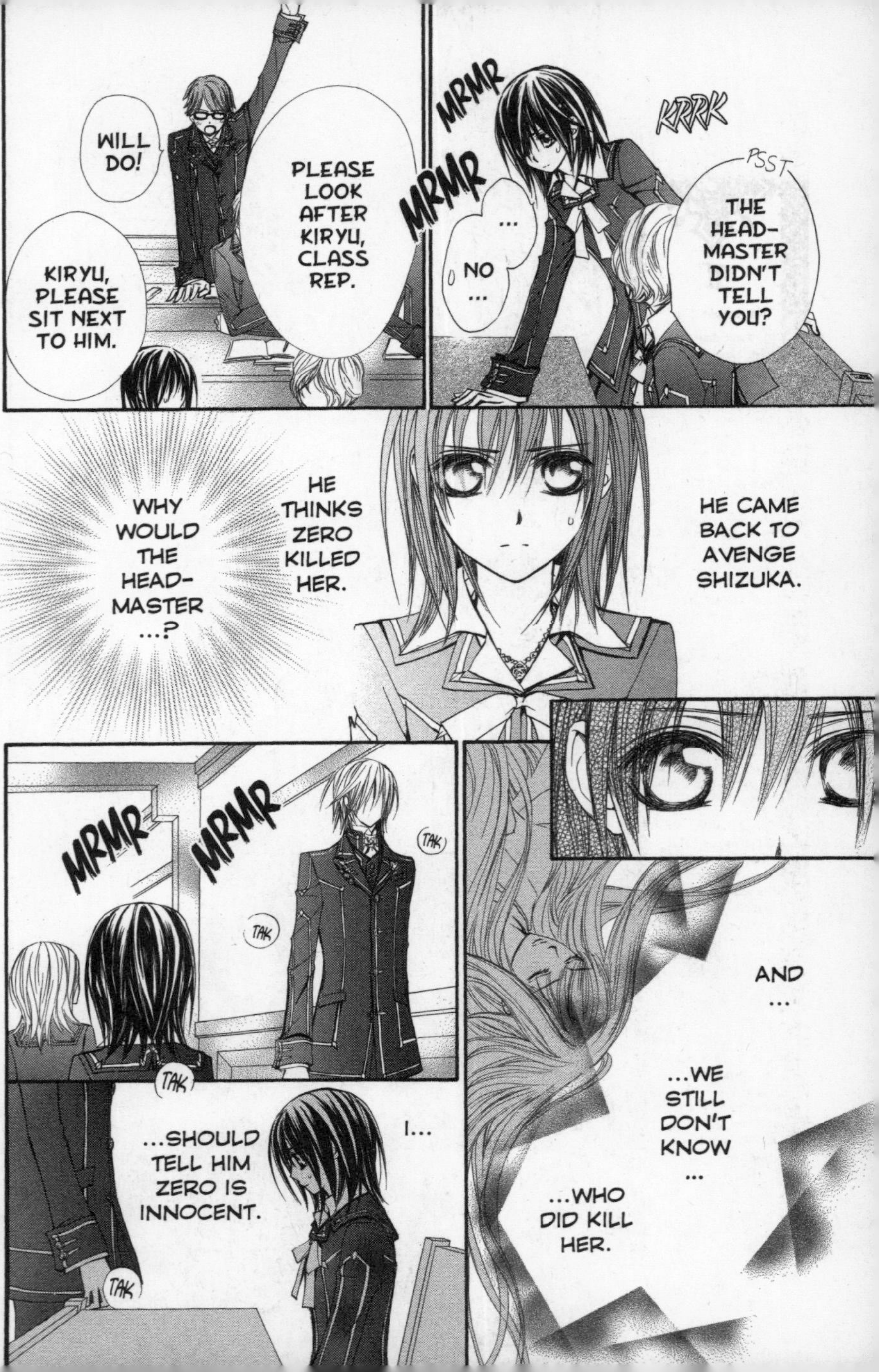
KRRK
PSST
THE HEAD-MASTER DIDN'T TELL YOU?
MRMR
MRMR
... NO ...
PLEASE LOOK AFTER KIRYU, CLASS REP.
WILL DO!
KIRYU, PLEASE SIT NEXT TO HIM.
HE CAME BACK TO AVENGE SHIZUKA.
HE THINKS ZERO KILLED HER.
WHY WOULD THE HEAD-MASTER ...?
AND ...
...WE STILL DON'T KNOW ...
...WHO DID KILL HER.
TAK
TAK
MRMR
MRMR
TAK
I...
...SHOULD TELL HIM ZERO IS INNOCENT.
TAK

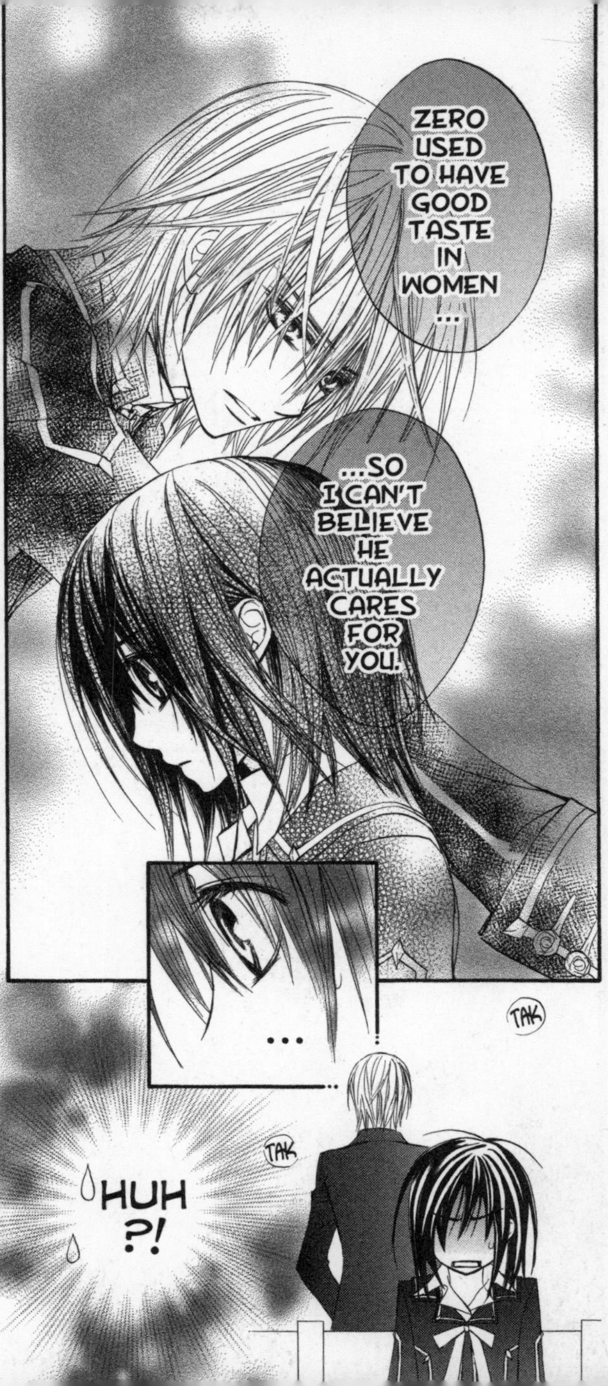
ZERO USED TO HAVE GOOD TASTE IN WOMEN...
...SO I CAN'T BELIEVE HE ACTUALLY CARES FOR YOU.
TAK
...
TAK
HUH?!

II

The anime...

In the beginning, I felt it was a festival happening far away...But as the premier approached, there were various things that I had to do as the mangaka. The days passed frantically, and before I knew it, I'd become just a viewer who was looking forward to the broadcast date.

...Yeah. I really feel happy about it.

People are working on the anime. People are cheering for the anime. I want to shout "Thank you so much!"

Director Sayama-san (he really cherishes the original manga) and all the staff's enthusiasm really inspired me. Woo! The manga can't lose!!!! Yeah!

The anime opening song (by ON/OFF) and the ending song (by Kanon Wakeshima-san) are very good songs too. I'm so very happy, what should I do?! Calm down.○○

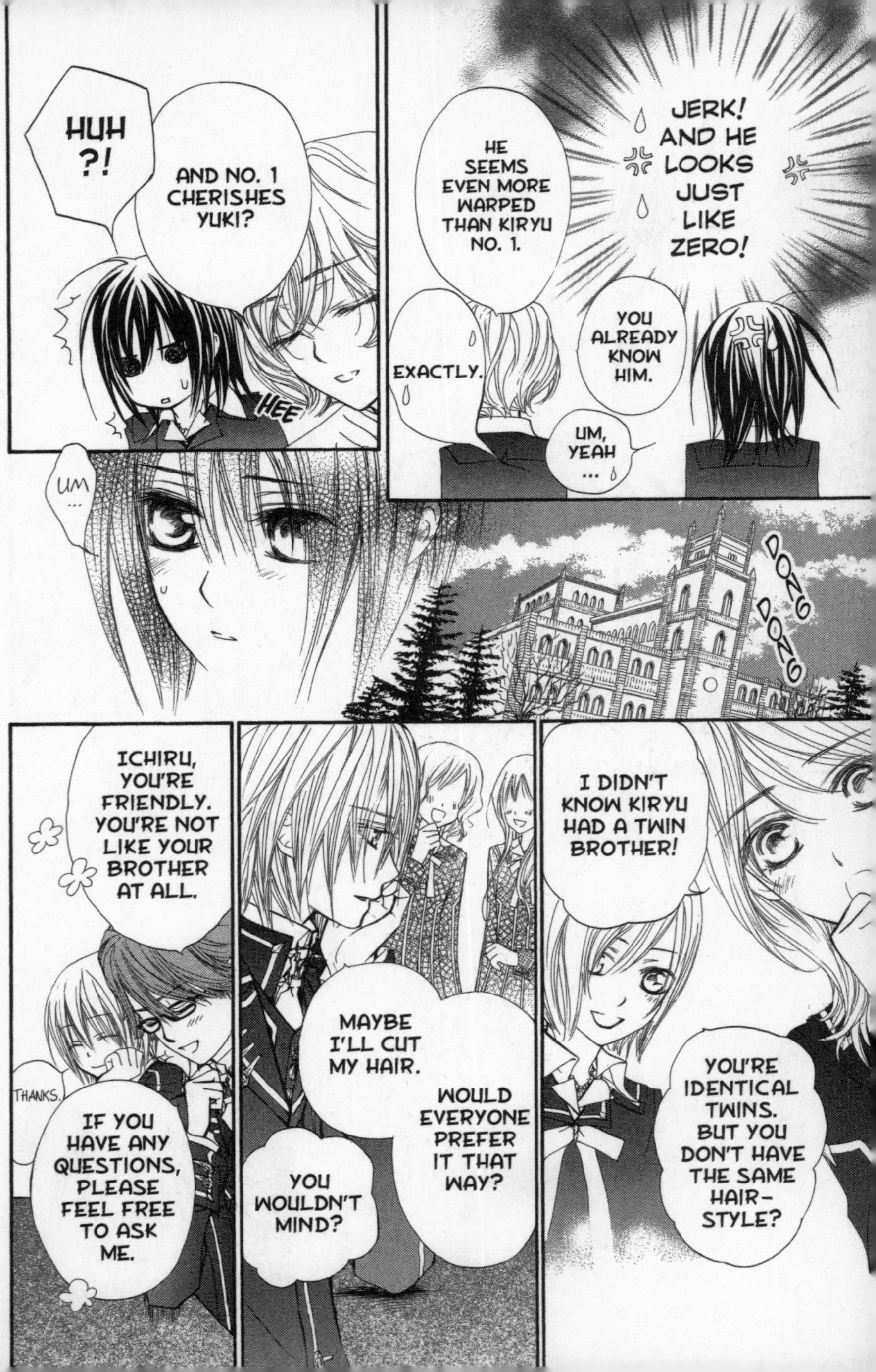
JERK! AND HE LOOKS JUST LIKE ZERO!
HE SEEMS EVEN MORE WARPED THAN KIRYU NO. 1.
YOU ALREADY KNOW HIM.
EXACTLY.
UM, YEAH ...
AND NO. 1 CHERISHES YUKI?
HUH ?!
HEE
DOZO
DOZO
DOZO
UM ...
I DIDN'T KNOW KIRYU HAD A TWIN BROTHER!
YOU'RE IDENTICAL TWINS. BUT YOU DON'T HAVE THE SAME HAIR-STYLE?
MAYBE I'LL CUT MY HAIR.
WOULD EVERYONE PREFER IT THAT WAY?
YOU WOULDN'T MIND?
ICHIRU, YOU'RE FRIENDLY. YOU'RE NOT LIKE YOUR BROTHER AT ALL.
THANKS.
IF YOU HAVE ANY QUESTIONS, PLEASE FEEL FREE TO ASK ME.

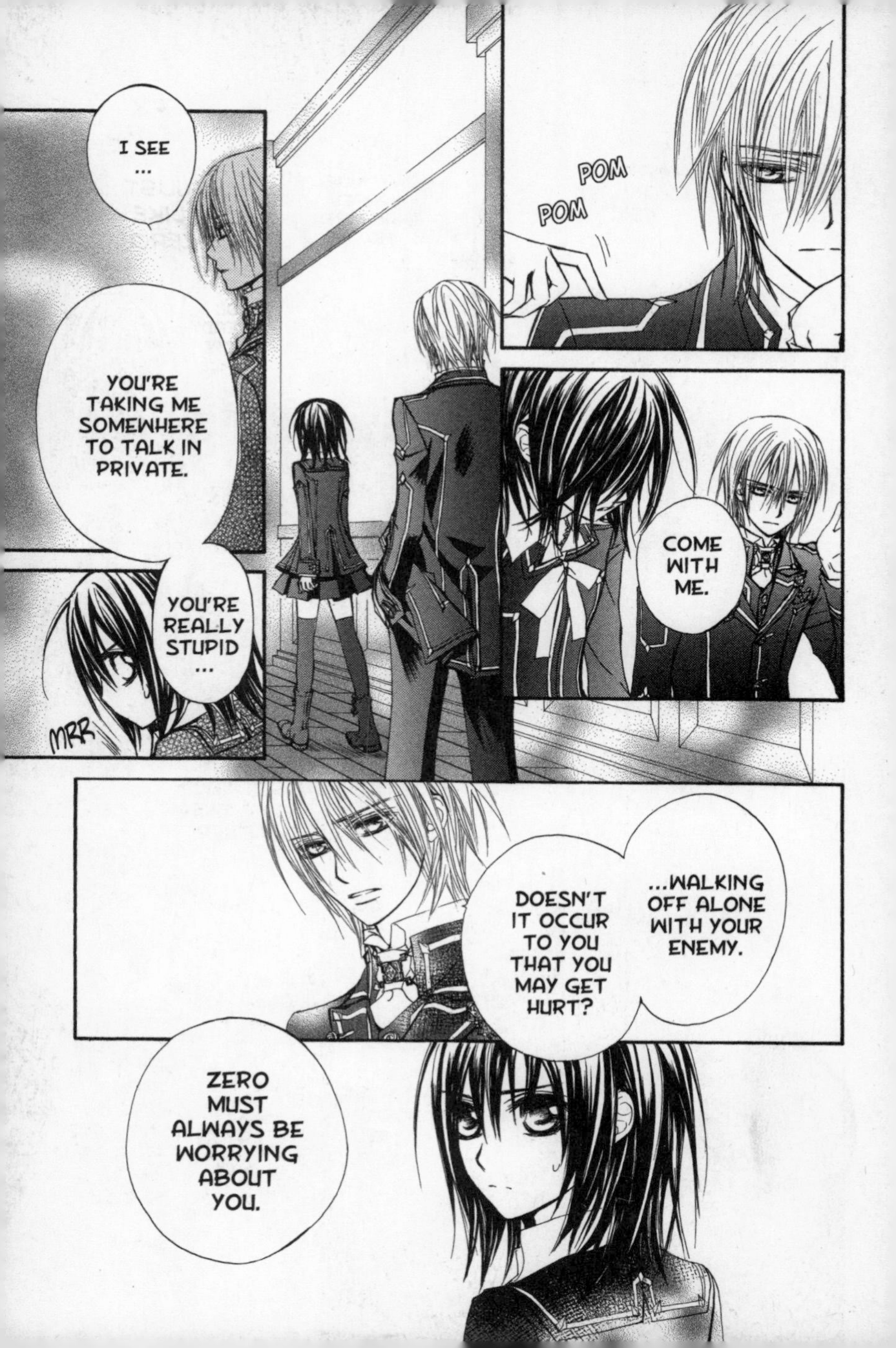
POM
POM
COME WITH ME.
I SEE ...
YOU'RE TAKING ME SOMEWHERE TO TALK IN PRIVATE.
YOU'RE REALLY STUPID ...
MRR
DOESN'T IT OCCUR TO YOU THAT YOU MAY GET HURT?
...WALKING OFF ALONE WITH YOUR ENEMY.
ZERO MUST ALWAYS BE WORRYING ABOUT YOU.

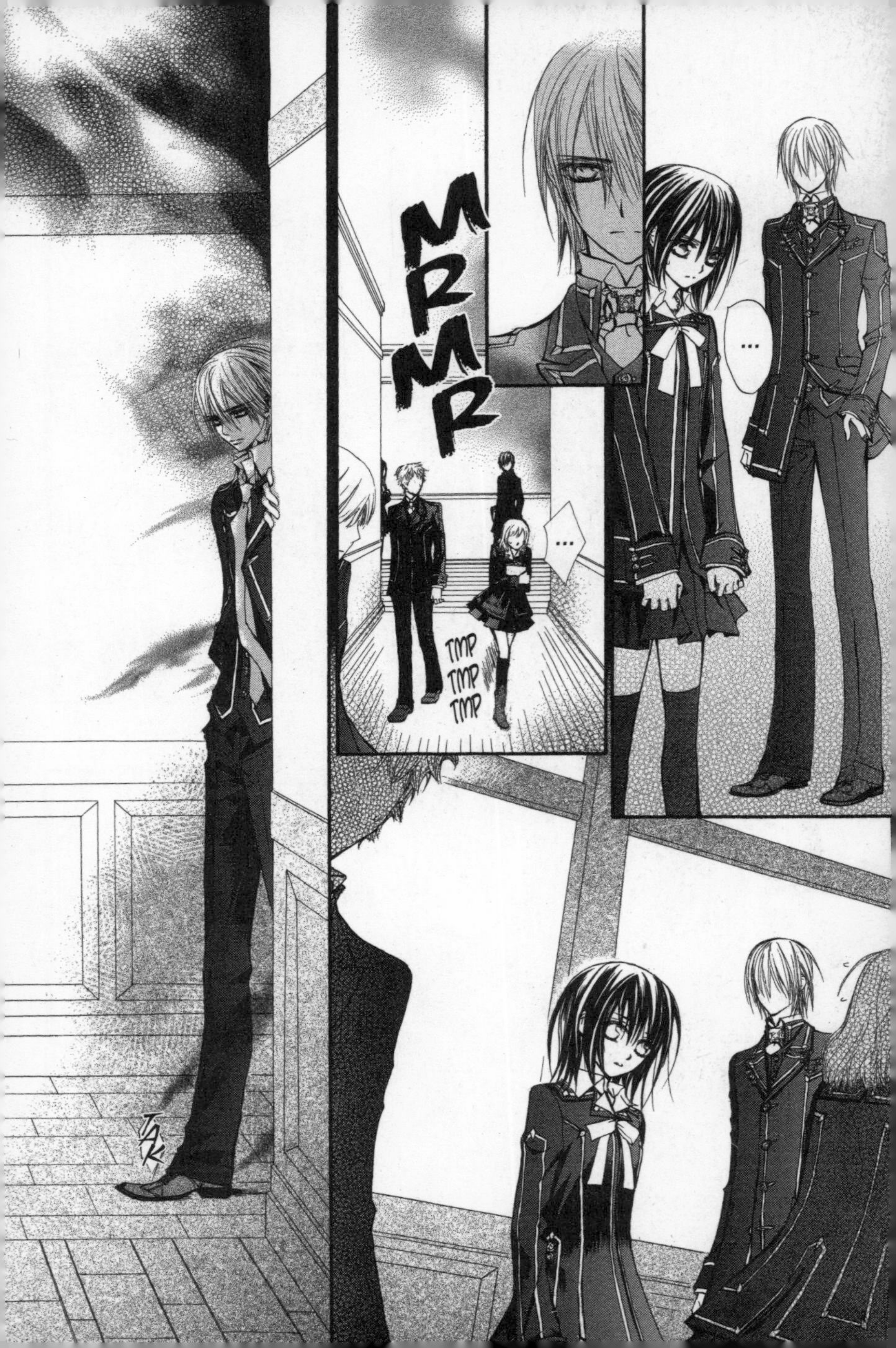
...
MRMR
...
TMP
TMP
TMP
TAK

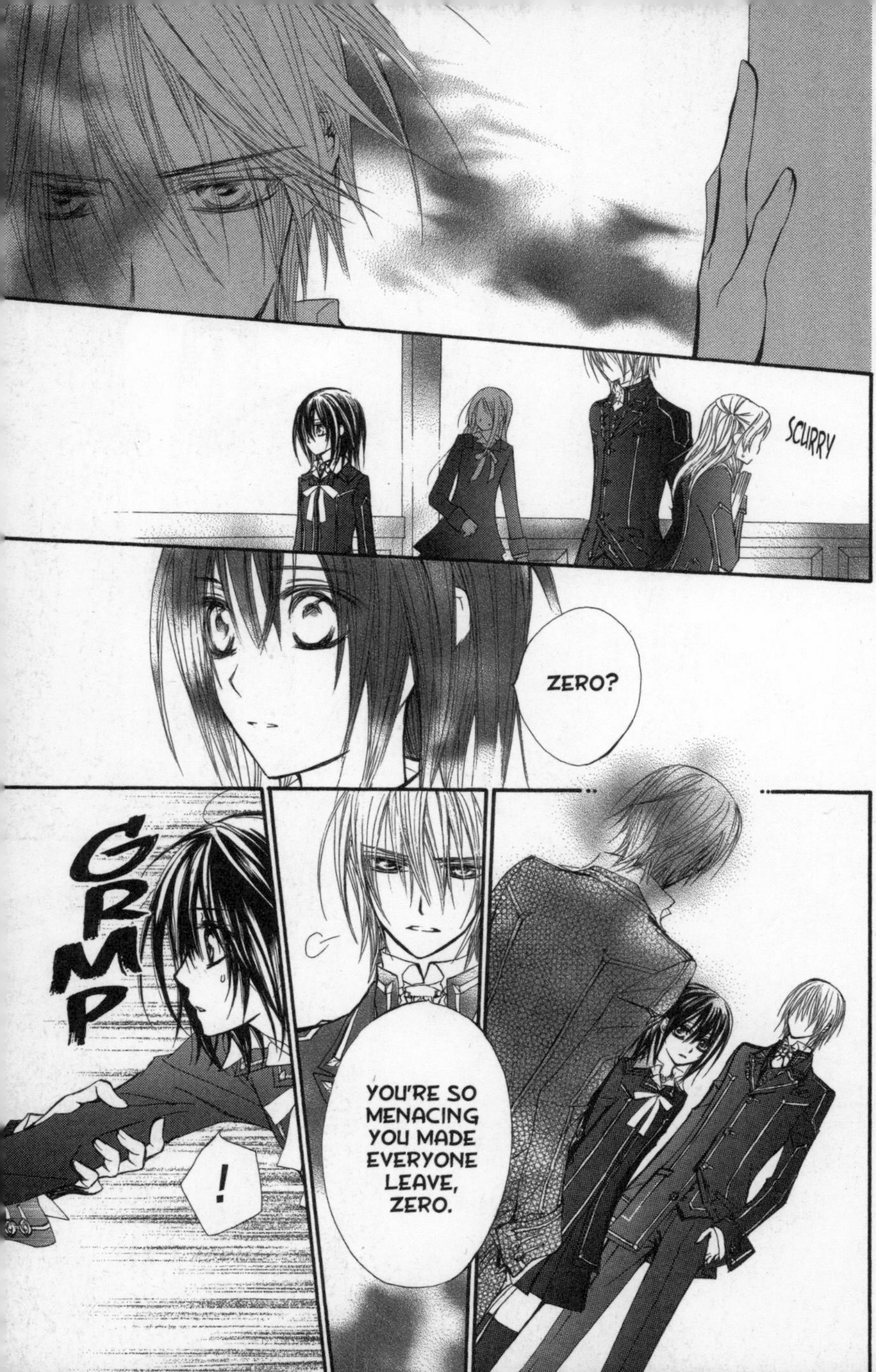
SCURRY
ZERO?
...
...
YOU'RE SO MENACING YOU MADE EVERYONE LEAVE, ZERO.
GRMP
!

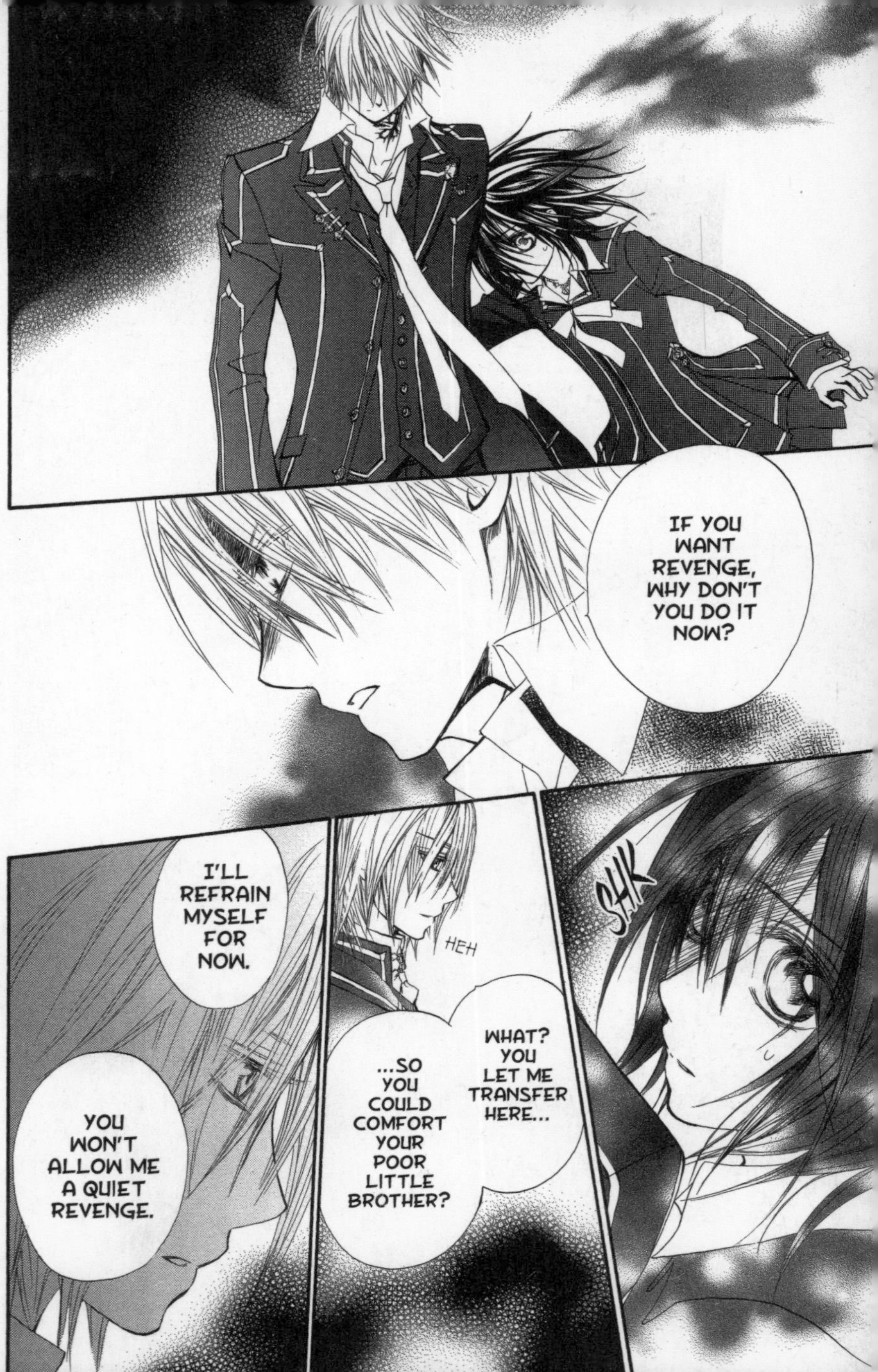
IF YOU WANT REVENGE, WHY DON'T YOU DO IT NOW?
SHK
HEH
WHAT? YOU LET ME TRANSFER HERE...
...SO YOU COULD COMFORT YOUR POOR LITTLE BROTHER?
I'LL REFRAIN MYSELF FOR NOW.
YOU WON'T ALLOW ME A QUIET REVENGE.

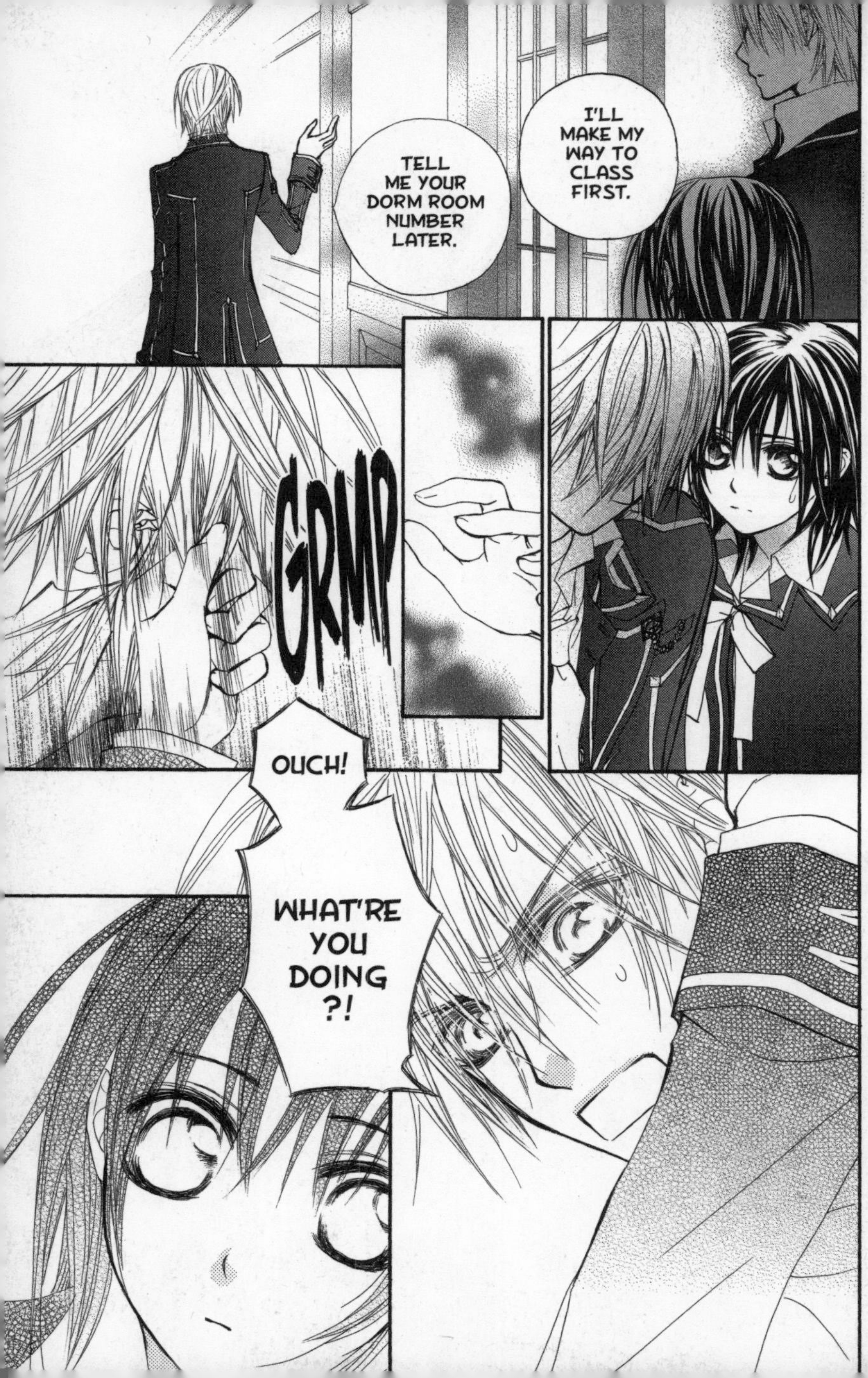
I'LL MAKE MY WAY TO CLASS FIRST.
TELL ME YOUR DORM ROOM NUMBER LATER.
GRMP
OUCH!
WHAT'RE YOU DOING ?!

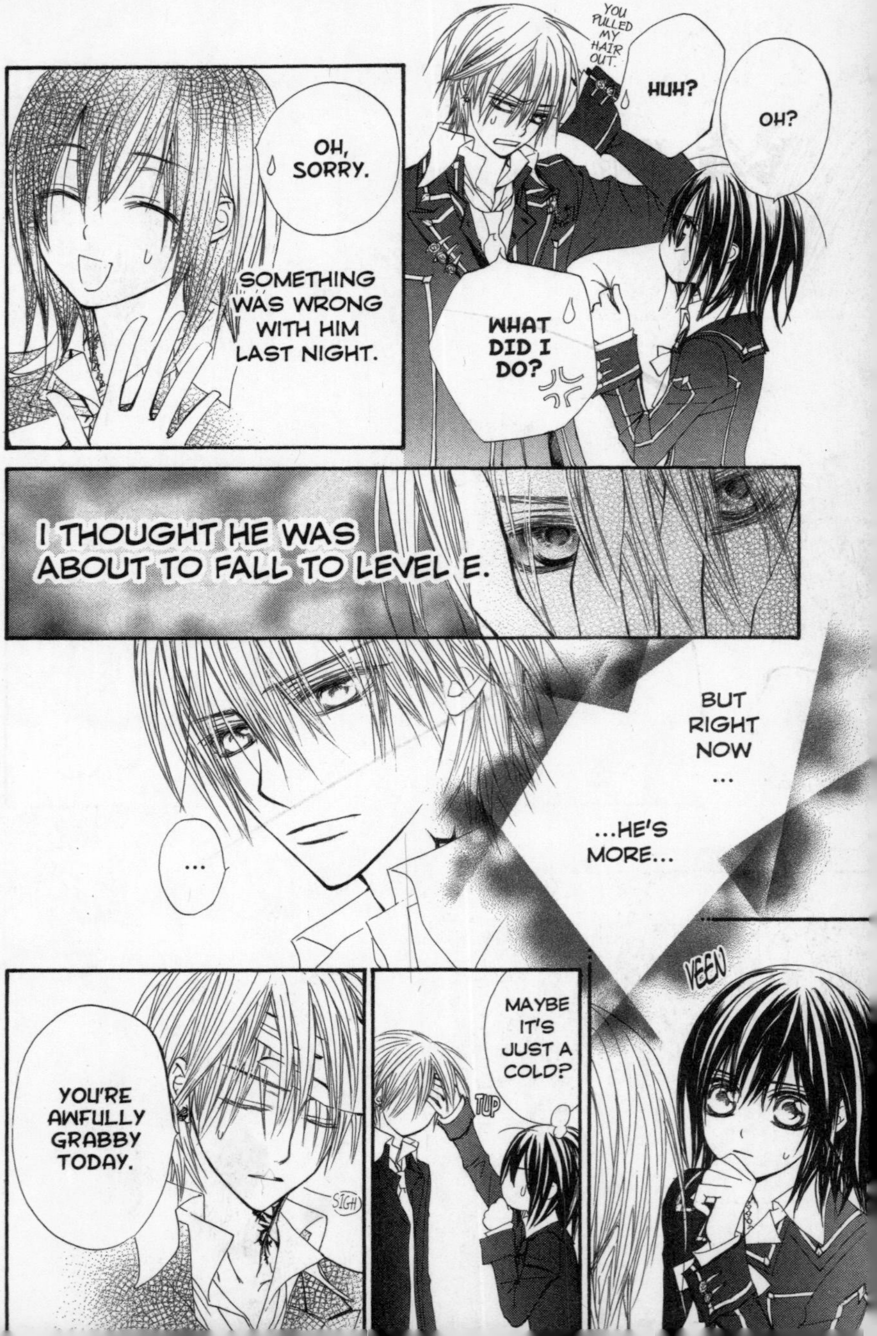
OH?
HUH?
YOU PULLED MY HAIR OUT.
WHAT DID I DO?
OH, SORRY.
SOMETHING WAS WRONG WITH HIM LAST NIGHT.
I THOUGHT HE WAS ABOUT TO FALL TO LEVEL E.
BUT RIGHT NOW ...
...HE'S MORE...
...
VEEN
MAYBE IT'S JUST A COLD?
TUP
YOU'RE AWFULLY GRABBY TODAY.
SIGH

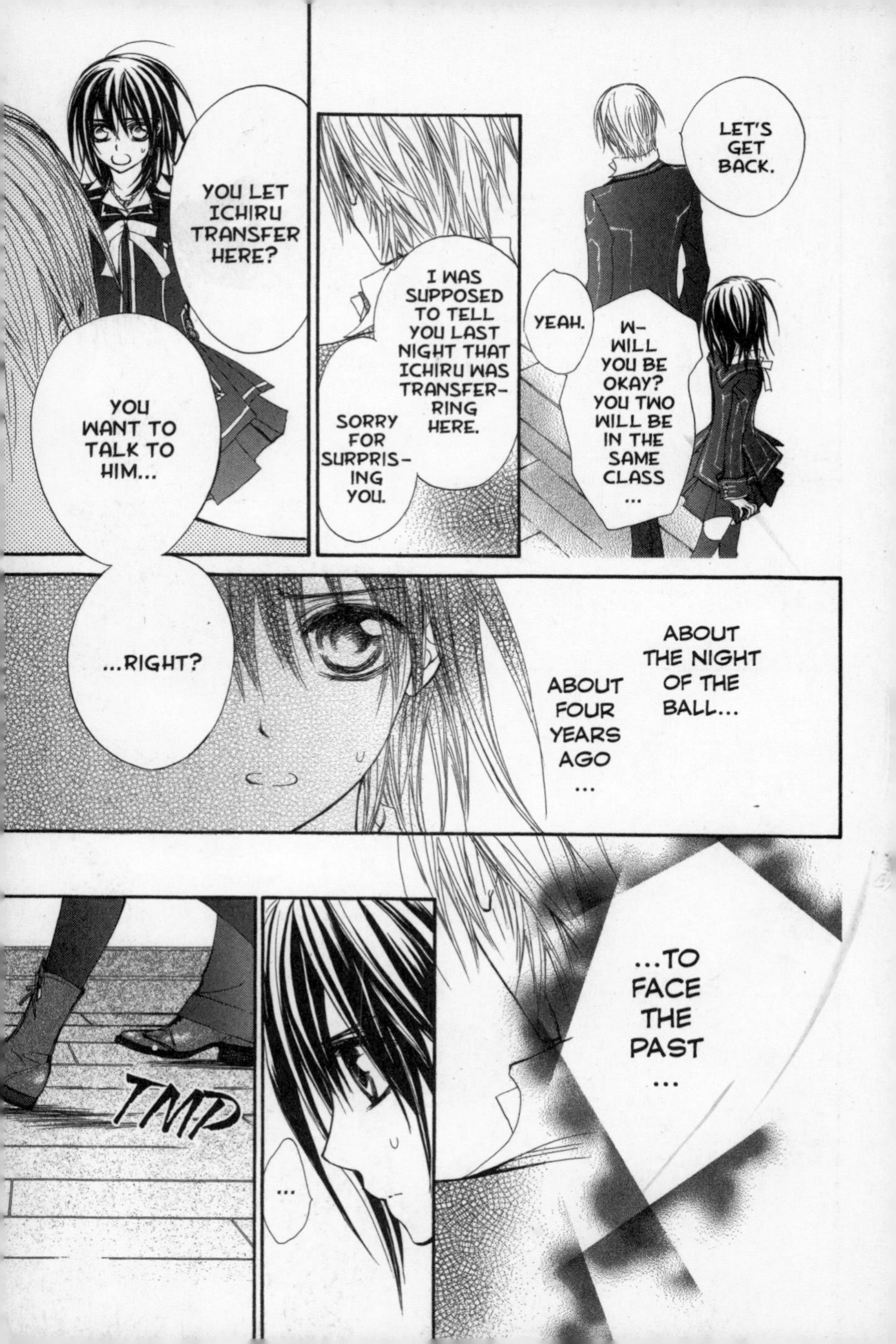
LET'S GET BACK.
YEAH.
W-WILL YOU BE OKAY? YOU TWO WILL BE IN THE SAME CLASS...
I WAS SUPPOSED TO TELL YOU LAST NIGHT THAT ICHIRU WAS TRANSFER-RING HERE.
SORRY FOR SURPRIS-ING YOU.
YOU LET ICHIRU TRANSFER HERE?
YOU WANT TO TALK TO HIM...
...RIGHT?
ABOUT THE NIGHT OF THE BALL...
ABOUT FOUR YEARS AGO...
...TO FACE THE PAST...
...
TMP

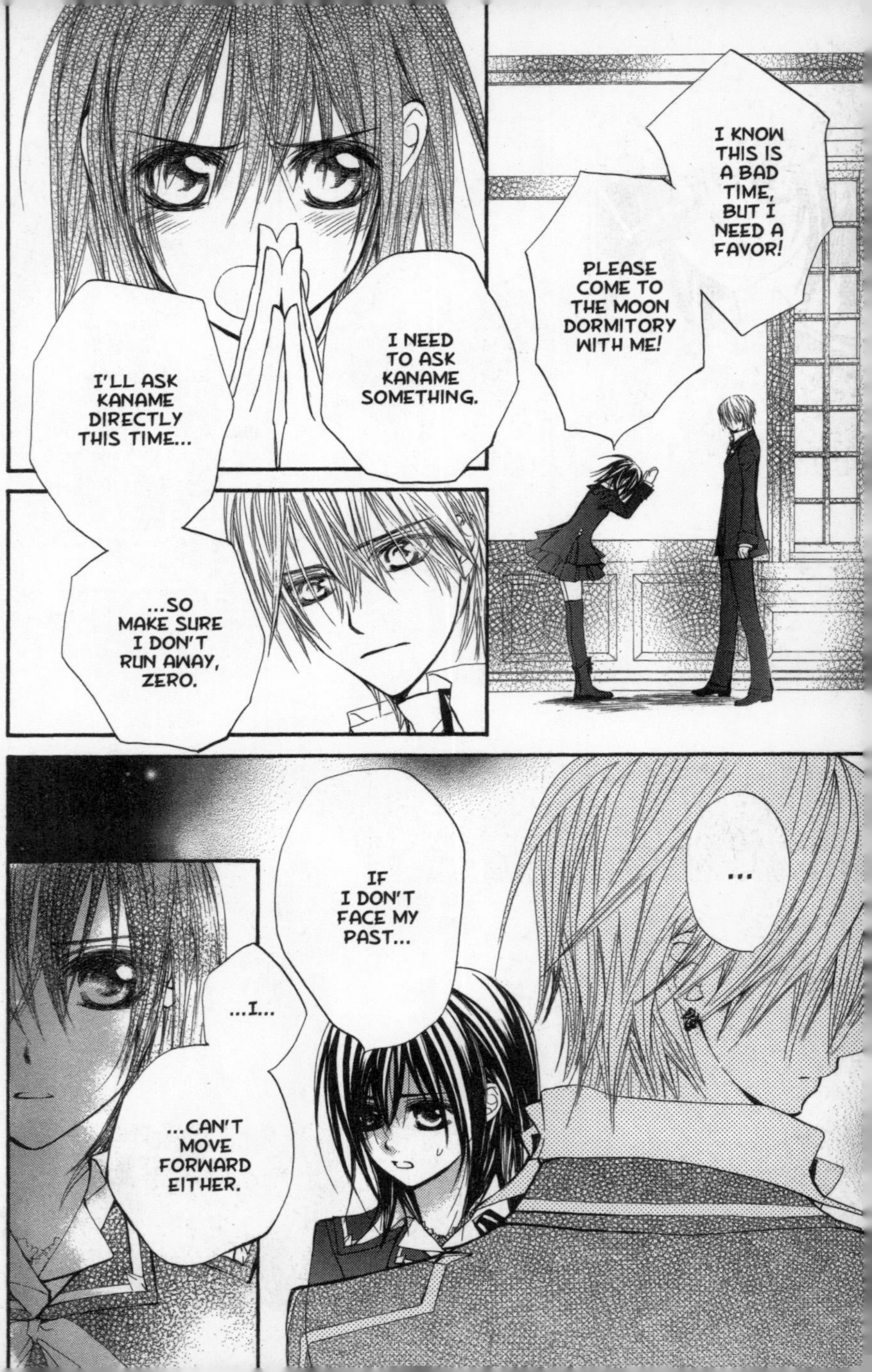
I KNOW THIS IS A BAD TIME, BUT I NEED A FAVOR!
PLEASE COME TO THE MOON DORMITORY WITH ME!
I NEED TO ASK KANAME SOMETHING.
I'LL ASK KANAME DIRECTLY THIS TIME...
...SO MAKE SURE I DON'T RUN AWAY, ZERO.
...
IF I DON'T FACE MY PAST...
...I...
...CAN'T MOVE FORWARD EITHER.

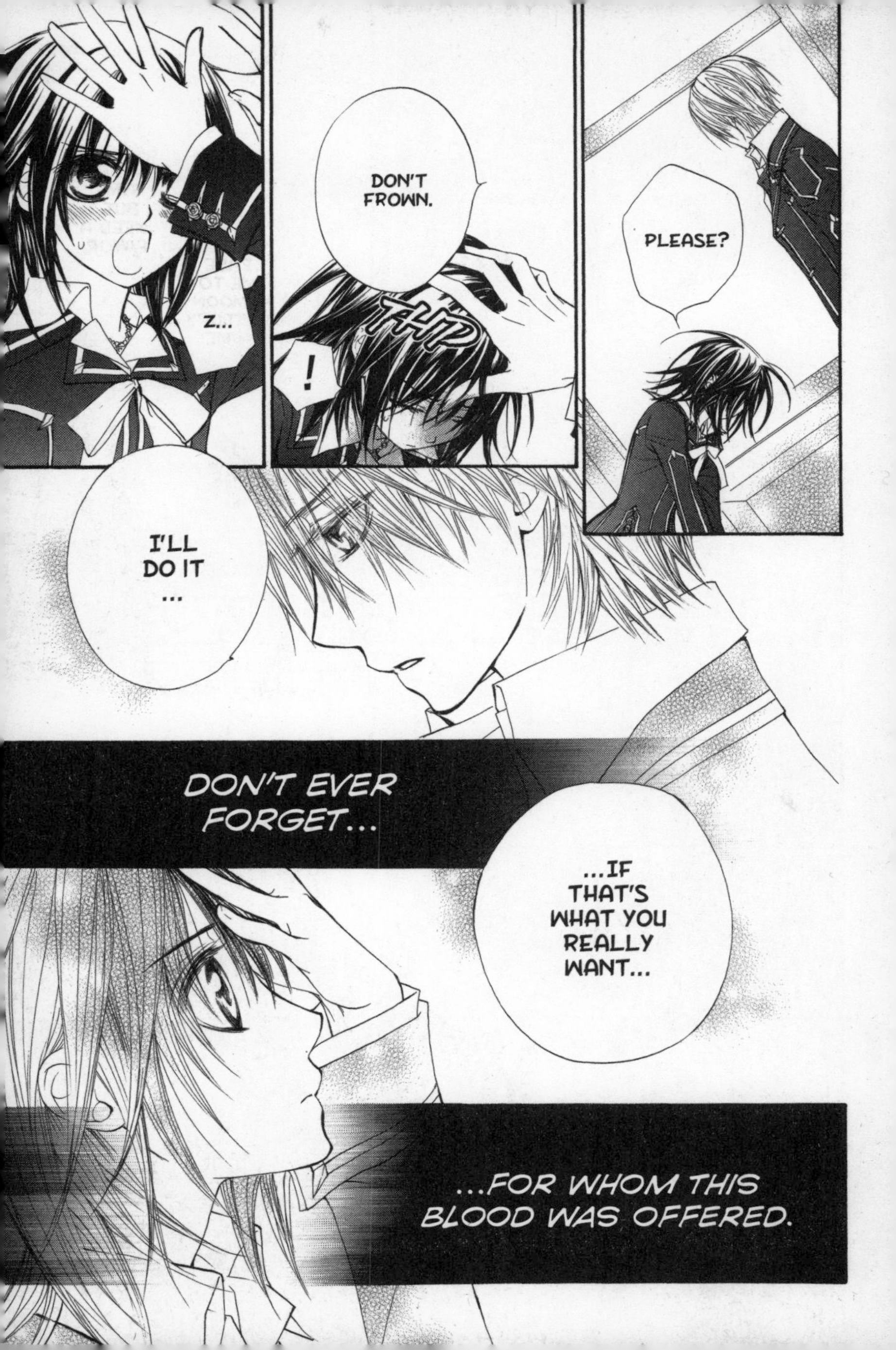

PLEASE?
DON'T FROWN.
!
Z...
I'LL DO IT ...
...IF THAT'S WHAT YOU REALLY WANT...
DON'T EVER FORGET...
...FOR WHOM THIS BLOOD WAS OFFERED.

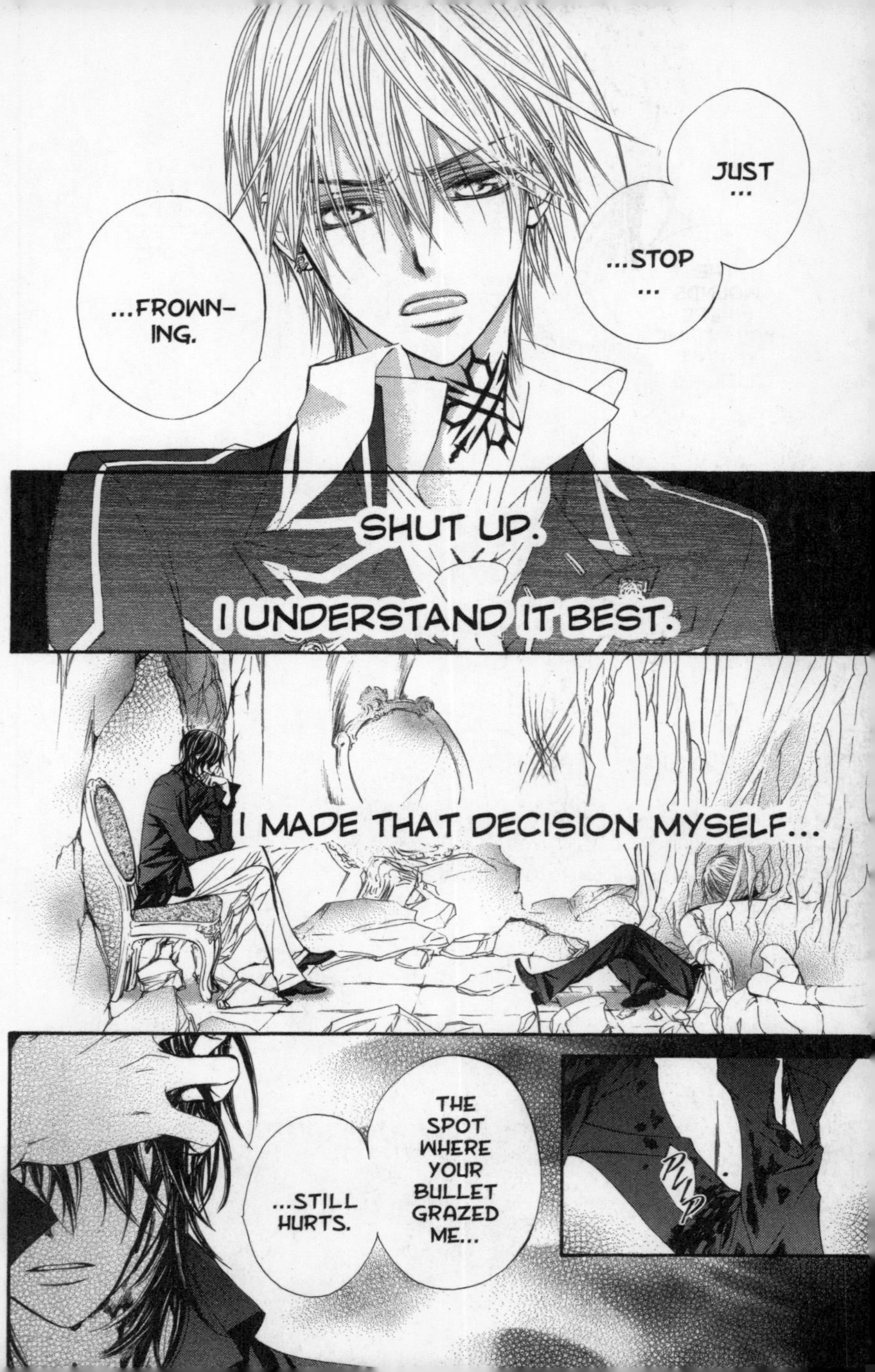
JUST ...
...STOP ...
...FROWN-ING.
SHUT UP.
I UNDERSTAND IT BEST.
I MADE THAT DECISION MYSELF...
PLIP
THE SPOT WHERE YOUR BULLET GRAZED ME...
...STILL HURTS.

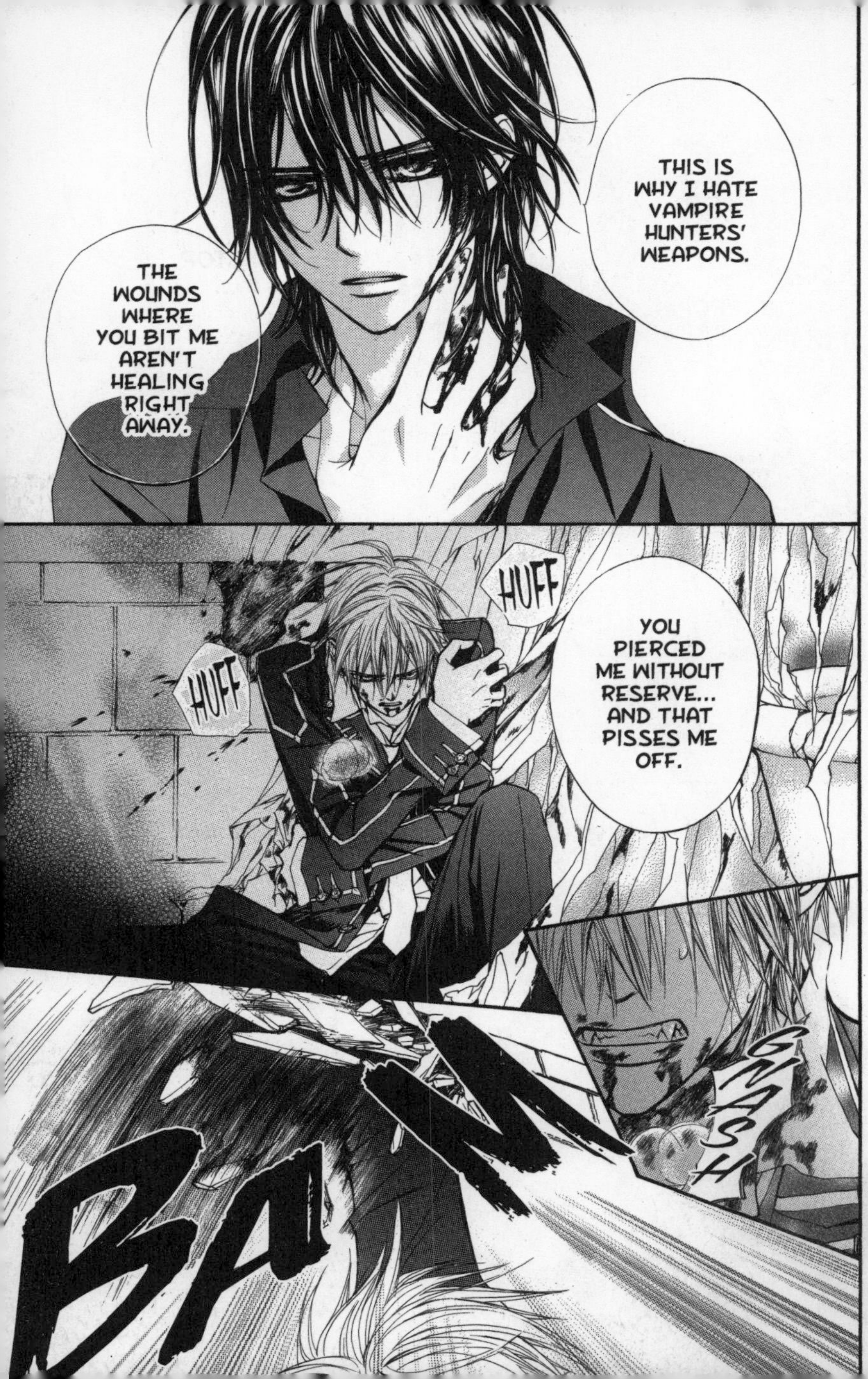
THIS IS WHY I HATE VAMPIRE HUNTERS' WEAPONS.
THE WOUNDS WHERE YOU BIT ME AREN'T HEALING RIGHT AWAY.
HUFF
YOU PIERCED ME WITHOUT RESERVE... AND THAT PISSES ME OFF.
HUFF
GNASH
BAM

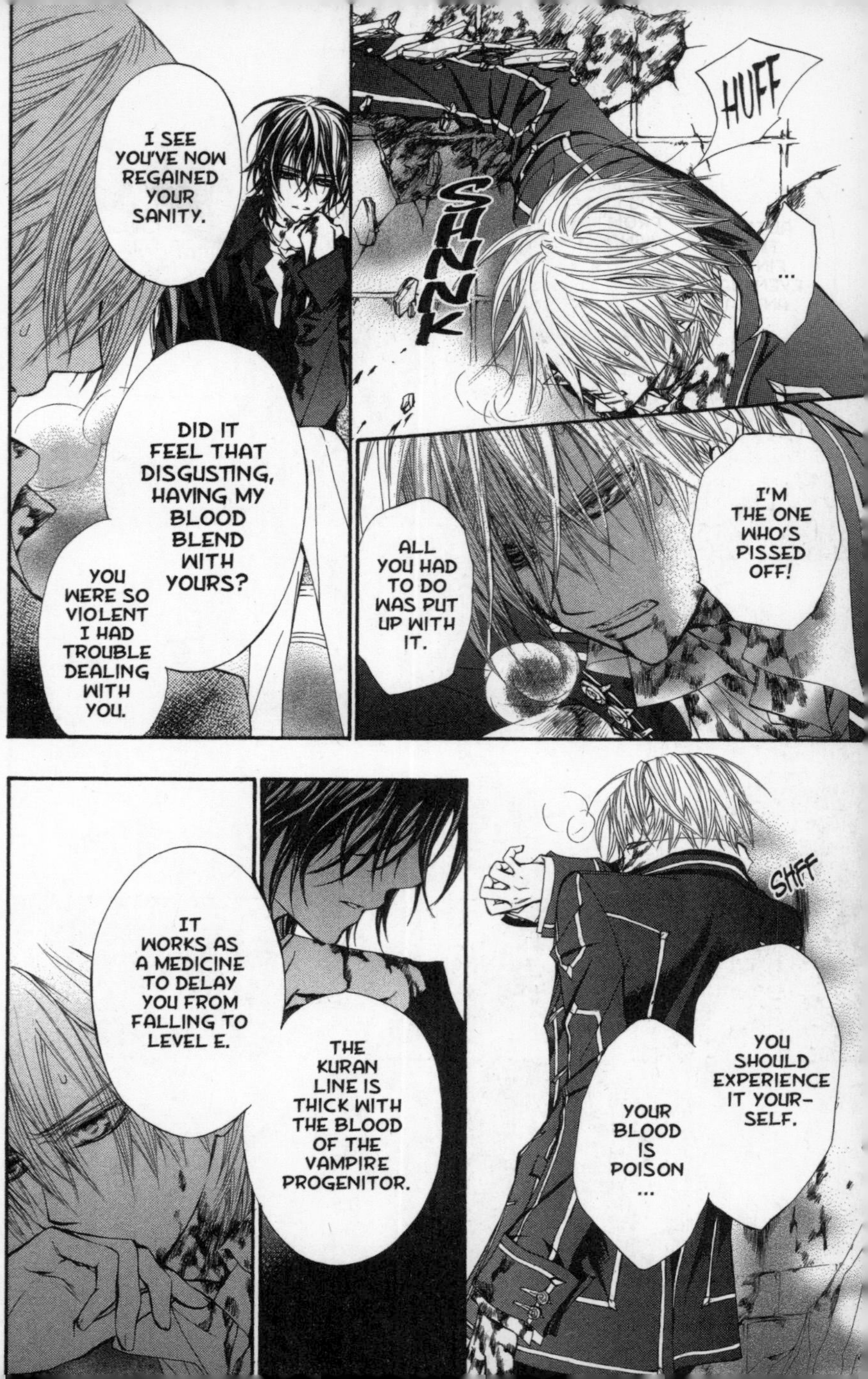
HUFF
SHNNK
...
I'M THE ONE WHO'S PISSED OFF!
ALL YOU HAD TO DO WAS PUT UP WITH IT.
I SEE YOU'VE NOW REGAINED YOUR SANITY.
DID IT FEEL THAT DISGUSTING, HAVING MY BLOOD BLEND WITH YOURS?
YOU WERE SO VIOLENT I HAD TROUBLE DEALING WITH YOU.
SHFF
YOU SHOULD EXPERIENCE IT YOUR-SELF.
YOUR BLOOD IS POISON ...
IT WORKS AS A MEDICINE TO DELAY YOU FROM FALLING TO LEVEL E.
THE KURAN LINE IS THICK WITH THE BLOOD OF THE VAMPIRE PROGENITOR.

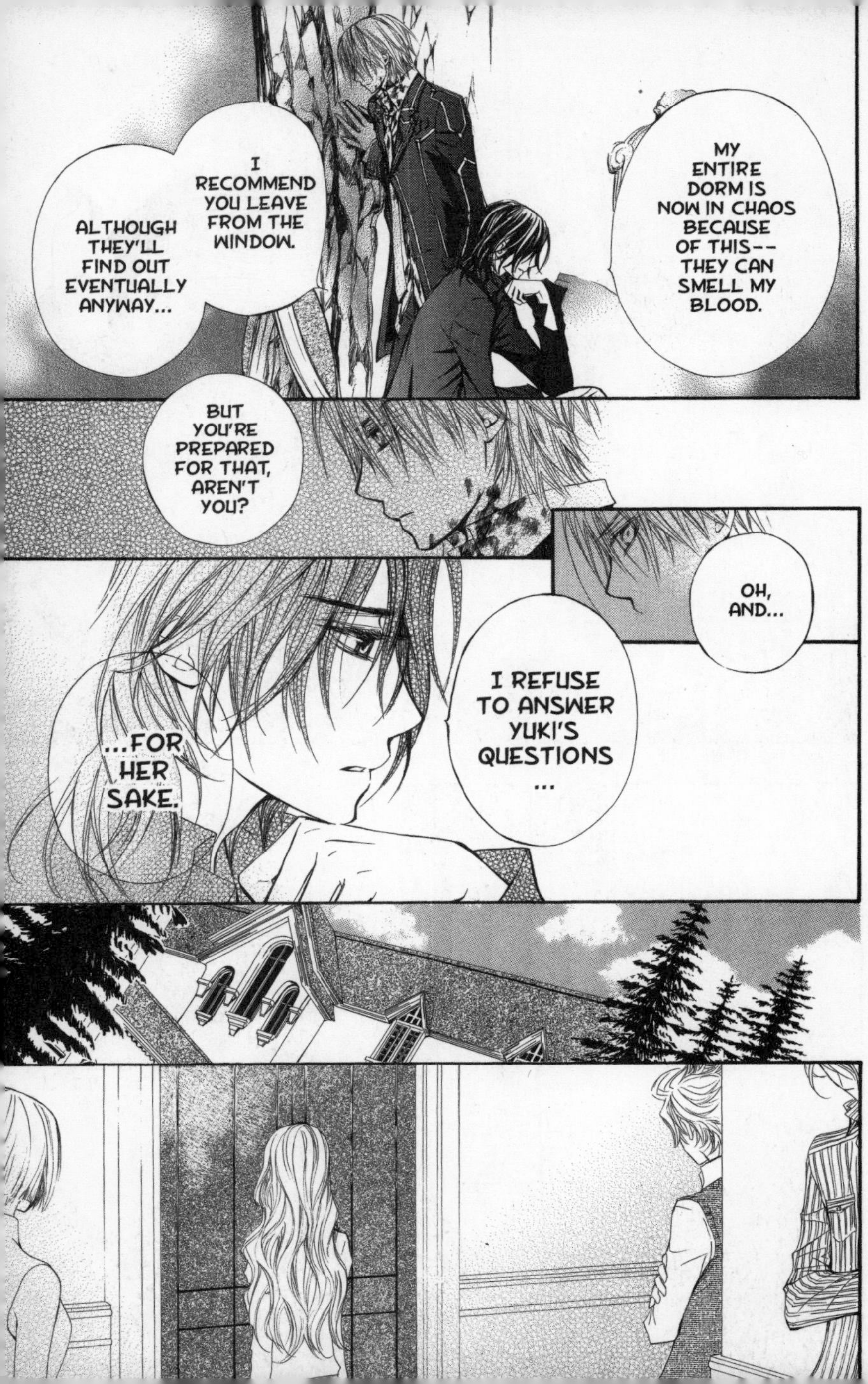
MY ENTIRE DORM IS NOW IN CHAOS BECAUSE OF THIS-- THEY CAN SMELL MY BLOOD.
I RECOMMEND YOU LEAVE FROM THE WINDOW.
ALTHOUGH THEY'LL FIND OUT EVENTUALLY ANYWAY...
BUT YOU'RE PREPARED FOR THAT, AREN'T YOU?
OH, AND...
I REFUSE TO ANSWER YUKI'S QUESTIONS ...
...FOR HER SAKE.

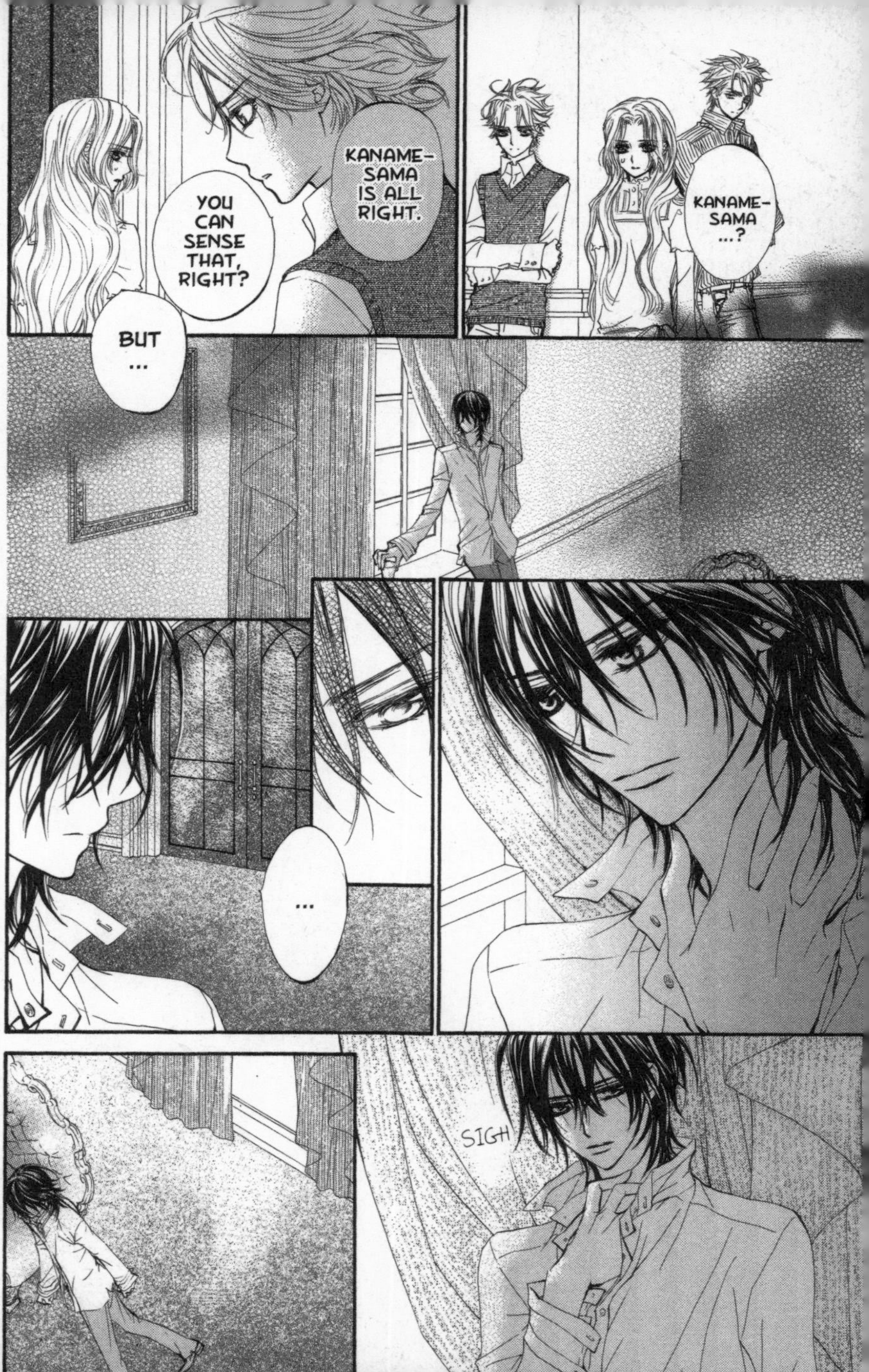
KANAME-SAMA ...?
KANAME-SAMA IS ALL RIGHT.
YOU CAN SENSE THAT, RIGHT?
BUT ...
...
SIGH

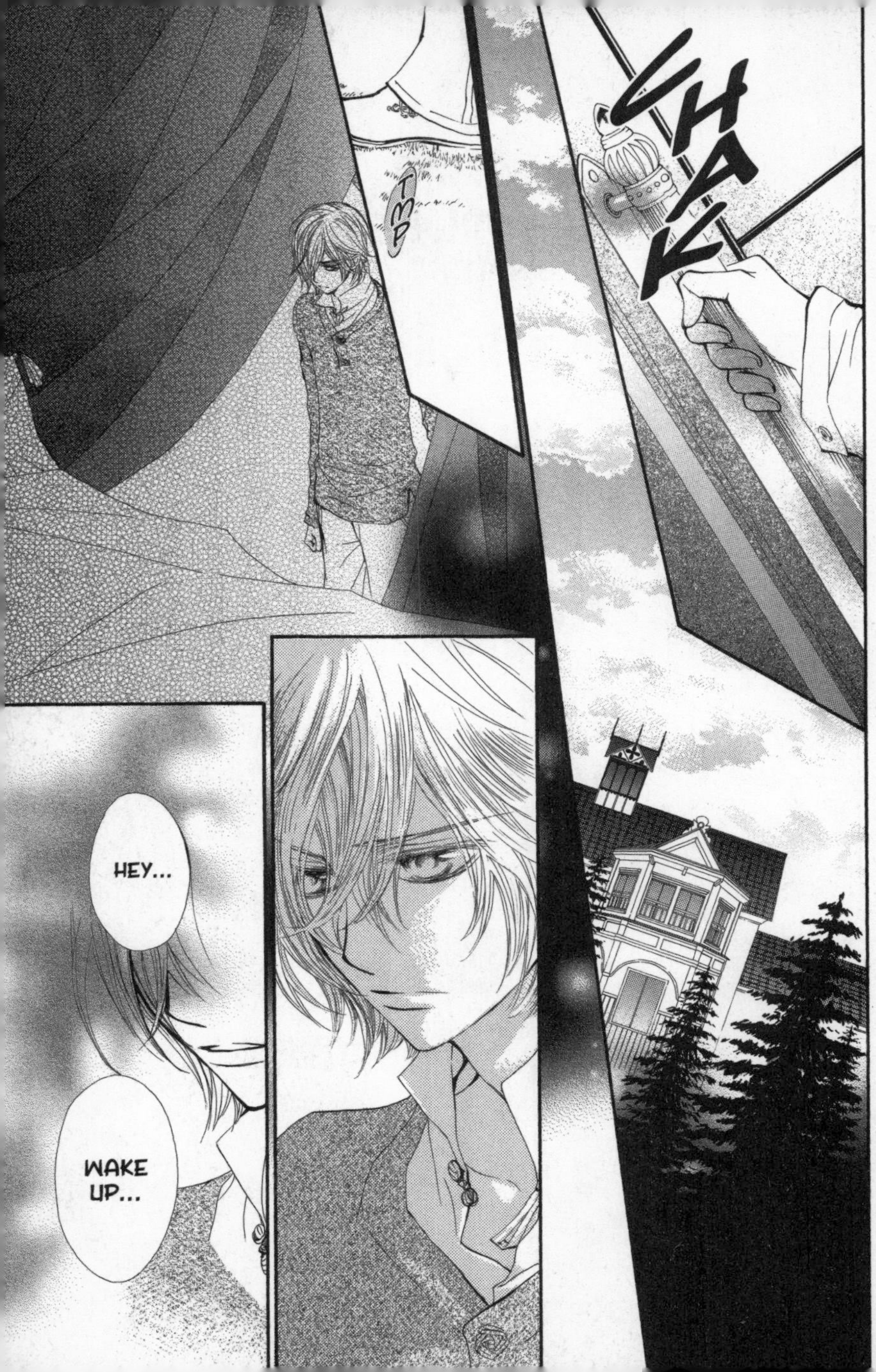
CHAK
TMP
HEY...
WAKE UP...

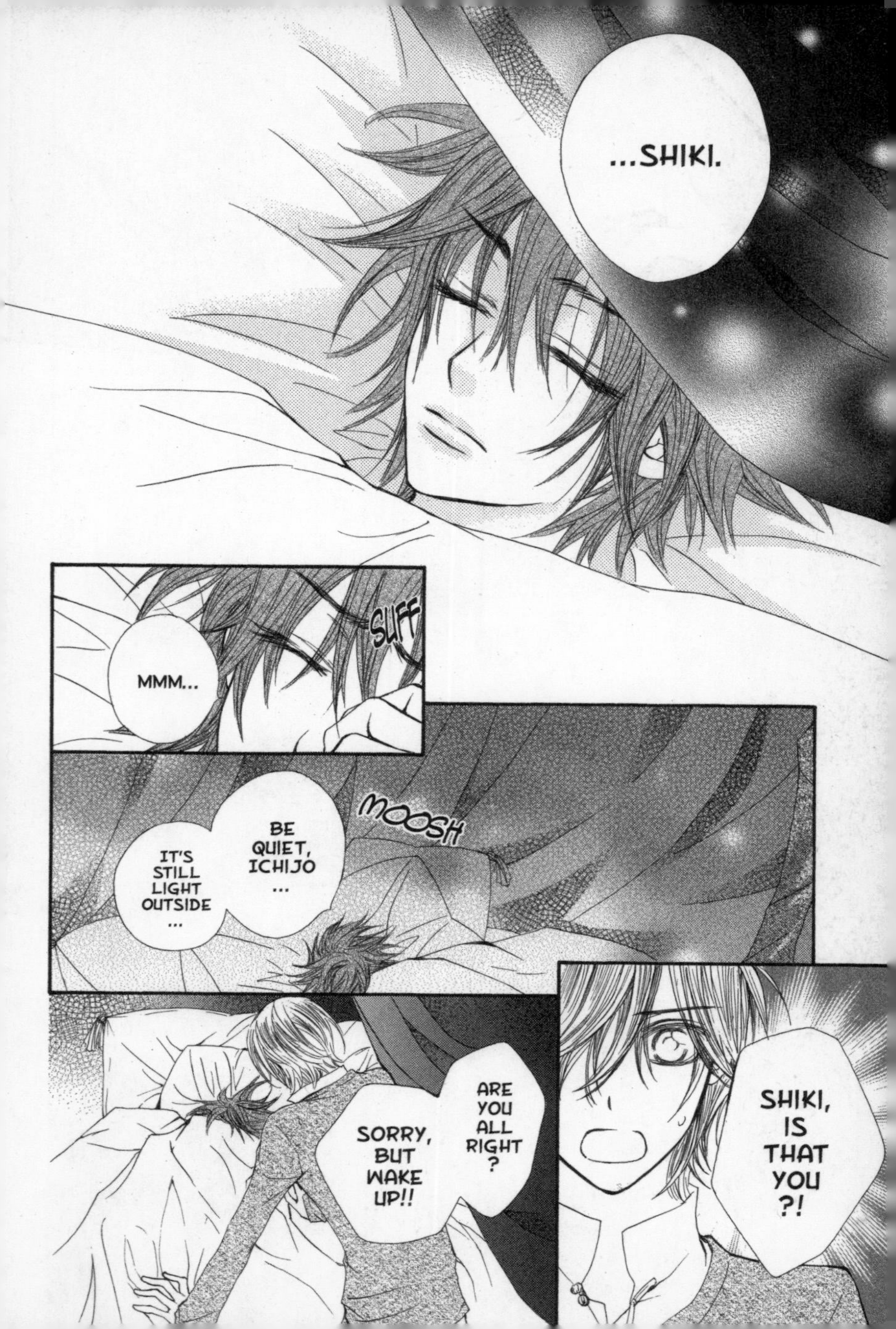
...SHIKI.
SNIFF
MMM...
MOOSH
BE QUIET, ICHIJO ...
IT'S STILL LIGHT OUTSIDE ...
SHIKI, IS THAT YOU ?!
ARE YOU ALL RIGHT ?
SORRY, BUT WAKE UP!!

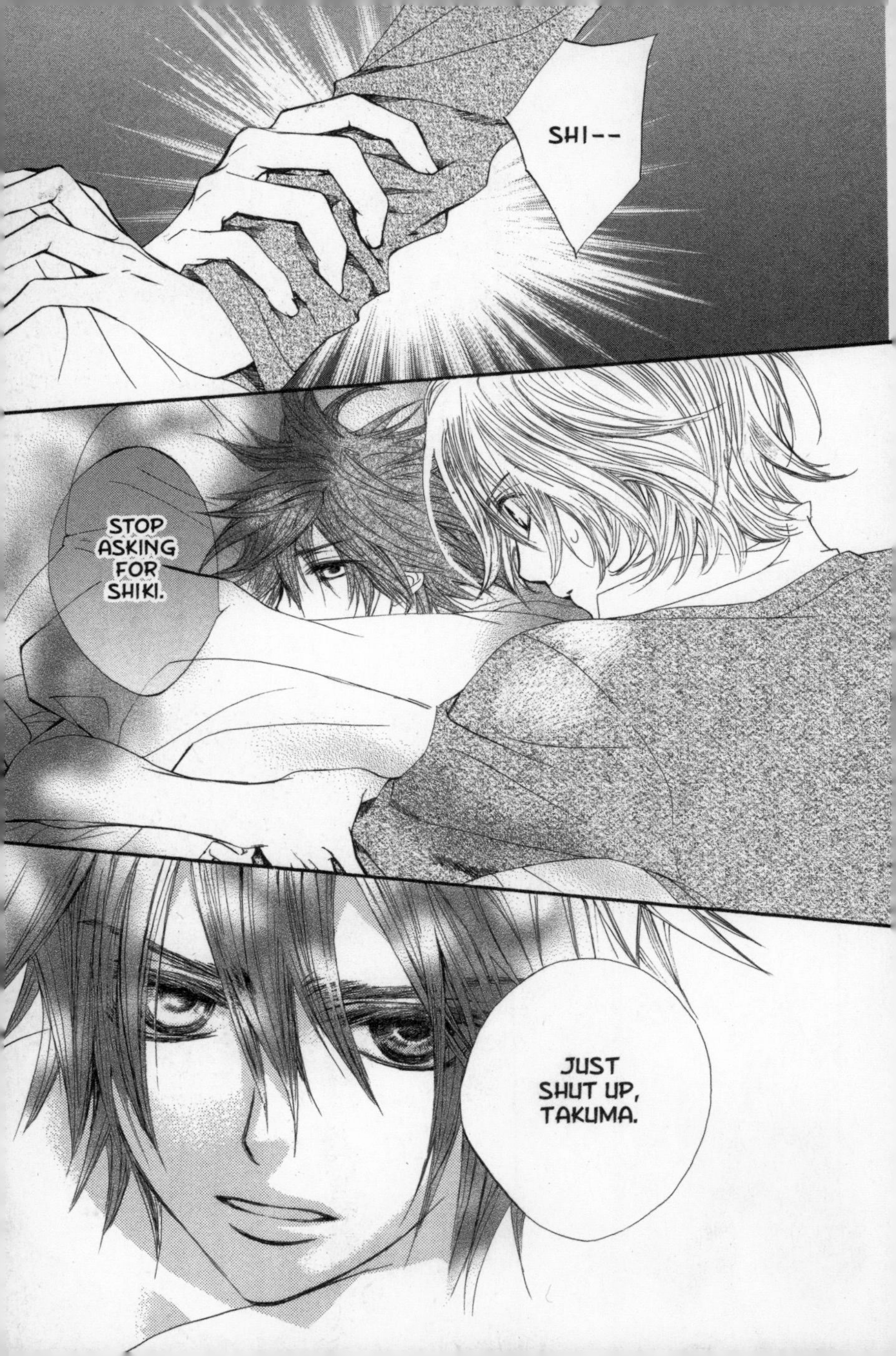
SHI--
STOP ASKING FOR SHIKI.
JUST SHUT UP, TAKUMA.

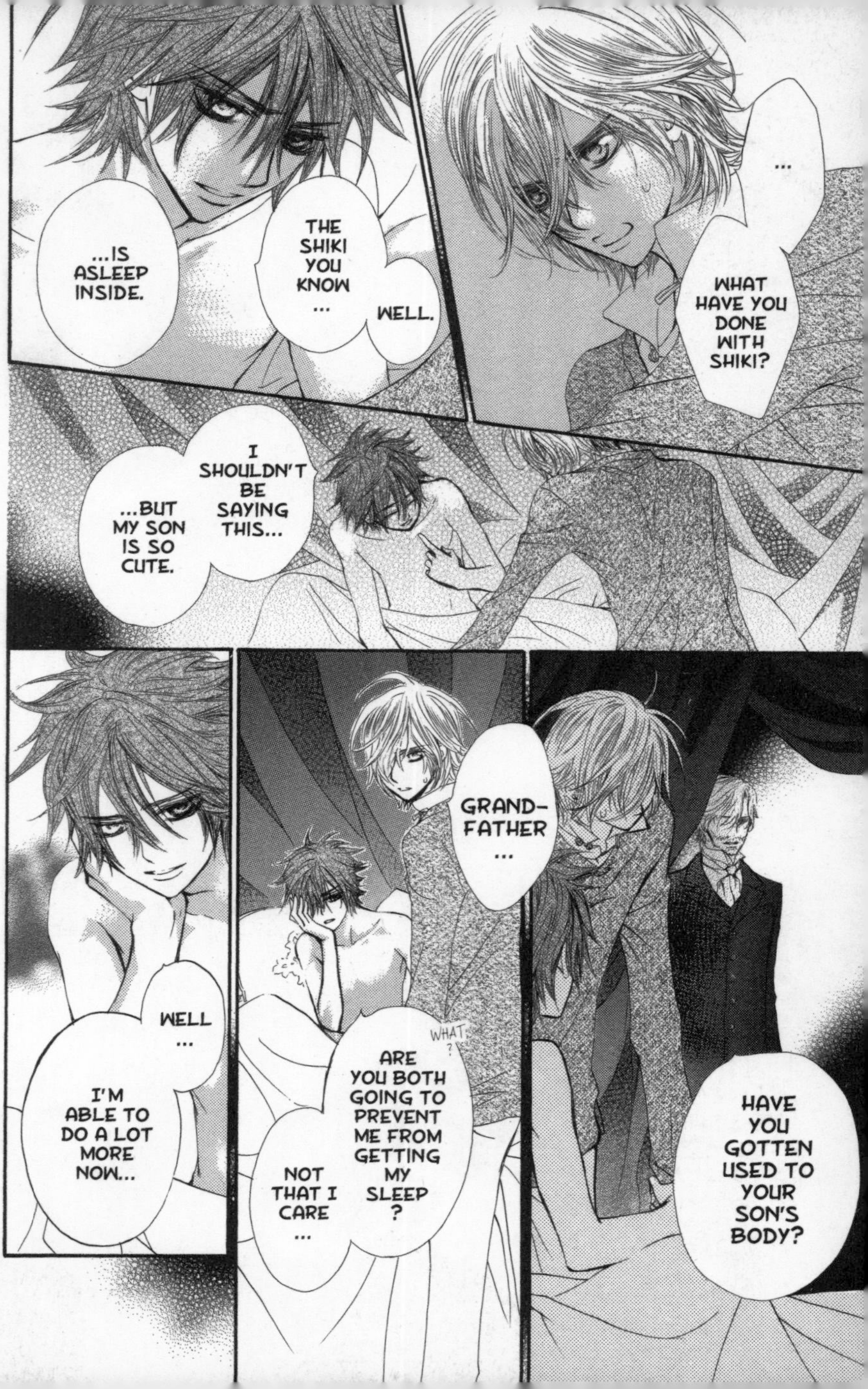
...
WHAT HAVE YOU DONE WITH SHIKI?
WELL.
THE SHIKI YOU KNOW ...
...IS ASLEEP INSIDE.
I SHOULDN'T BE SAYING THIS...
...BUT MY SON IS SO CUTE.
GRANDFATHER ...
HAVE YOU GOTTEN USED TO YOUR SON'S BODY?
WHAT?
ARE YOU BOTH GOING TO PREVENT ME FROM GETTING MY SLEEP?
NOT THAT I CARE ...
WELL ...
I'M ABLE TO DO A LOT MORE NOW...

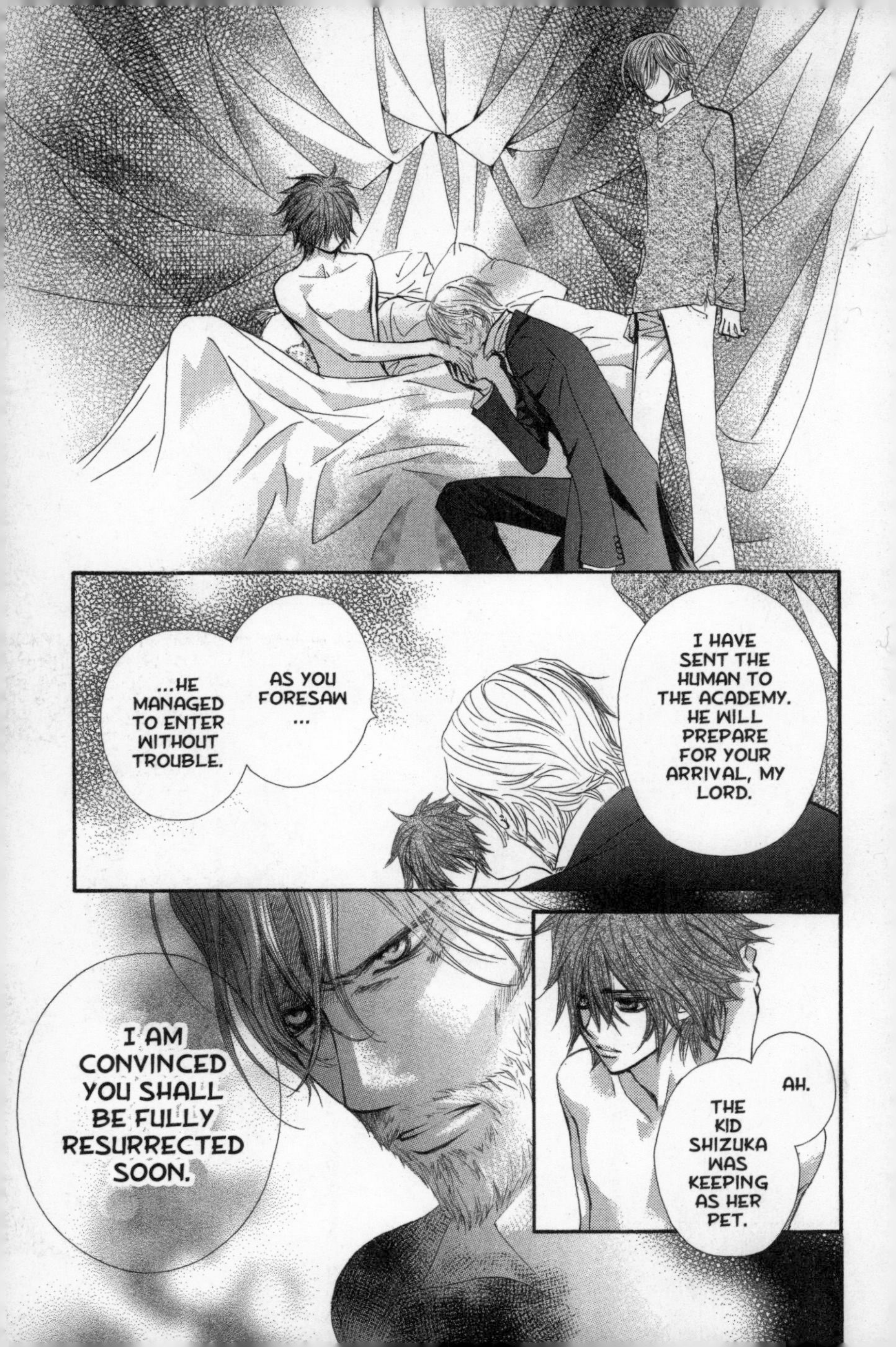
I HAVE SENT THE HUMAN TO THE ACADEMY. HE WILL PREPARE FOR YOUR ARRIVAL, MY LORD.
AS YOU FORESAW ...
...HE MANAGED TO ENTER WITHOUT TROUBLE.
AH.
THE KID SHIZUKA WAS KEEPING AS HER PET.
I AM CONVINCED YOU SHALL BE FULLY RESURRECTED SOON.

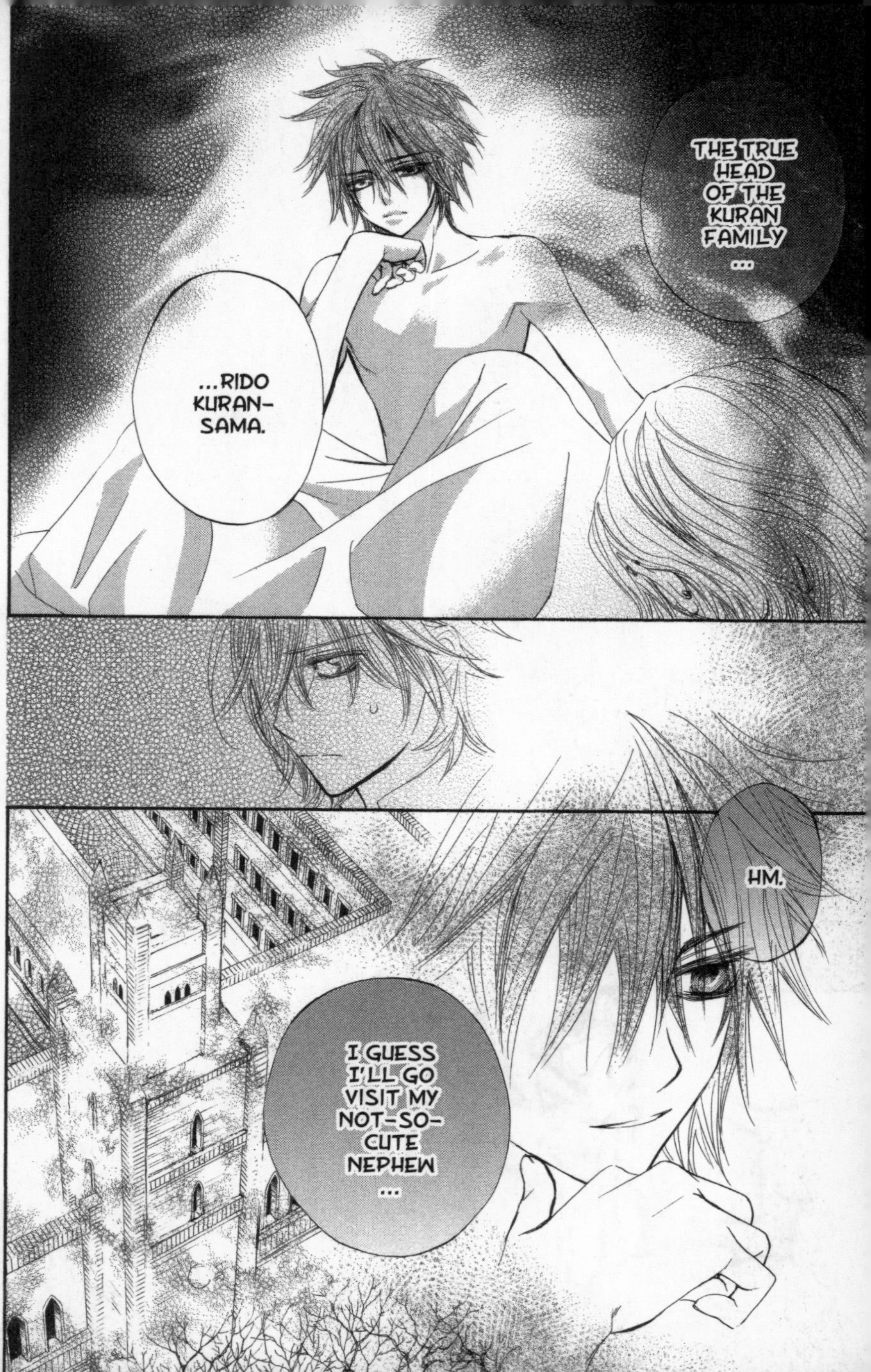
THE TRUE HEAD OF THE KURAN FAMILY ...
...RIDO KURAN-SAMA.
HM.
I GUESS I'LL GO VISIT MY NOT-SO-CUTE NEPHEW ...

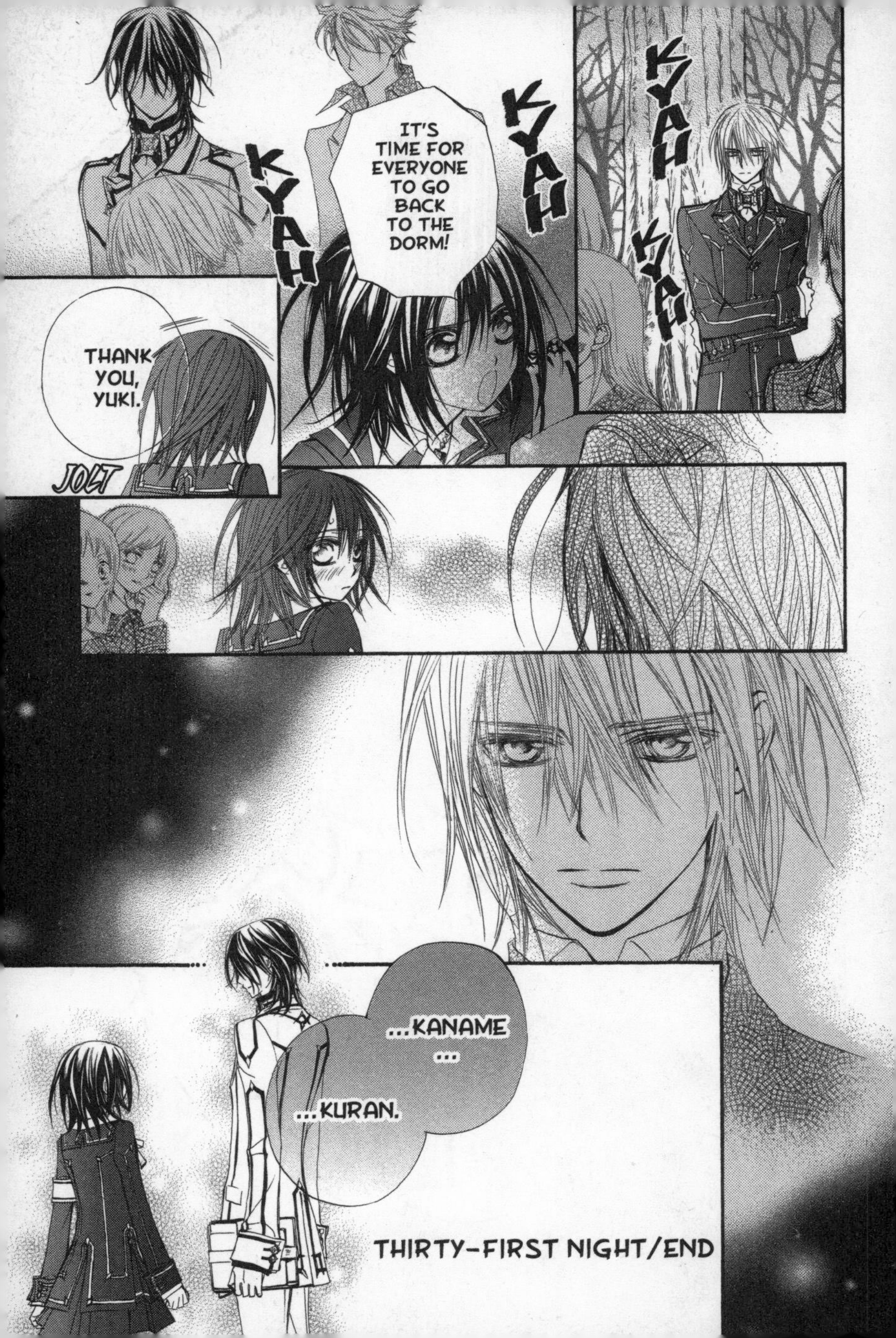

KYAH
KYAH
KYAH
IT'S TIME FOR EVERYONE TO GO BACK TO THE DORM!
KYAH
THANK YOU, YUKI.
JOLT
...KANAME ...
...KURAN.
THIRTY-FIRST NIGHT/END

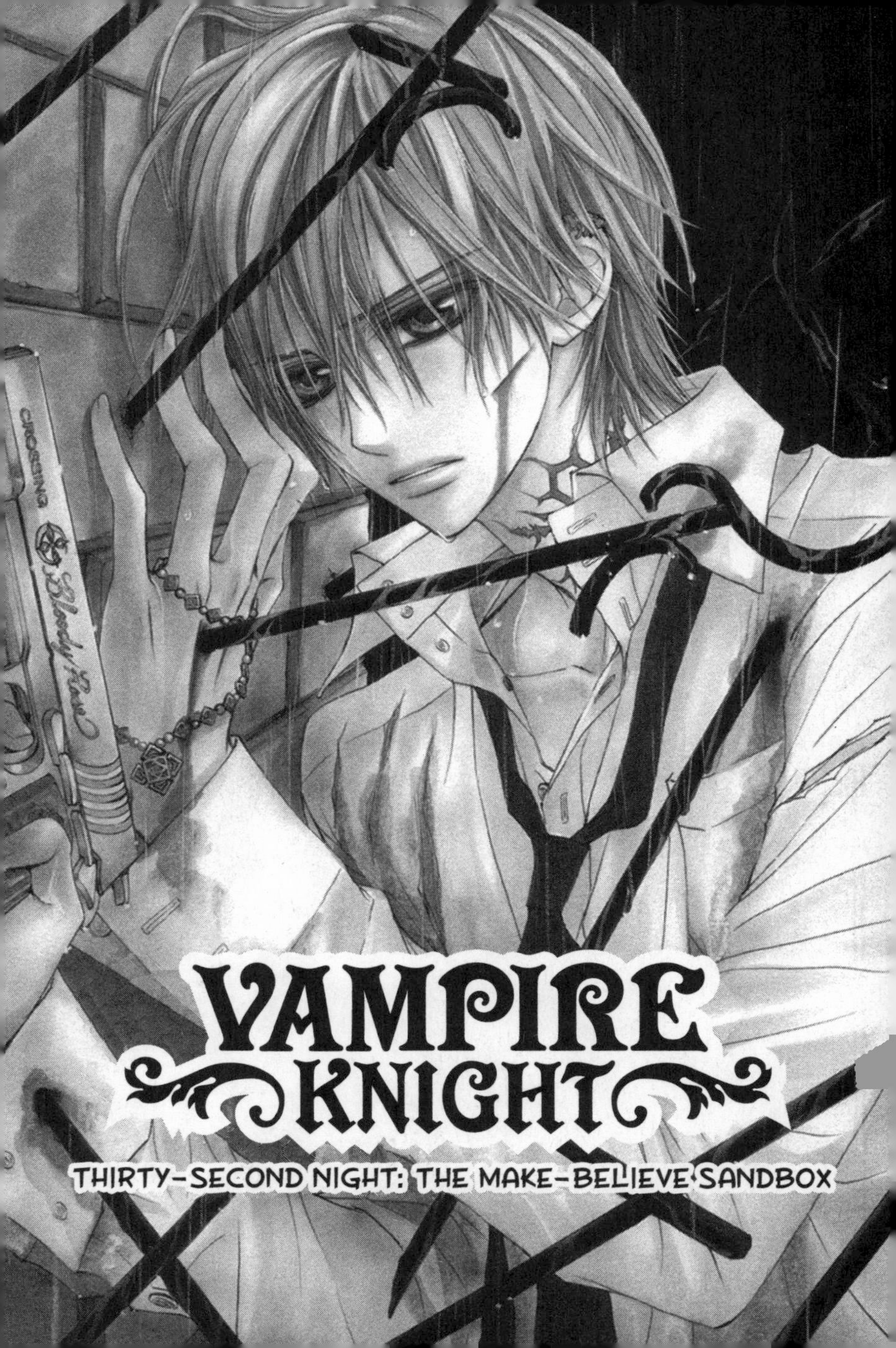
VAMPIRE KNIGHT
THIRTY-SECOND NIGHT: THE MAKE-BELIEVE SANDBOX

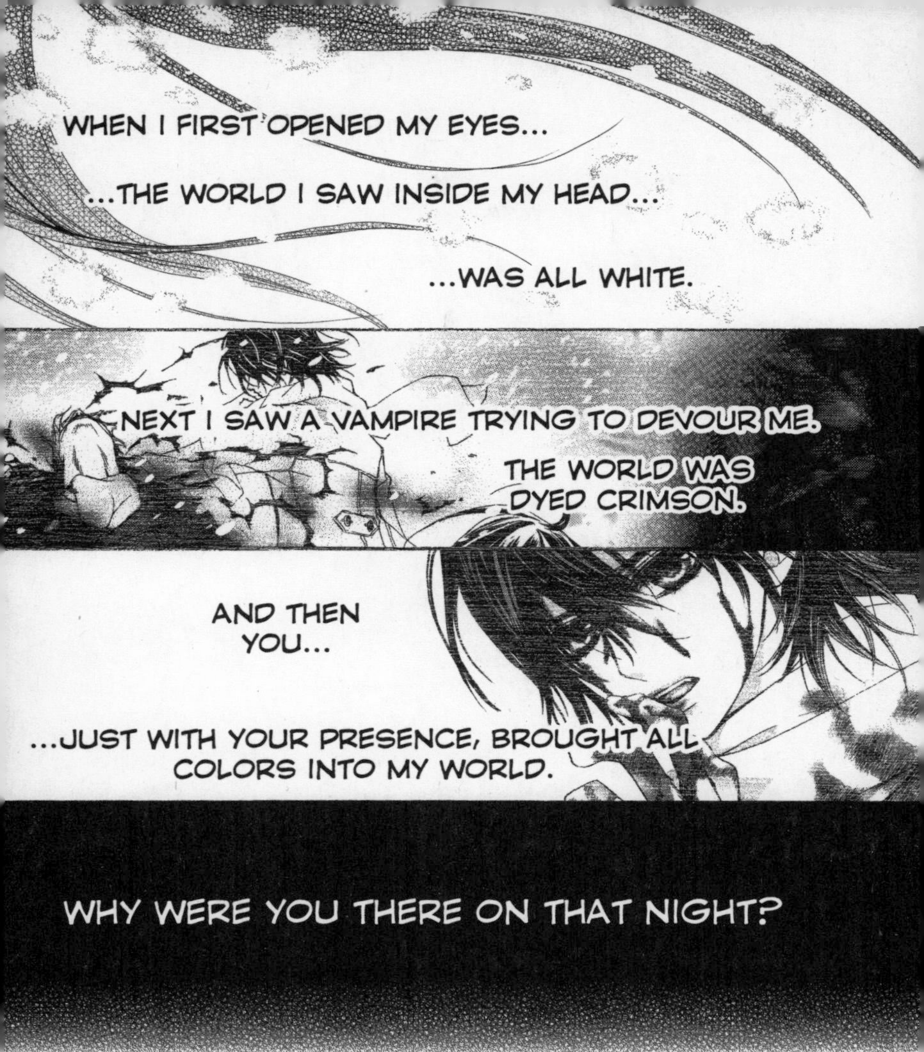
WHEN I FIRST OPENED MY EYES...
...THE WORLD I SAW INSIDE MY HEAD...
...WAS ALL WHITE.
NEXT I SAW A VAMPIRE TRYING TO DEVOUR ME.
THE WORLD WAS DYED CRIMSON.
AND THEN YOU...
...JUST WITH YOUR PRESENCE, BROUGHT ALL COLORS INTO MY WORLD.
WHY WERE YOU THERE ON THAT NIGHT?

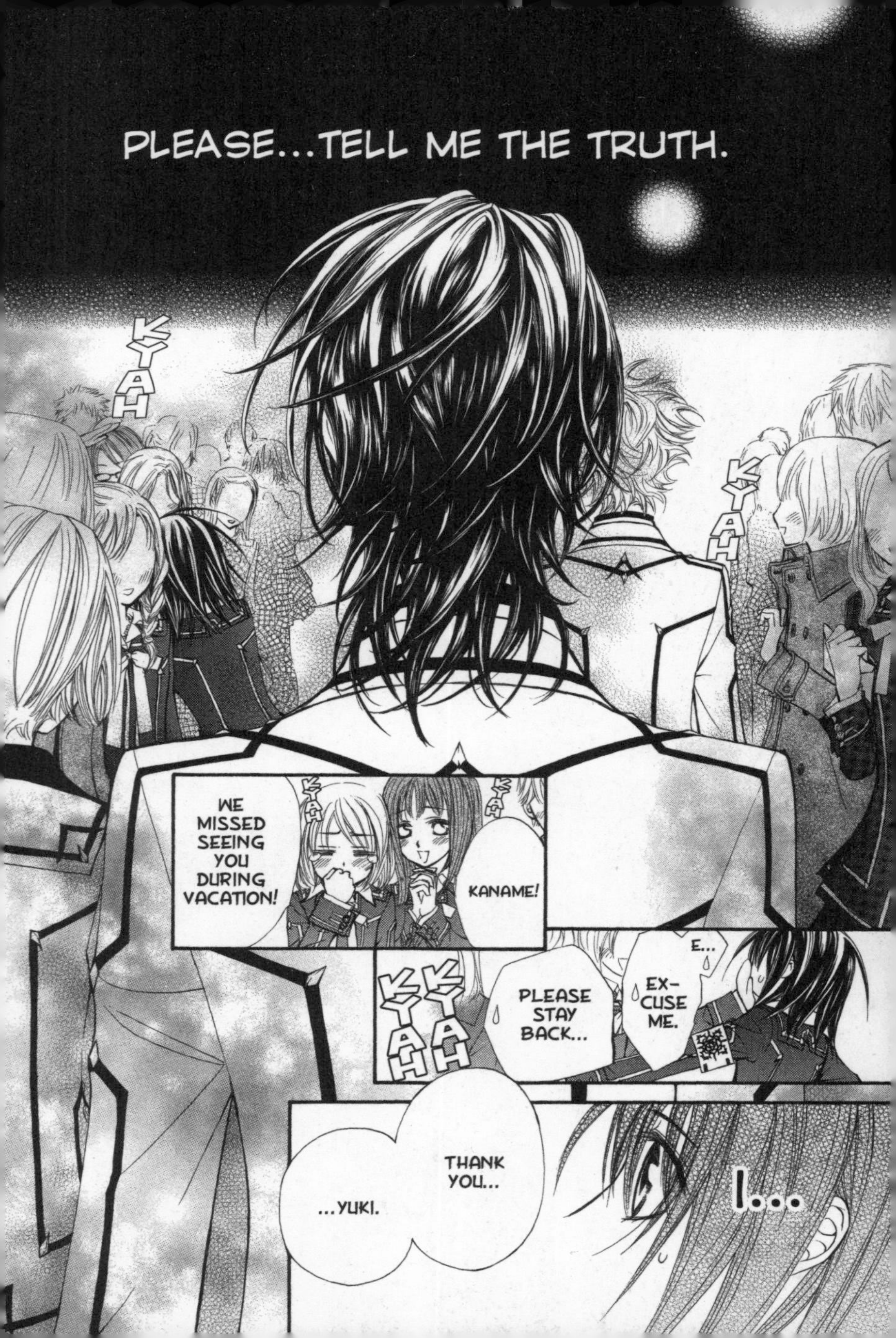
PLEASE...TELL ME THE TRUTH.
KYAH
KYAH
KYAH
KYAH
KANAME!
WE MISSED SEEING YOU DURING VACATION!
E...
EX-CUSE ME.
PLEASE STAY BACK...
KYAAH
KYAAH
I...
THANK YOU...
...YUKI.

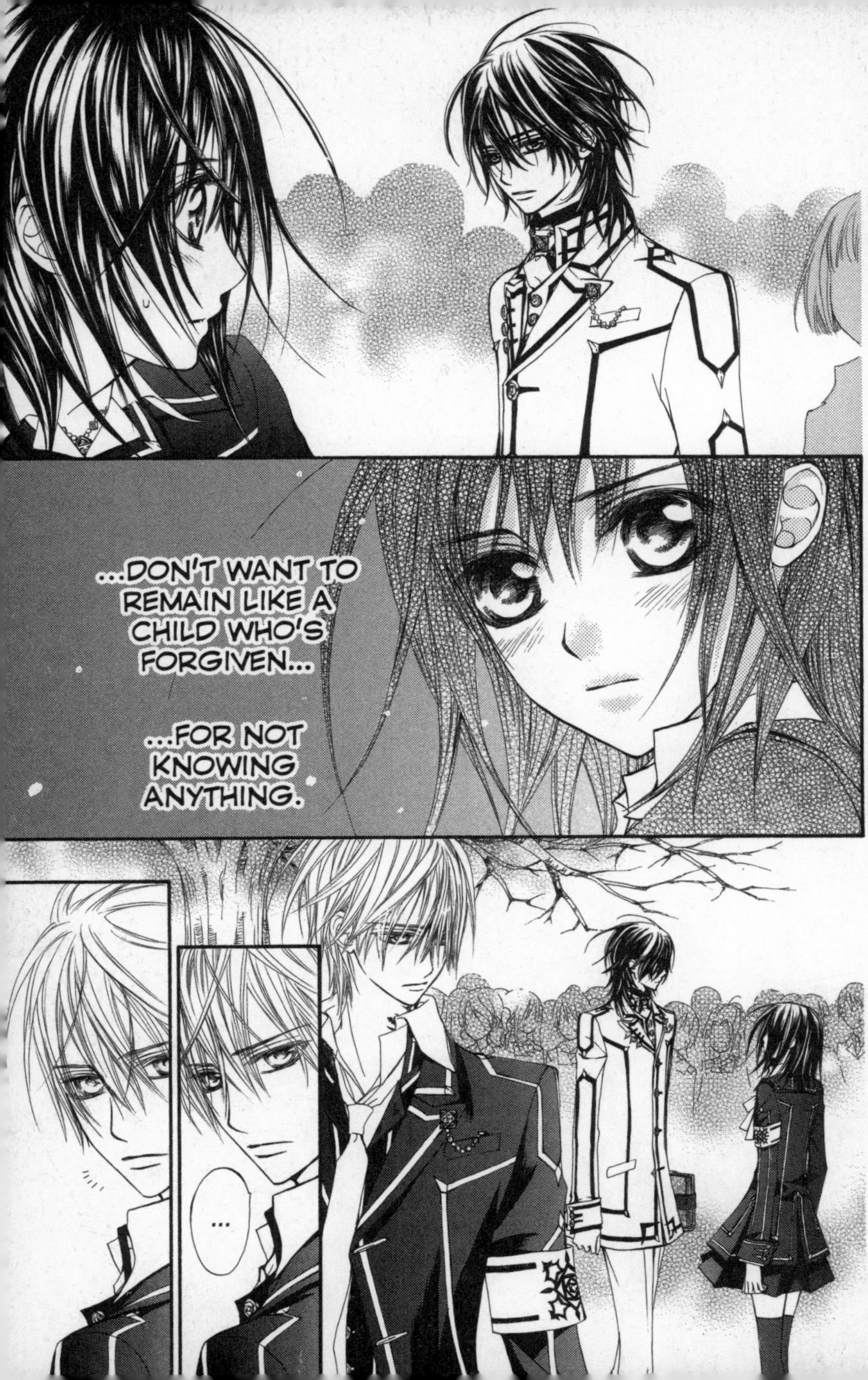
...DON'T WANT TO REMAIN LIKE A CHILD WHO'S FORGIVEN...
...FOR NOT KNOWING ANYTHING.
...

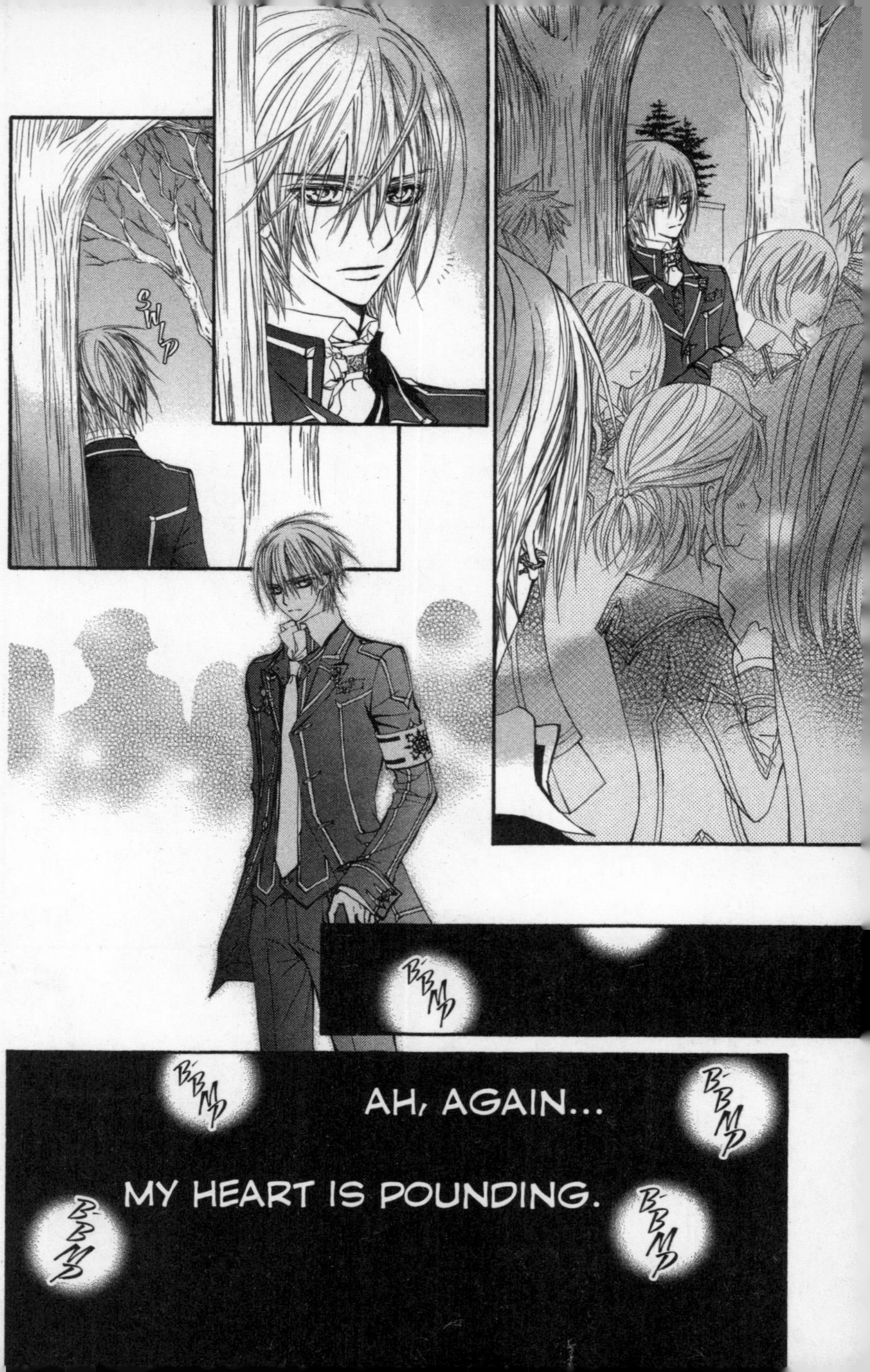
SWIP
B-BMP
B-BMP
AH, AGAIN...
B-BMP
MY HEART IS POUNDING.
B-BMP

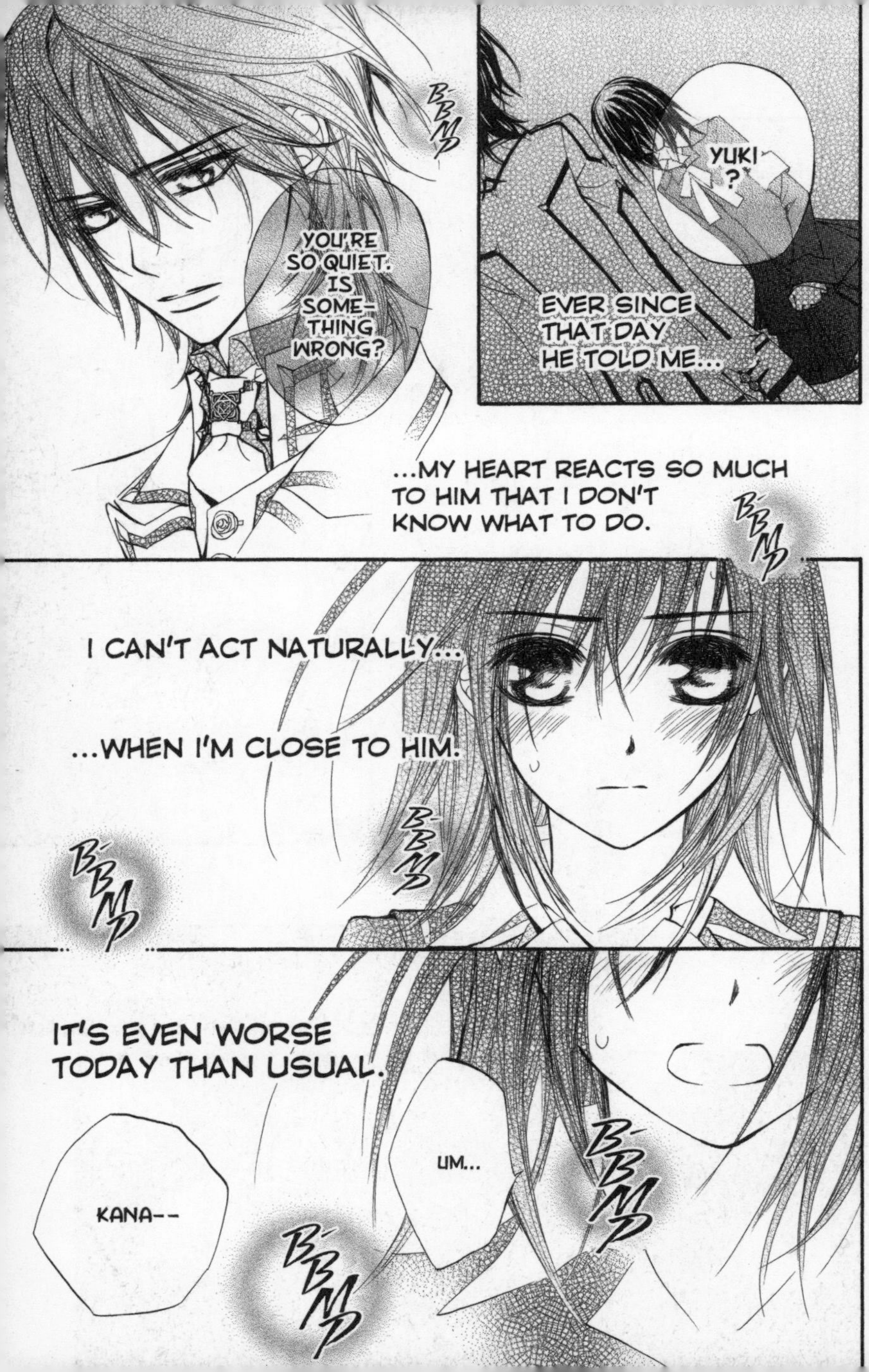
YUKI?
EVER SINCE THAT DAY HE TOLD ME...
B-BMP
YOU'RE SO QUIET. IS SOMETHING WRONG?
...MY HEART REACTS SO MUCH TO HIM THAT I DON'T KNOW WHAT TO DO.
B-BMP
I CAN'T ACT NATURALLY...
...WHEN I'M CLOSE TO HIM.
B-BMP
B-BMP
IT'S EVEN WORSE TODAY THAN USUAL.
B-BMP
UM...
KANA--
B-BMP

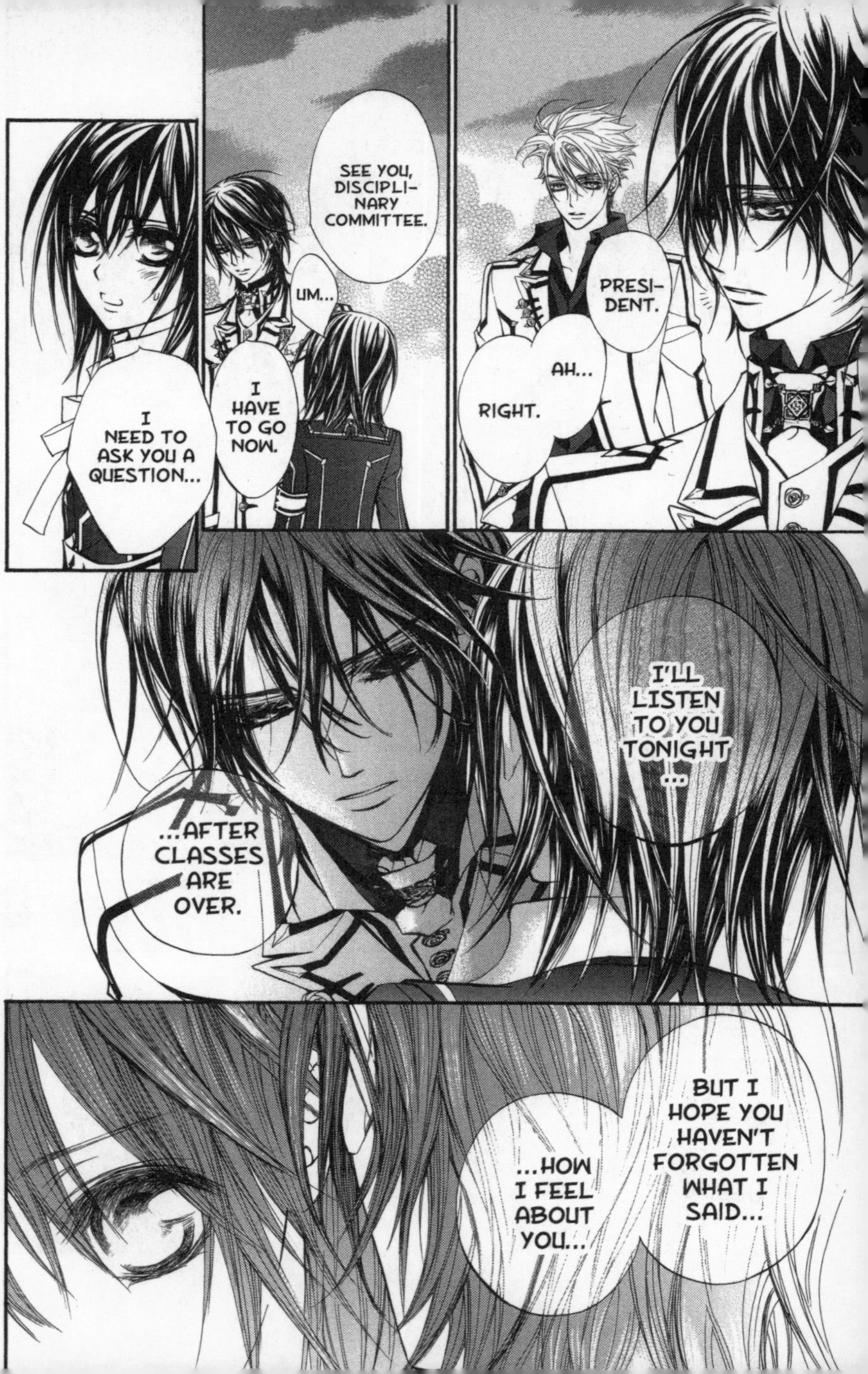
PRESI-DENT.
AH... RIGHT.
SEE YOU, DISCIPLI-NARY COMMITTEE.
UM...
I HAVE TO GO NOW.
I NEED TO ASK YOU A QUESTION...
I'LL LISTEN TO YOU TONIGHT...
...AFTER CLASSES ARE OVER.
BUT I HOPE YOU HAVEN'T FORGOTTEN WHAT I SAID...
...HOW I FEEL ABOUT YOU...

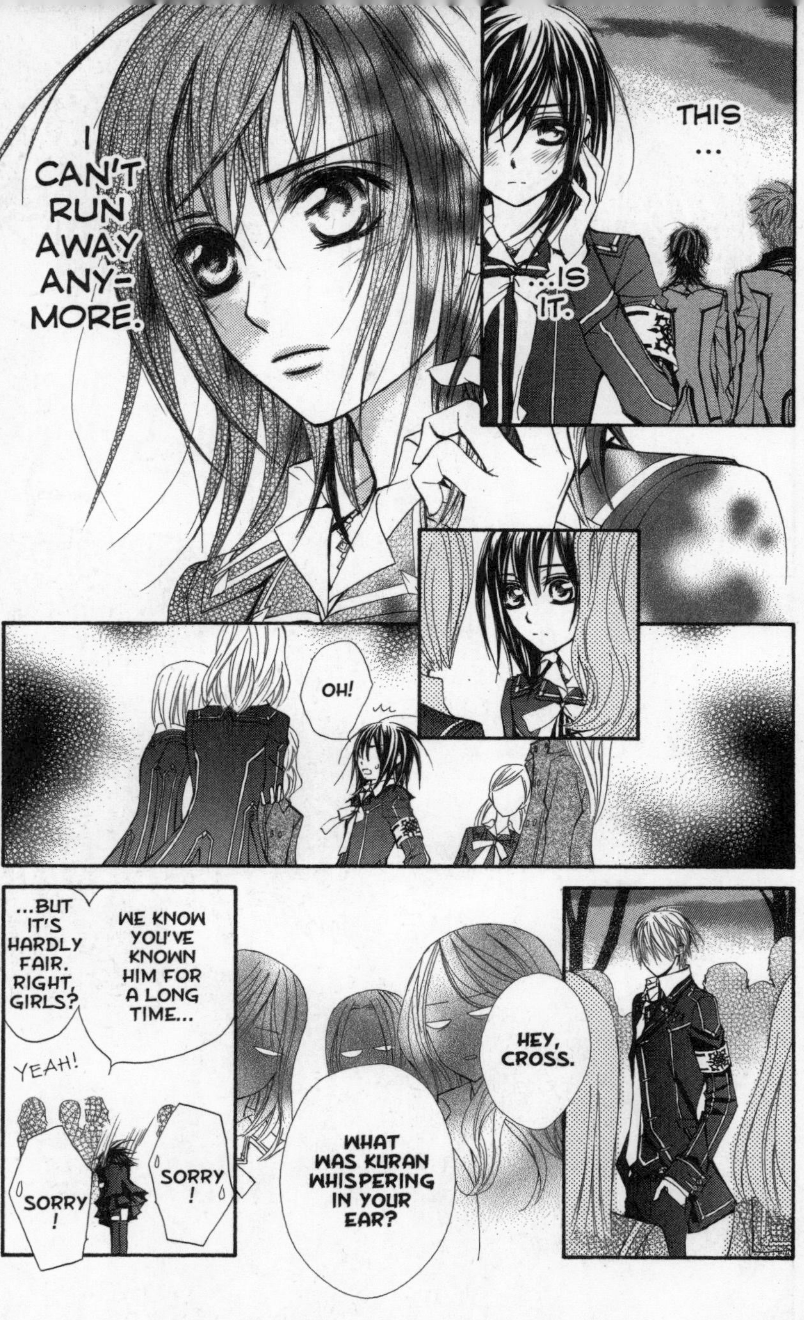
THIS ...
...IS IT.
I CAN'T RUN AWAY ANY-MORE.
OH!
HEY, CROSS.
WHAT WAS KURAN WHISPERING IN YOUR EAR?
WE KNOW YOU'VE KNOWN HIM FOR A LONG TIME...
...BUT IT'S HARDLY FAIR. RIGHT, GIRLS?
YEAH!
SORRY!
SORRY!

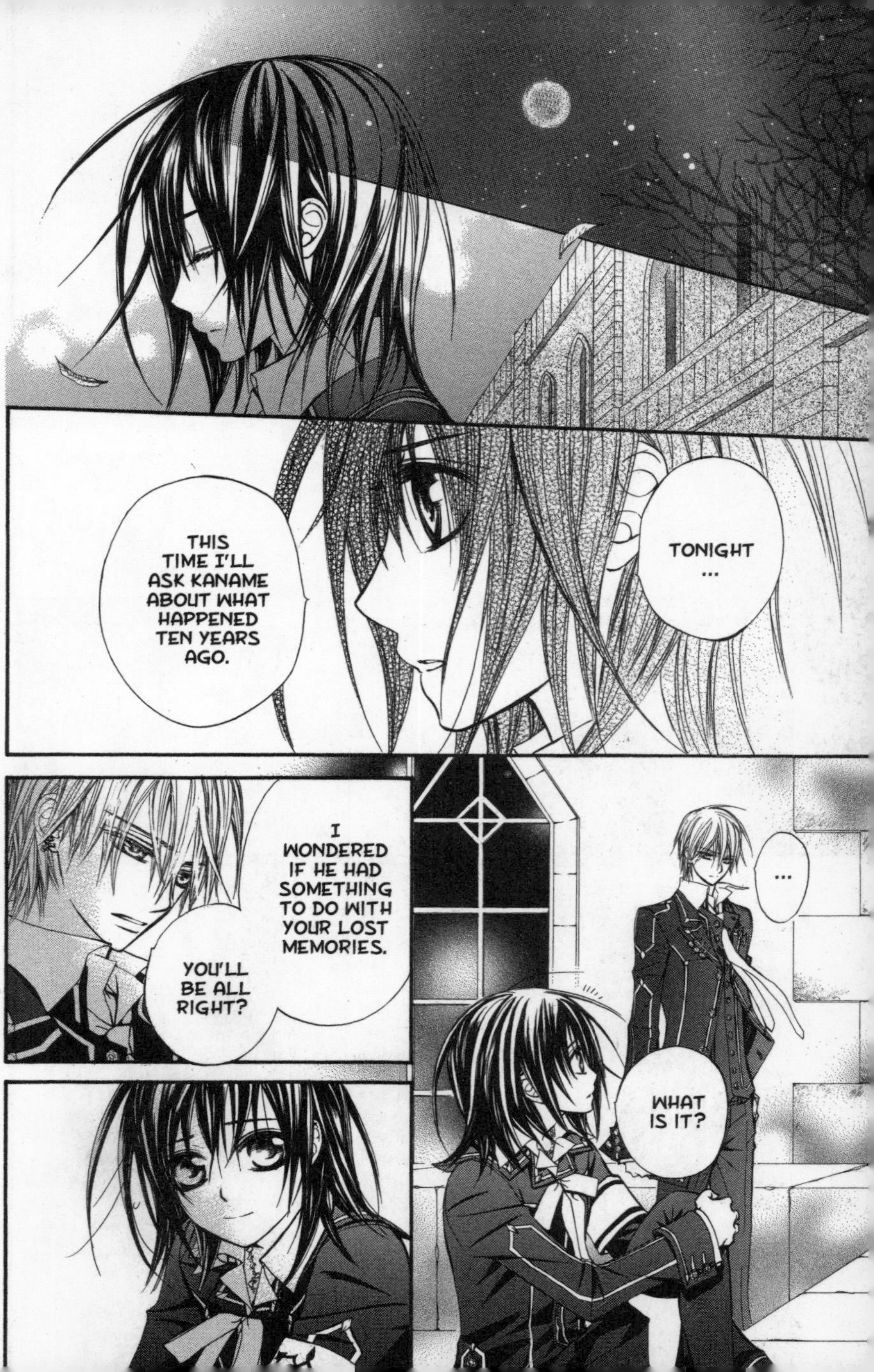
TONIGHT ...
THIS TIME I'LL ASK KANAME ABOUT WHAT HAPPENED TEN YEARS AGO.
...
WHAT IS IT?
I WONDERED IF HE HAD SOMETHING TO DO WITH YOUR LOST MEMORIES.
YOU'LL BE ALL RIGHT?

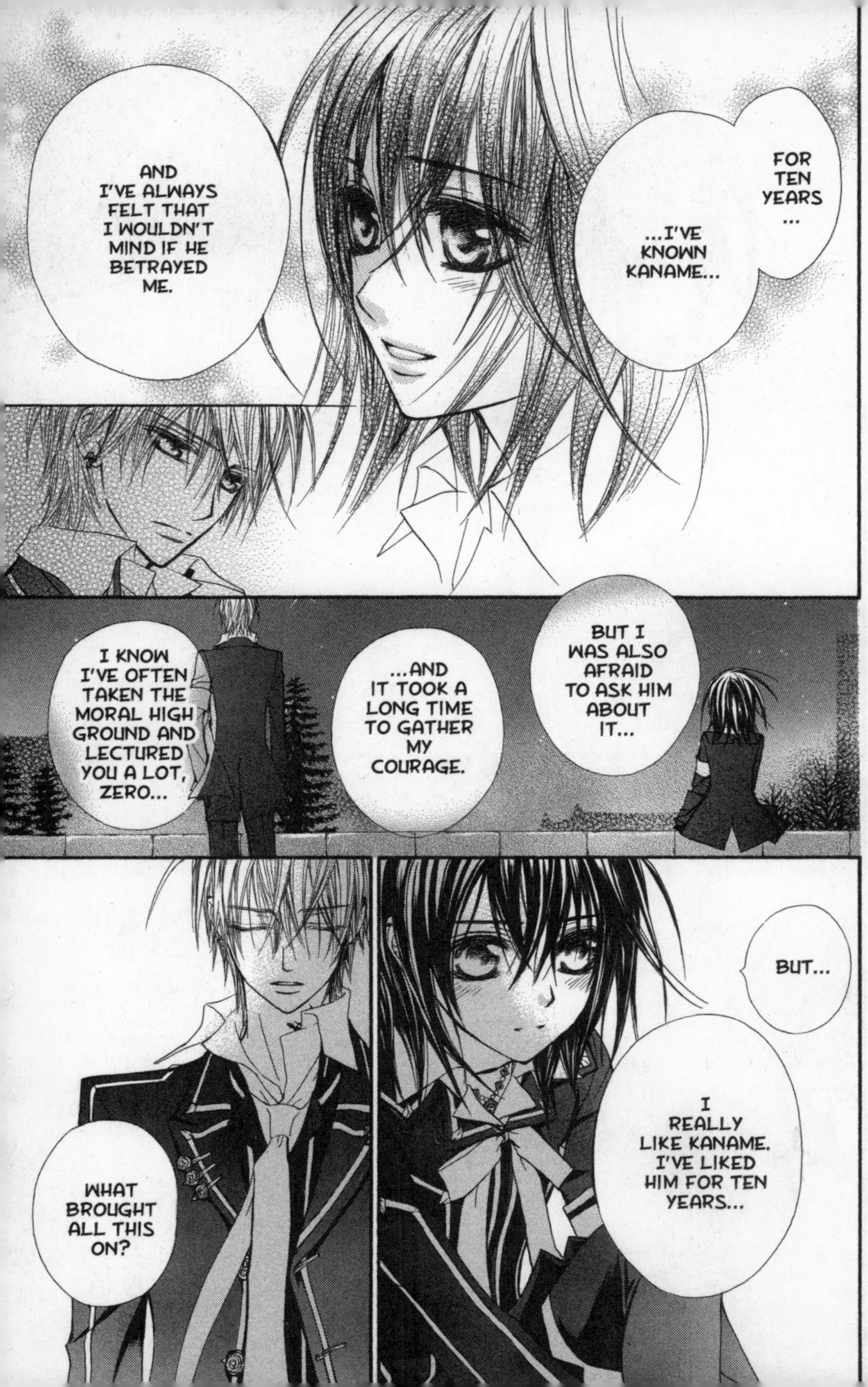
FOR TEN YEARS ...
...I'VE KNOWN KANAME...
AND I'VE ALWAYS FELT THAT I WOULDN'T MIND IF HE BETRAYED ME.
BUT I WAS ALSO AFRAID TO ASK HIM ABOUT IT...
...AND IT TOOK A LONG TIME TO GATHER MY COURAGE.
I KNOW I'VE OFTEN TAKEN THE MORAL HIGH GROUND AND LECTURED YOU A LOT, ZERO...
BUT...
I REALLY LIKE KANAME. I'VE LIKED HIM FOR TEN YEARS...
WHAT BROUGHT ALL THIS ON?

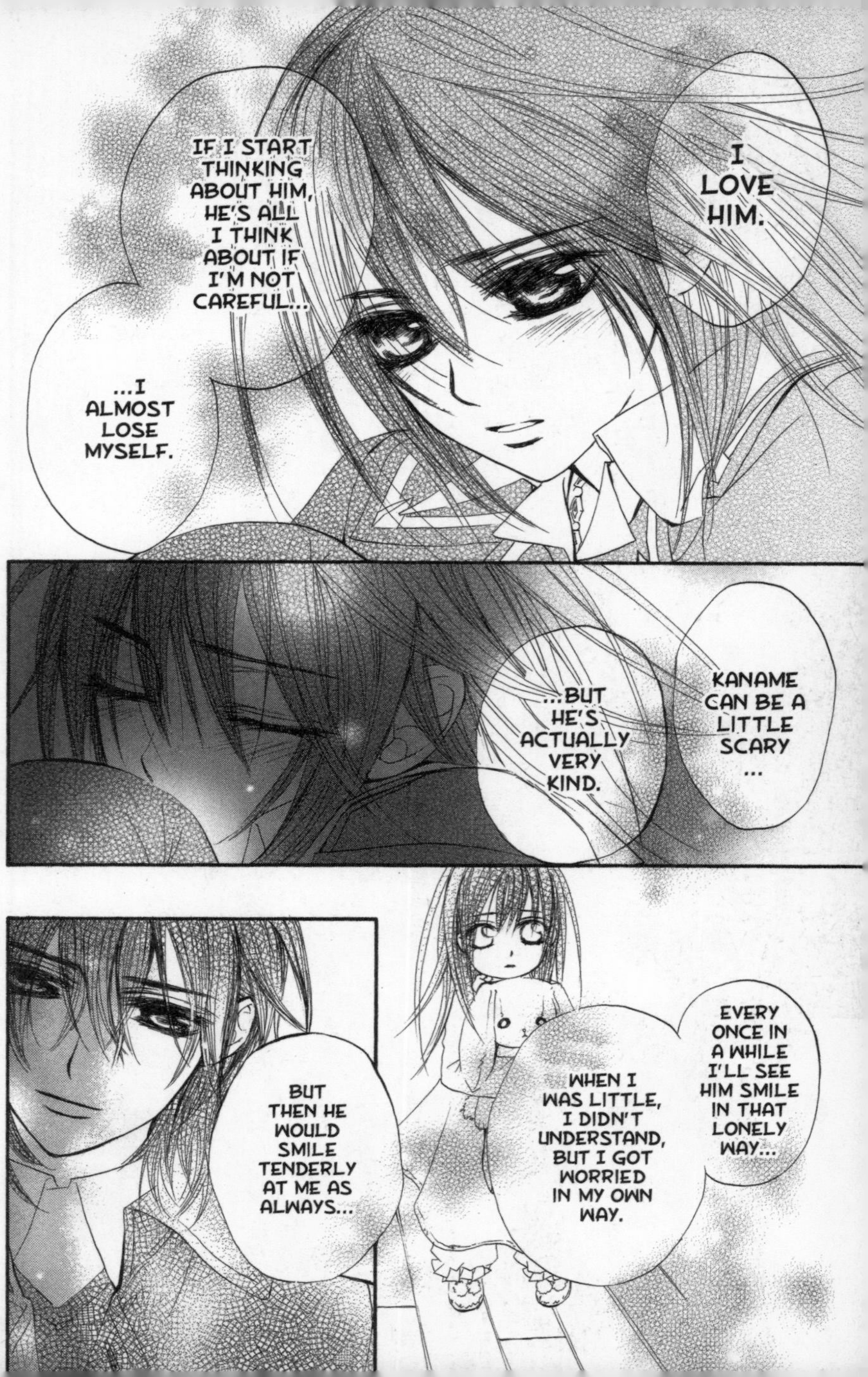
I LOVE HIM.
IF I START THINKING ABOUT HIM, HE'S ALL I THINK ABOUT IF I'M NOT CAREFUL...
...I ALMOST LOSE MYSELF.
KANAME CAN BE A LITTLE SCARY...
...BUT HE'S ACTUALLY VERY KIND.
EVERY ONCE IN A WHILE I'LL SEE HIM SMILE IN THAT LONELY WAY...
WHEN I WAS LITTLE, I DIDN'T UNDERSTAND, BUT I GOT WORRIED IN MY OWN WAY.
BUT THEN HE WOULD SMILE TENDERLY AT ME AS ALWAYS...

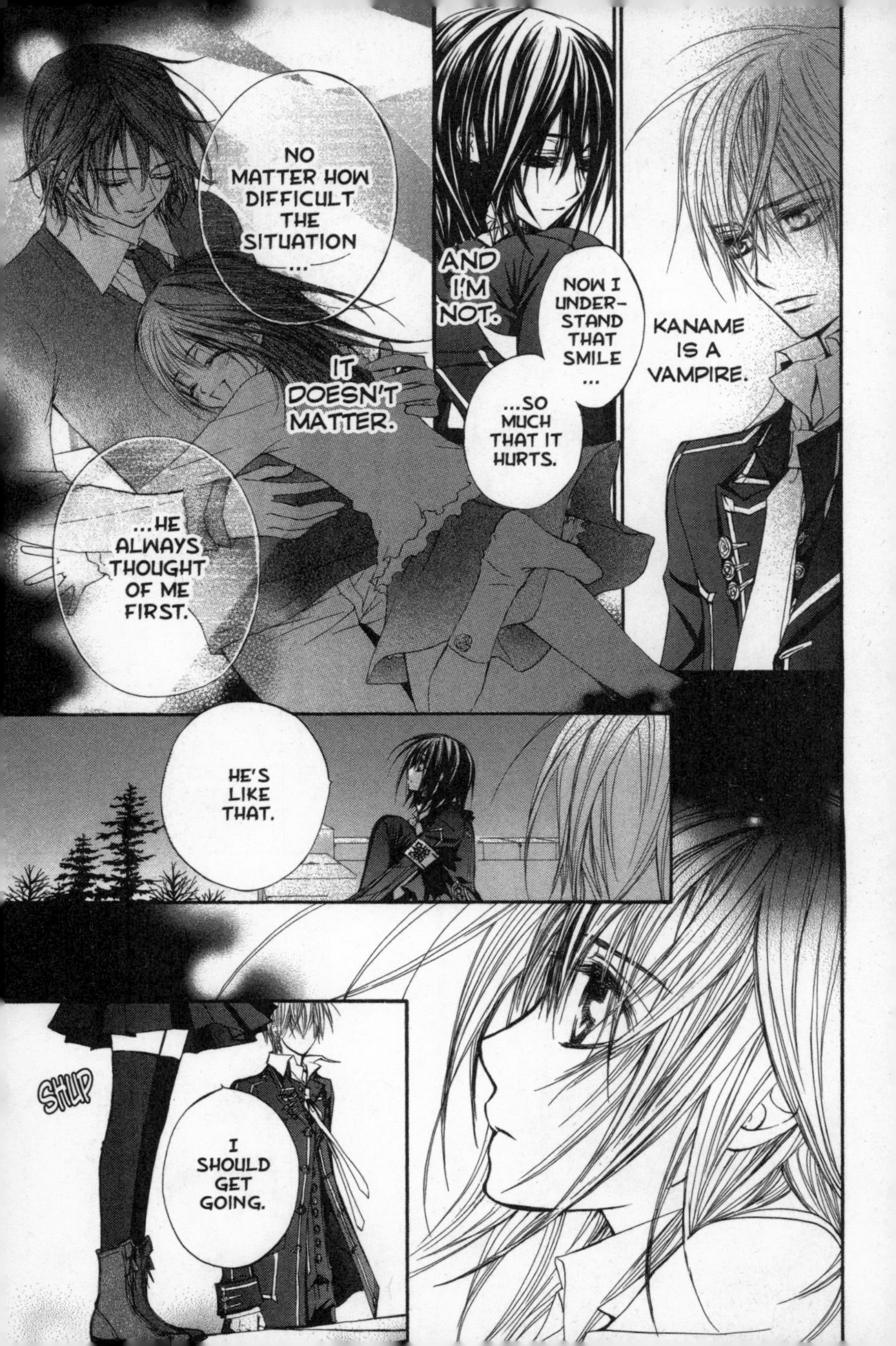
KANAME IS A VAMPIRE.
AND I'M NOT.
NOW I UNDERSTAND THAT SMILE...
...SO MUCH THAT IT HURTS.
NO MATTER HOW DIFFICULT THE SITUATION...
IT DOESN'T MATTER.
...HE ALWAYS THOUGHT OF ME FIRST.
HE'S LIKE THAT.
SHUP
I SHOULD GET GOING.

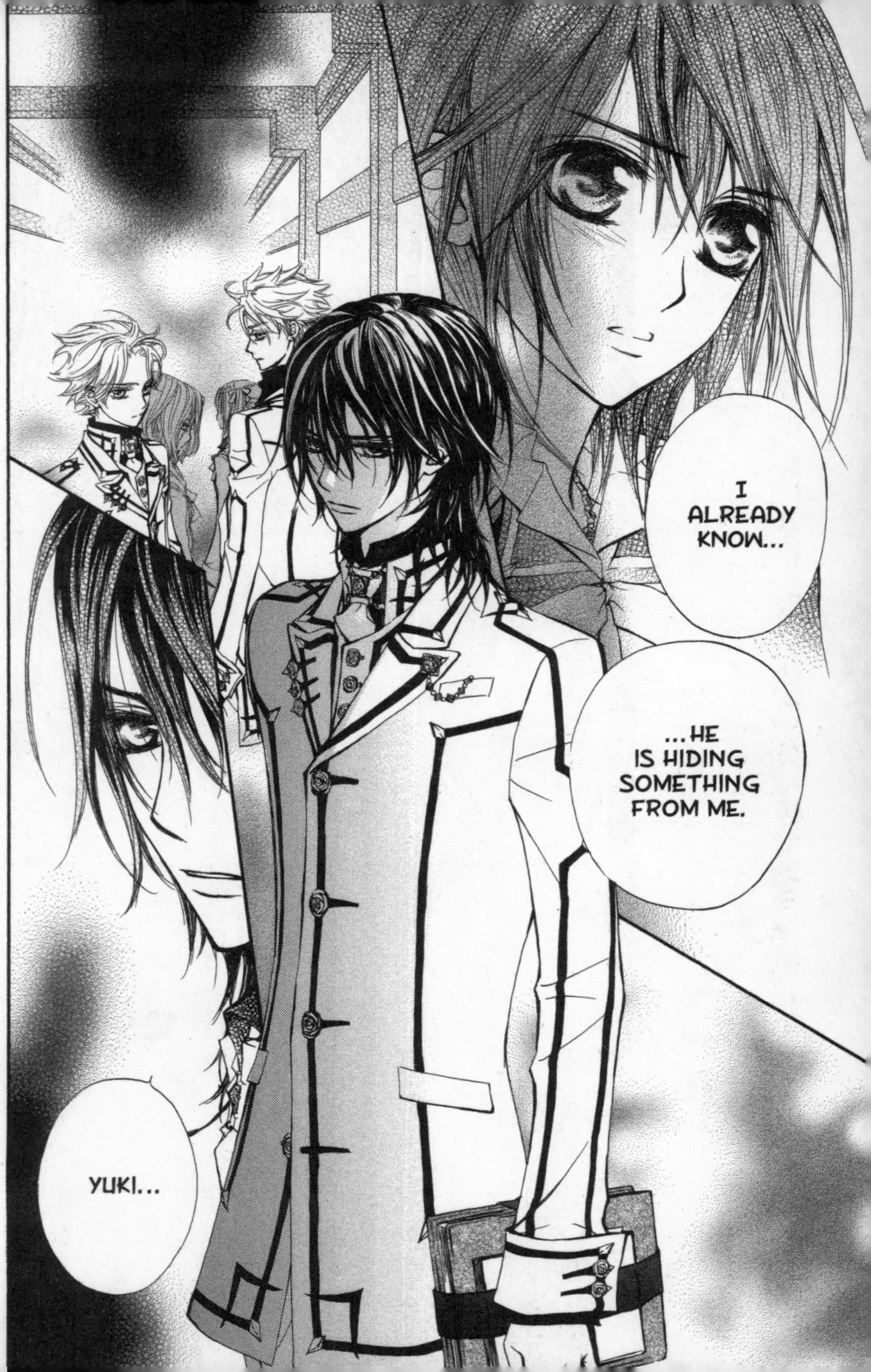
I ALREADY KNOW...
...HE IS HIDING SOMETHING FROM ME.
YUKI...

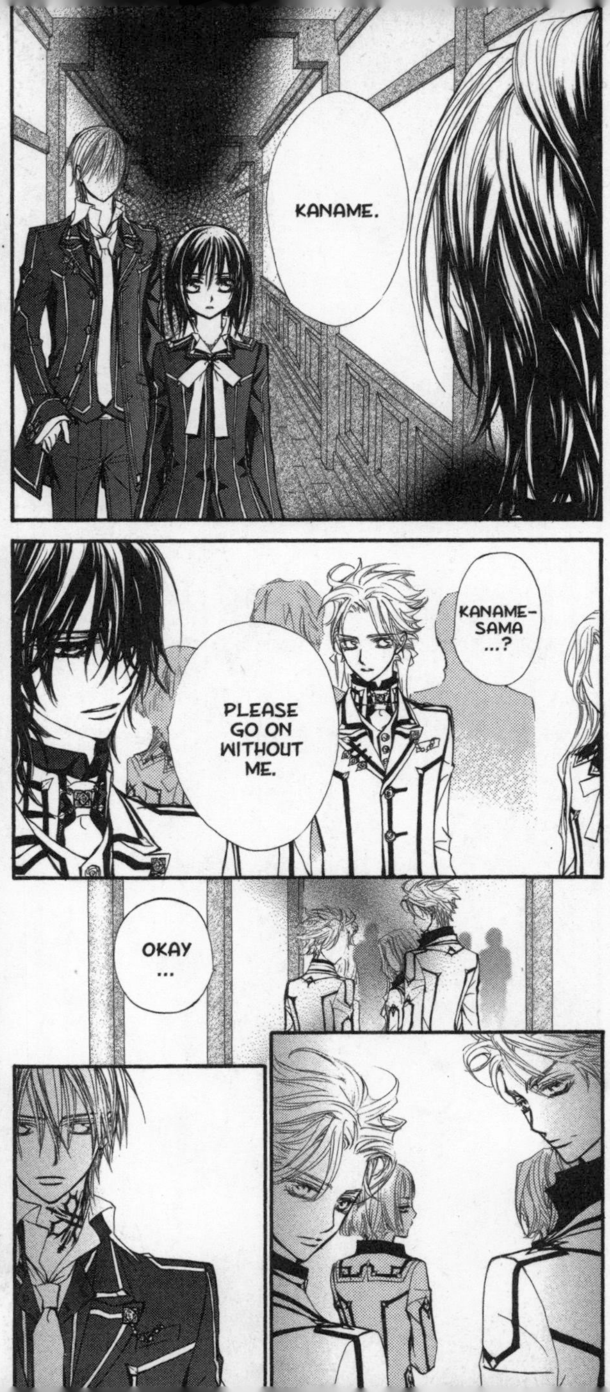
KANAME.
KANAME-SAMA ...?
PLEASE GO ON WITHOUT ME.
OKAY ...

III

I think there are people who know about it already, or may have even bought it already...

A novel was published the same day this volume went on sale in Japan!

Ayuna Fujisaki-san wrote the novel. She's a novelist as well as a scriptwriter. (She's writing scripts for the *Vampire Knight* anime too. ^^) I'm really honored!

She's someone who weaves words to slip you into a world in an instant. In the novel she explored this world and a facet of the characters in depth, thoroughly expressing their feelings of sadness and helplessness... I was drawn into it to the end. Fujisaki-sama, thank you! I recommend it to everyone.

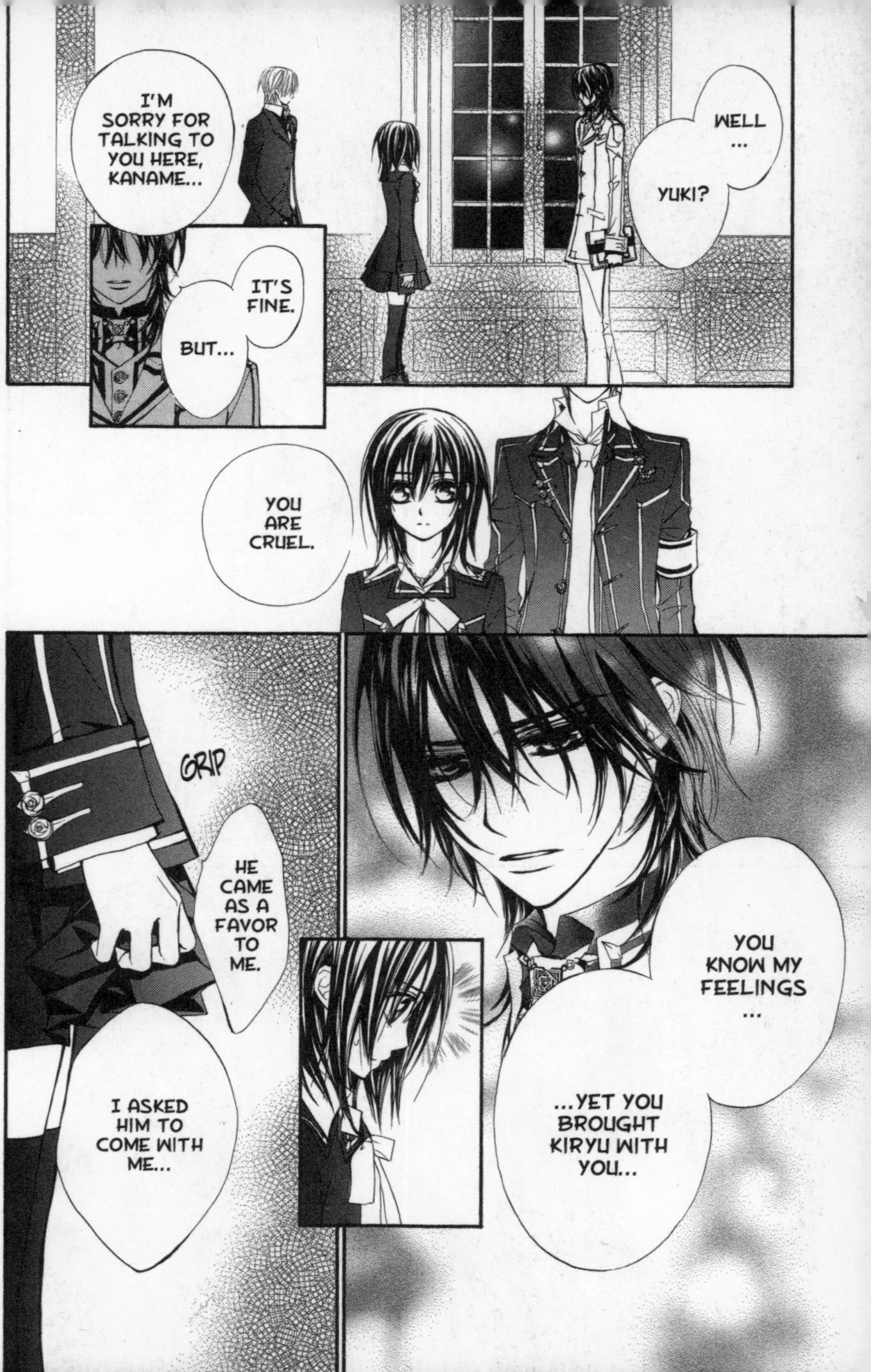
WELL ... YUKI?
I'M SORRY FOR TALKING TO YOU HERE, KANAME...
IT'S FINE. BUT...
YOU ARE CRUEL.
YOU KNOW MY FEELINGS ...
...YET YOU BROUGHT KIRYU WITH YOU...
GRIP
HE CAME AS A FAVOR TO ME.
I ASKED HIM TO COME WITH ME...

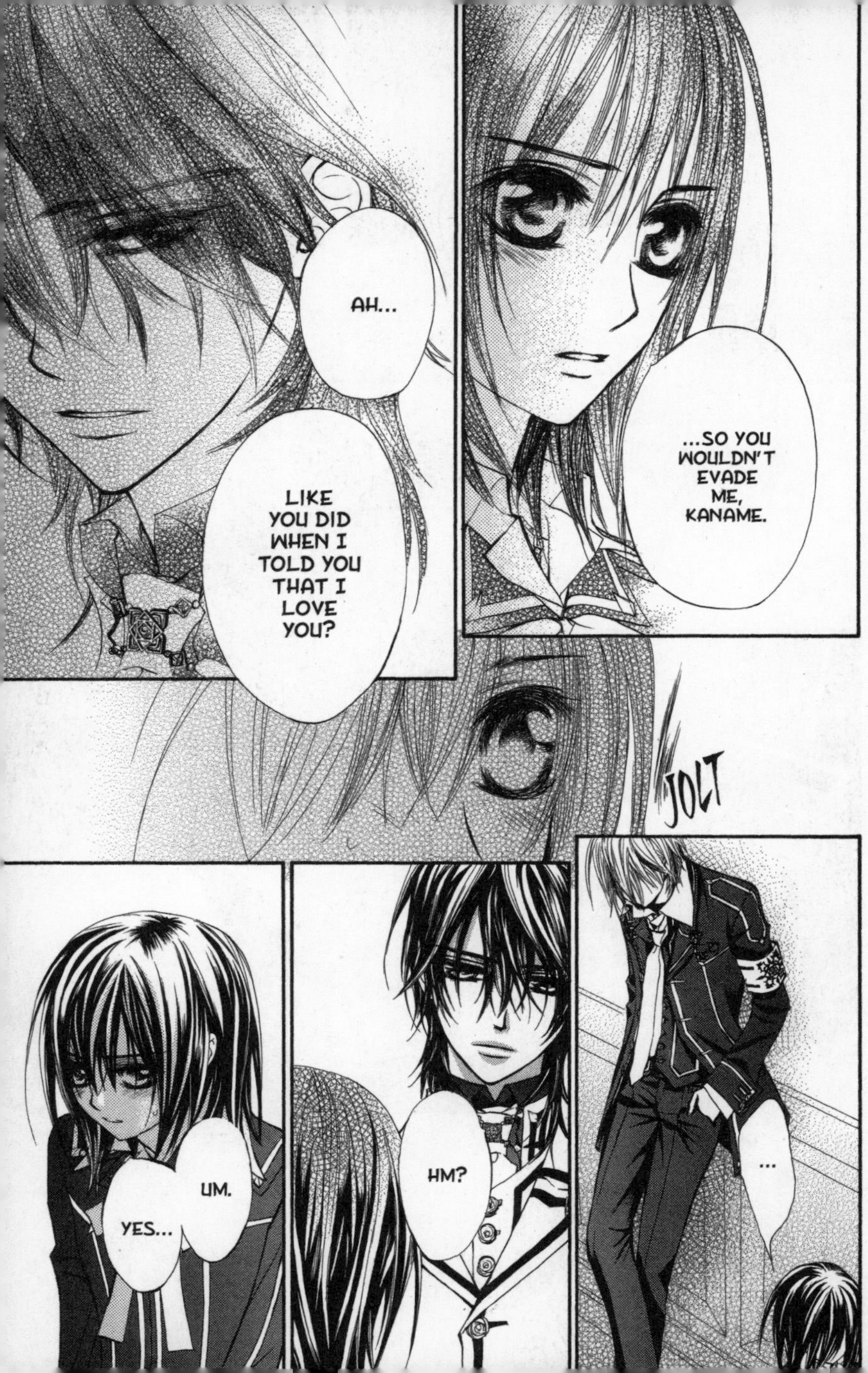
...SO YOU WOULDN'T EVADE ME, KANAME.
AH...
LIKE YOU DID WHEN I TOLD YOU THAT I LOVE YOU?
JOLT
...
HM?
UM.
YES...

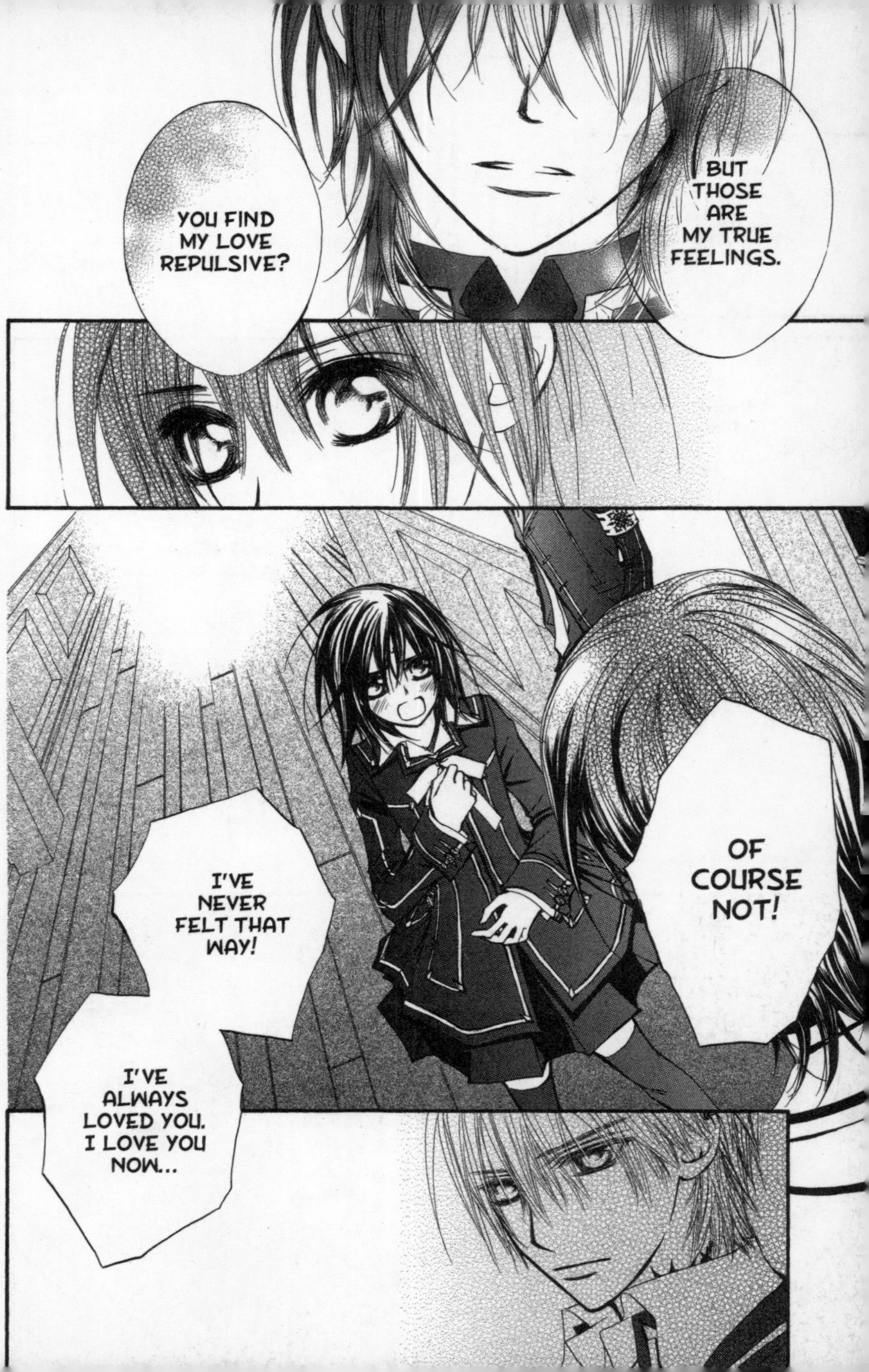
BUT THOSE ARE MY TRUE FEELINGS.
YOU FIND MY LOVE REPULSIVE?
OF COURSE NOT!
I'VE NEVER FELT THAT WAY!
I'VE ALWAYS LOVED YOU. I LOVE YOU NOW...

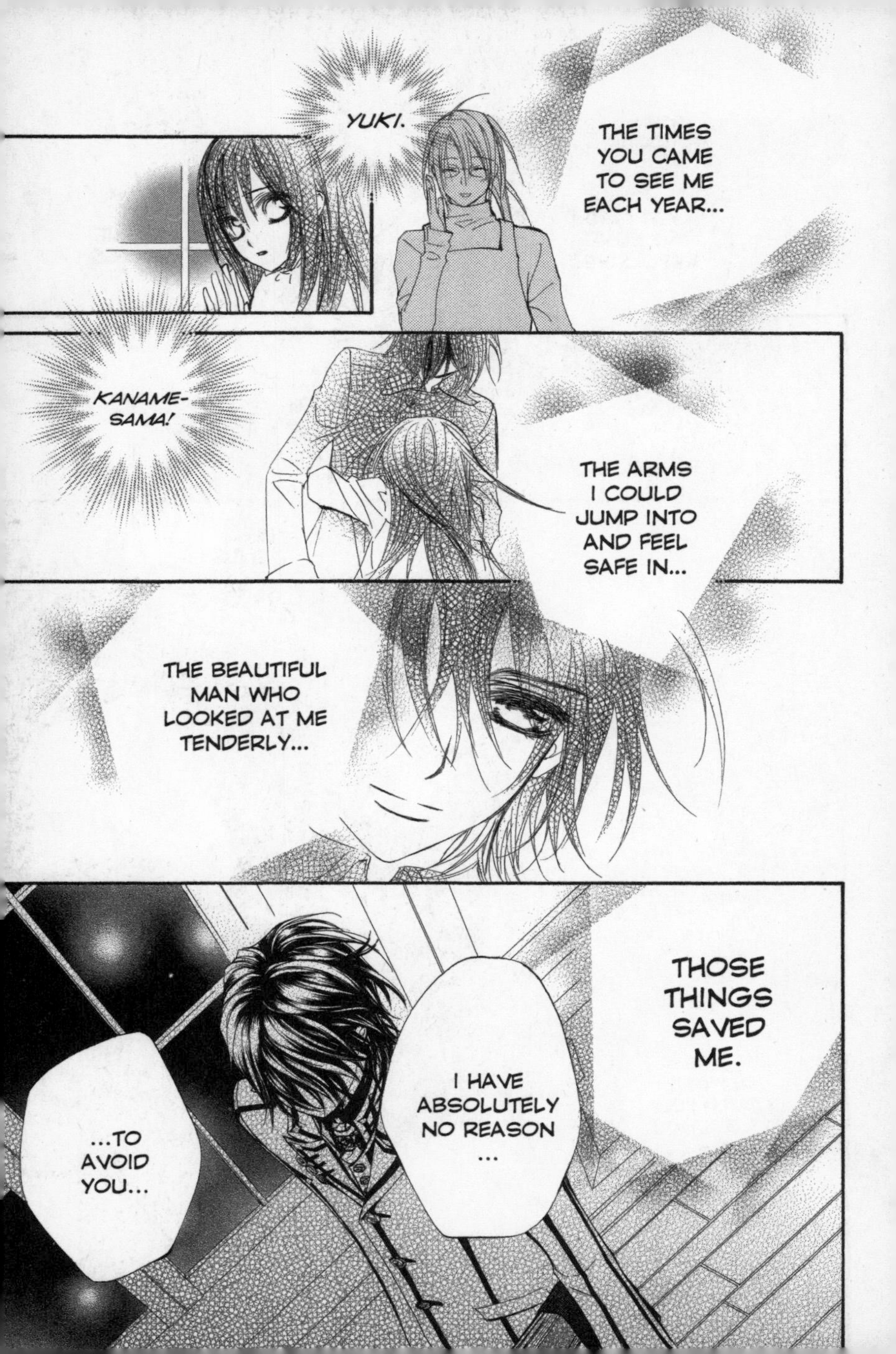
THE TIMES YOU CAME TO SEE ME EACH YEAR...
YUKI.
THE ARMS I COULD JUMP INTO AND FEEL SAFE IN...
KANAME-SAMA!
THE BEAUTIFUL MAN WHO LOOKED AT ME TENDERLY...
THOSE THINGS SAVED ME.
I HAVE ABSOLUTELY NO REASON ...
...TO AVOID YOU...

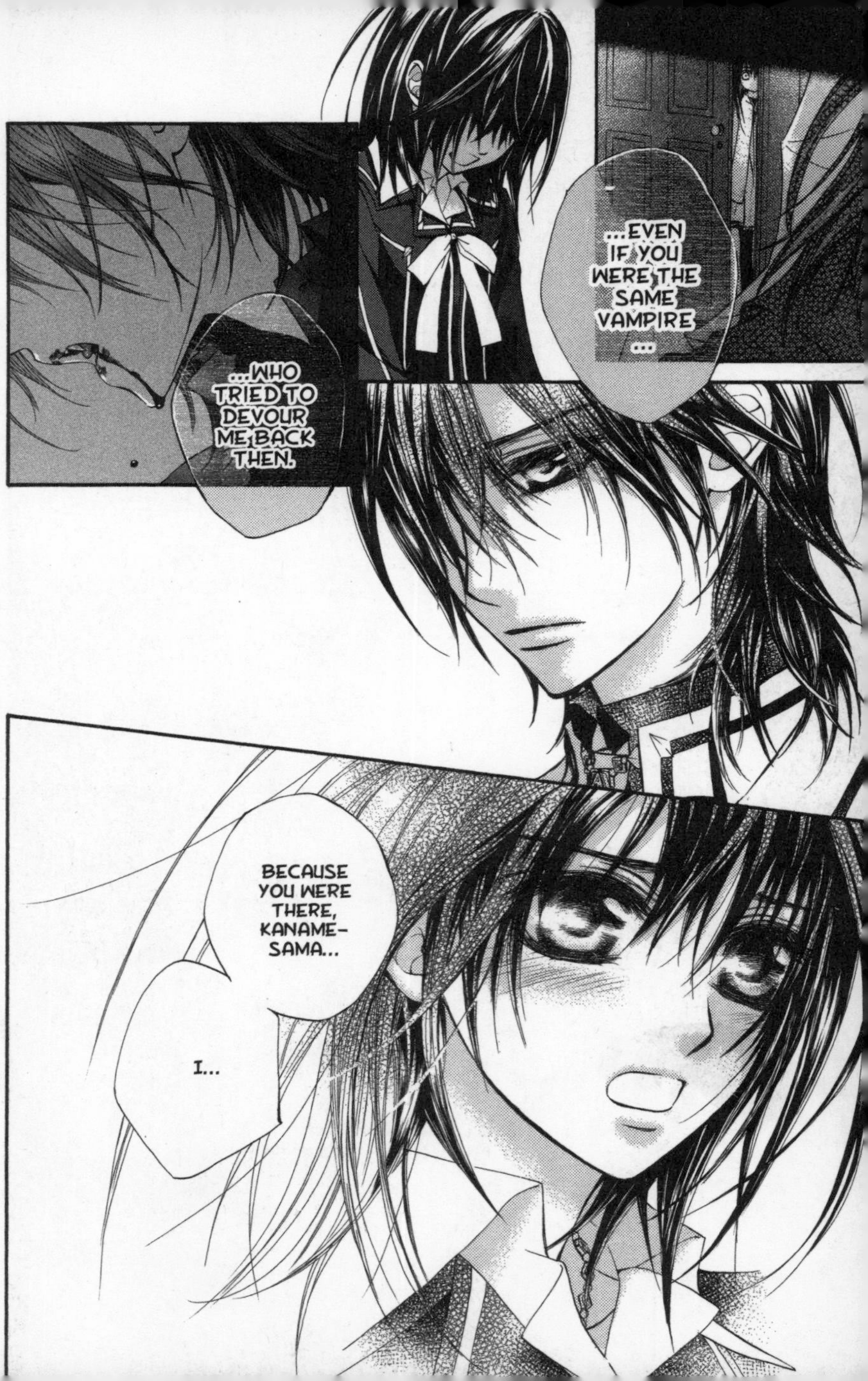
...EVEN IF YOU WERE THE SAME VAMPIRE ...
...WHO TRIED TO DEVOUR ME BACK THEN.
BECAUSE YOU WERE THERE, KANAME-SAMA...
I...

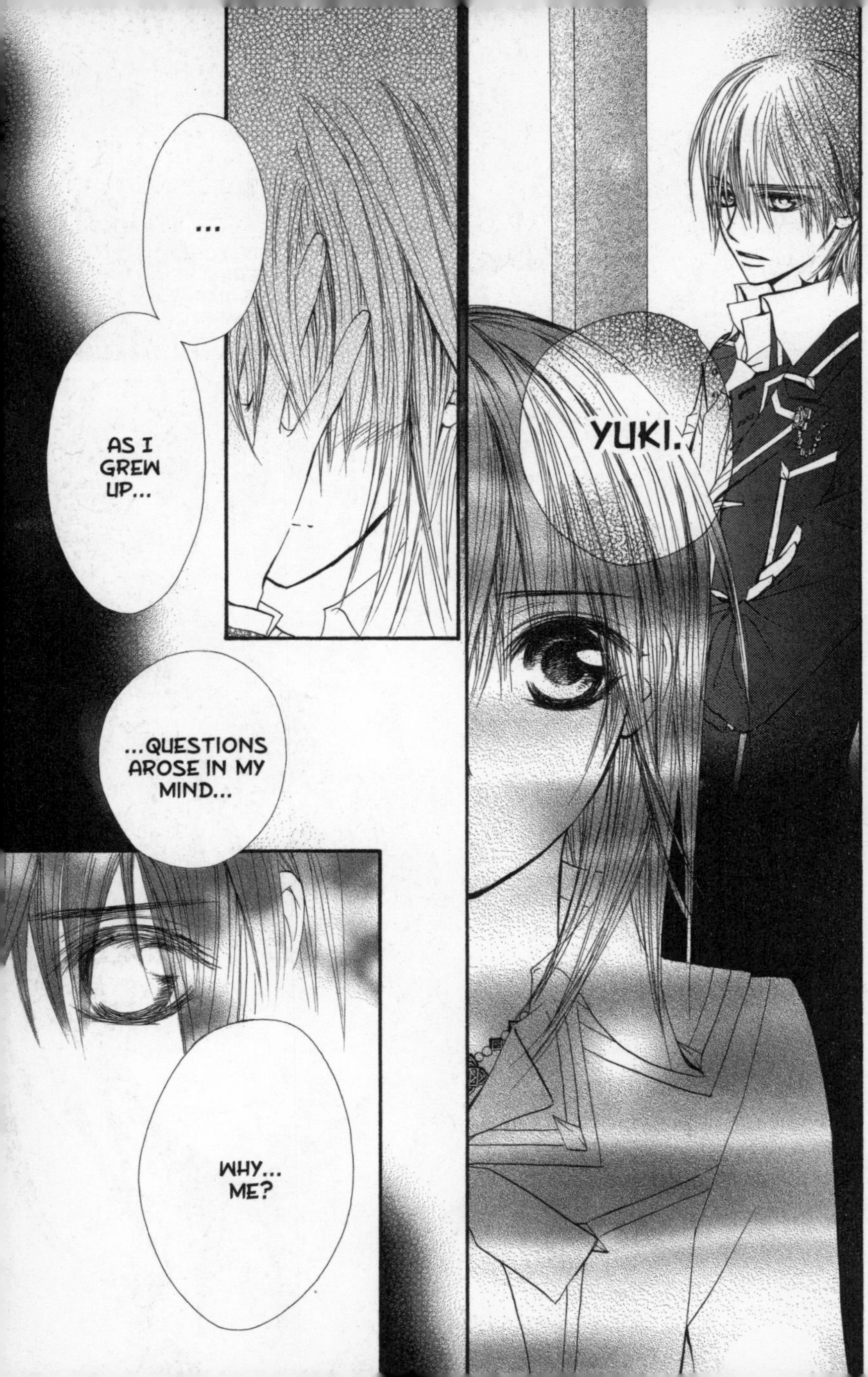
YUKI.
...
AS I GREW UP...
...QUESTIONS AROSE IN MY MIND...
WHY... ME?

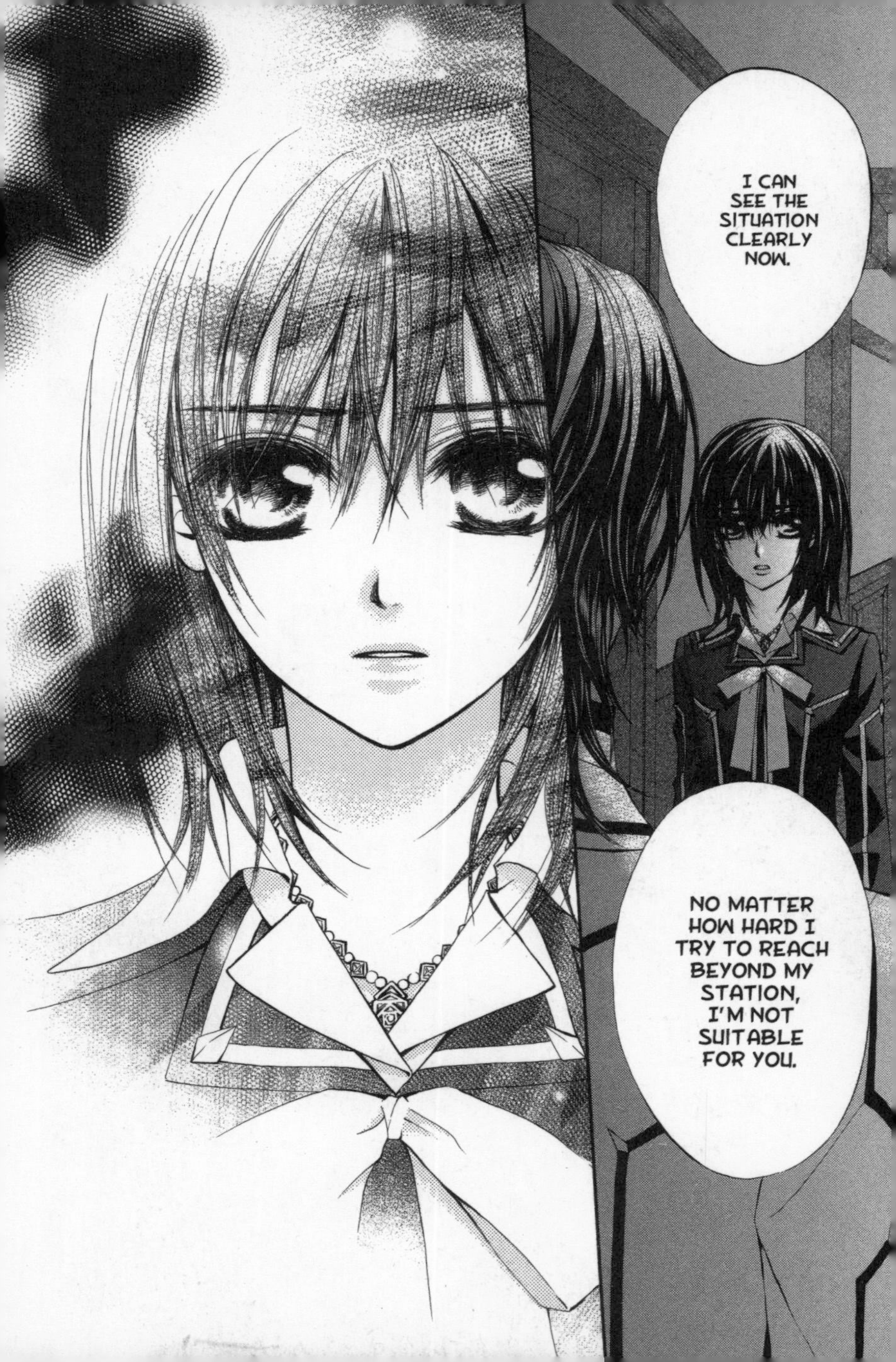
I CAN SEE THE SITUATION CLEARLY NOW.
NO MATTER HOW HARD I TRY TO REACH BEYOND MY STATION, I'M NOT SUITABLE FOR YOU.

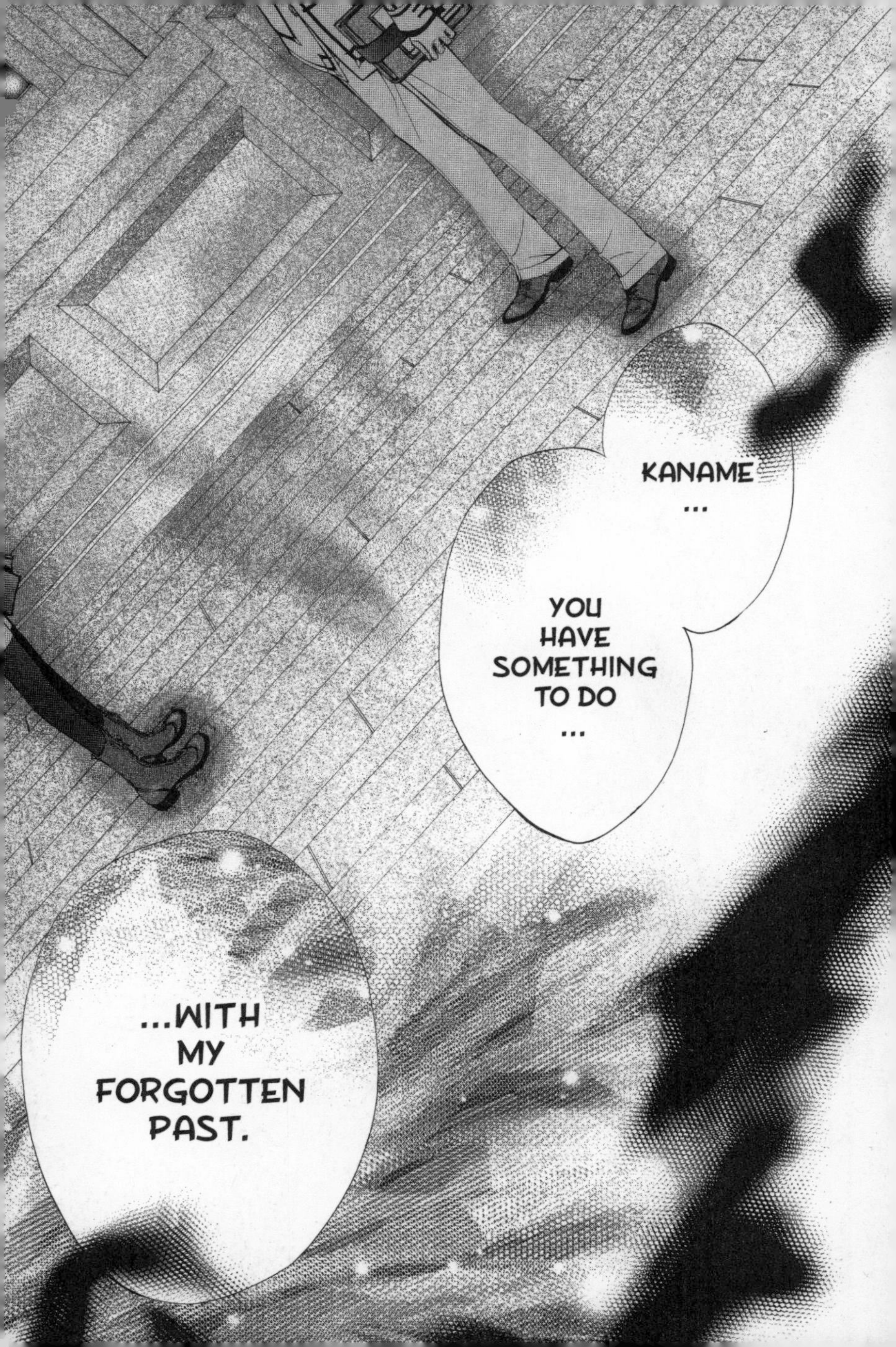
KANAME ...
YOU HAVE SOMETHING TO DO ...
...WITH MY FORGOTTEN PAST.

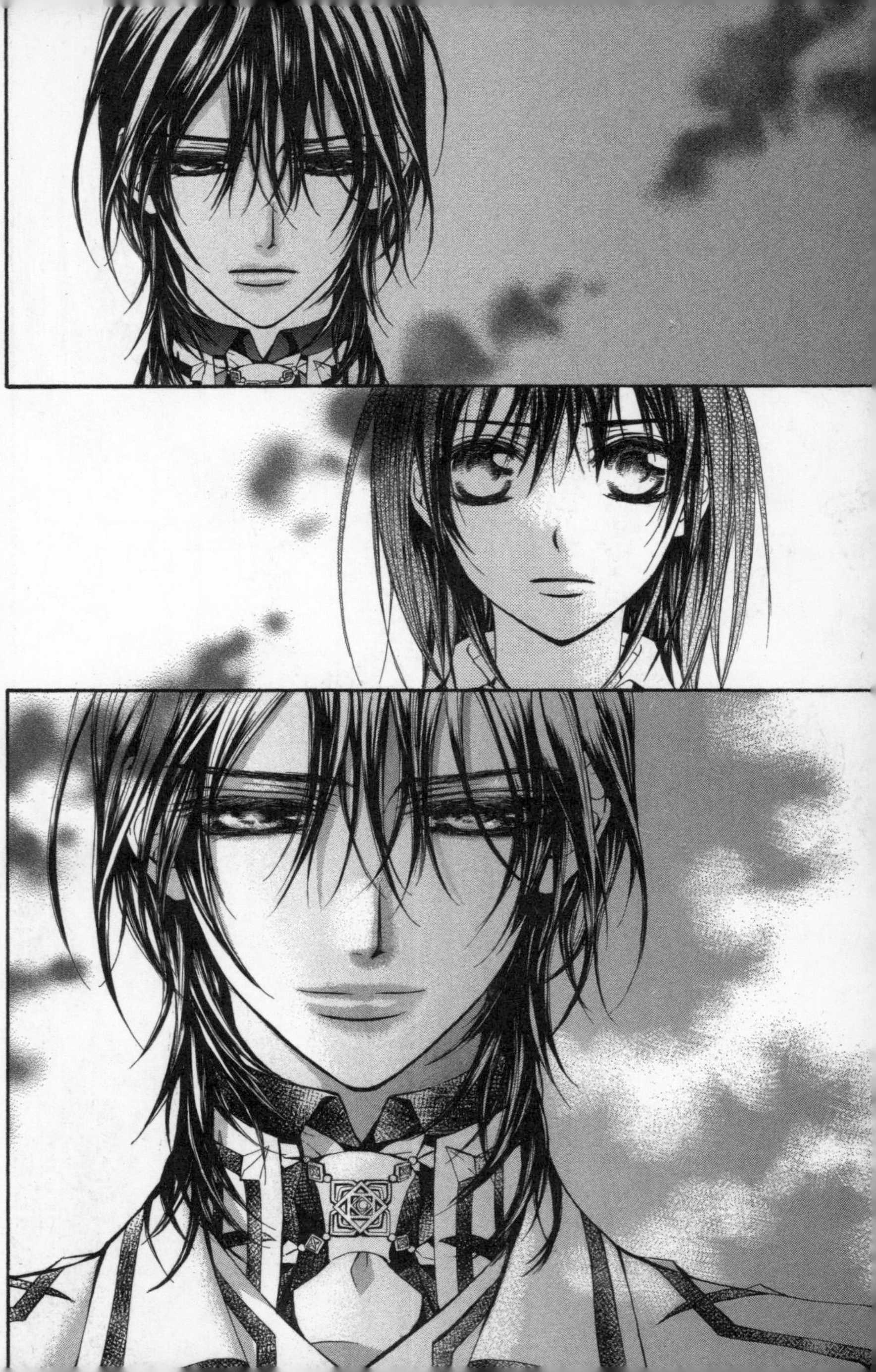

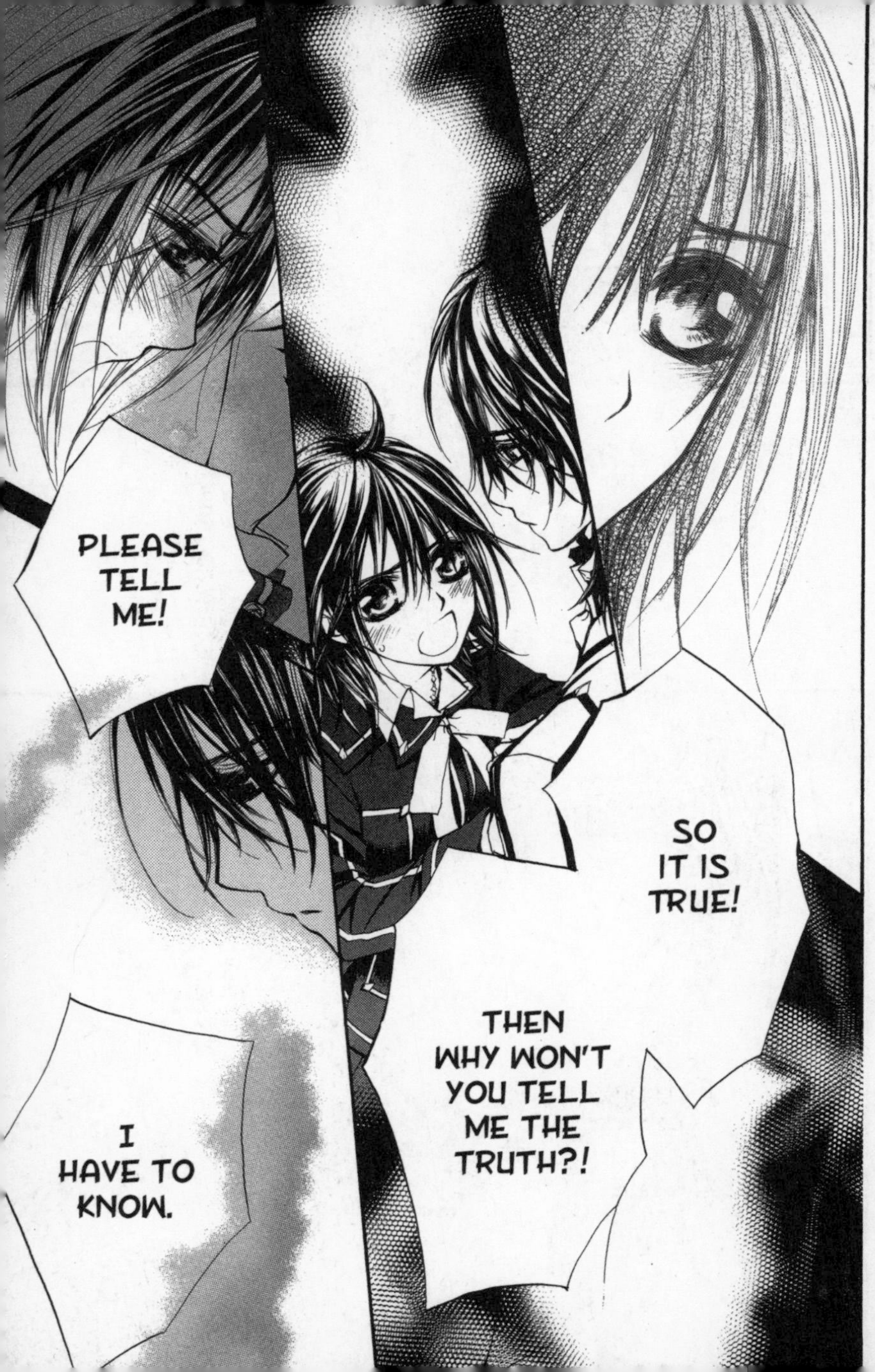
SO IT IS TRUE!
THEN WHY WON'T YOU TELL ME THE TRUTH?!
PLEASE TELL ME!
I HAVE TO KNOW.

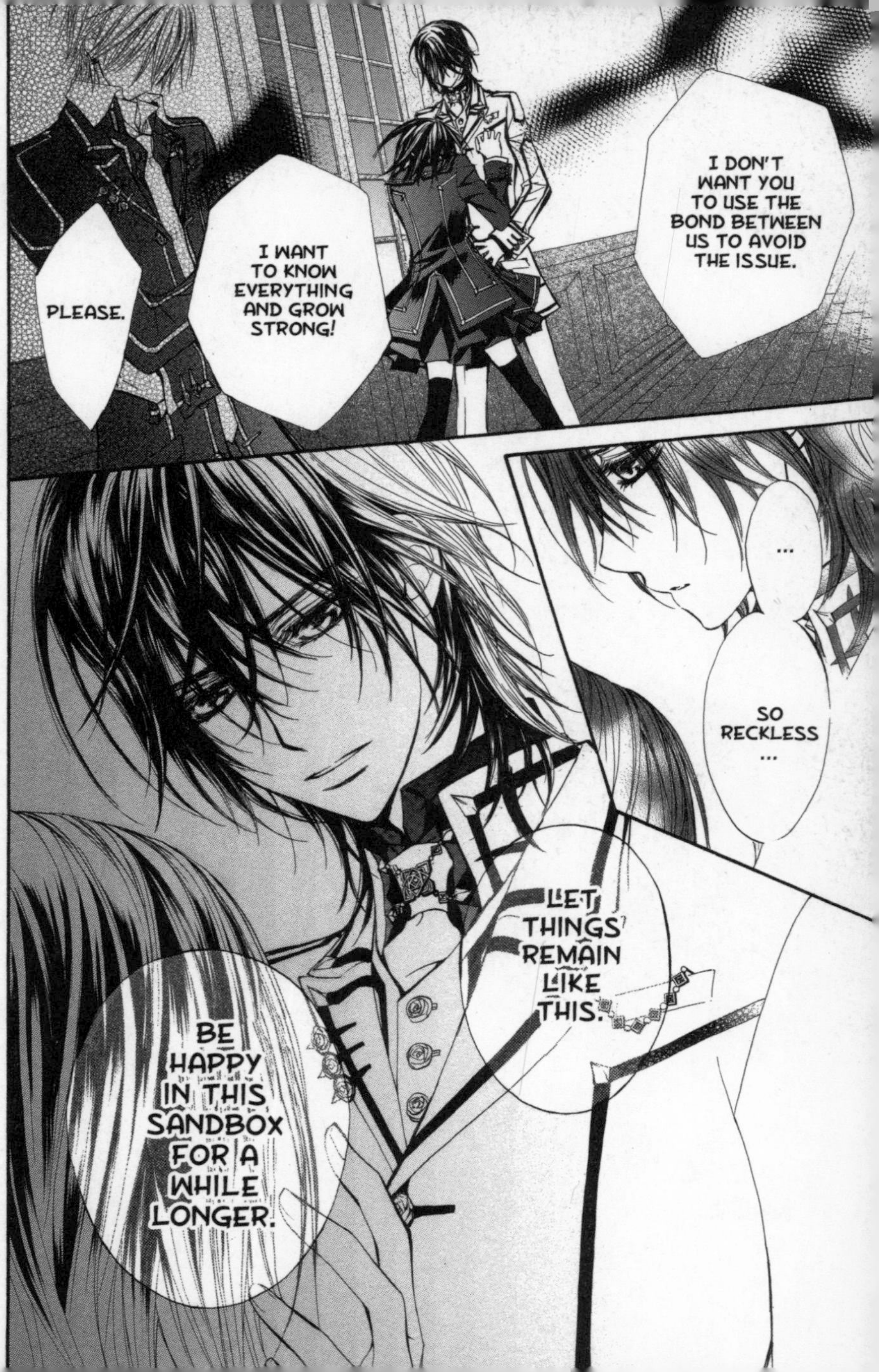
I DON'T WANT YOU TO USE THE BOND BETWEEN US TO AVOID THE ISSUE.
I WANT TO KNOW EVERYTHING AND GROW STRONG!
PLEASE.
...
SO RECKLESS ...
LET THINGS REMAIN LIKE THIS.
BE HAPPY IN THIS SANDBOX FOR A WHILE LONGER.

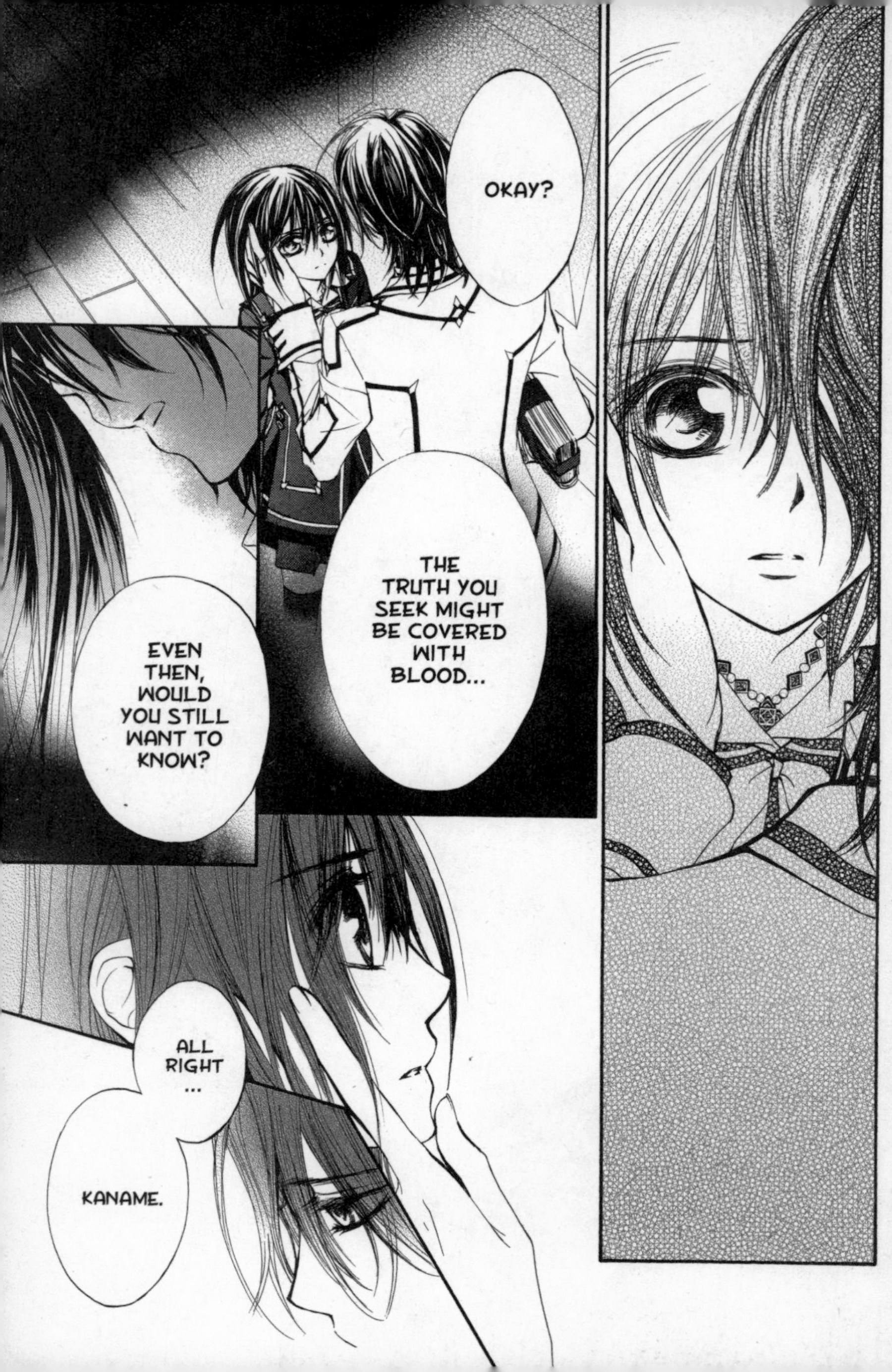
OKAY?
THE TRUTH YOU SEEK MIGHT BE COVERED WITH BLOOD...
EVEN THEN, WOULD YOU STILL WANT TO KNOW?
ALL RIGHT ...
KANAME.

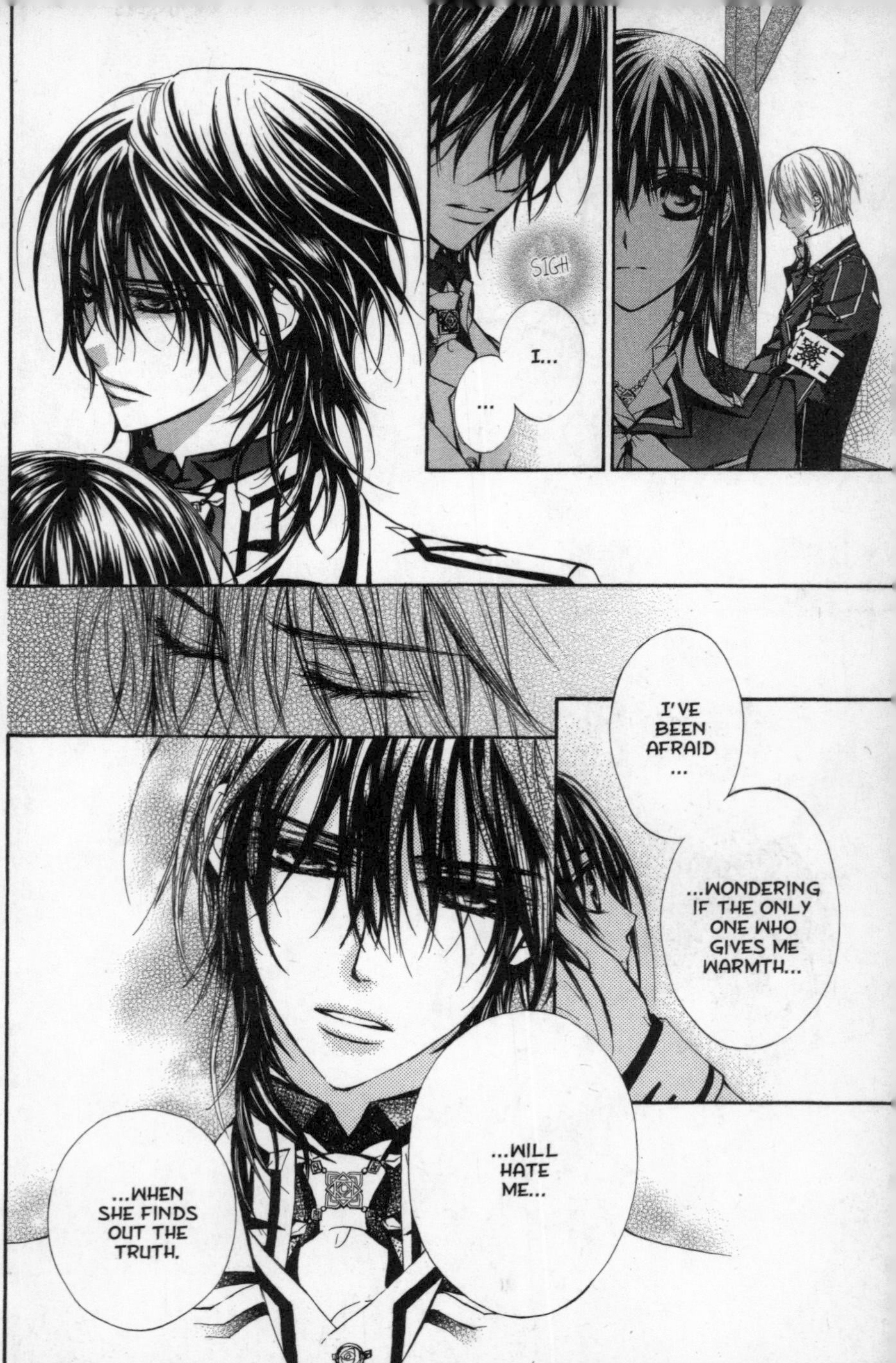
SIGH
I...
...
I'VE BEEN AFRAID ...
...WONDERING IF THE ONLY ONE WHO GIVES ME WARMTH...
...WILL HATE ME...
...WHEN SHE FINDS OUT THE TRUTH.

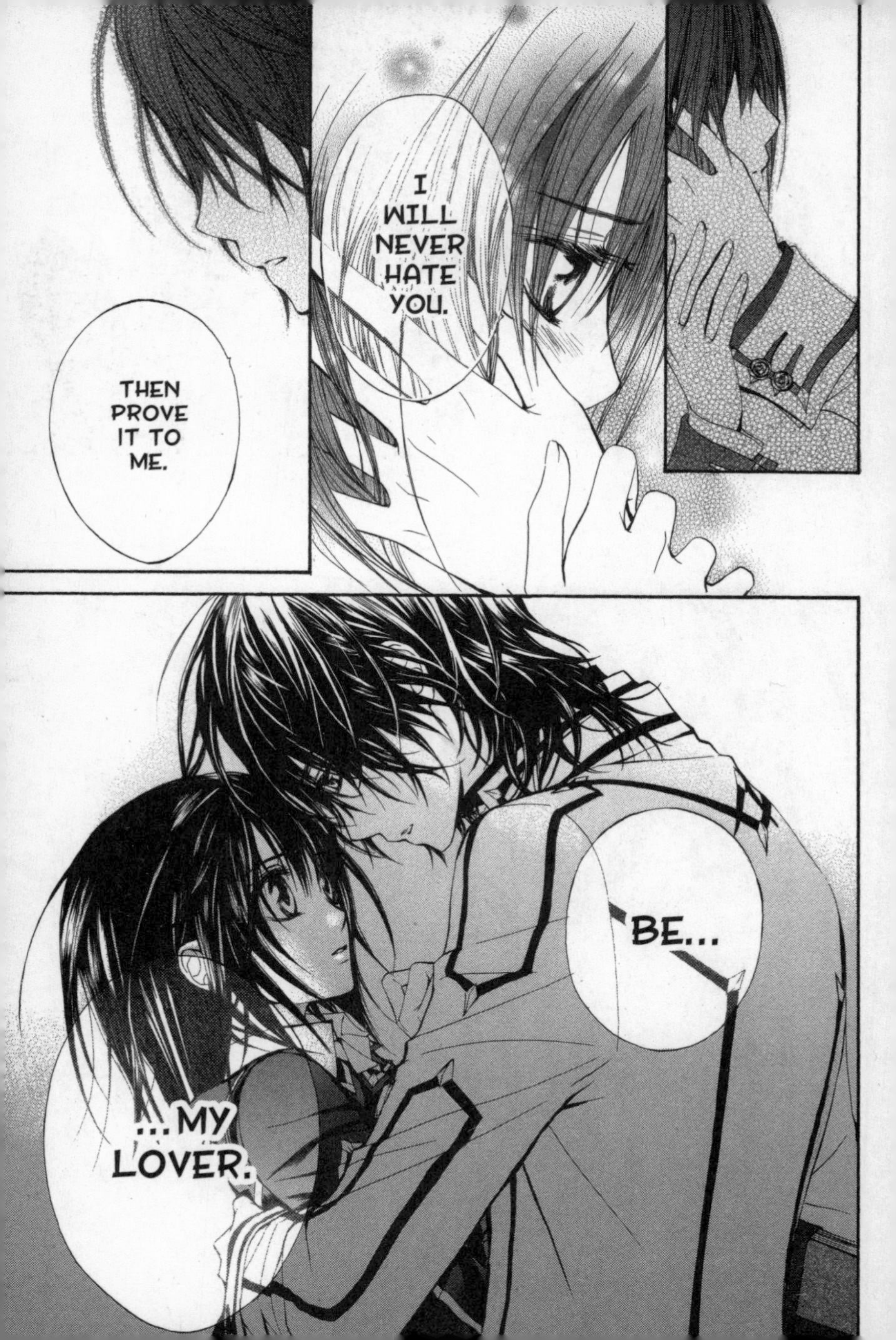
I WILL NEVER HATE YOU.
THEN PROVE IT TO ME.
BE...
...MY LOVER.

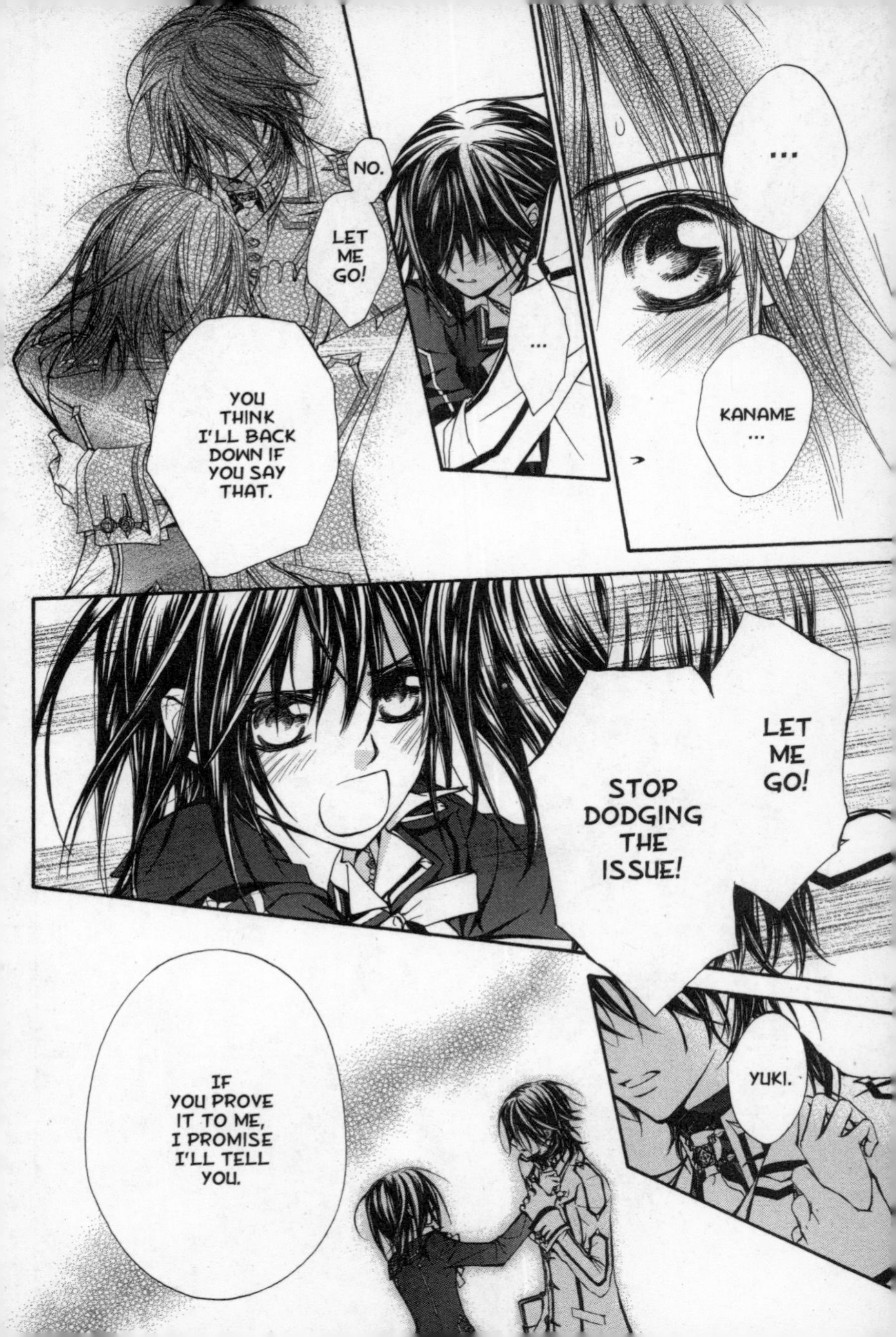
...
KANAME ...
...
NO.
LET ME GO!
YOU THINK I'LL BACK DOWN IF YOU SAY THAT.
LET ME GO!
STOP DODGING THE ISSUE!
YUKI.
IF YOU PROVE IT TO ME, I PROMISE I'LL TELL YOU.

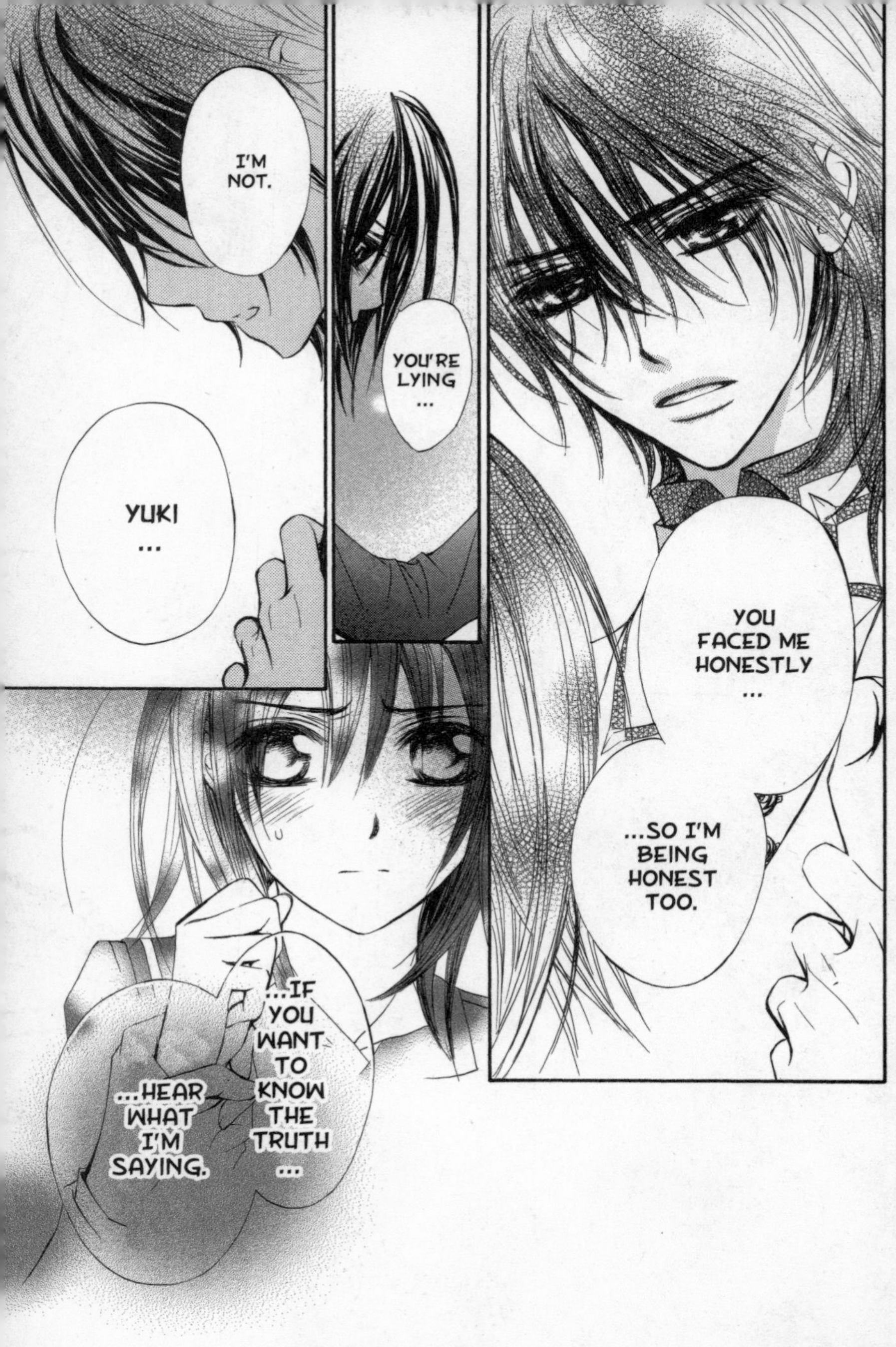
YOU FACED ME HONESTLY ...
...SO I'M BEING HONEST TOO.
YOU'RE LYING ...
I'M NOT.
YUKI ...
...IF YOU WANT TO KNOW THE TRUTH ...
...HEAR WHAT I'M SAYING.

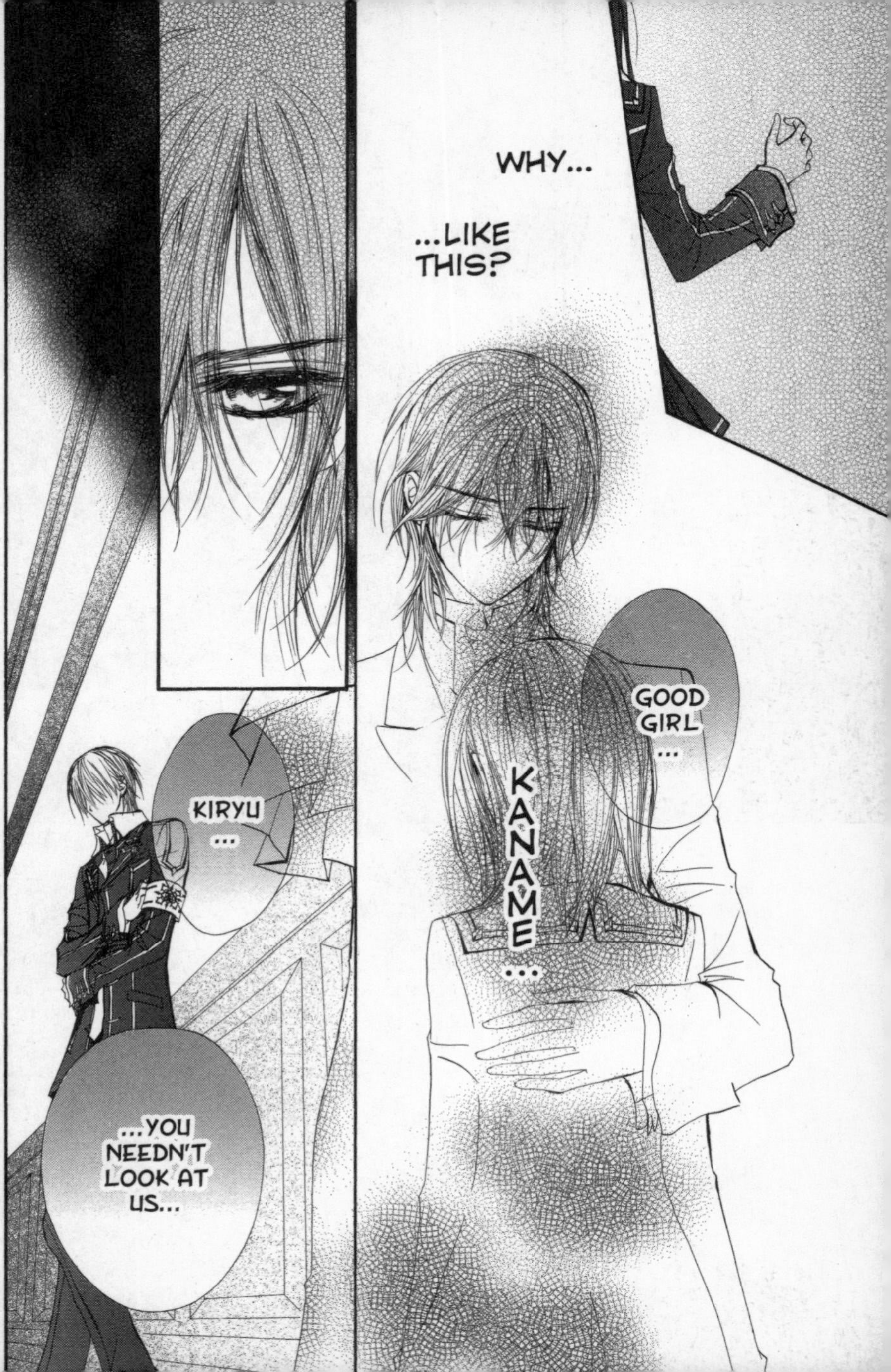
WHY...
...LIKE THIS?
GOOD GIRL...
KANAME...
KIRYU...
...YOU NEEDN'T LOOK AT US...

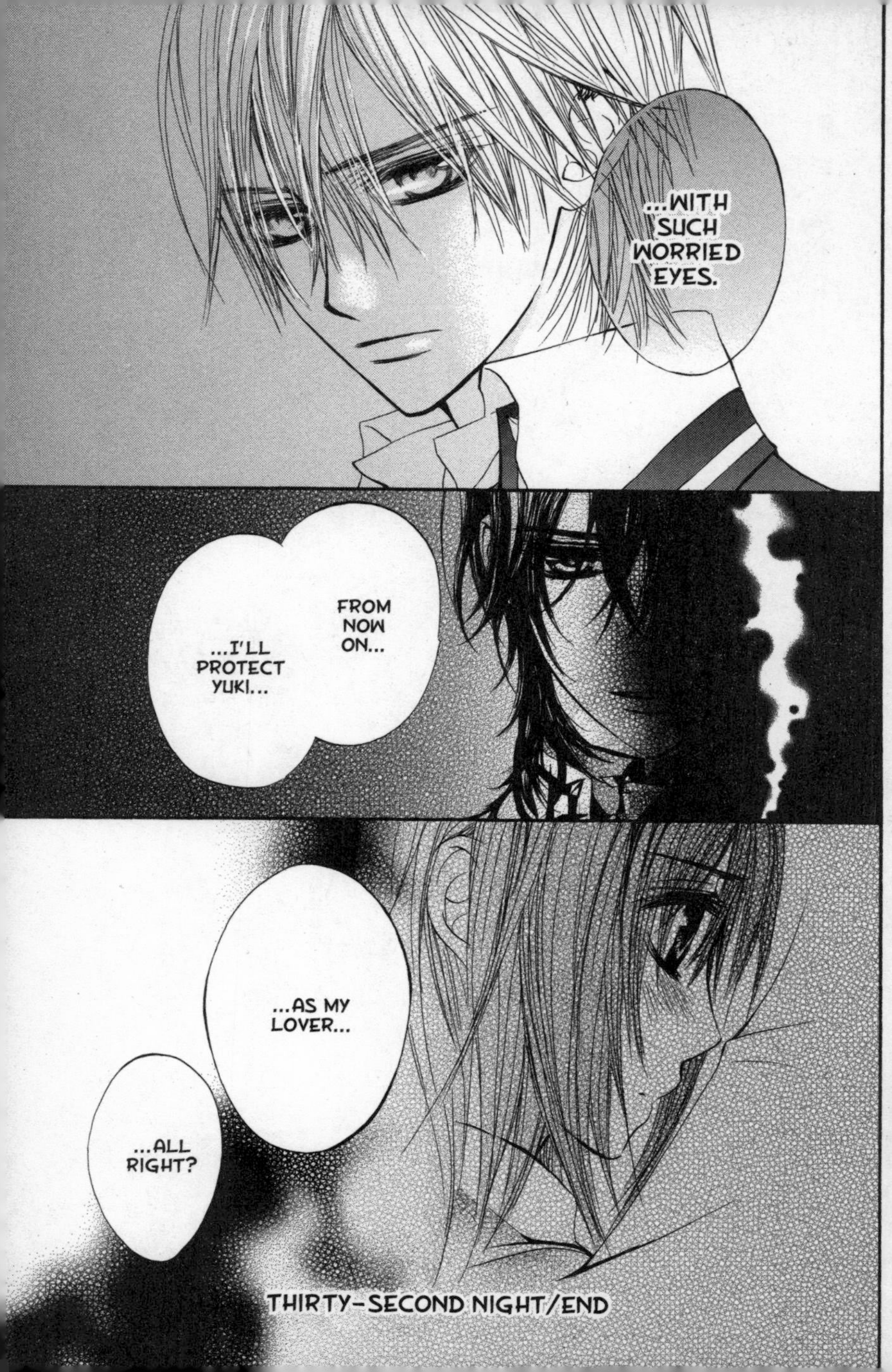
...WITH SUCH WORRIED EYES.
FROM NOW ON...
...I'LL PROTECT YUKI...
...AS MY LOVER...
...ALL RIGHT?
THIRTY-SECOND NIGHT/END

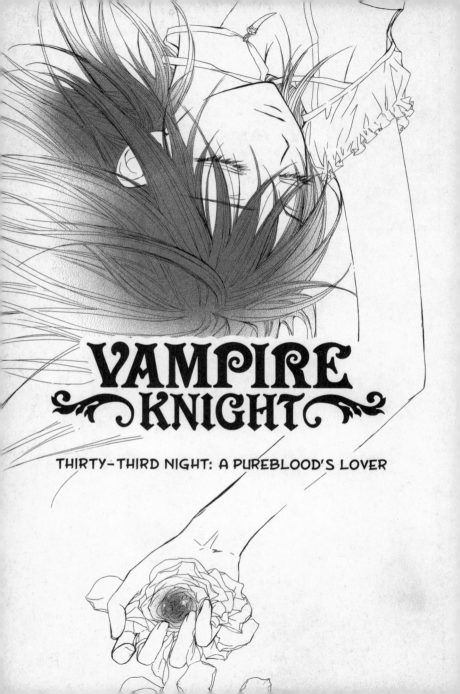

VAMPIRE KNIGHT

THIRTY-THIRD NIGHT: A PUREBLOOD'S LOVER

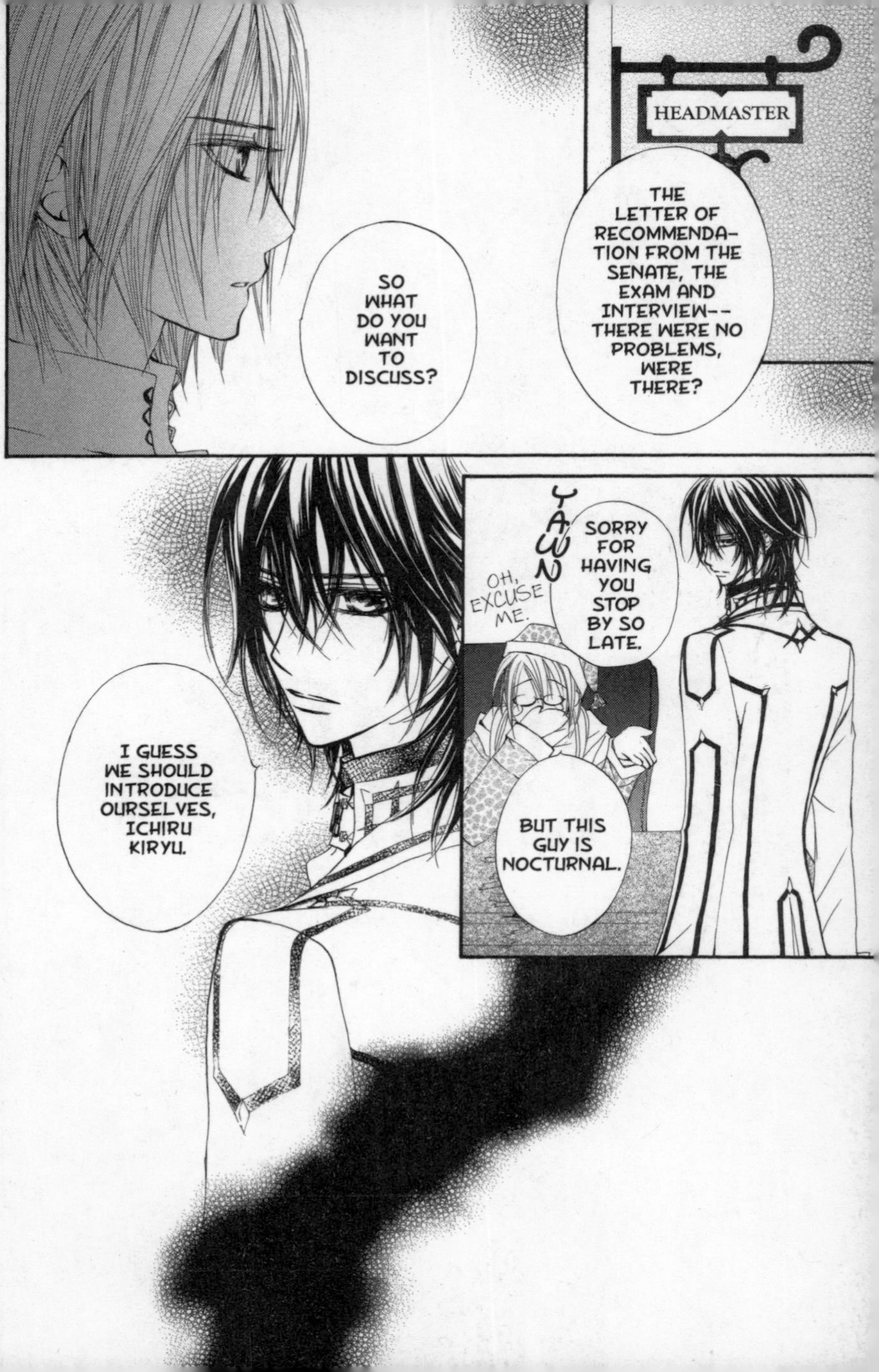
HEADMASTER
THE LETTER OF RECOMMENDATION FROM THE SENATE, THE EXAM AND INTERVIEW-- THERE WERE NO PROBLEMS, WERE THERE?
SO WHAT DO YOU WANT TO DISCUSS?
SORRY FOR HAVING YOU STOP BY SO LATE.
YAWN
OH, EXCUSE ME.
BUT THIS GUY IS NOCTURNAL.
I GUESS WE SHOULD INTRODUCE OURSELVES, ICHIRU KIRYU.

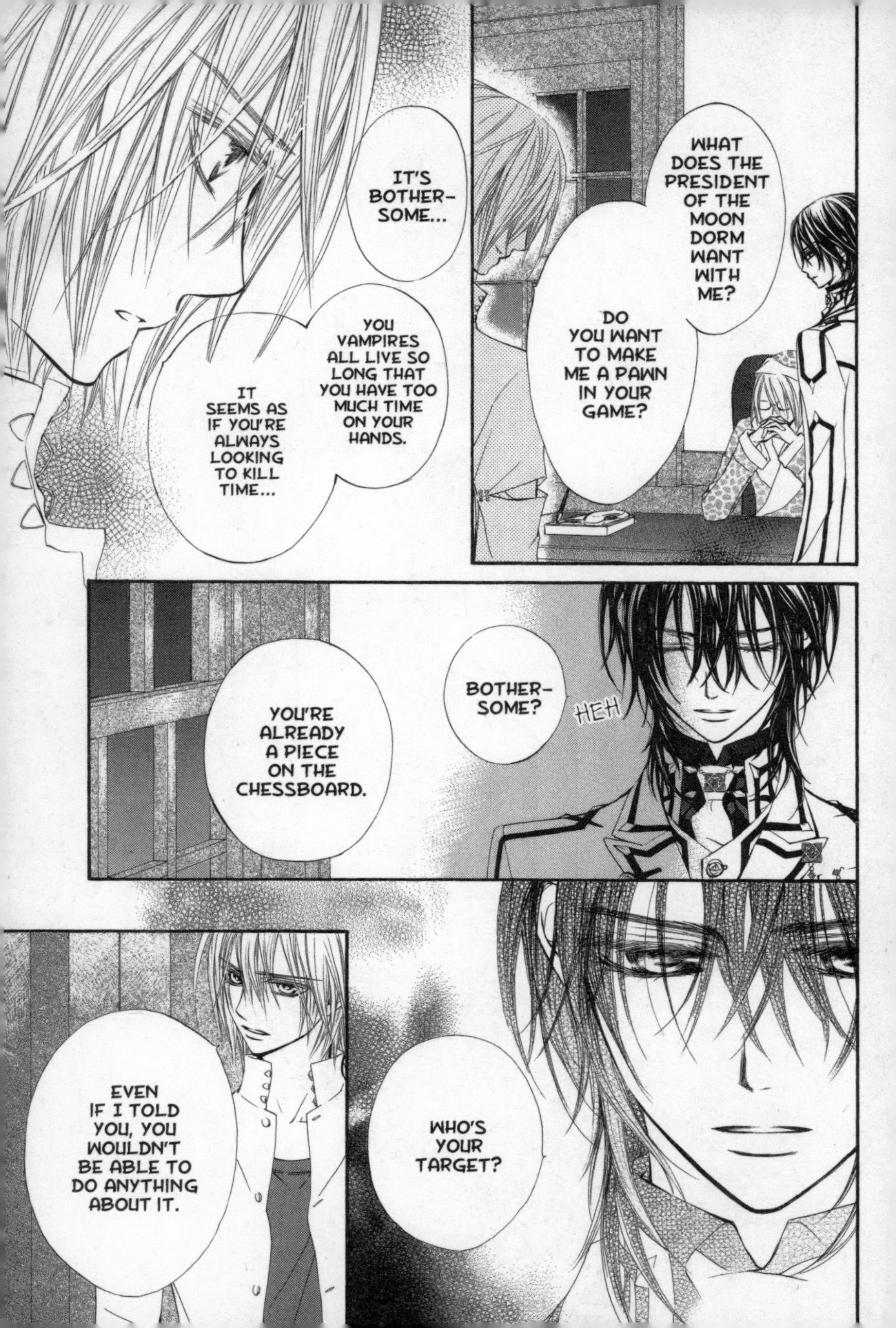
WHAT DOES THE PRESIDENT OF THE MOON DORM WANT WITH ME?
DO YOU WANT TO MAKE ME A PAWN IN YOUR GAME?
IT'S BOTHER-SOME...
YOU VAMPIRES ALL LIVE SO LONG THAT YOU HAVE TOO MUCH TIME ON YOUR HANDS.
IT SEEMS AS IF YOU'RE ALWAYS LOOKING TO KILL TIME...
HEH
BOTHER-SOME?
YOU'RE ALREADY A PIECE ON THE CHESSBOARD.
WHO'S YOUR TARGET?
EVEN IF I TOLD YOU, YOU WOULDN'T BE ABLE TO DO ANYTHING ABOUT IT.

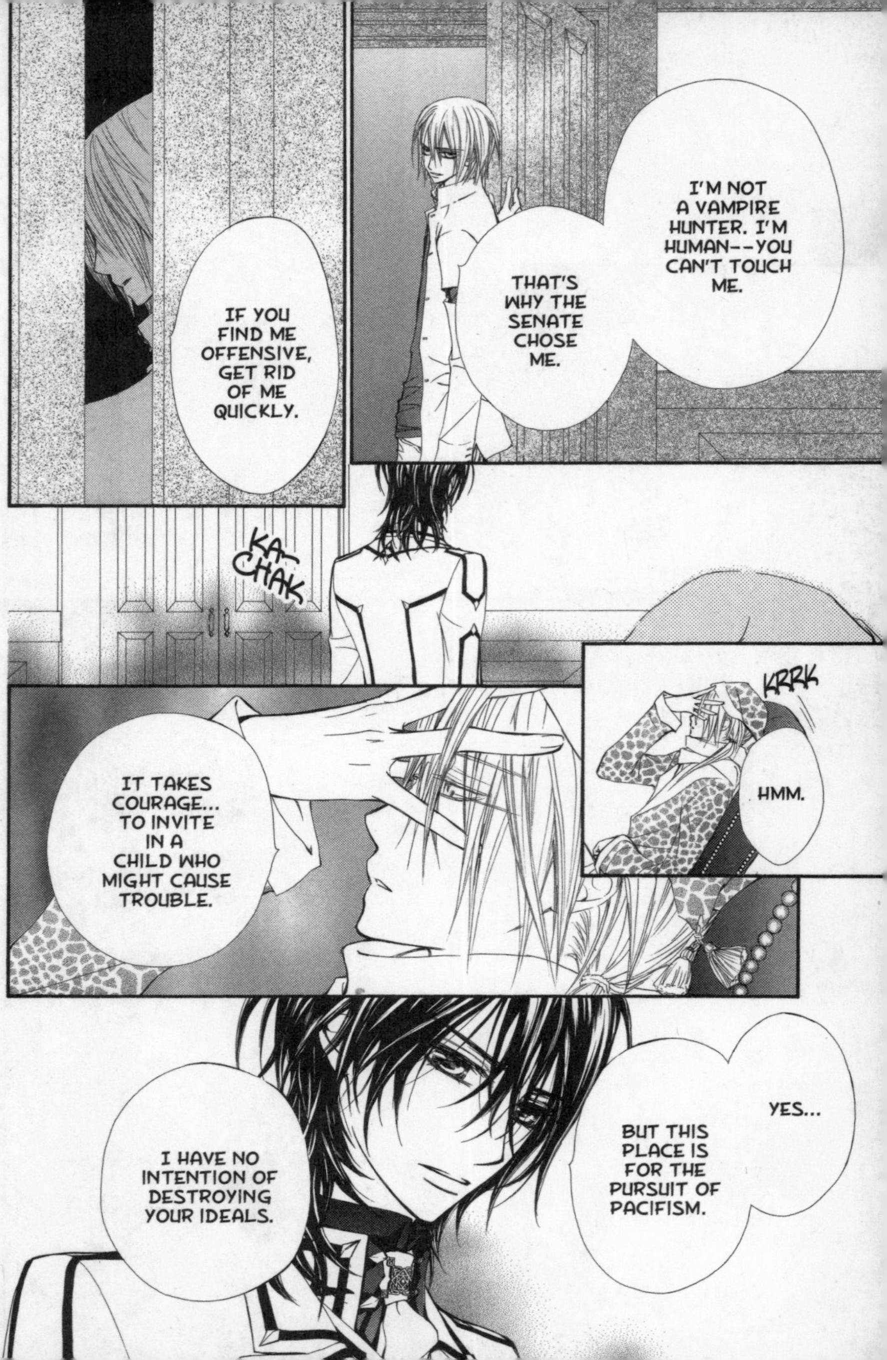
I'M NOT A VAMPIRE HUNTER. I'M HUMAN--YOU CAN'T TOUCH ME.
THAT'S WHY THE SENATE CHOSE ME.
IF YOU FIND ME OFFENSIVE, GET RID OF ME QUICKLY.
KA-CHAK
KRRK
HMM.
IT TAKES COURAGE... TO INVITE IN A CHILD WHO MIGHT CAUSE TROUBLE.
YES...
BUT THIS PLACE IS FOR THE PURSUIT OF PACIFISM.
I HAVE NO INTENTION OF DESTROYING YOUR IDEALS.

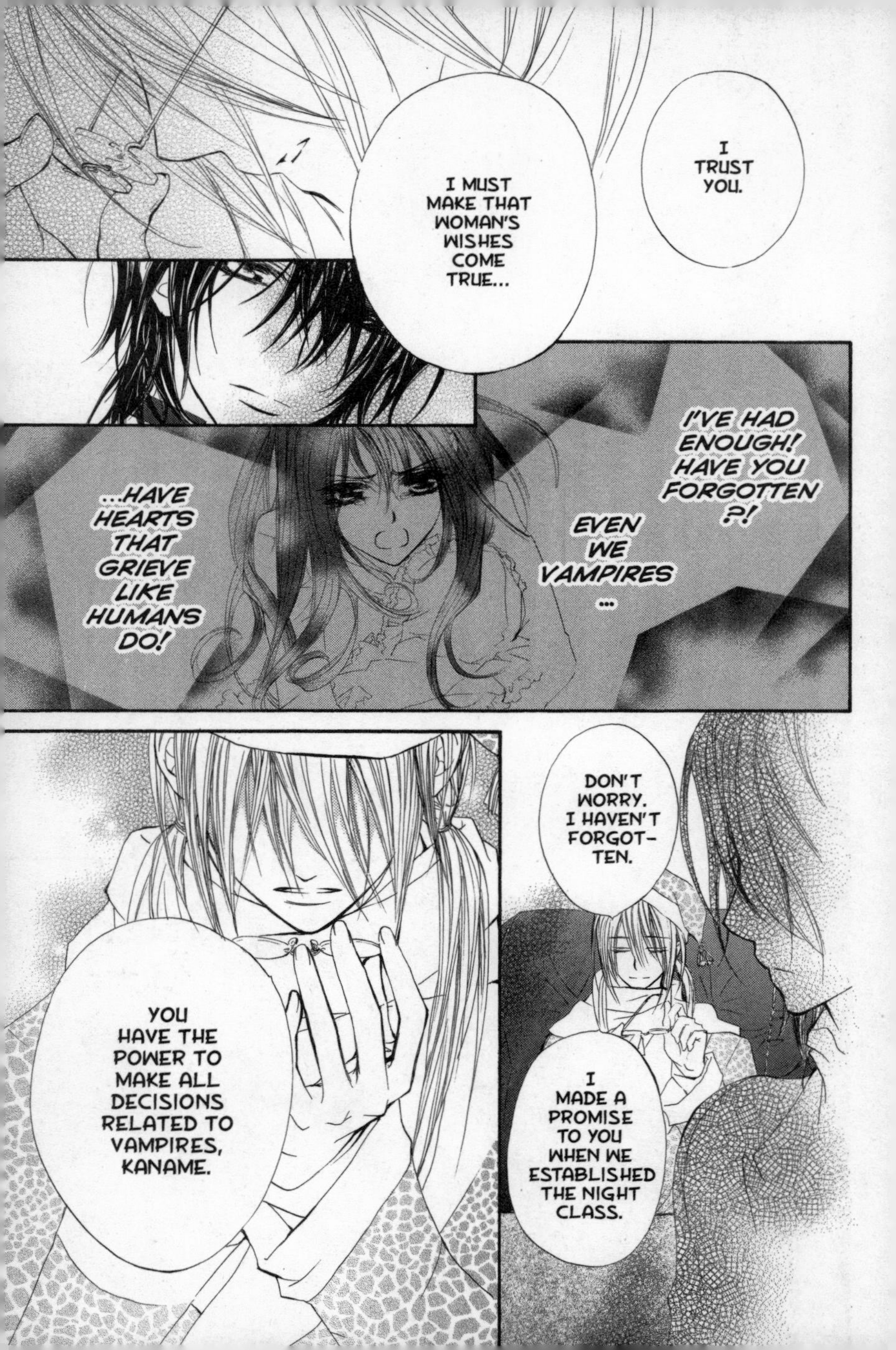
I TRUST YOU.
I MUST MAKE THAT WOMAN'S WISHES COME TRUE...
I'VE HAD ENOUGH! HAVE YOU FORGOTTEN ?!
EVEN WE VAMPIRES ...
...HAVE HEARTS THAT GRIEVE LIKE HUMANS DO!
DON'T WORRY. I HAVEN'T FORGOT-TEN.
I MADE A PROMISE TO YOU WHEN WE ESTABLISHED THE NIGHT CLASS.
YOU HAVE THE POWER TO MAKE ALL DECISIONS RELATED TO VAMPIRES, KANAME.

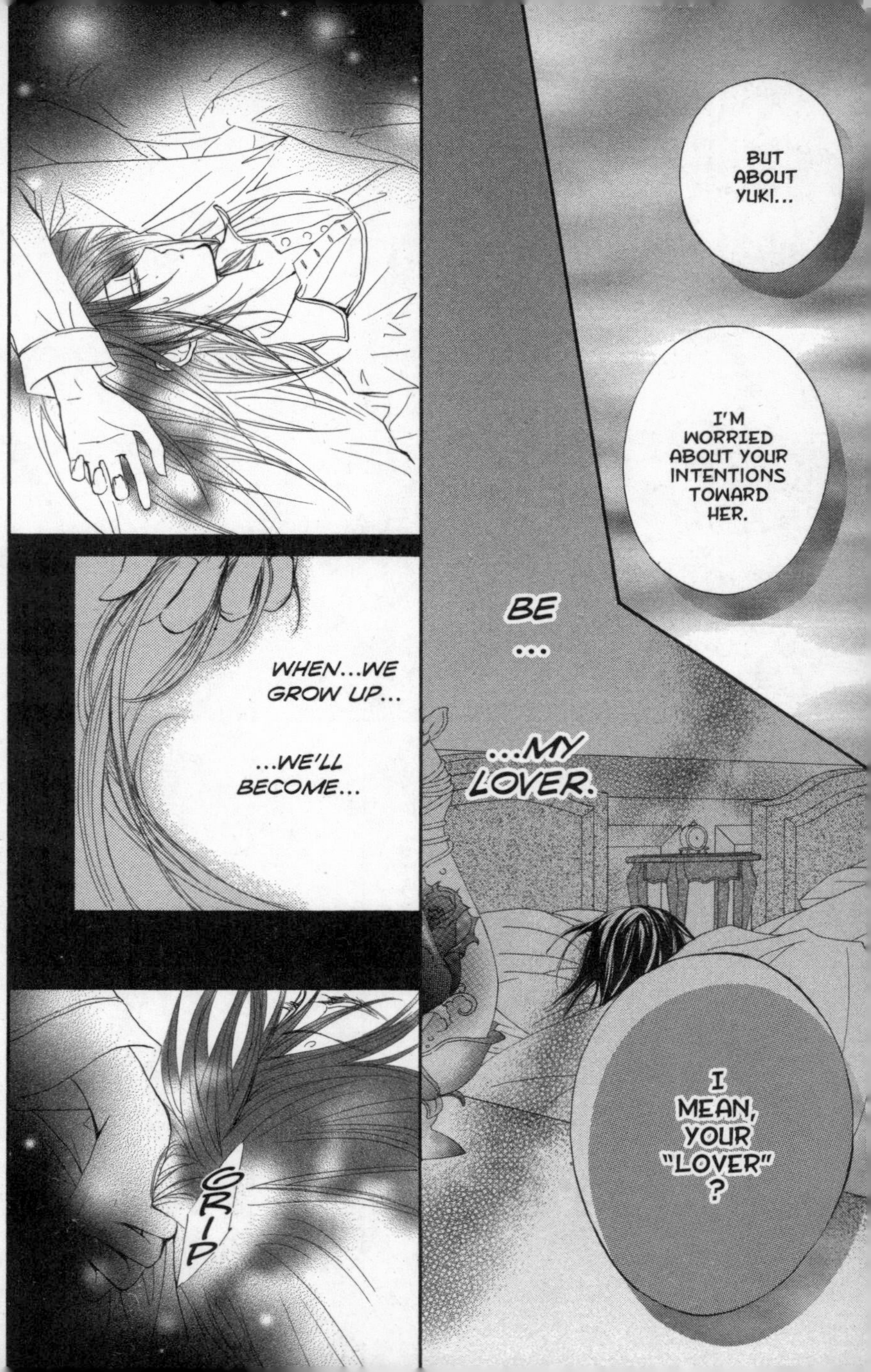
BUT ABOUT YUKI...
I'M WORRIED ABOUT YOUR INTENTIONS TOWARD HER.
BE ...
...MY LOVER.
I MEAN, YOUR "LOVER"?
WHEN...WE GROW UP...
...WE'LL BECOME...
GRIP

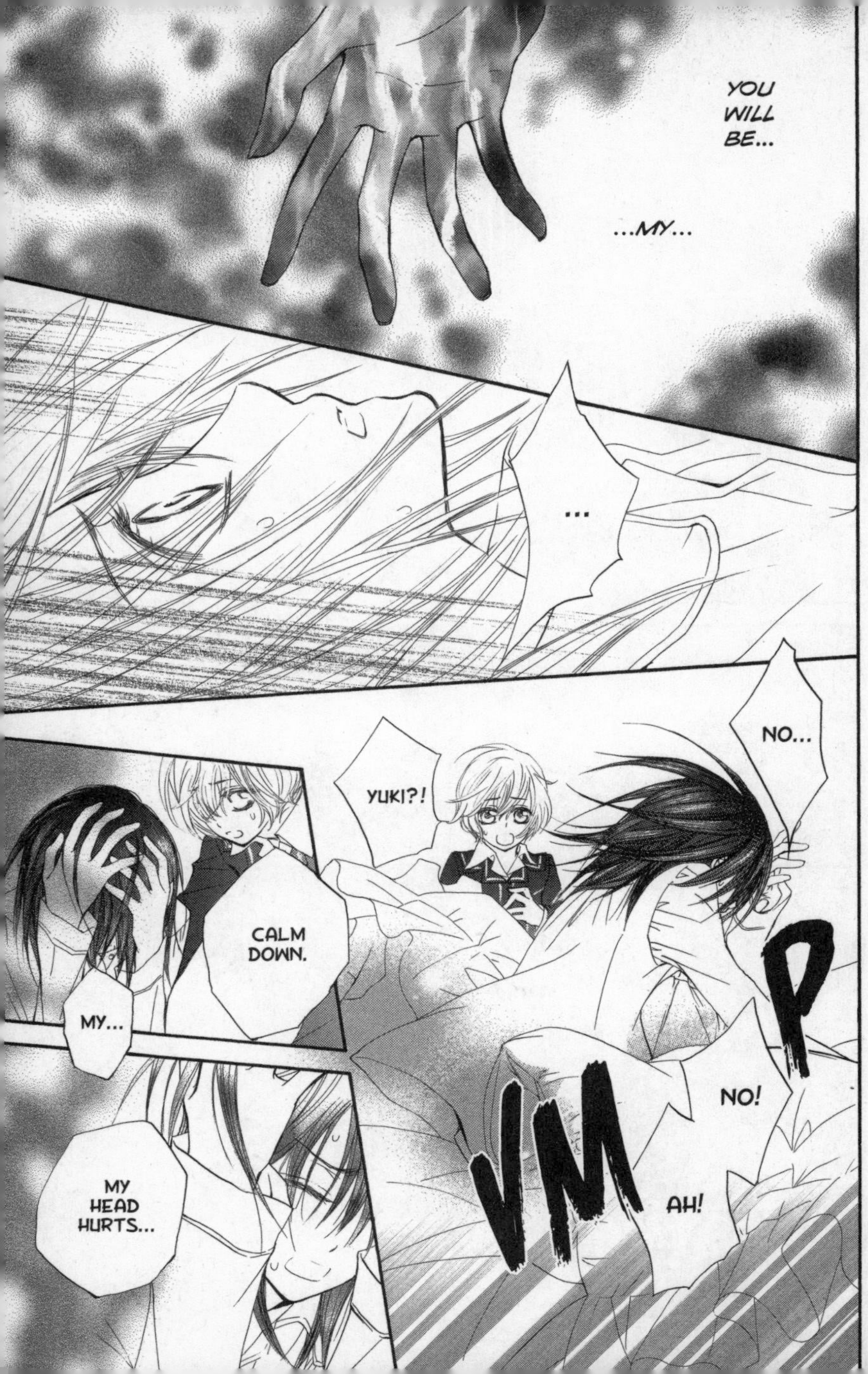
YOU WILL BE...
...MY...
...
NO...
YUKI?!
VMP
NO!
AH!
CALM DOWN.
MY...
MY HEAD HURTS...

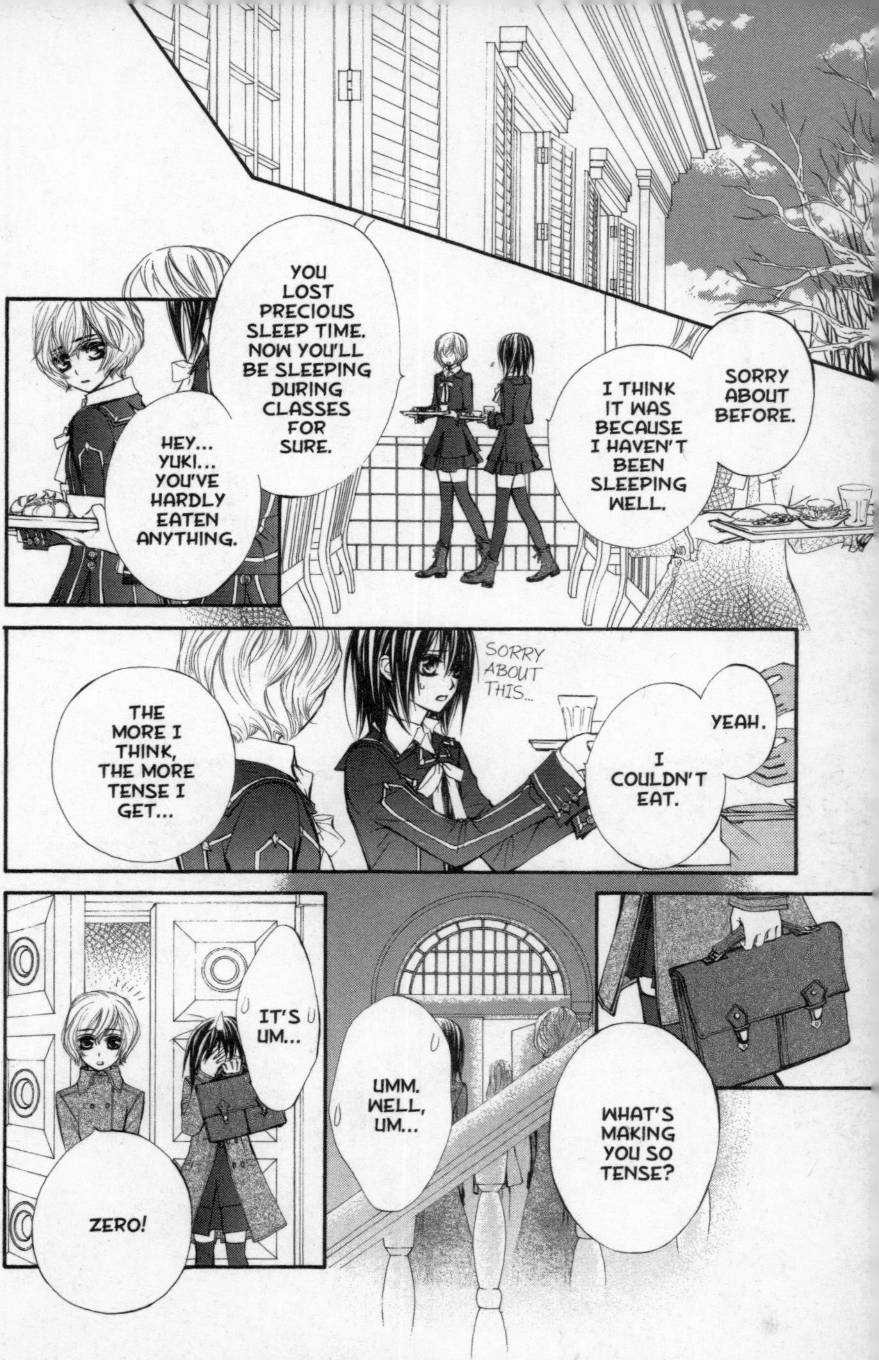
SORRY ABOUT BEFORE.
I THINK IT WAS BECAUSE I HAVEN'T BEEN SLEEPING WELL.
YOU LOST PRECIOUS SLEEP TIME. NOW YOU'LL BE SLEEPING DURING CLASSES FOR SURE.
HEY... YUKI... YOU'VE HARDLY EATEN ANYTHING.
YEAH.
I COULDN'T EAT.
SORRY ABOUT THIS...
THE MORE I THINK, THE MORE TENSE I GET...
WHAT'S MAKING YOU SO TENSE?
UMM. WELL, UM...
IT'S UM...
ZERO!

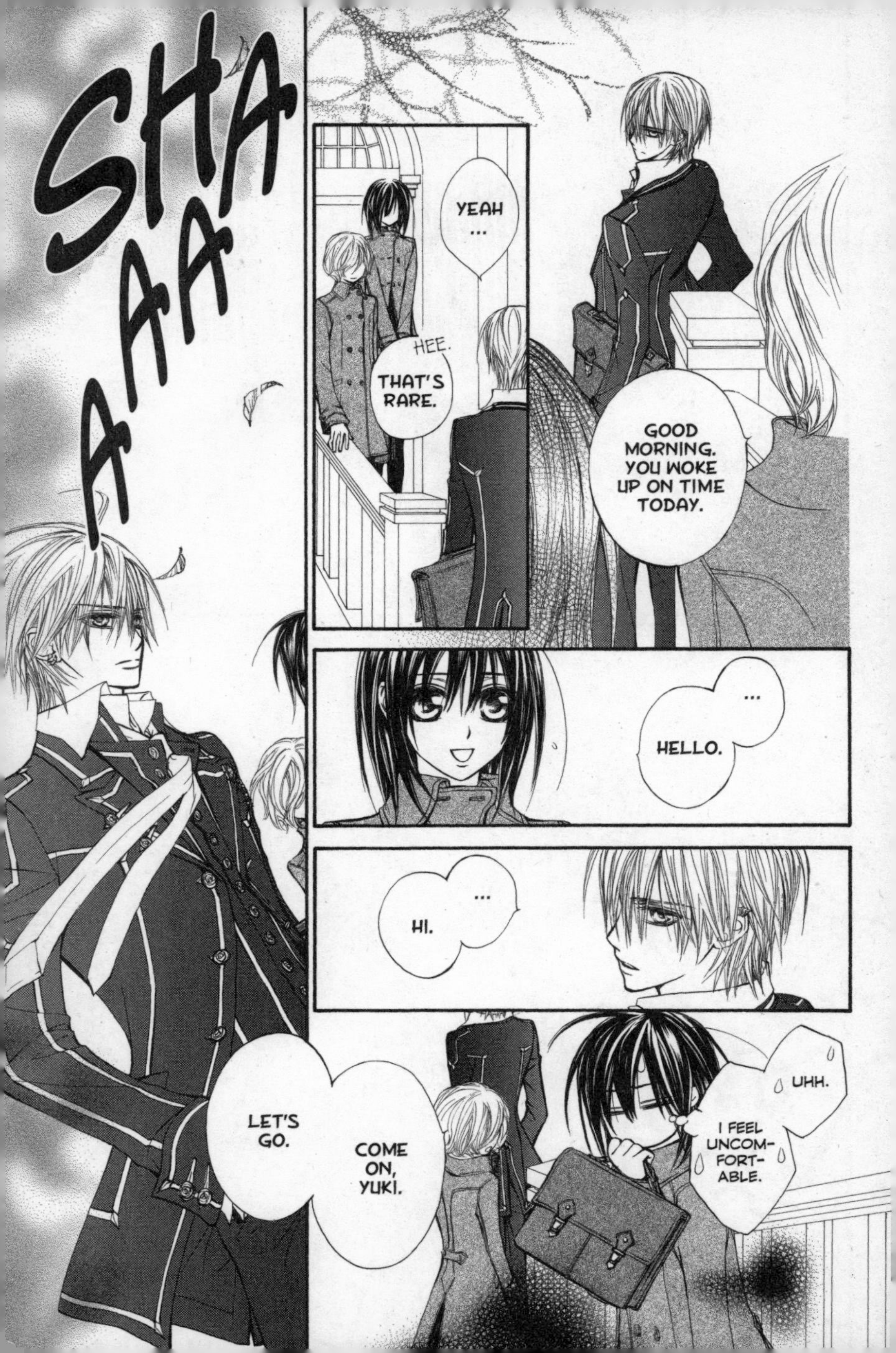
GOOD MORNING. YOU WOKE UP ON TIME TODAY.
YEAH ...
HEE.
THAT'S RARE.
... HELLO.
... HI.
UHH.
I FEEL UNCOM-FORT-ABLE.
COME ON, YUKI.
LET'S GO.
SHA AAA

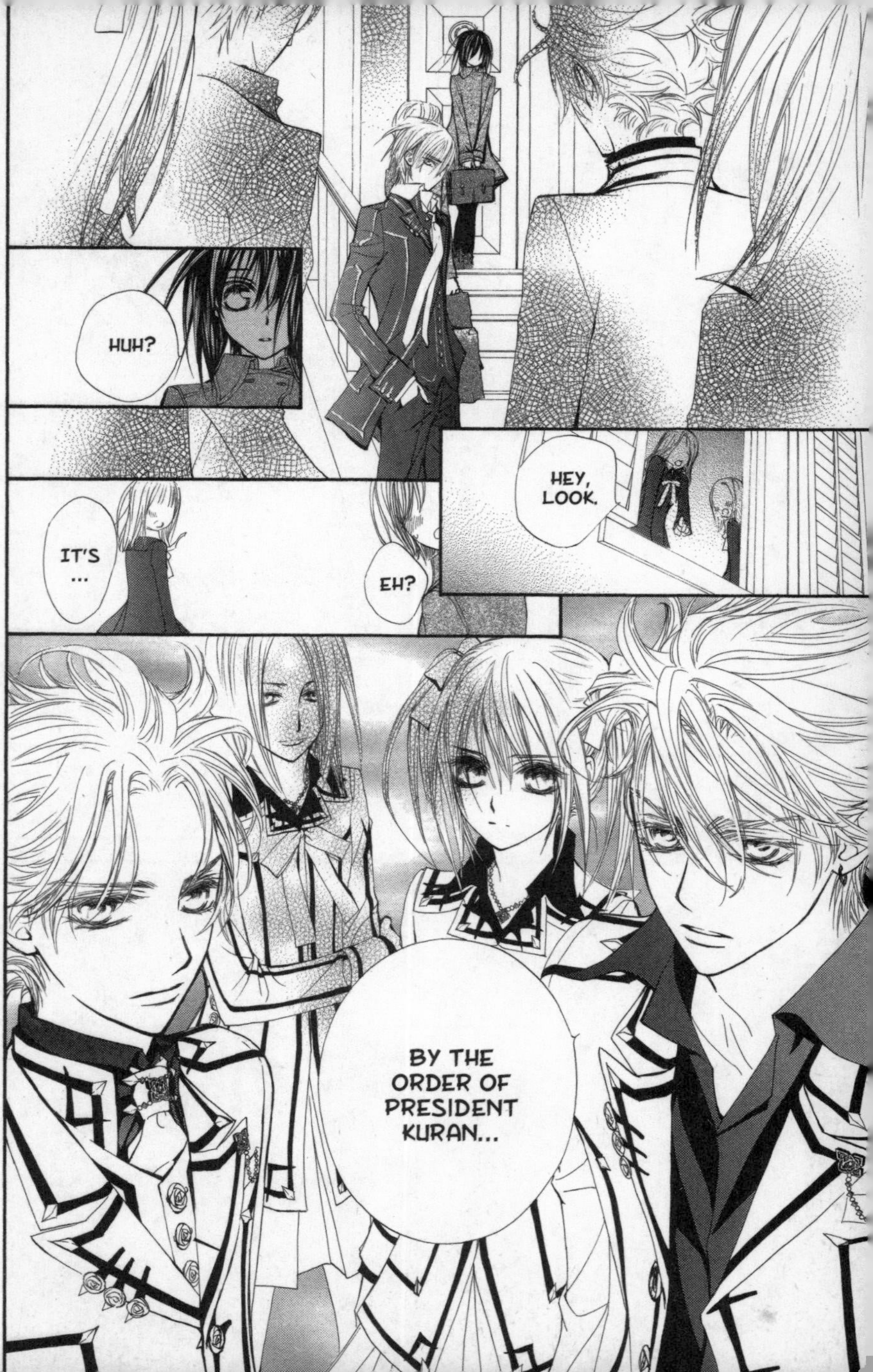
HUH?
HEY, LOOK.
EH?
IT'S ...
BY THE ORDER OF PRESIDENT KURAN...

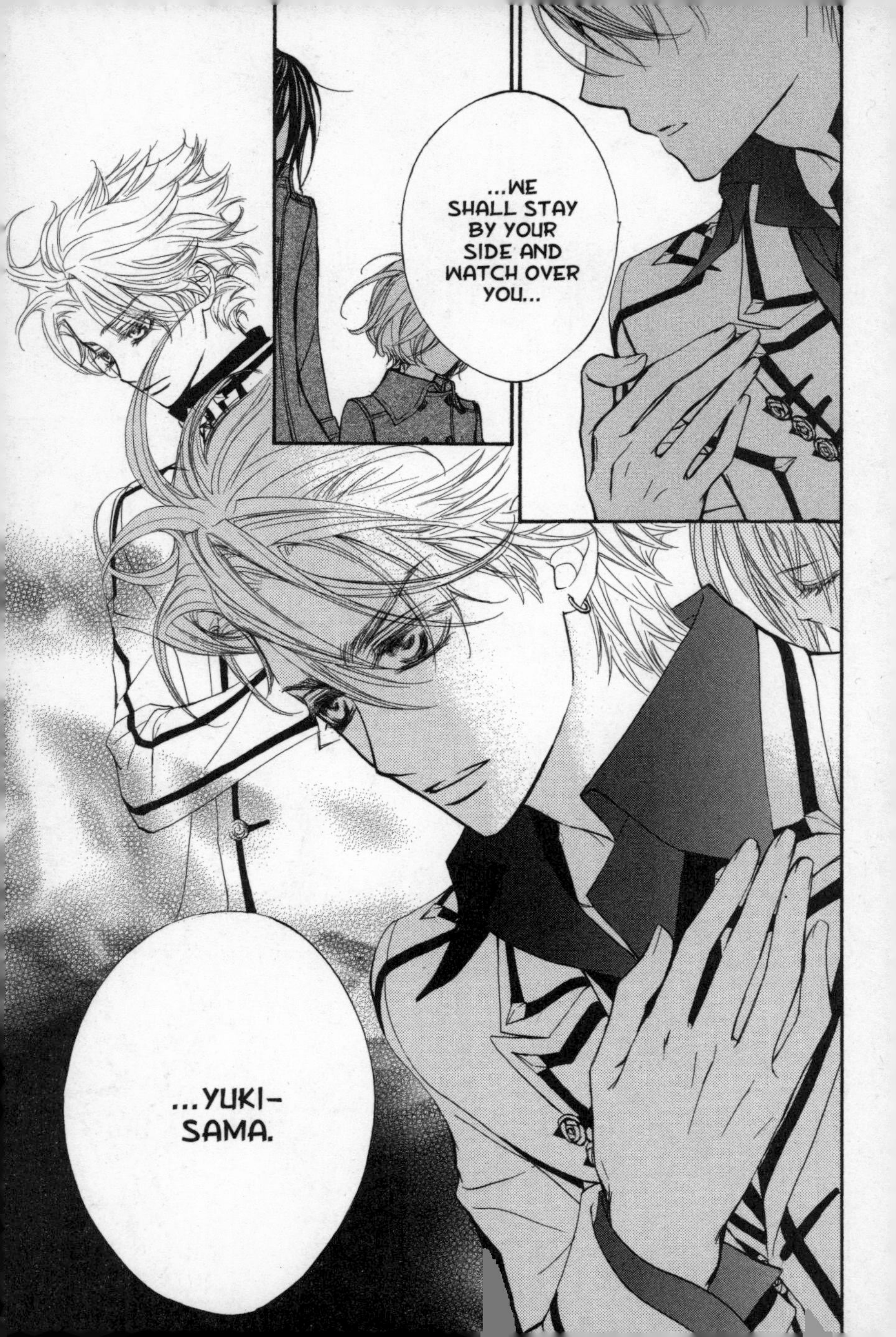
...WE SHALL STAY BY YOUR SIDE AND WATCH OVER YOU...
...YUKI-SAMA.

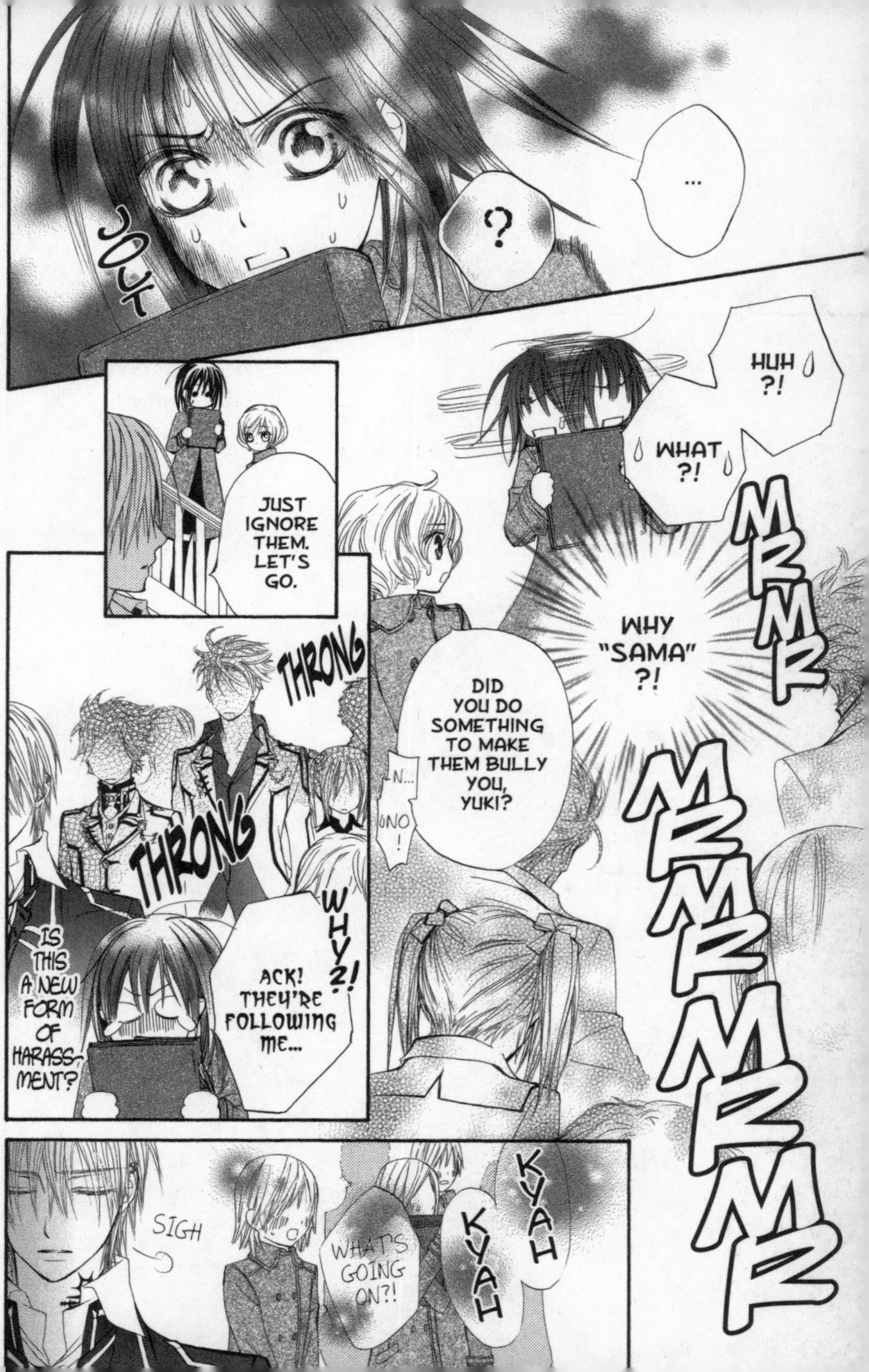

...
?
JOLT
HUH?!
WHAT?!
JUST IGNORE THEM. LET'S GO.
MZMZ
MZMZMZMZ
WHY "SAMA"?!
DID YOU DO SOMETHING TO MAKE THEM BULLY YOU, YUKI?
N... NO!
THRONG
THRONG
WHY?!
ACK! THEY'RE FOLLOWING ME...
IS THIS A NEW FORM OF HARASSMENT?
KYAH
KYAH
WHAT'S GOING ON?!
SIGH

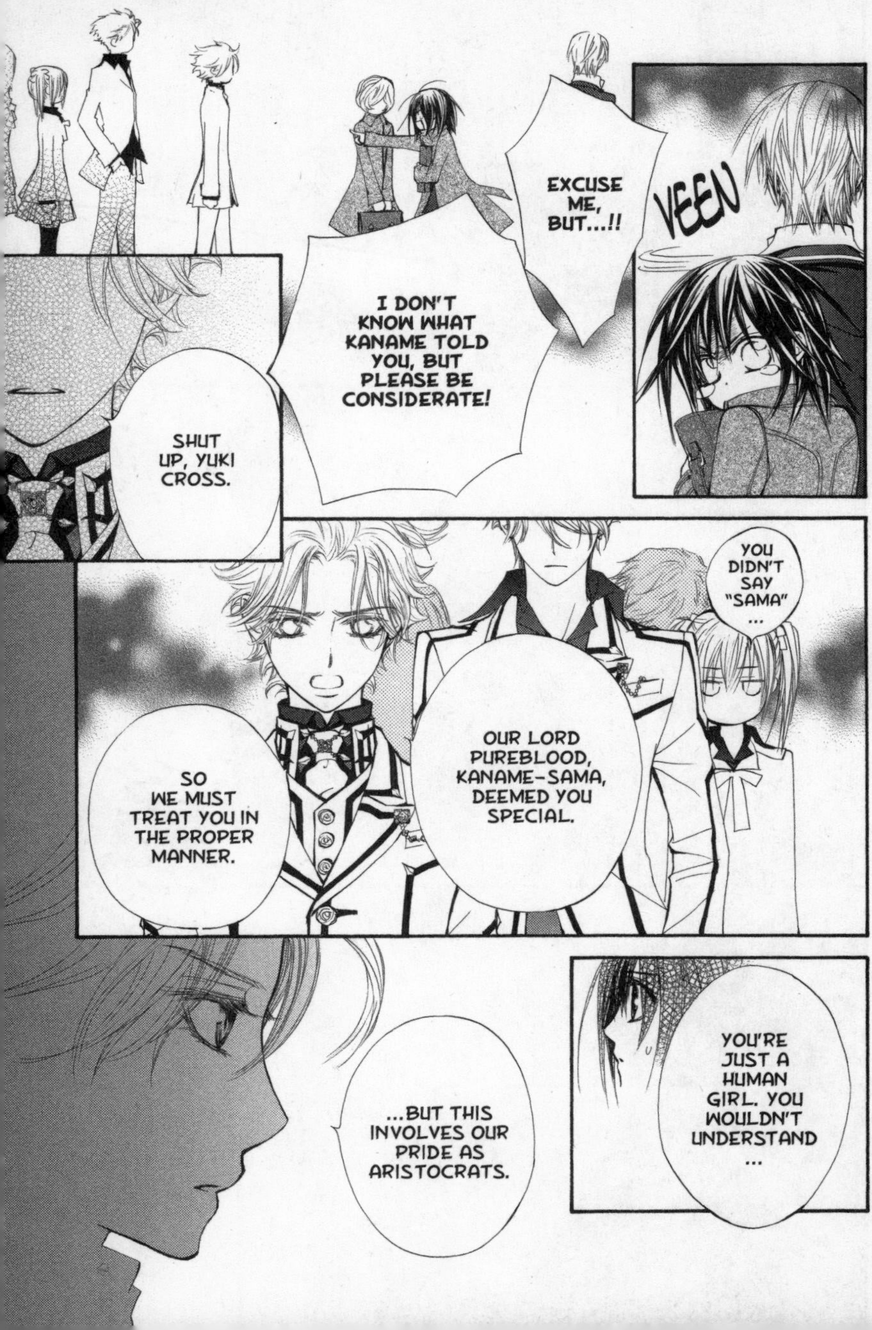
VEEN
EXCUSE ME, BUT...!!
I DON'T KNOW WHAT KANAME TOLD YOU, BUT PLEASE BE CONSIDERATE!
SHUT UP, YUKI CROSS.
YOU DIDN'T SAY "SAMA"...
OUR LORD PUREBLOOD, KANAME-SAMA, DEEMED YOU SPECIAL.
SO WE MUST TREAT YOU IN THE PROPER MANNER.
YOU'RE JUST A HUMAN GIRL. YOU WOULDN'T UNDERSTAND...
...BUT THIS INVOLVES OUR PRIDE AS ARISTOCRATS.

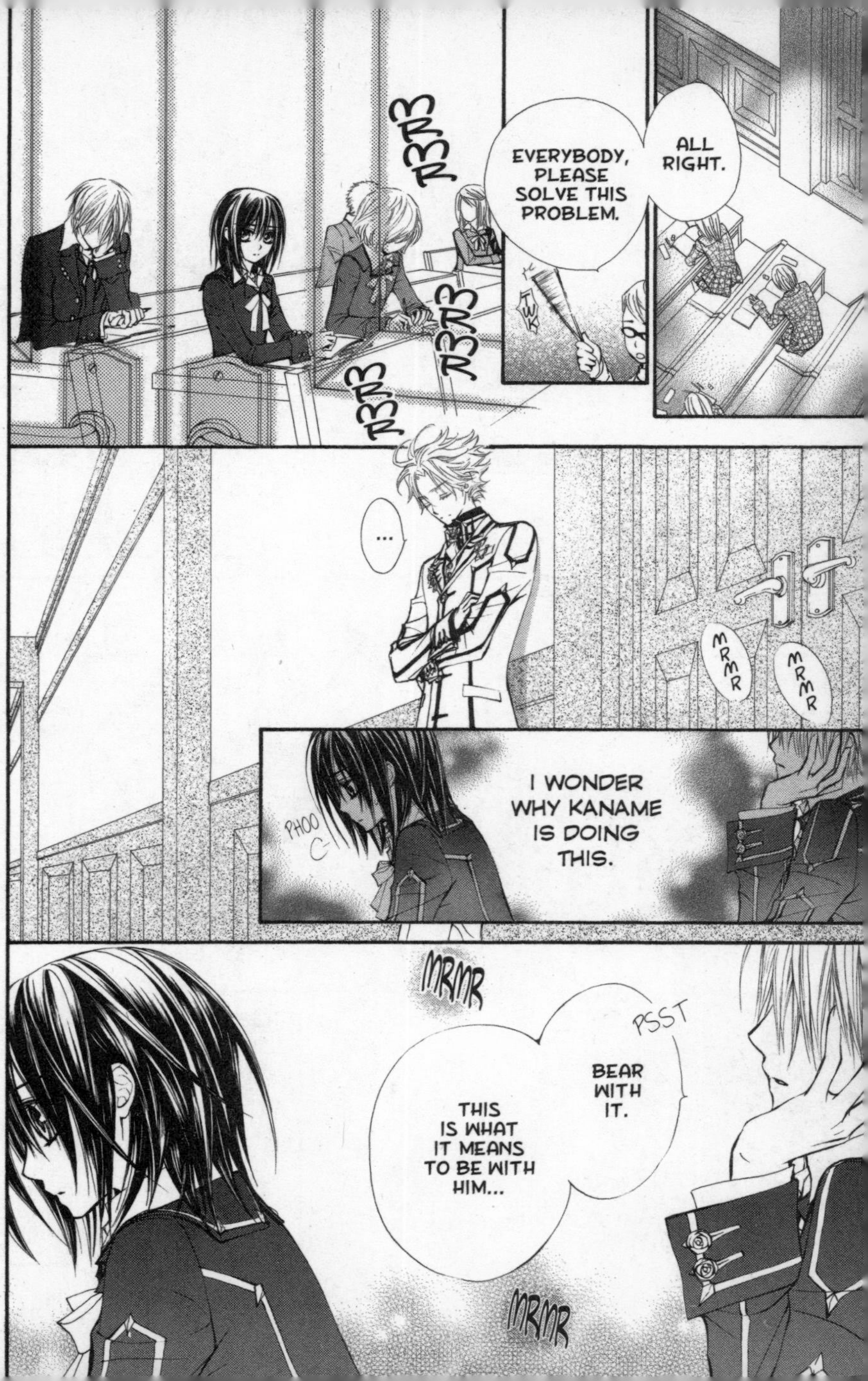
ALL RIGHT.
EVERYBODY, PLEASE SOLVE THIS PROBLEM.
TWK
MRMR
MRMR
MRMR
...
MRMR
MRMR
I WONDER WHY KANAME IS DOING THIS.
PHOO
MRMR
PSST
BEAR WITH IT.
THIS IS WHAT IT MEANS TO BE WITH HIM...
MRMR

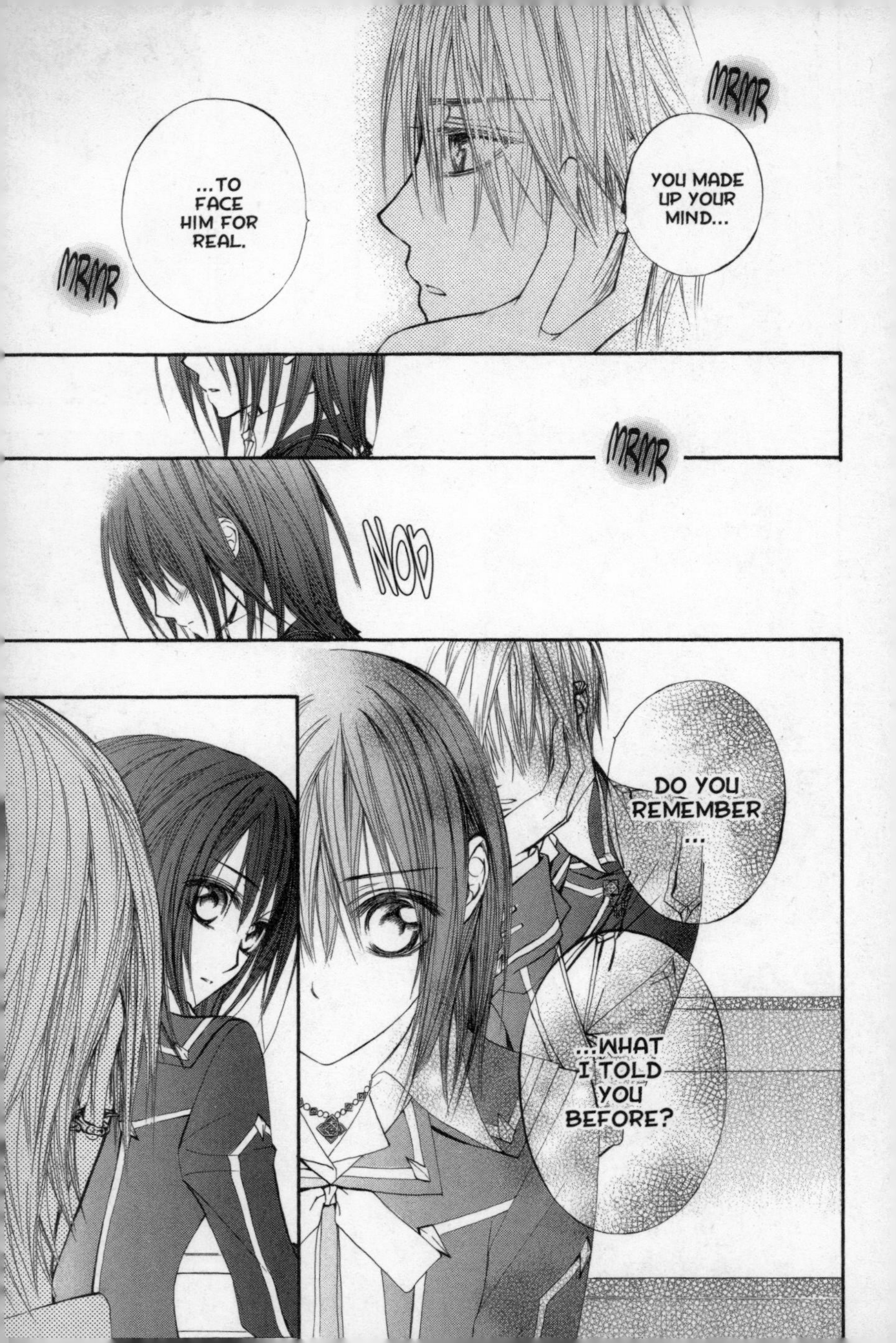
MRMR
YOU MADE UP YOUR MIND...
...TO FACE HIM FOR REAL.
MRMR
MRMR
NOD
DO YOU REMEMBER ...
...WHAT I TOLD YOU BEFORE?

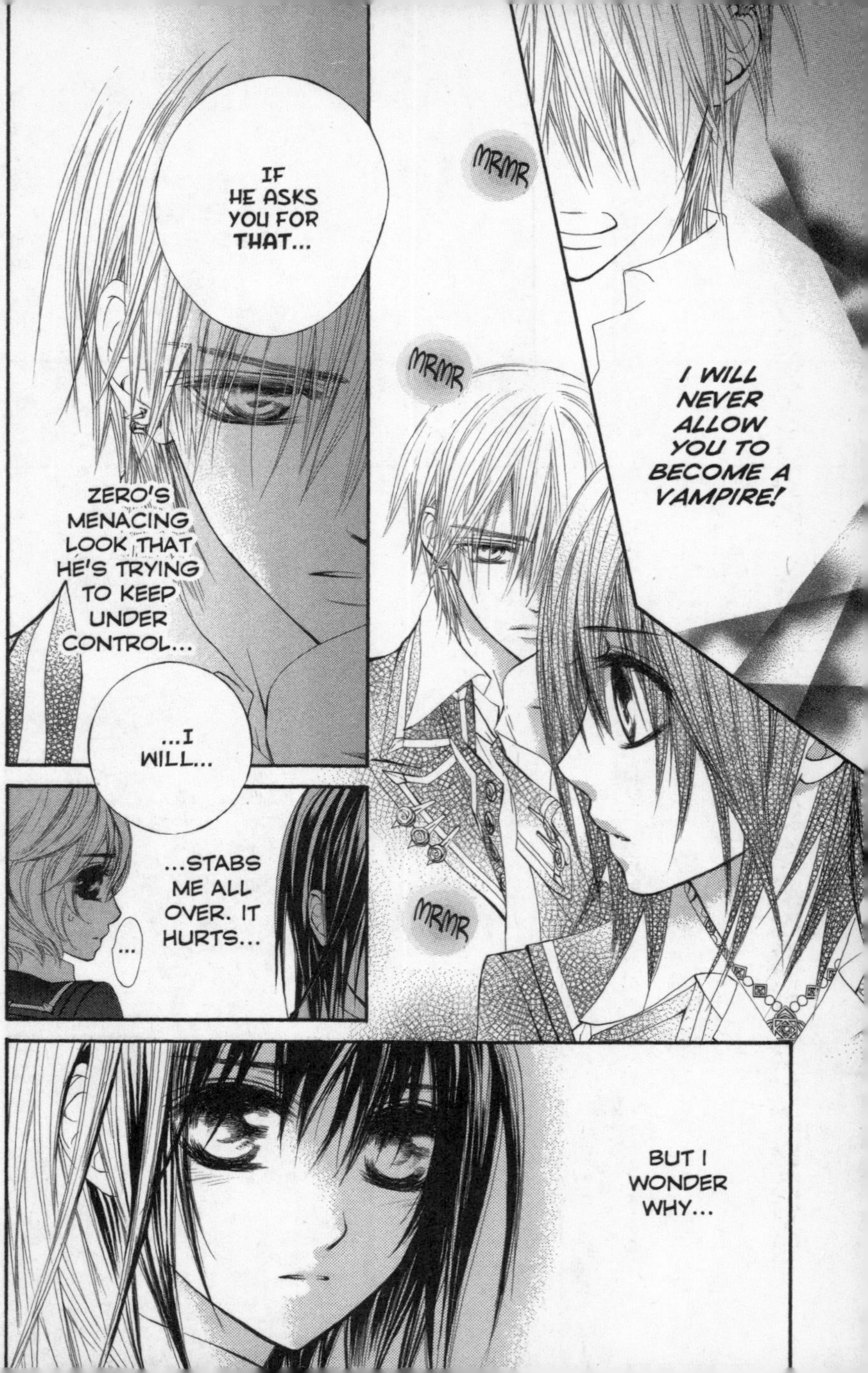
MRMR
I WILL NEVER ALLOW YOU TO BECOME A VAMPIRE!
MRMR
MRMR
IF HE ASKS YOU FOR THAT...
ZERO'S MENACING LOOK THAT HE'S TRYING TO KEEP UNDER CONTROL...
...I WILL...
...STABS ME ALL OVER. IT HURTS...
...
BUT I WONDER WHY...

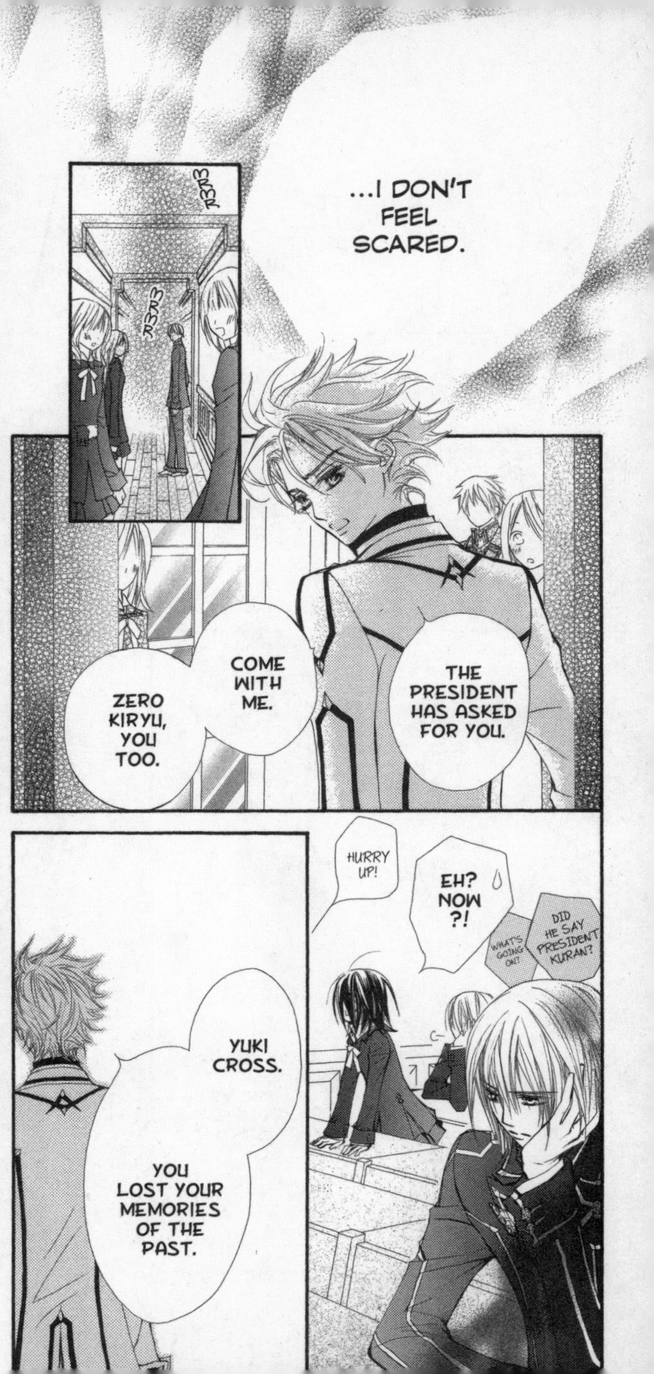
...I DON'T FEEL SCARED.
MRMR
MRMR
THE PRESIDENT HAS ASKED FOR YOU.
COME WITH ME.
ZERO KIRYU, YOU TOO.
DID HE SAY PRESIDENT KURAN?
WHAT'S GOING ON?
EH? NOW?!
HURRY UP!
YUKI CROSS.
YOU LOST YOUR MEMORIES OF THE PAST.

IV

In volume 6, I was having trouble thinking of what to write in these sidebars. There were a couple of people who wrote to me, worrying about it and making suggestions for what to write about... Thank you! I'll use them to inspire me later on!

This time I'll answer the most popular questions here. ^^

Q. Who's your favorite character? Which characters do you find easy to draw?

➡ I like Kaname's parents. (Like how they have the same aura as when I was drawing *Merupuri*?) And they're easy to draw... The one who's hard to draw is...yes, Kaname...

Q. How can I improve my drawing?

➡ This makes me think. This is a theme that will always exist for me too. There are various issues I need to deal with.

- I have my peculiarities, so it takes forever until I can sketch. Or...
- When I'm pressed for time, the differences among characters become blurry. Or...
- I can hardly do drawings that I'm satisfied with!!

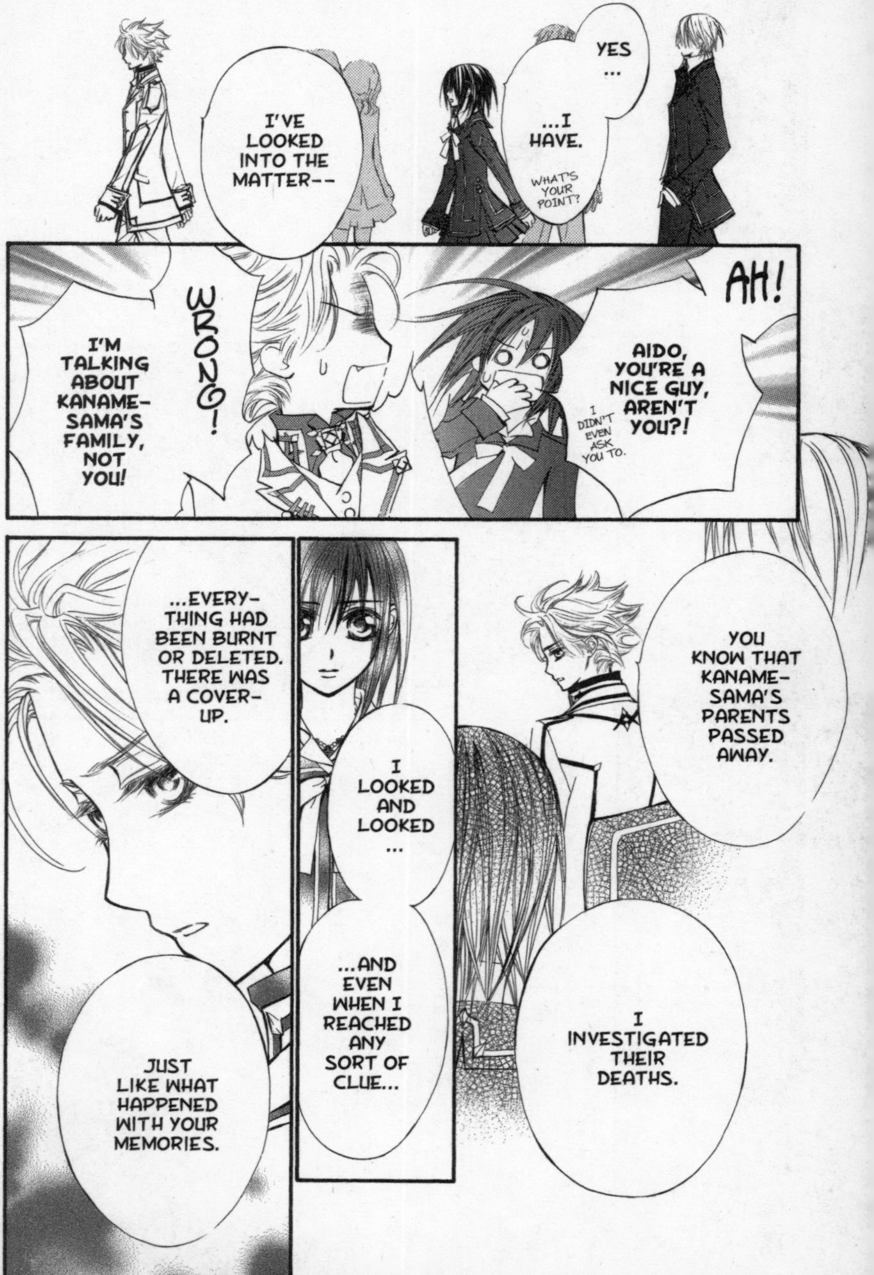
YES ... ...I HAVE.
WHAT'S YOUR POINT?
I'VE LOOKED INTO THE MATTER--
AH!
AIDO, YOU'RE A NICE GUY, AREN'T YOU?!
I DIDN'T EVEN ASK YOU TO.
WRONG!
I'M TALKING ABOUT KANAME-SAMA'S FAMILY, NOT YOU!
YOU KNOW THAT KANAME-SAMA'S PARENTS PASSED AWAY.
I INVESTIGATED THEIR DEATHS.
I LOOKED AND LOOKED ...
...AND EVEN WHEN I REACHED ANY SORT OF CLUE...
...EVERY-THING HAD BEEN BURNT OR DELETED. THERE WAS A COVER-UP.
JUST LIKE WHAT HAPPENED WITH YOUR MEMORIES.

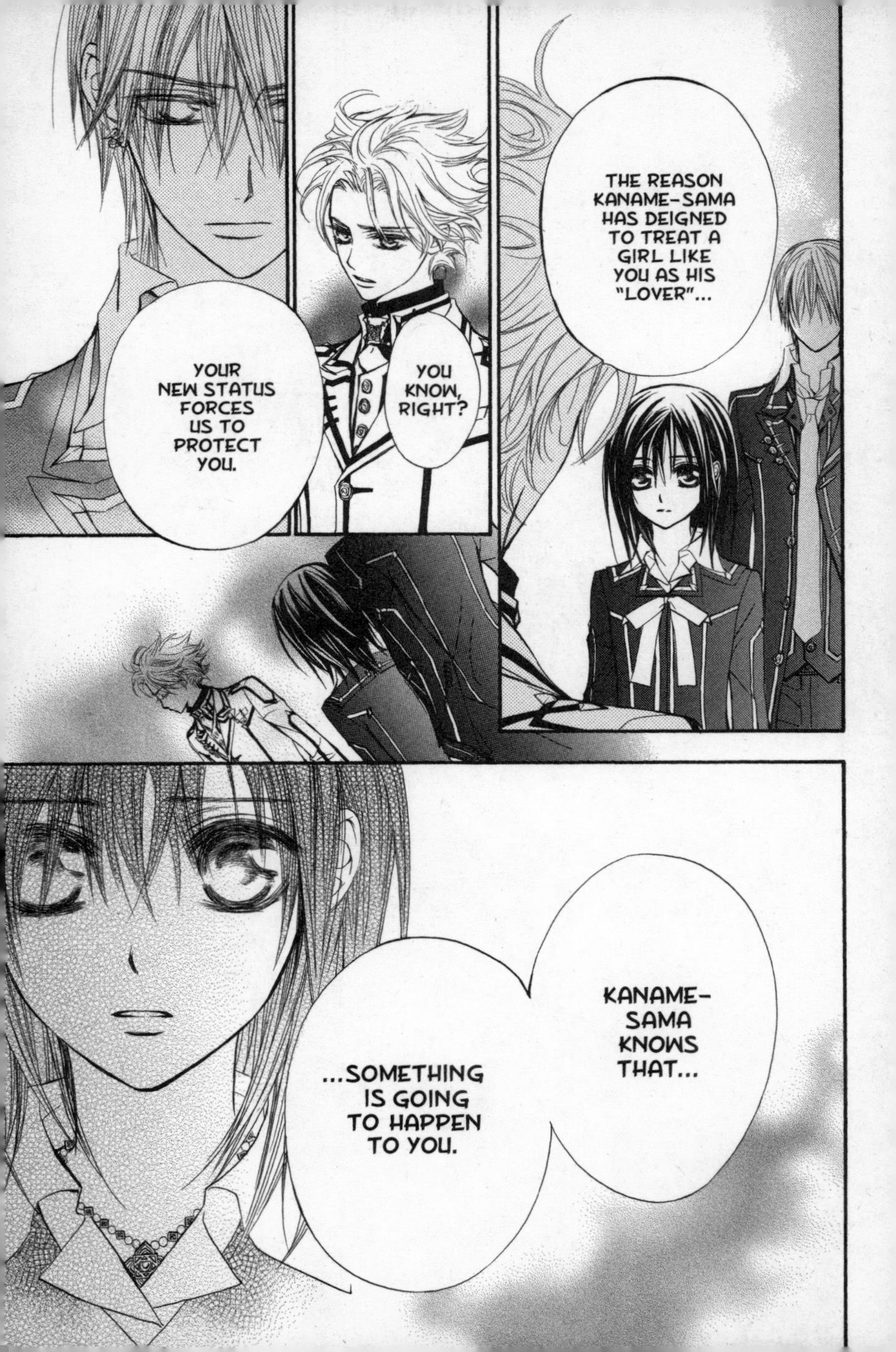
THE REASON KANAME-SAMA HAS DEIGNED TO TREAT A GIRL LIKE YOU AS HIS "LOVER"...
YOU KNOW, RIGHT?
YOUR NEW STATUS FORCES US TO PROTECT YOU.
KANAME-SAMA KNOWS THAT...
...SOMETHING IS GOING TO HAPPEN TO YOU.

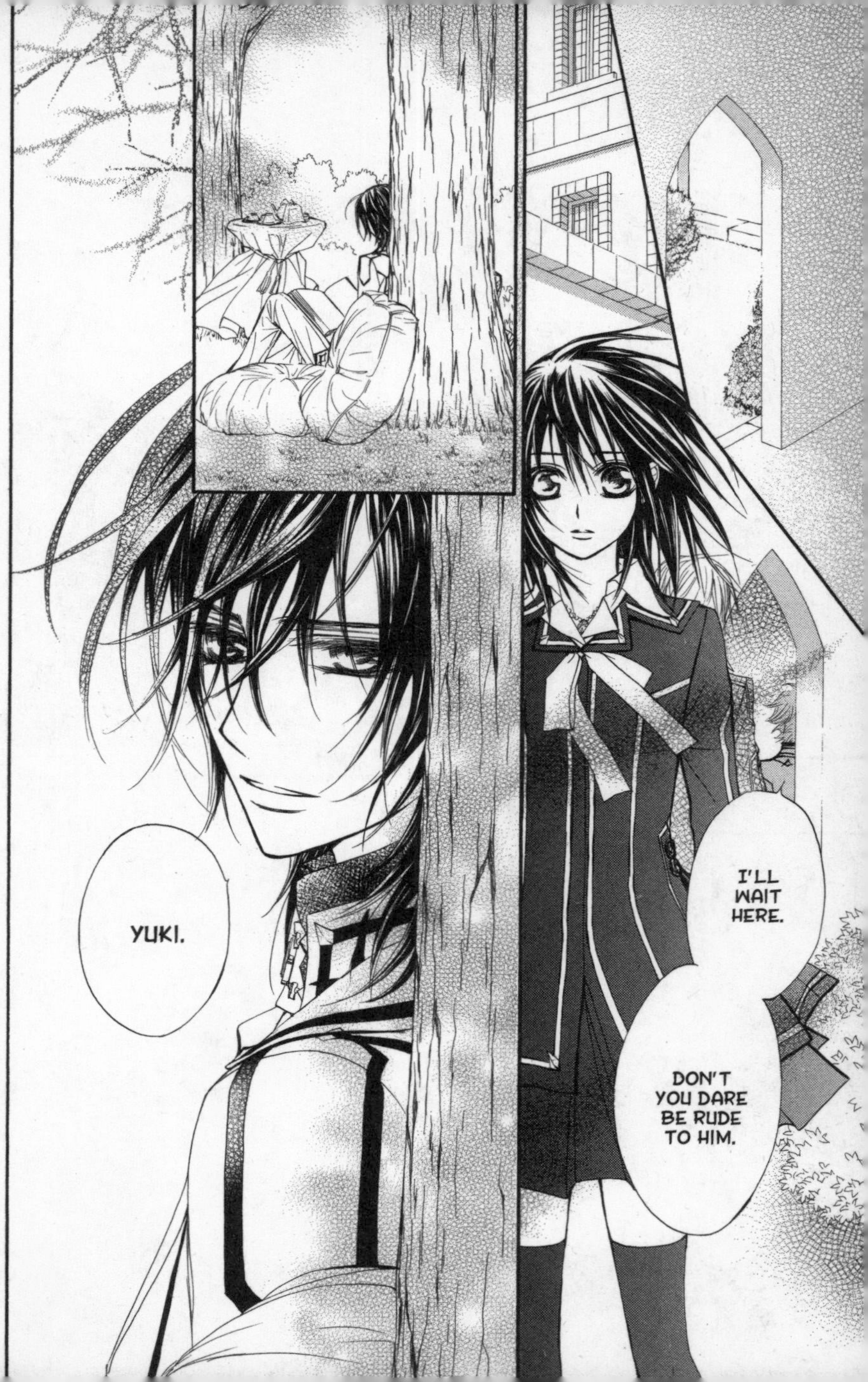
I'LL WAIT HERE.
DON'T YOU DARE BE RUDE TO HIM.
YUKI.

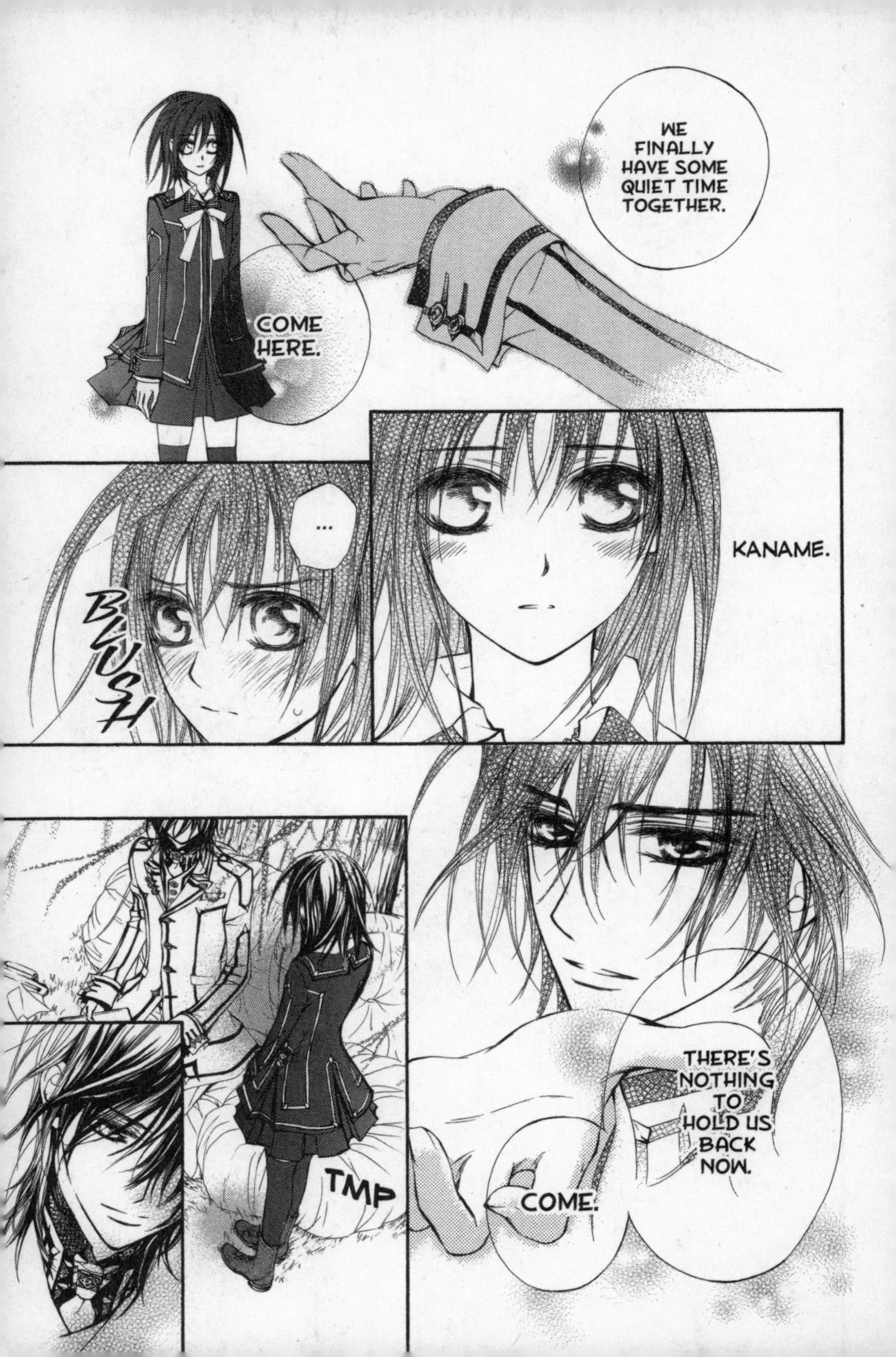
WE FINALLY HAVE SOME QUIET TIME TOGETHER.
COME HERE.
KANAME.
...
BLUSH
THERE'S NOTHING TO HOLD US BACK NOW.
COME.
TMP

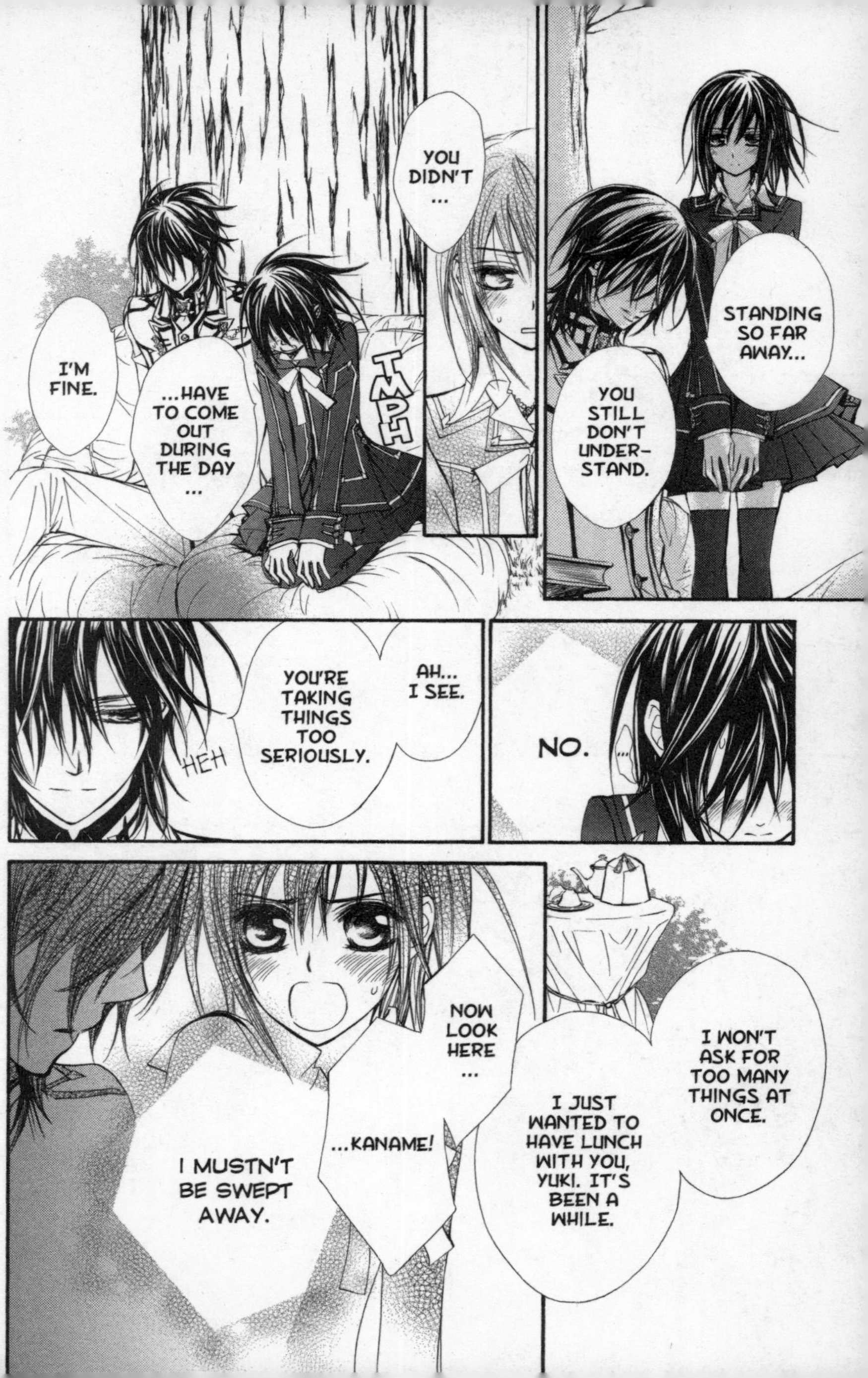

STANDING SO FAR AWAY...
YOU STILL DON'T UNDER-STAND.
YOU DIDN'T ...
TMPH
...HAVE TO COME OUT DURING THE DAY ...
I'M FINE.
...
NO.
AH... I SEE.
YOU'RE TAKING THINGS TOO SERIOUSLY.
HEH
I WON'T ASK FOR TOO MANY THINGS AT ONCE.
I JUST WANTED TO HAVE LUNCH WITH YOU, YUKI. IT'S BEEN A WHILE.
NOW LOOK HERE ...
...KANAME!
I MUSTN'T BE SWEPT AWAY.

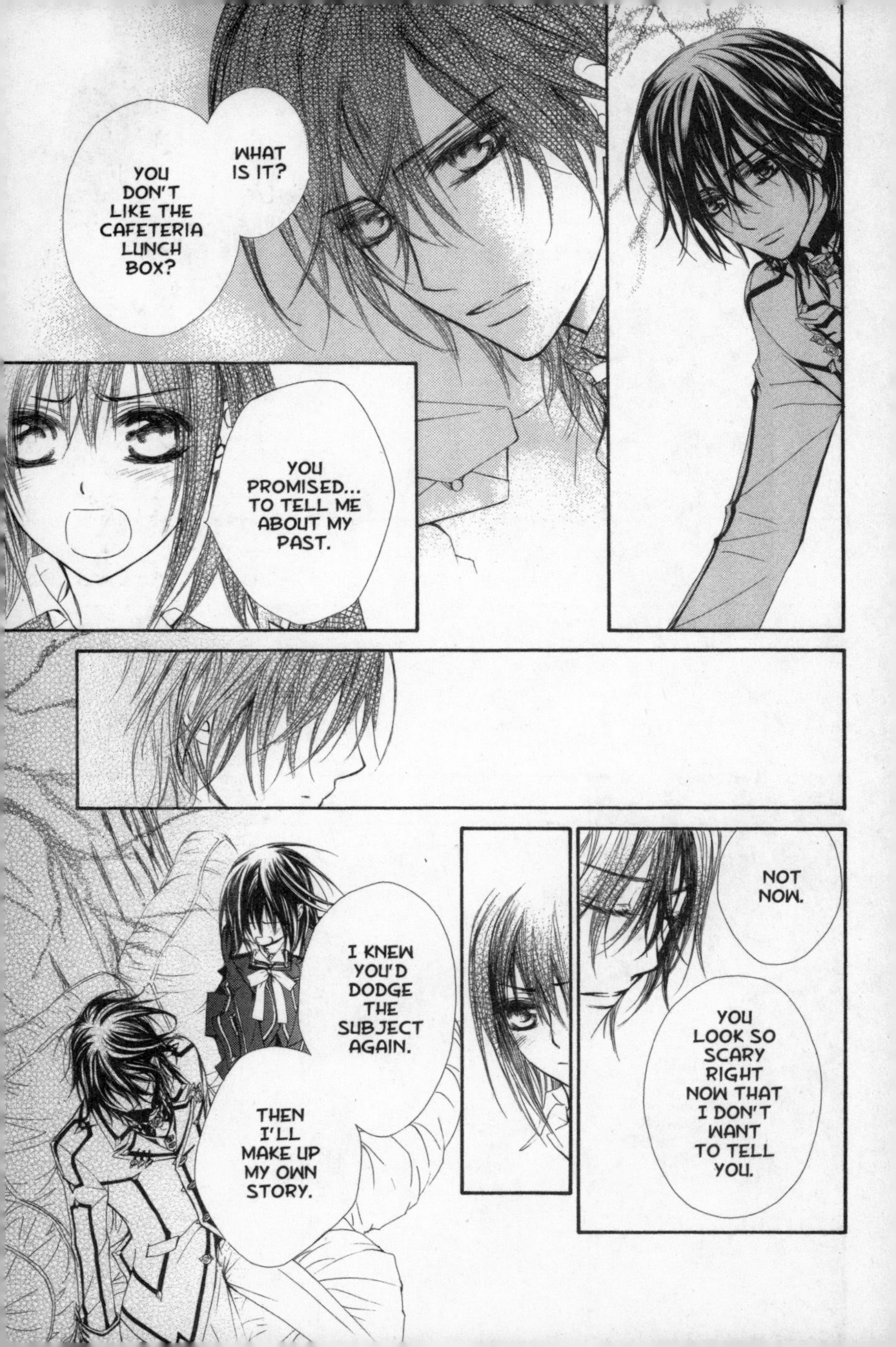
WHAT IS IT?
YOU DON'T LIKE THE CAFETERIA LUNCH BOX?
YOU PROMISED... TO TELL ME ABOUT MY PAST.
NOT NOW.
YOU LOOK SO SCARY RIGHT NOW THAT I DON'T WANT TO TELL YOU.
I KNEW YOU'D DODGE THE SUBJECT AGAIN.
THEN I'LL MAKE UP MY OWN STORY.

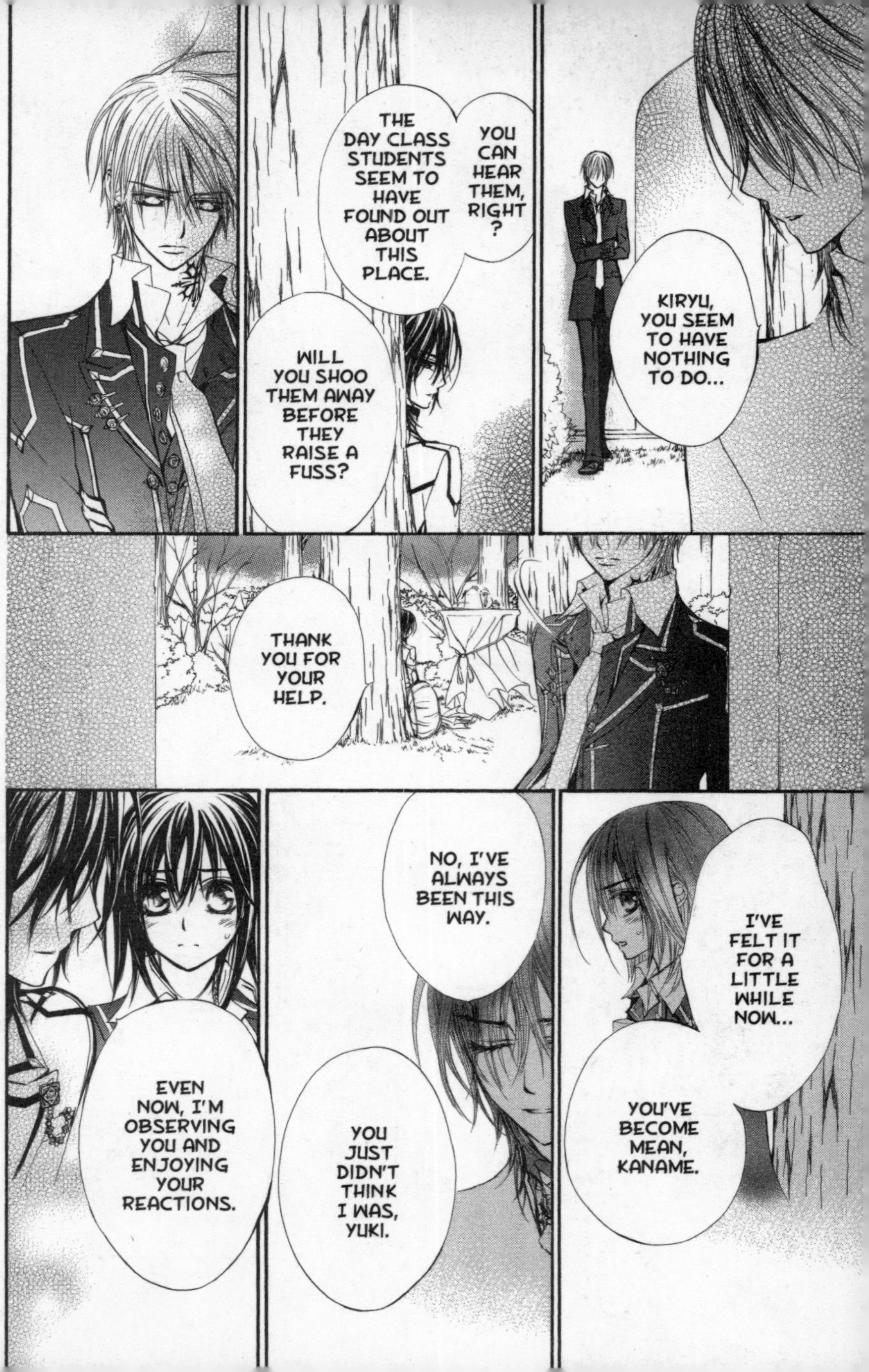
KIRYU, YOU SEEM TO HAVE NOTHING TO DO...
THE DAY CLASS STUDENTS SEEM TO HAVE FOUND OUT ABOUT THIS PLACE.
YOU CAN HEAR THEM, RIGHT?
WILL YOU SHOO THEM AWAY BEFORE THEY RAISE A FUSS?
THANK YOU FOR YOUR HELP.
I'VE FELT IT FOR A LITTLE WHILE NOW...
YOU'VE BECOME MEAN, KANAME.
NO, I'VE ALWAYS BEEN THIS WAY.
YOU JUST DIDN'T THINK I WAS, YUKI.
EVEN NOW, I'M OBSERVING YOU AND ENJOYING YOUR REACTIONS.

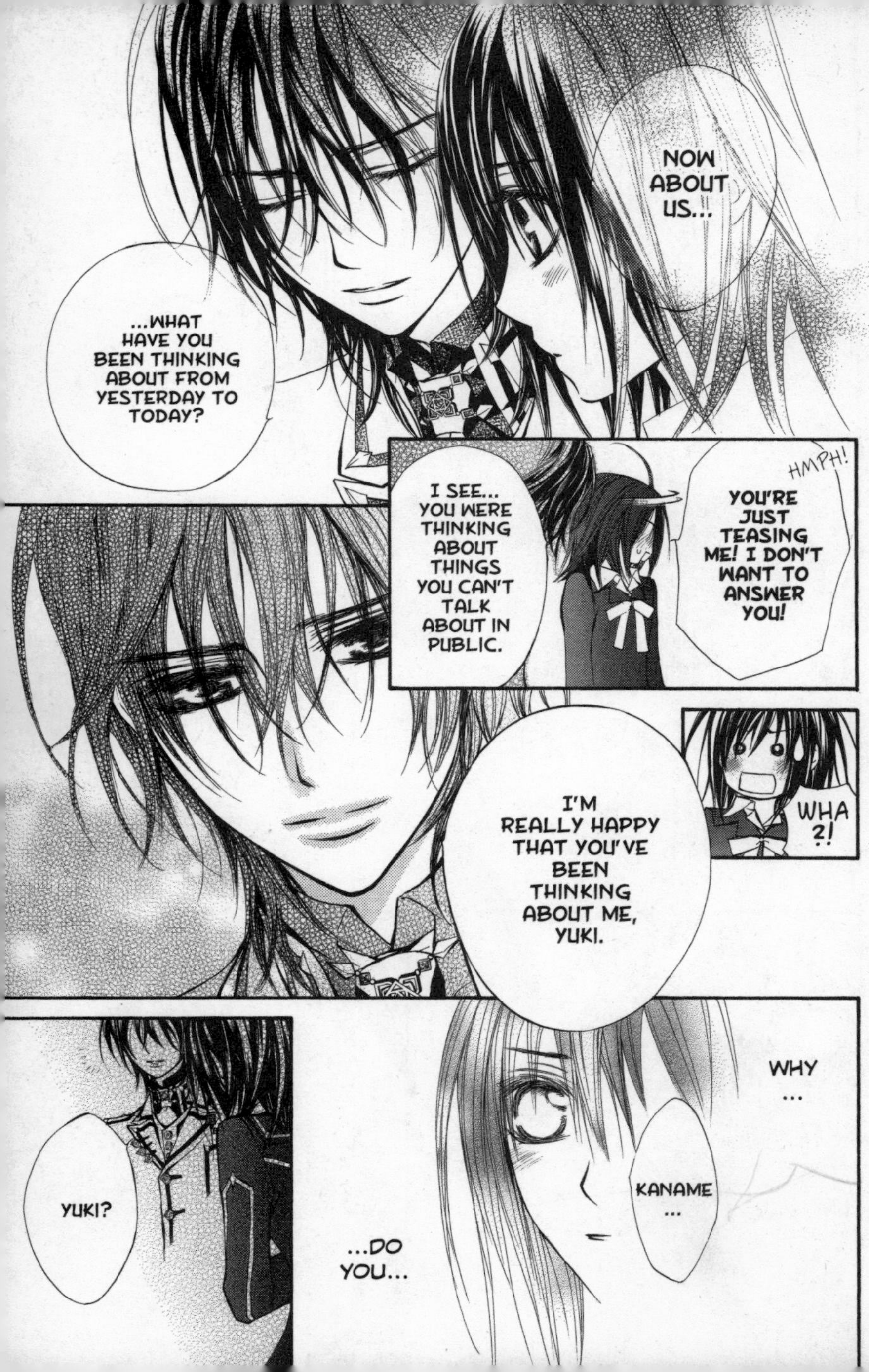
NOW ABOUT US...
...WHAT HAVE YOU BEEN THINKING ABOUT FROM YESTERDAY TO TODAY?
HMPH!
YOU'RE JUST TEASING ME! I DON'T WANT TO ANSWER YOU!
I SEE... YOU WERE THINKING ABOUT THINGS YOU CAN'T TALK ABOUT IN PUBLIC.
WHA?!
I'M REALLY HAPPY THAT YOU'VE BEEN THINKING ABOUT ME, YUKI.
WHY...
KANAME...
...DO YOU...
YUKI?

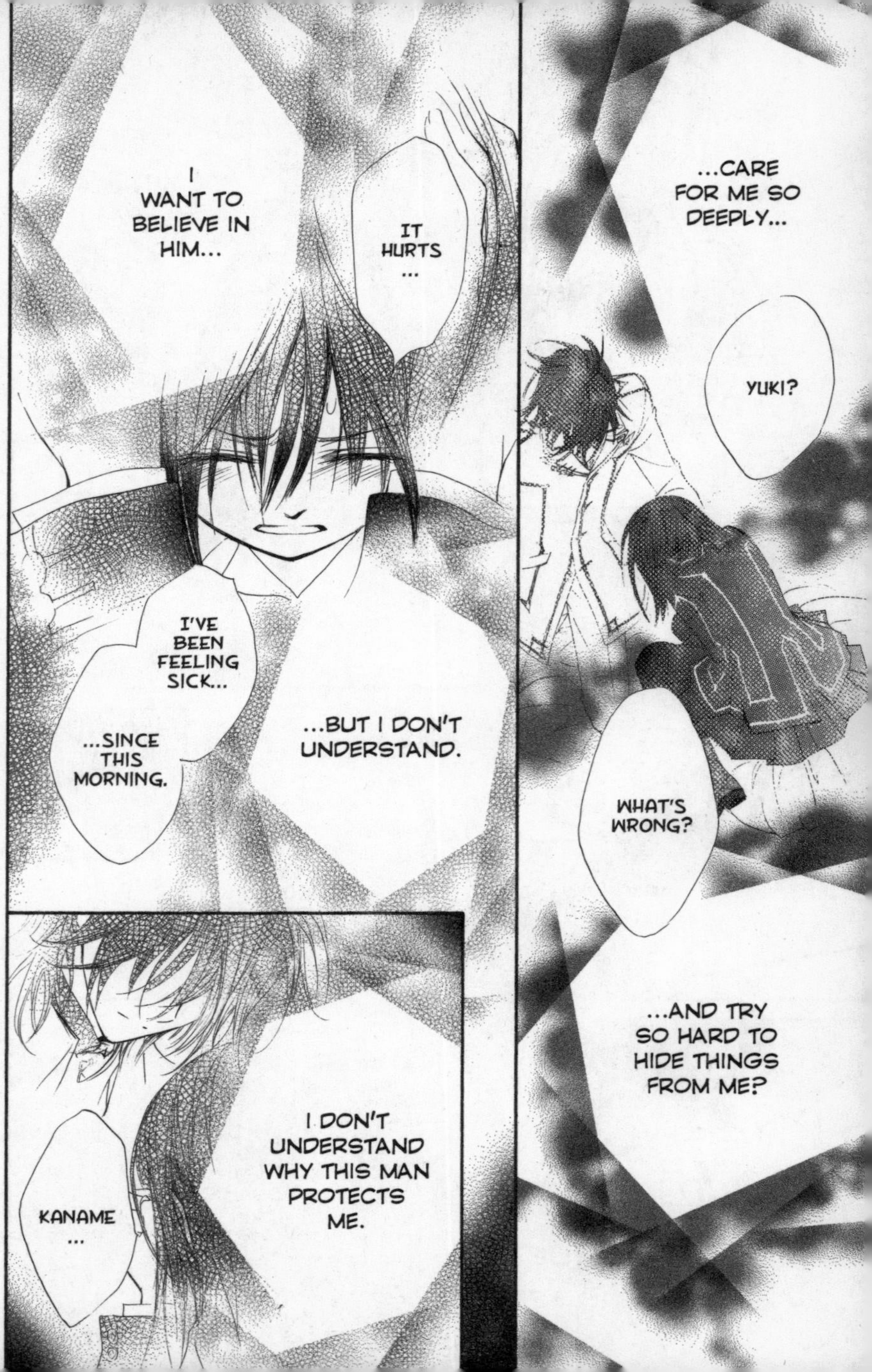
IT HURTS...
I WANT TO BELIEVE IN HIM...
I'VE BEEN FEELING SICK...
...SINCE THIS MORNING.
...BUT I DON'T UNDERSTAND.
I DON'T UNDERSTAND WHY THIS MAN PROTECTS ME.
KANAME...
...CARE FOR ME SO DEEPLY...
YUKI?
WHAT'S WRONG?
...AND TRY SO HARD TO HIDE THINGS FROM ME?

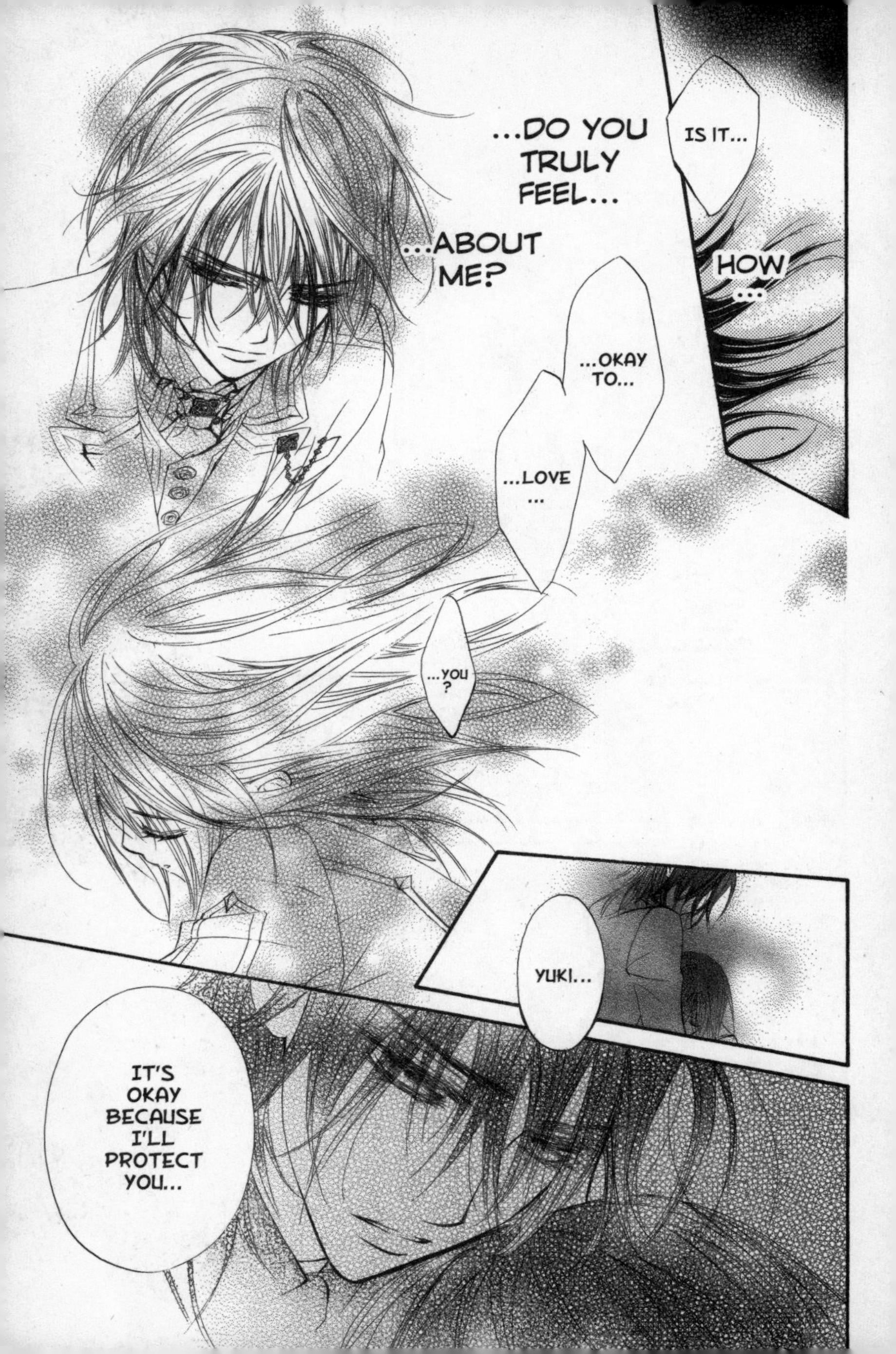
IS IT...
HOW...
...DO YOU TRULY FEEL...
...ABOUT ME?
...OKAY TO...
...LOVE...
...YOU?
YUKI...
IT'S OKAY BECAUSE I'LL PROTECT YOU...

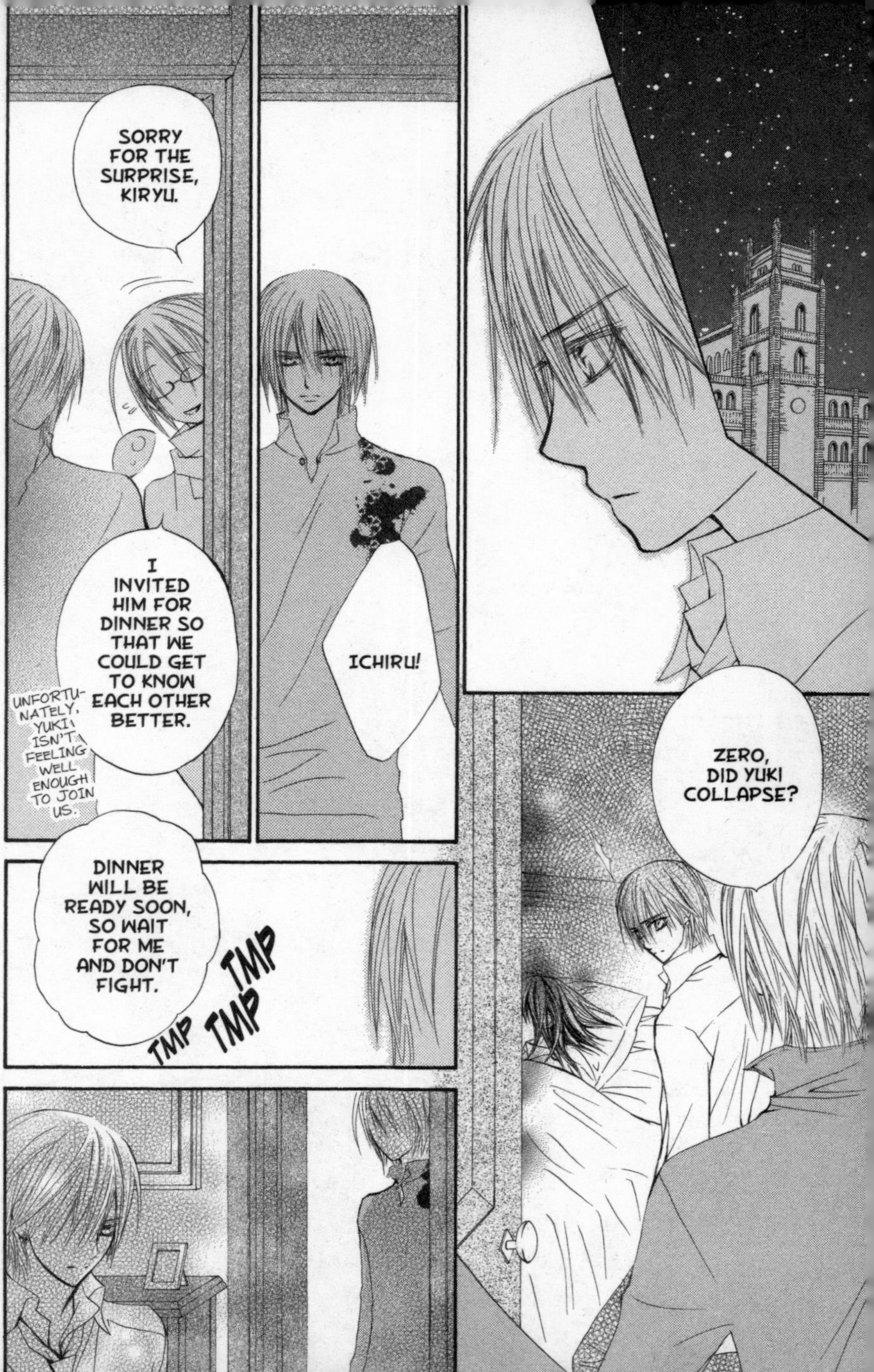
ICHIRU!
SORRY FOR THE SURPRISE, KIRYU.
I INVITED HIM FOR DINNER SO THAT WE COULD GET TO KNOW EACH OTHER BETTER.
UNFORTUNATELY, YUKI ISN'T FEELING WELL ENOUGH TO JOIN US.
ZERO, DID YUKI COLLAPSE?
DINNER WILL BE READY SOON, SO WAIT FOR ME AND DON'T FIGHT.
TMP TMP TMP

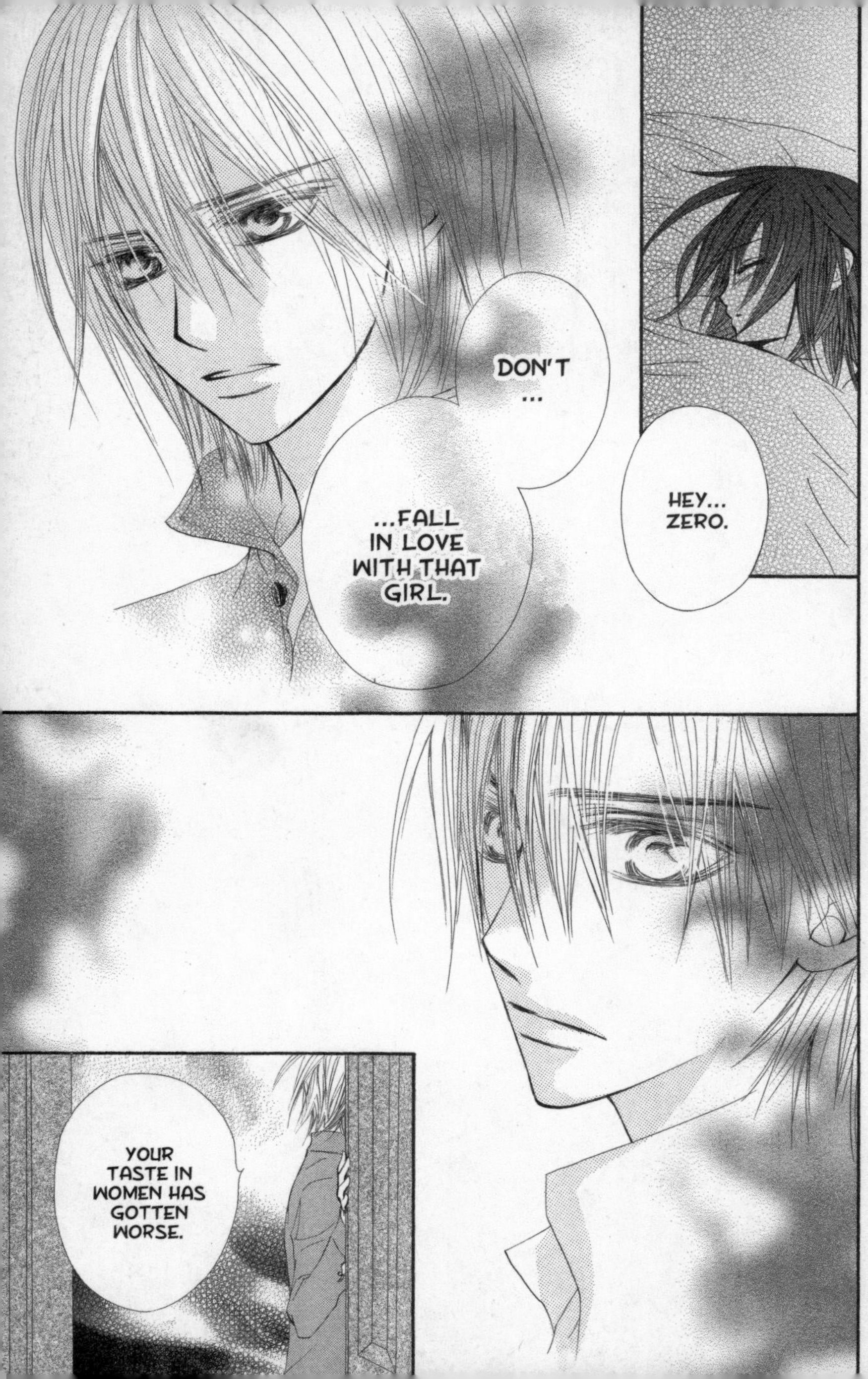
HEY... ZERO.
DON'T ...
...FALL IN LOVE WITH THAT GIRL.
YOUR TASTE IN WOMEN HAS GOTTEN WORSE.

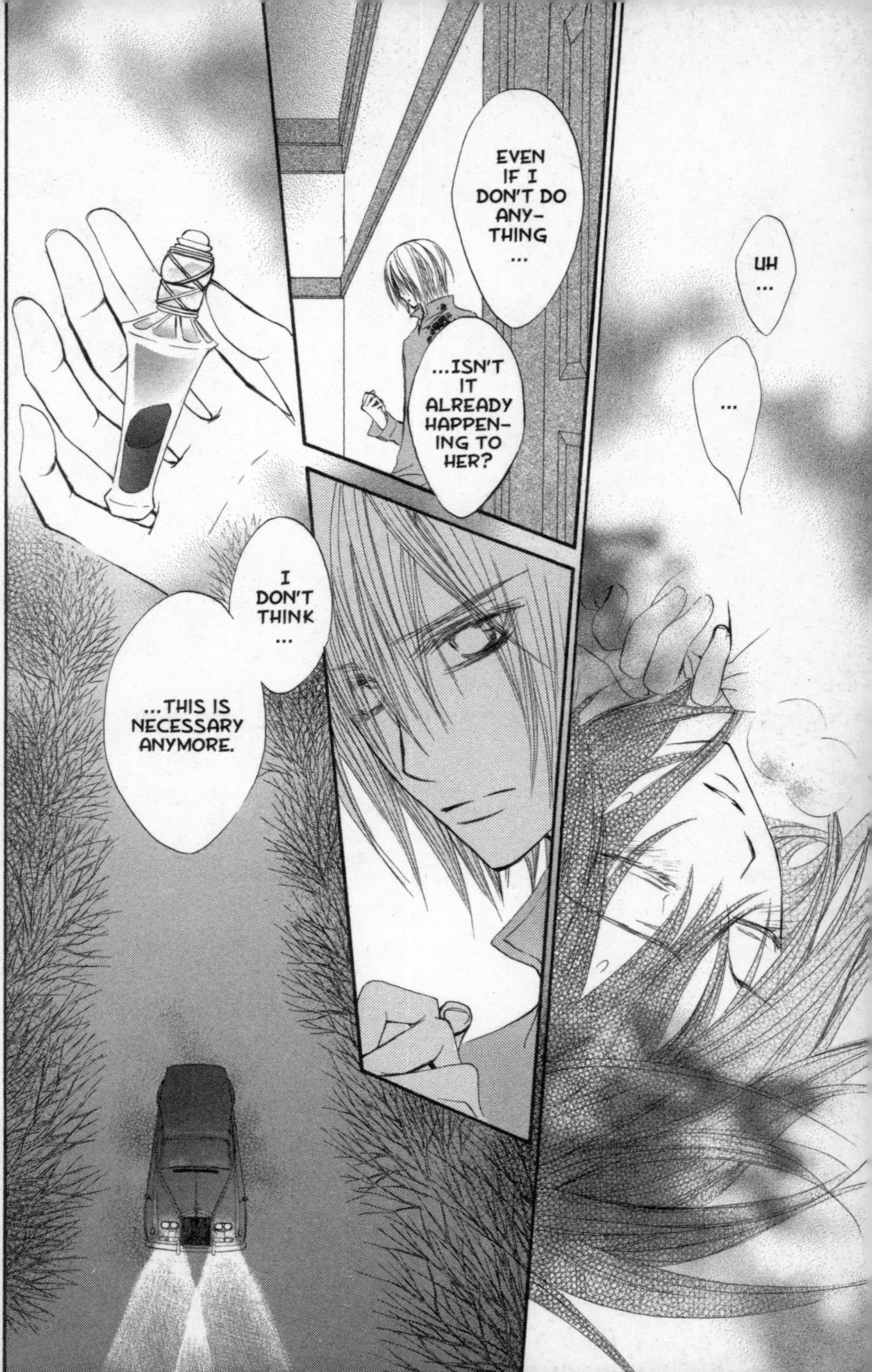
UH...
...
EVEN IF I DON'T DO ANYTHING...
...ISN'T IT ALREADY HAPPENING TO HER?
I DON'T THINK...
...THIS IS NECESSARY ANYMORE.

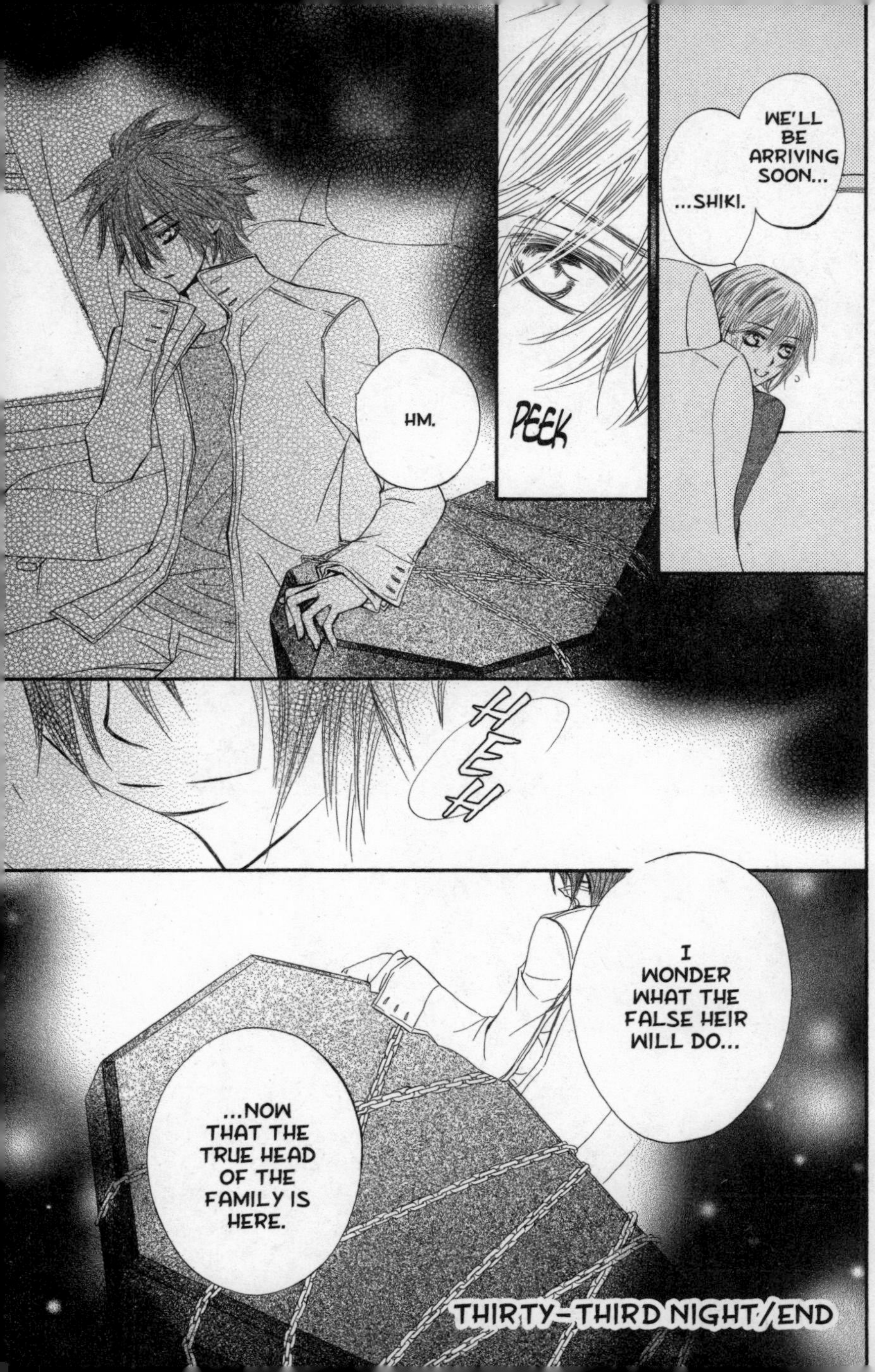
WE'LL BE ARRIVING SOON...
...SHIKI.
PEEK
HM.
HEH
I WONDER WHAT THE FALSE HEIR WILL DO...
...NOW THAT THE TRUE HEAD OF THE FAMILY IS HERE.
THIRTY-THIRD NIGHT/END

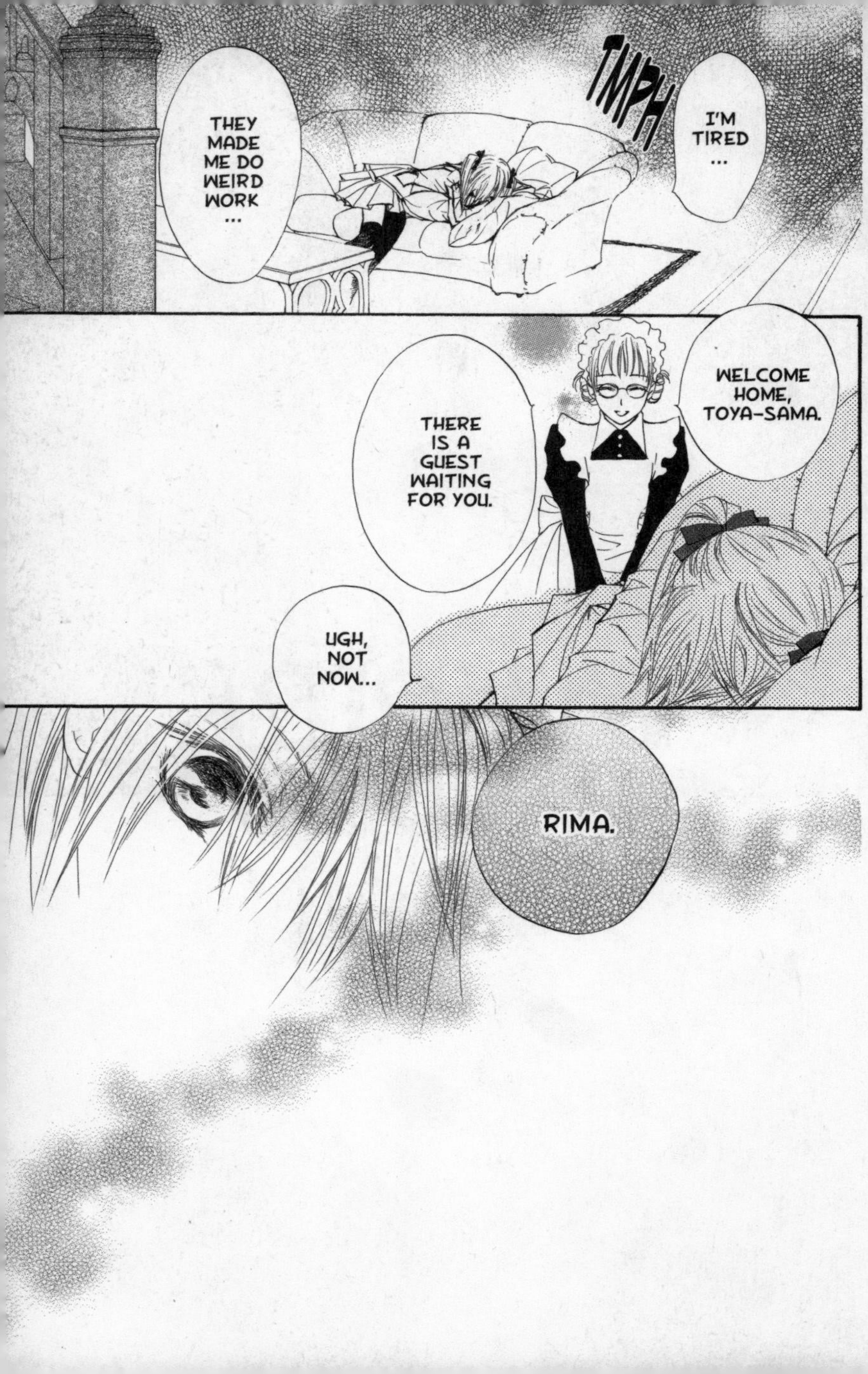
TMPH
I'M TIRED ...
THEY MADE ME DO WEIRD WORK ...
WELCOME HOME, TOYA-SAMA.
THERE IS A GUEST WAITING FOR YOU.
UGH, NOT NOW...
RIMA.

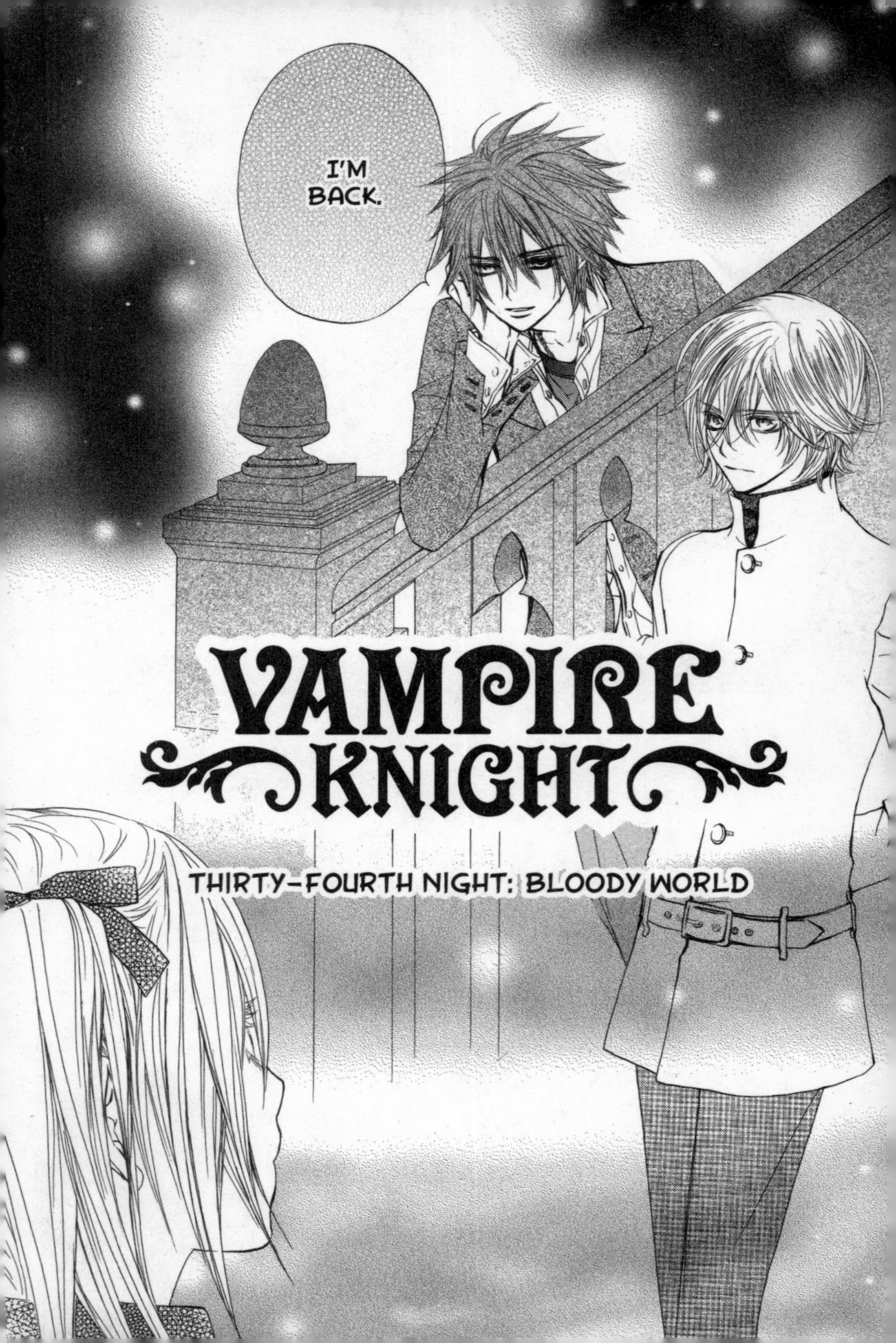
I'M BACK.
VAMPIRE KNIGHT
THIRTY-FOURTH NIGHT: BLOODY WORLD

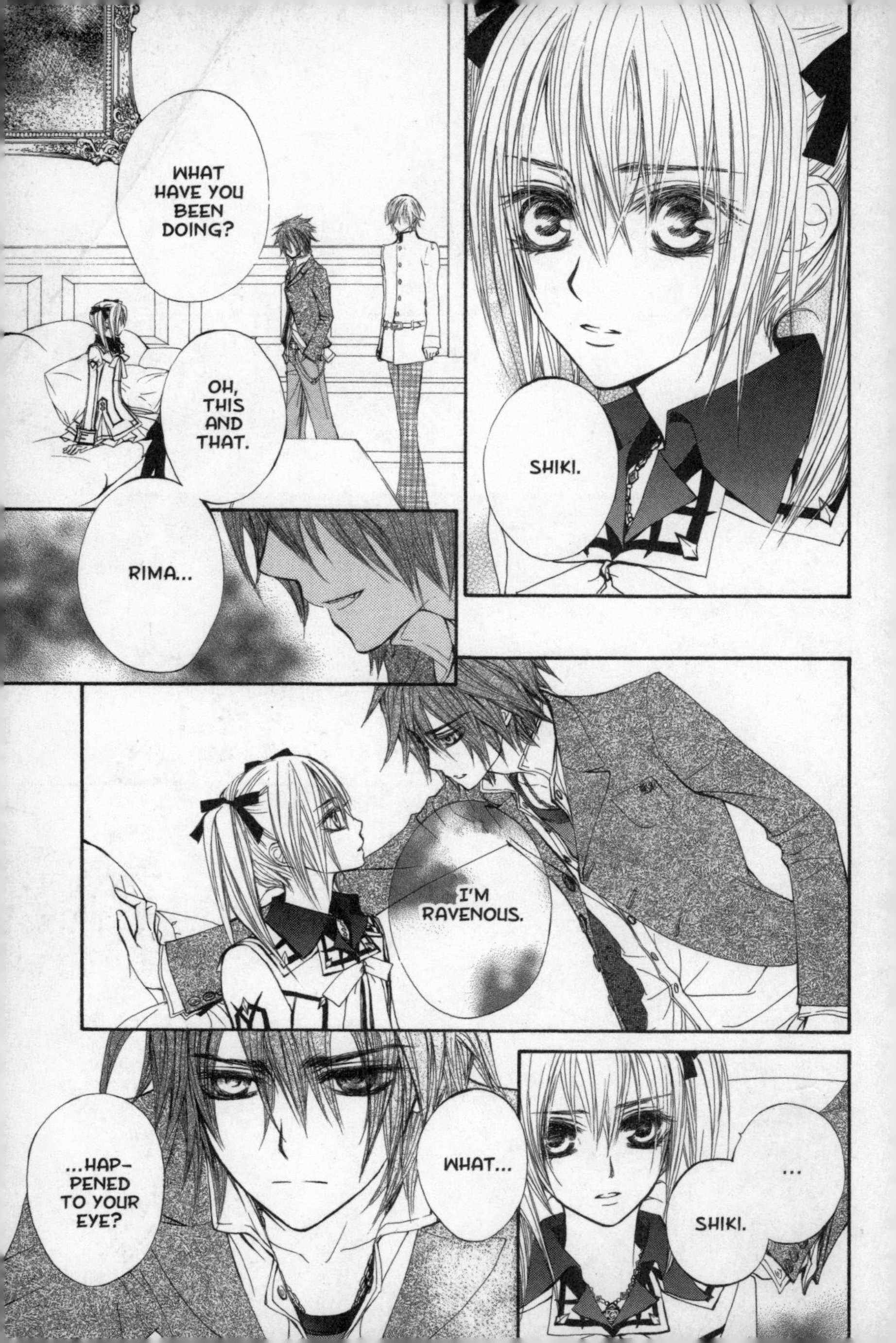
SHIKI.
WHAT HAVE YOU BEEN DOING?
OH, THIS AND THAT.
RIMA...
I'M RAVENOUS.
...
SHIKI.
WHAT...
...HAP-PENED TO YOUR EYE?

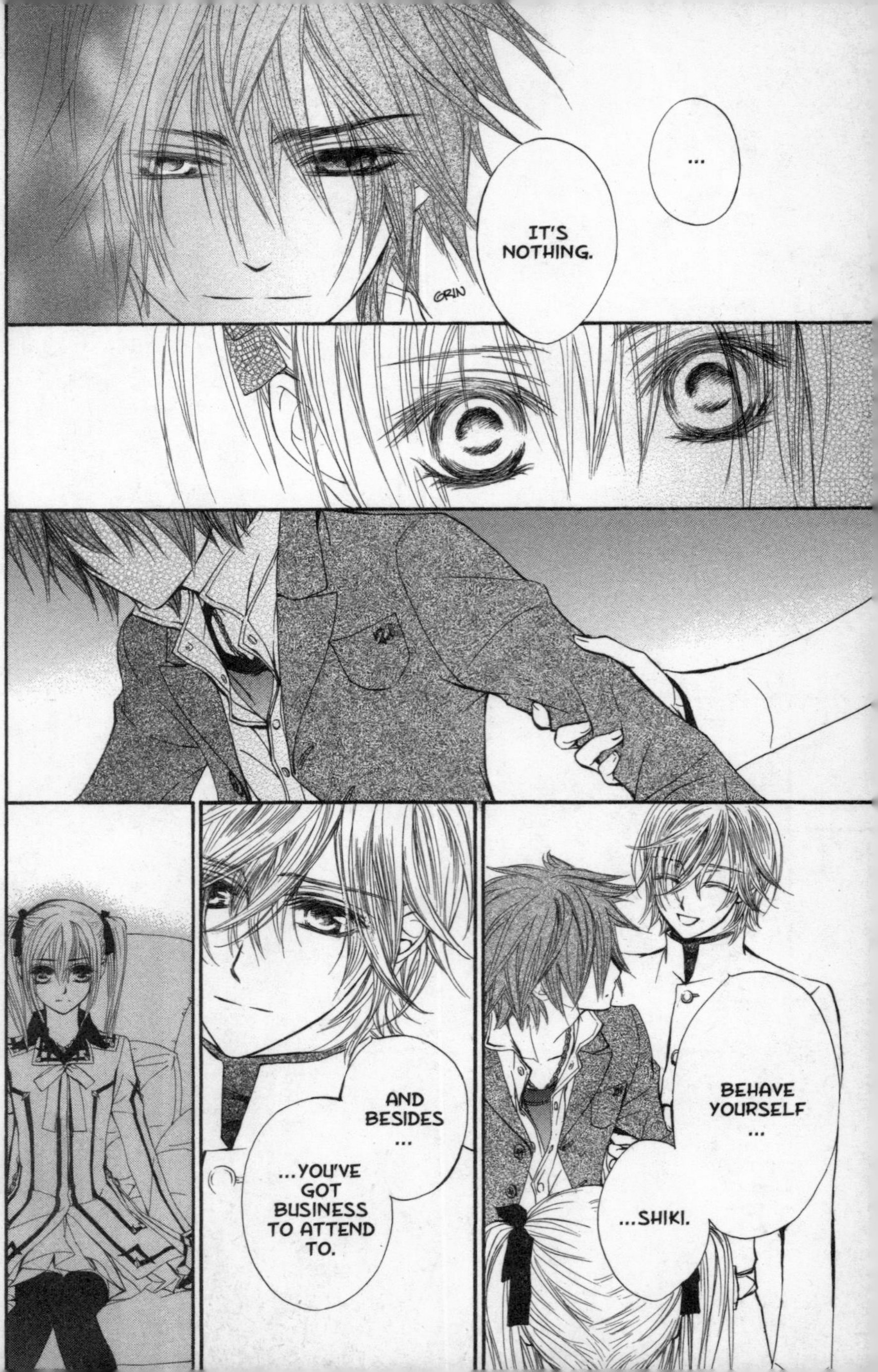
...
IT'S NOTHING.
GRIN
BEHAVE YOURSELF ...
...SHIKI.
AND BESIDES ...
...YOU'VE GOT BUSINESS TO ATTEND TO.

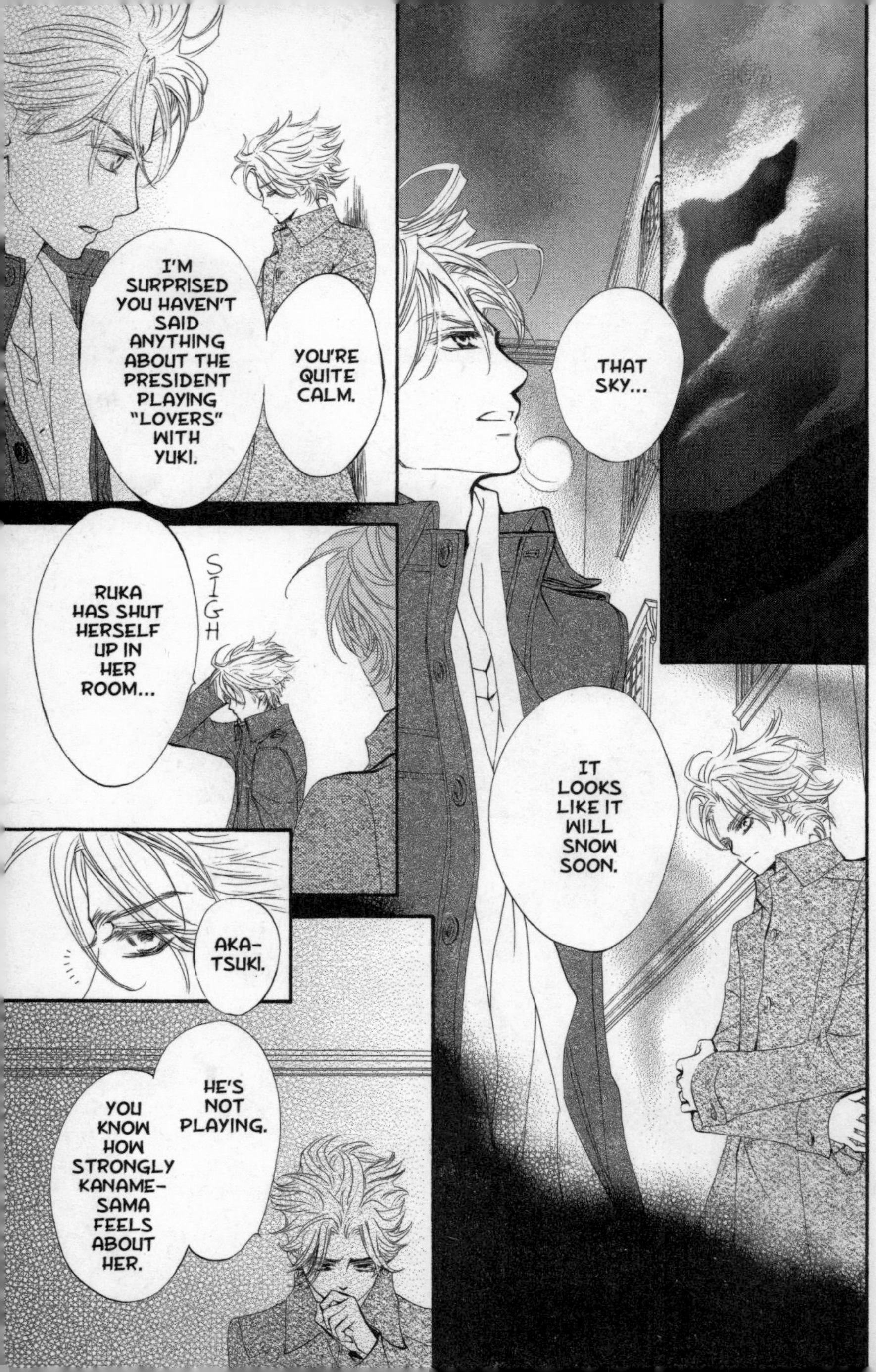
THAT SKY...
IT LOOKS LIKE IT WILL SNOW SOON.
YOU'RE QUITE CALM.
I'M SURPRISED YOU HAVEN'T SAID ANYTHING ABOUT THE PRESIDENT PLAYING "LOVERS" WITH YUKI.
SIGH
RUKA HAS SHUT HERSELF UP IN HER ROOM...
AKA-TSUKI.
HE'S NOT PLAYING.
YOU KNOW HOW STRONGLY KANAME-SAMA FEELS ABOUT HER.

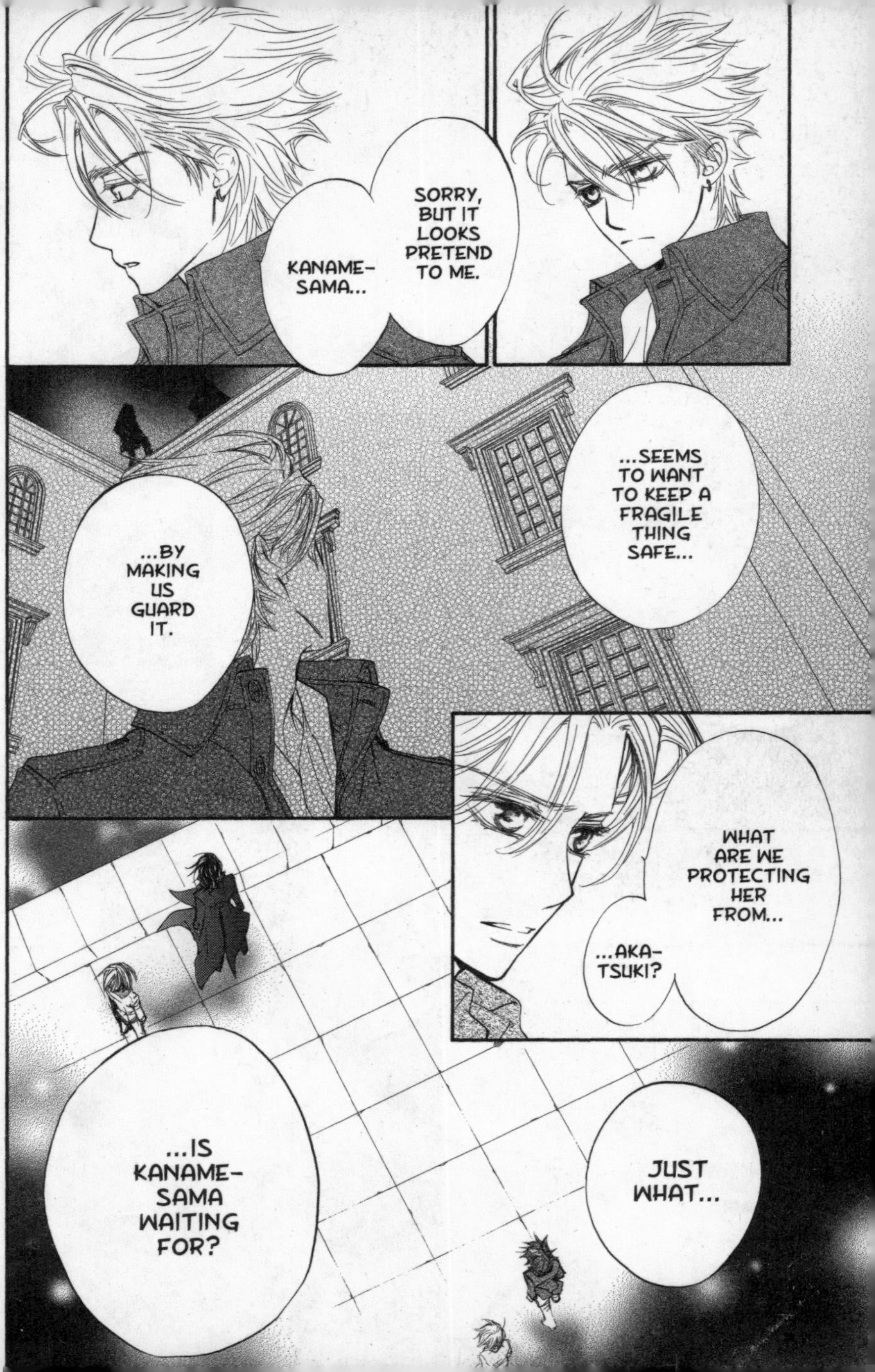
SORRY, BUT IT LOOKS PRETEND TO ME.
KANAME-SAMA...
...SEEMS TO WANT TO KEEP A FRAGILE THING SAFE...
...BY MAKING US GUARD IT.
WHAT ARE WE PROTECTING HER FROM...
...AKA-TSUKI?
JUST WHAT...
...IS KANAME-SAMA WAITING FOR?

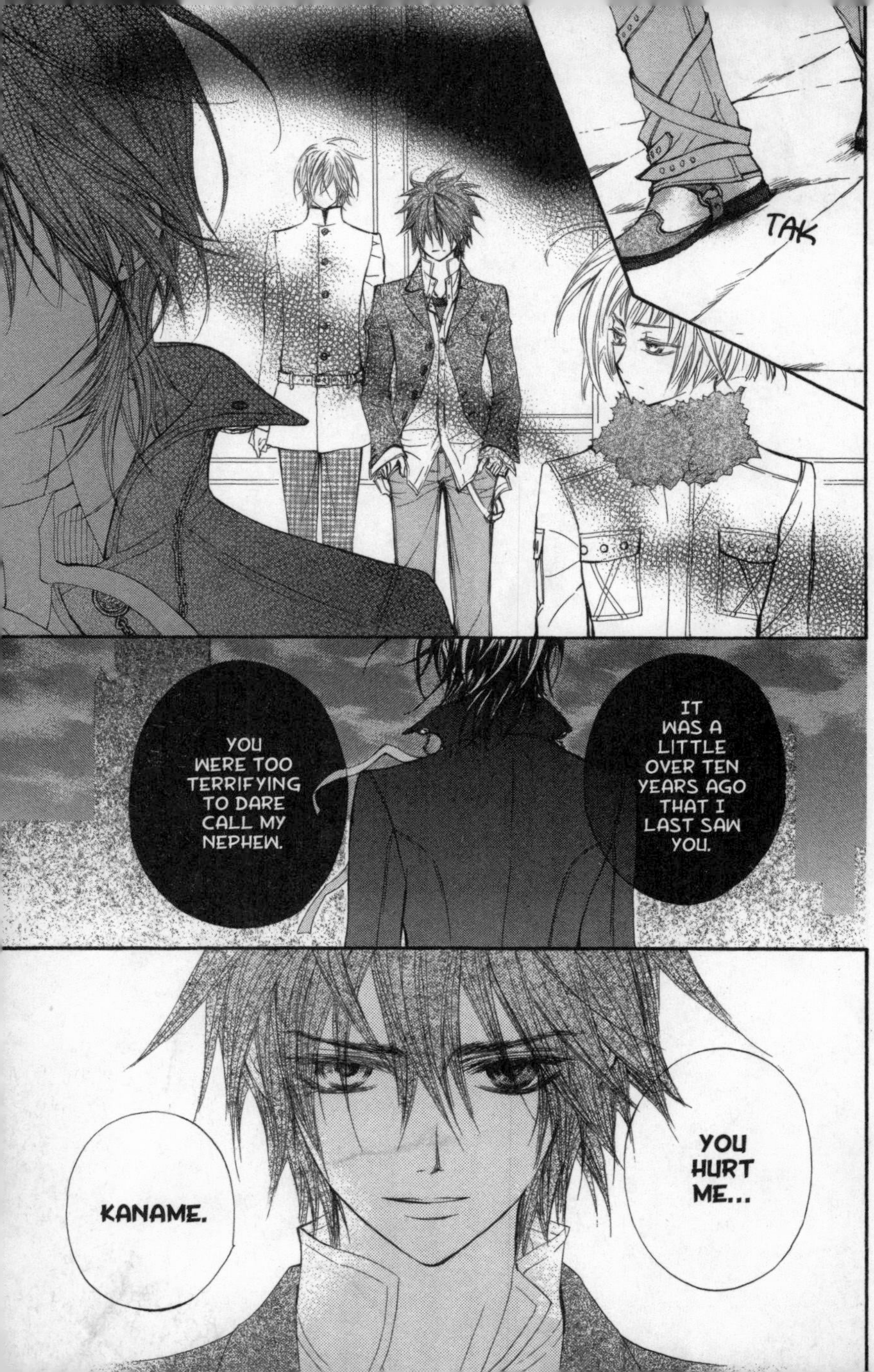
TAK
IT WAS A LITTLE OVER TEN YEARS AGO THAT I LAST SAW YOU.
YOU WERE TOO TERRIFYING TO DARE CALL MY NEPHEW.
YOU HURT ME...
KANAME.

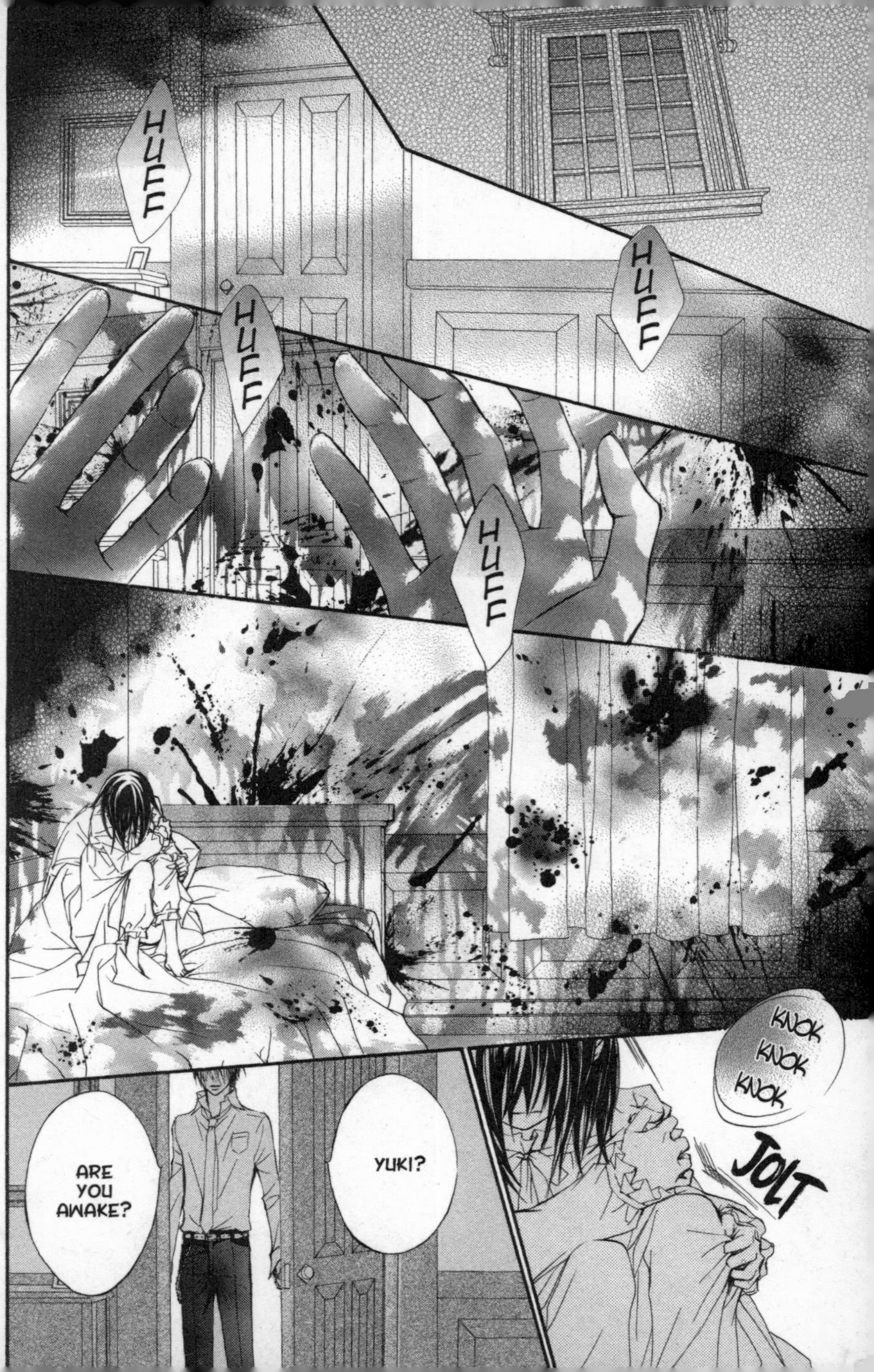
HUFF
HUFF
HUFF
HUFF
KNOK KNOK KNOK
JOLT
YUKI?
ARE YOU AWAKE?

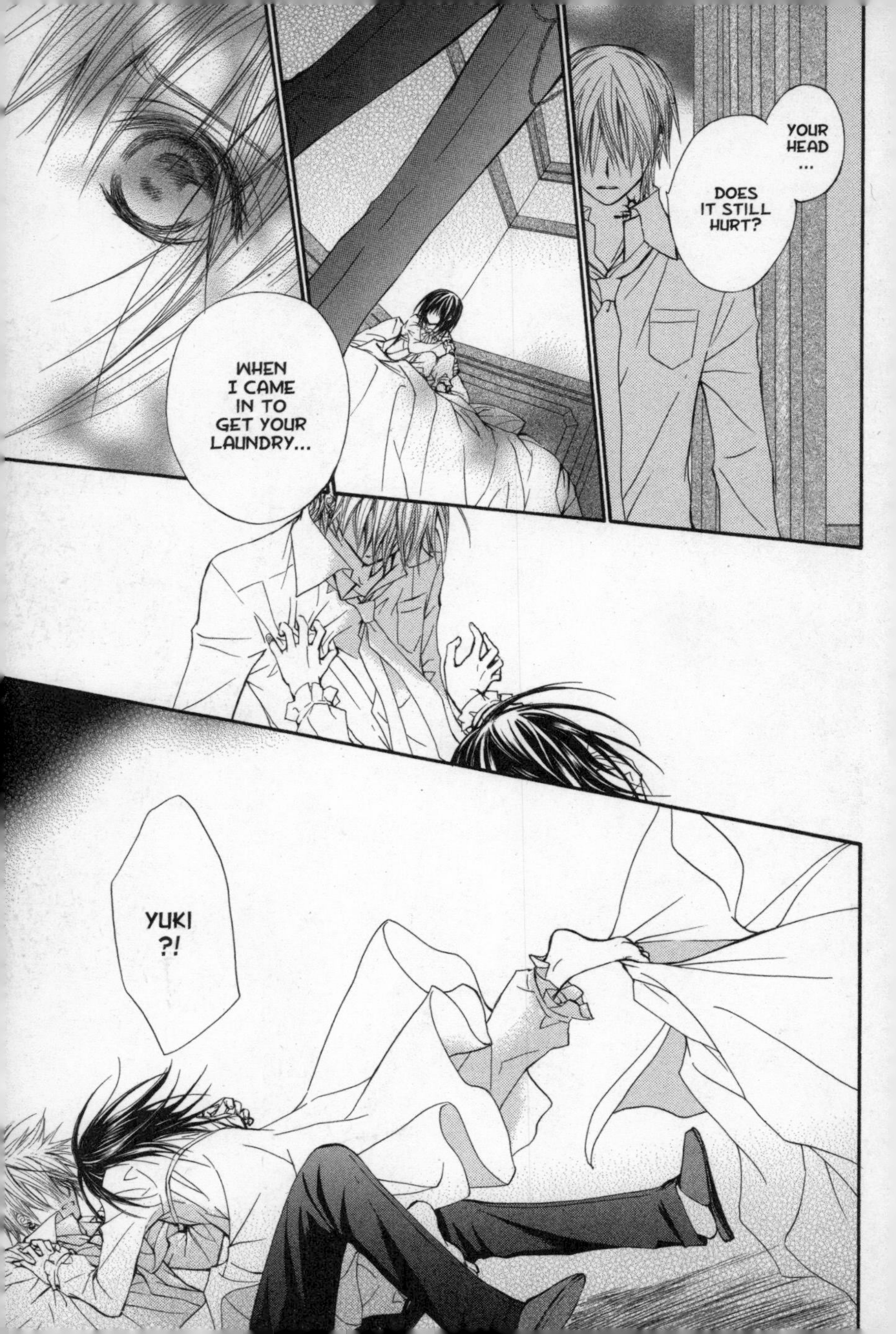
YOUR HEAD ...
DOES IT STILL HURT?
WHEN I CAME IN TO GET YOUR LAUNDRY...
YUKI ?!

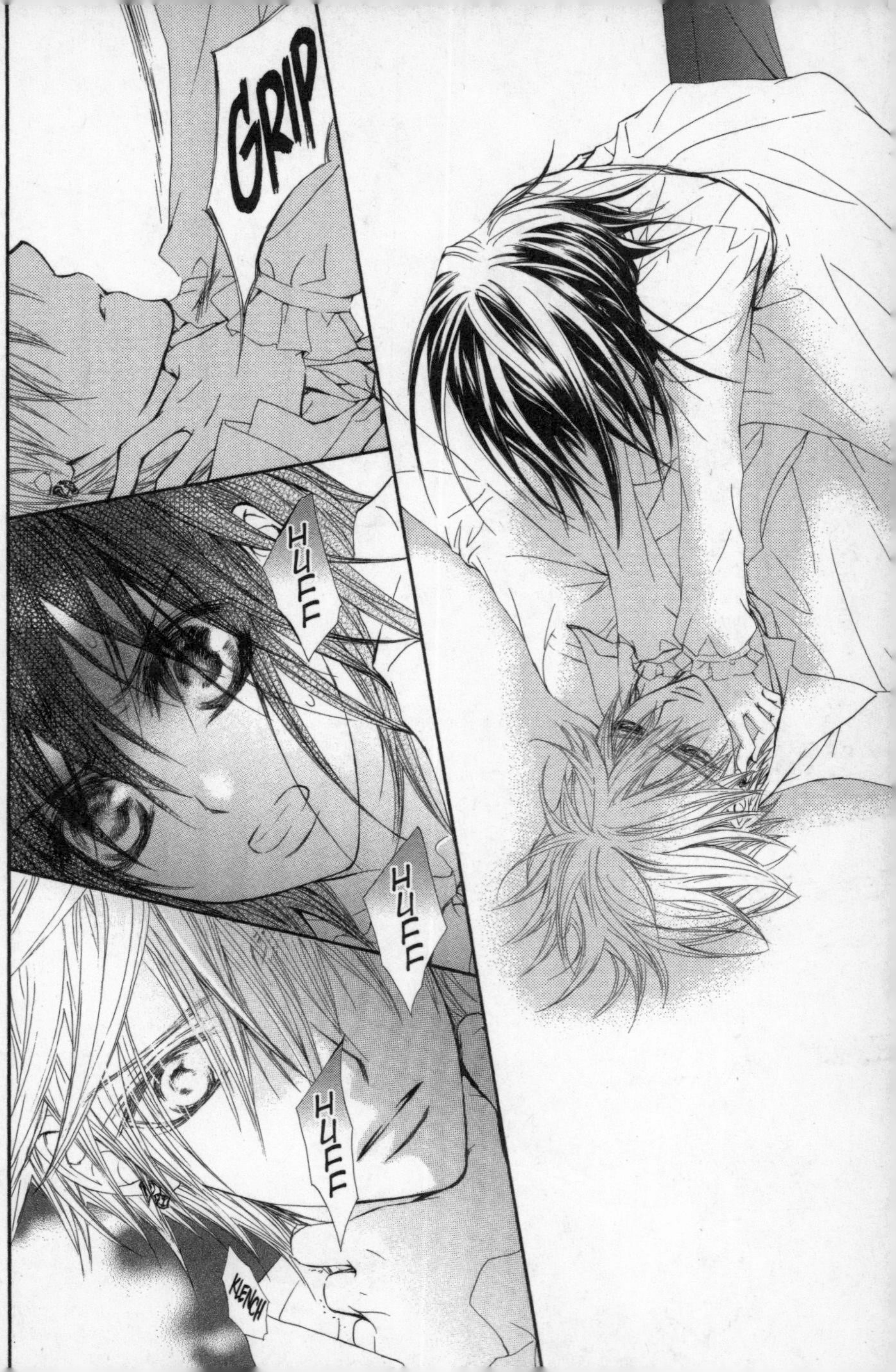
GRIP
HUFF
HUFF
HUFF
KLENCH

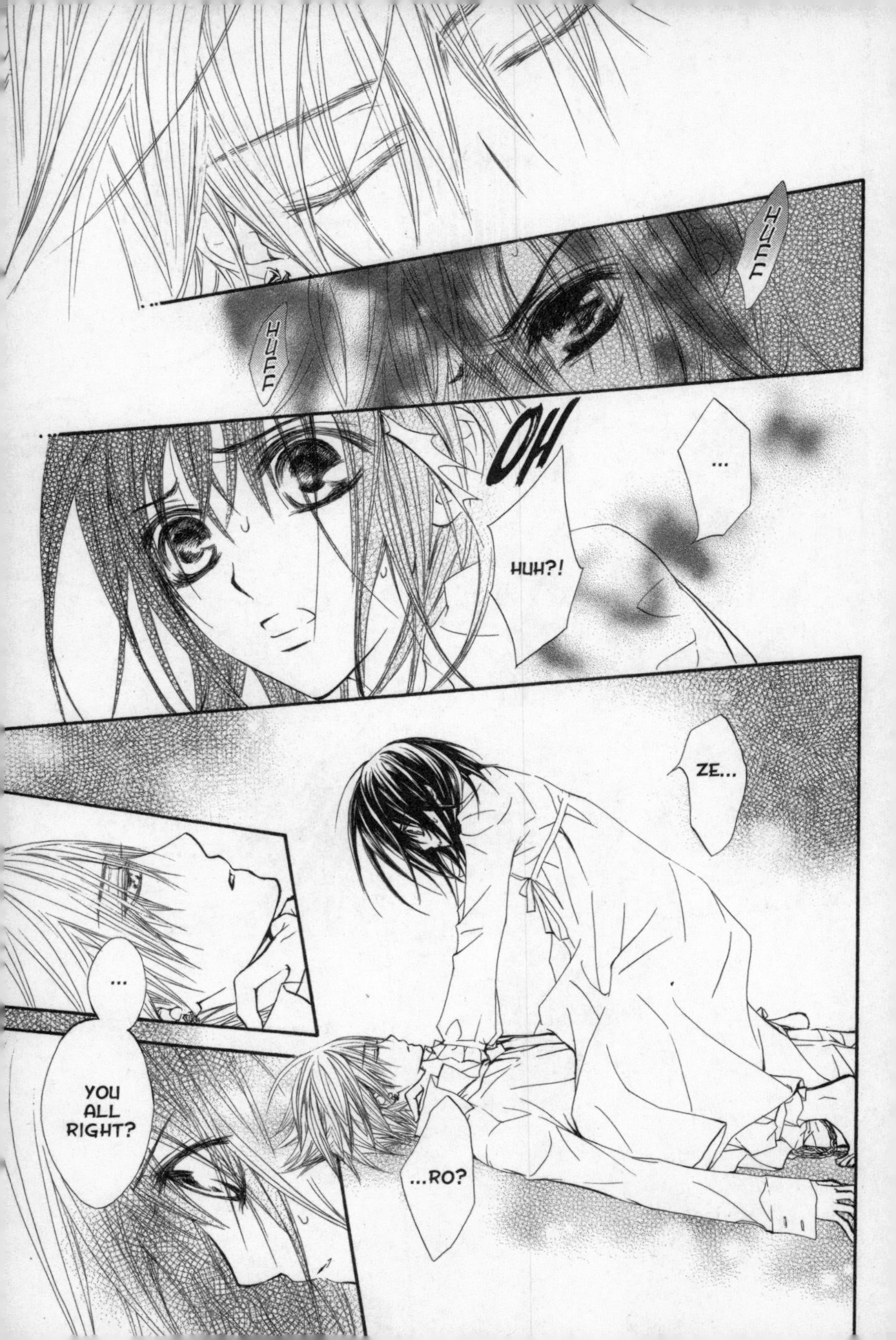
HUFF
HUFF
...
...
OH
HUH?!
...
ZE...
...RO?
...
YOU ALL RIGHT?

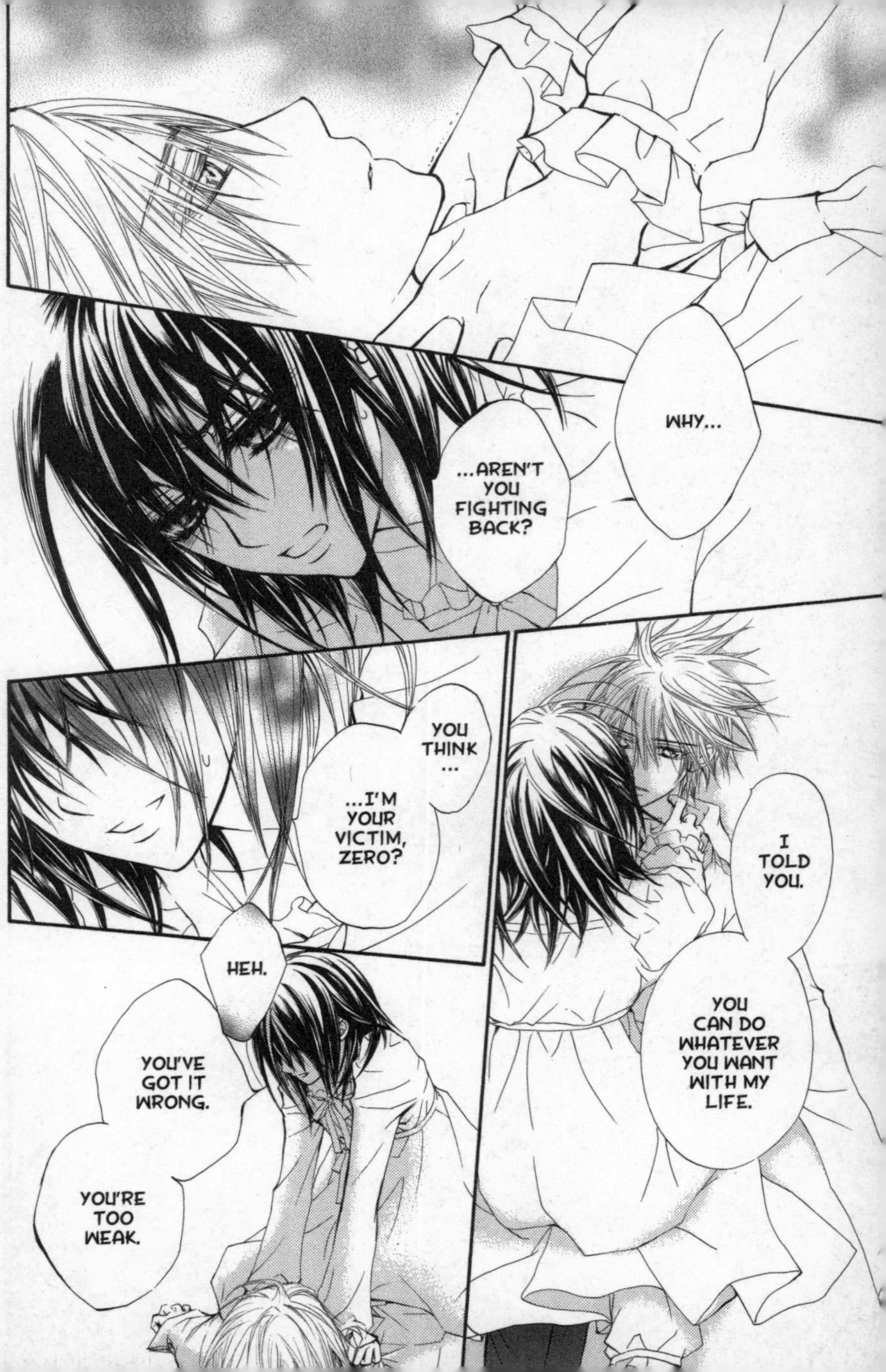
WHY...
...AREN'T YOU FIGHTING BACK?
I TOLD YOU.
YOU CAN DO WHATEVER YOU WANT WITH MY LIFE.
YOU THINK...
...I'M YOUR VICTIM, ZERO?
HEH.
YOU'VE GOT IT WRONG.
YOU'RE TOO WEAK.

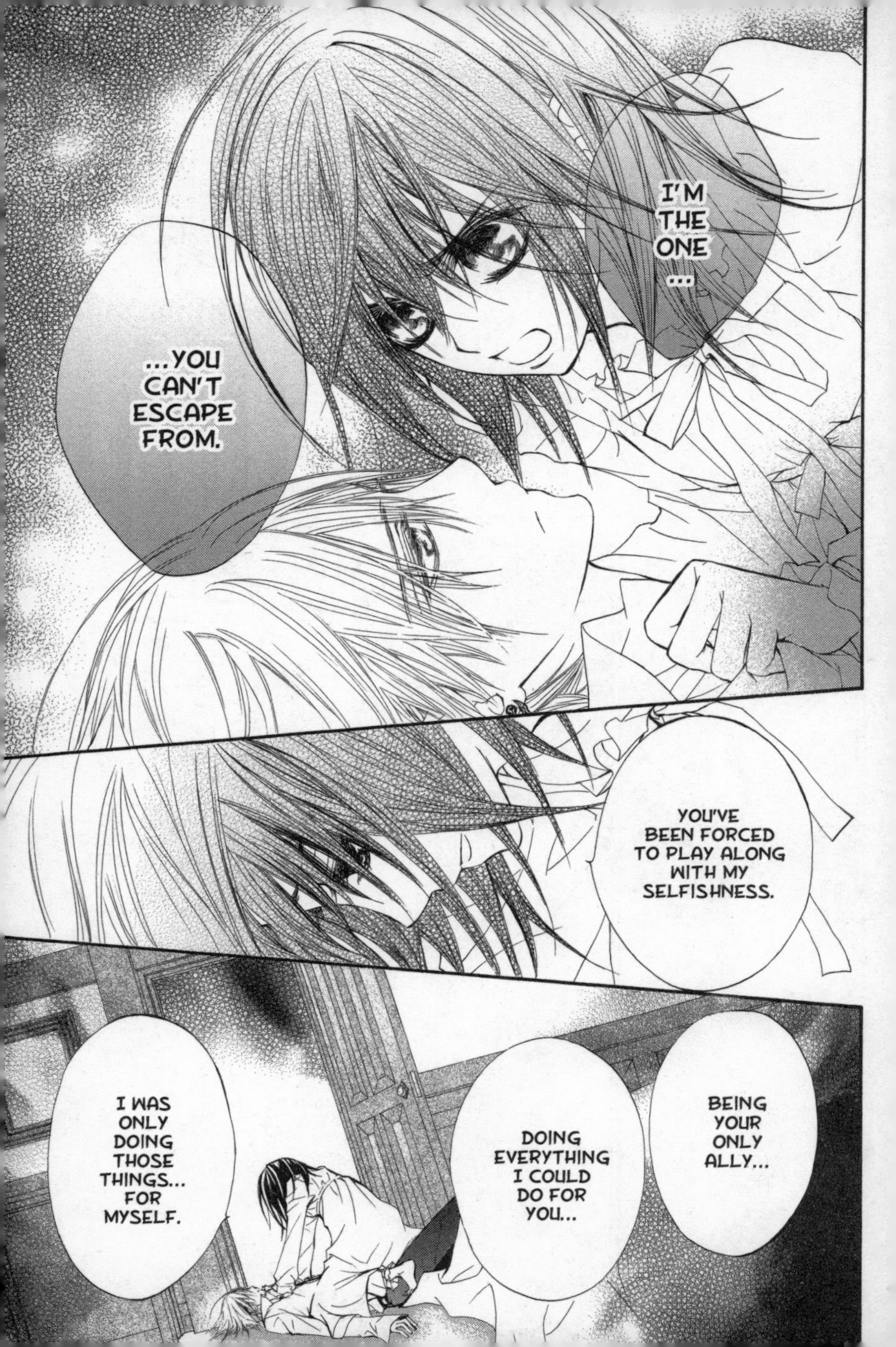
I'M THE ONE ...
...YOU CAN'T ESCAPE FROM.
YOU'VE BEEN FORCED TO PLAY ALONG WITH MY SELFISHNESS.
BEING YOUR ONLY ALLY...
DOING EVERYTHING I COULD DO FOR YOU...
I WAS ONLY DOING THOSE THINGS... FOR MYSELF.

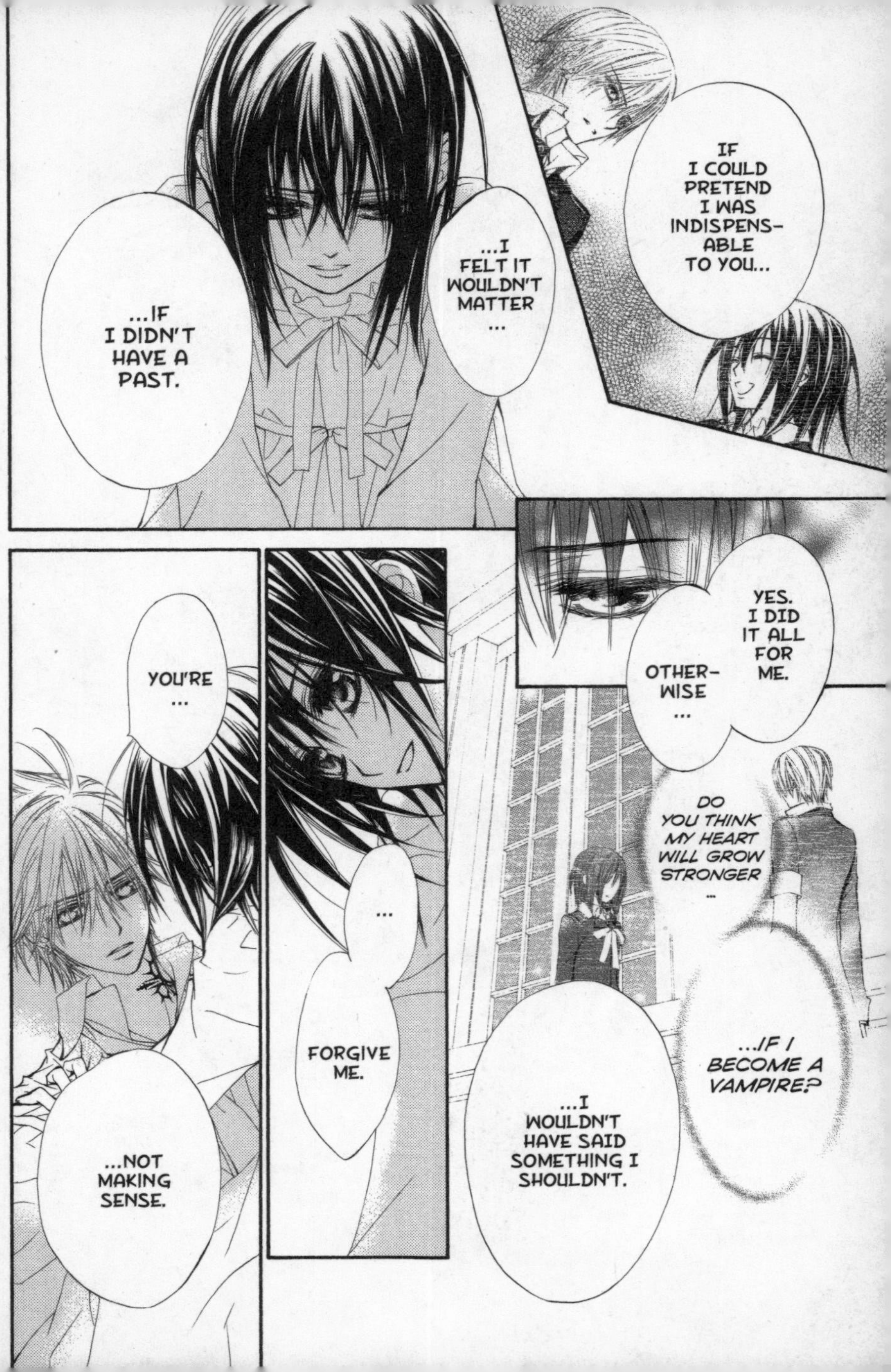
IF I COULD PRETEND I WAS INDISPENSABLE TO YOU...
...I FELT IT WOULDN'T MATTER ...
...IF I DIDN'T HAVE A PAST.
YES. I DID IT ALL FOR ME.
OTHERWISE ...
DO YOU THINK MY HEART WILL GROW STRONGER ...
...IF I BECOME A VAMPIRE?
...I WOULDN'T HAVE SAID SOMETHING I SHOULDN'T.
...
FORGIVE ME.
YOU'RE ...
...NOT MAKING SENSE.

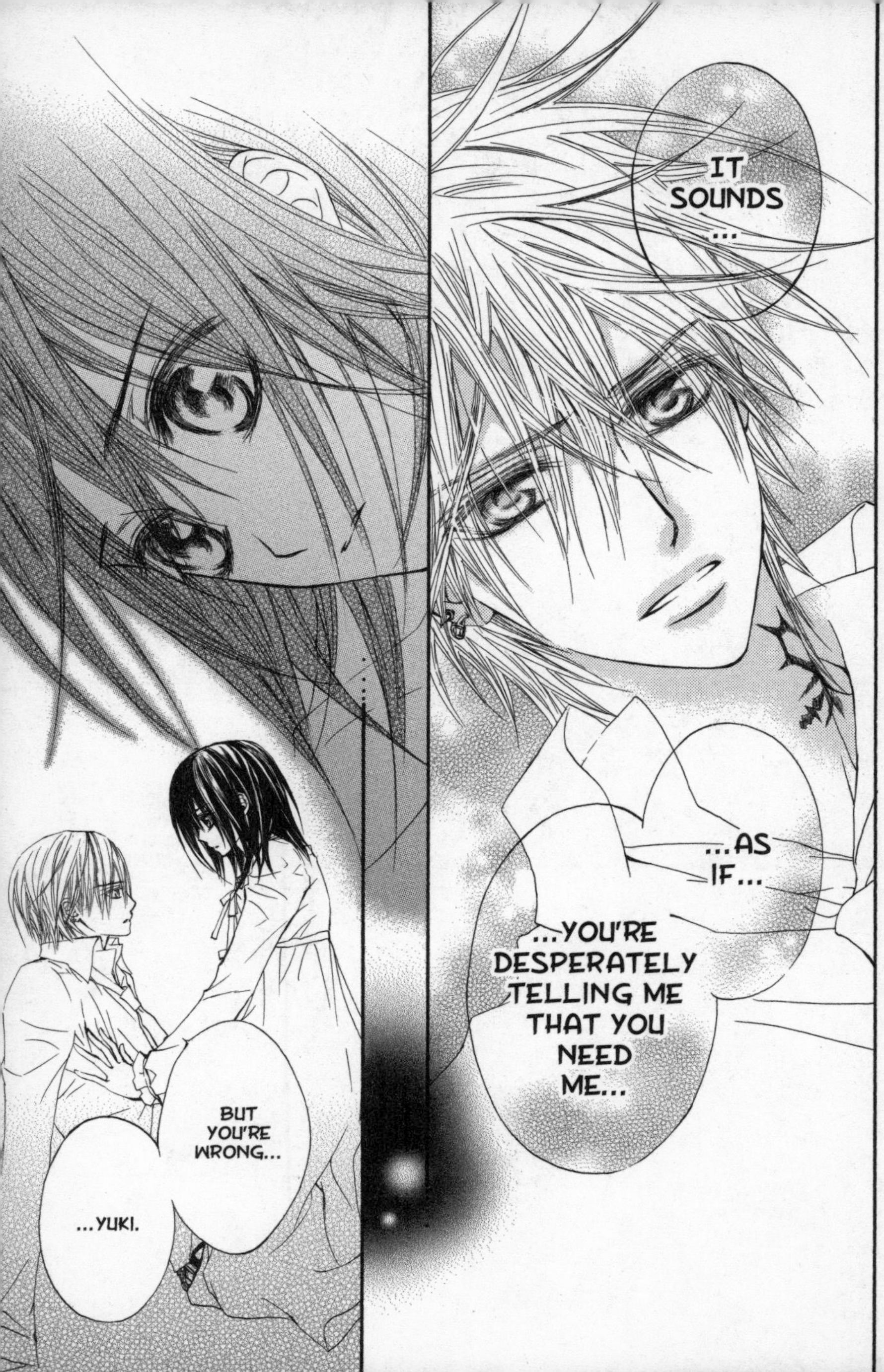
IT SOUNDS...
...AS IF...
...YOU'RE DESPERATELY TELLING ME THAT YOU NEED ME...
BUT YOU'RE WRONG...
...YUKI.

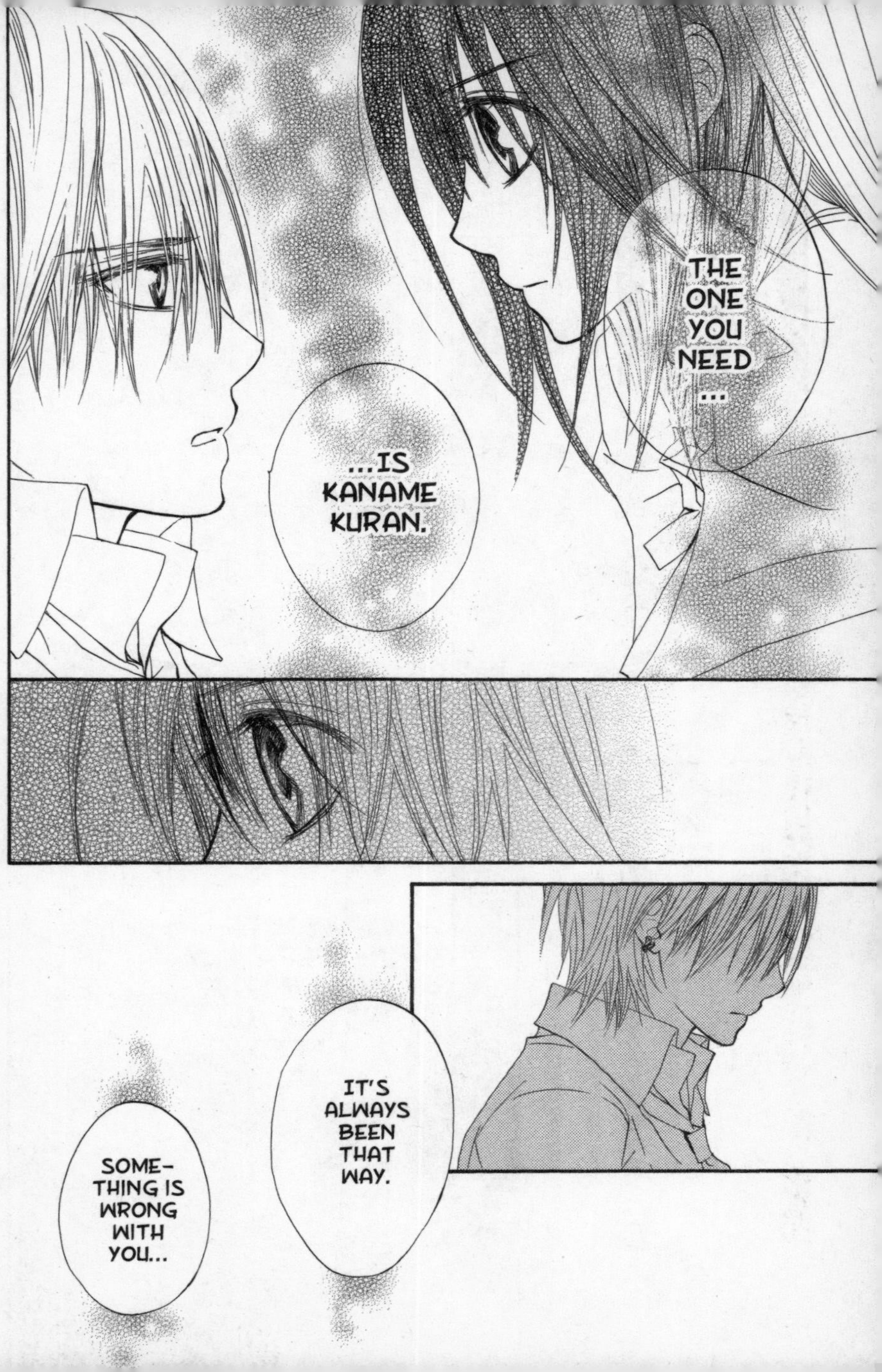
THE ONE YOU NEED...
...IS KANAME KURAN.
IT'S ALWAYS BEEN THAT WAY.
SOME-THING IS WRONG WITH YOU...

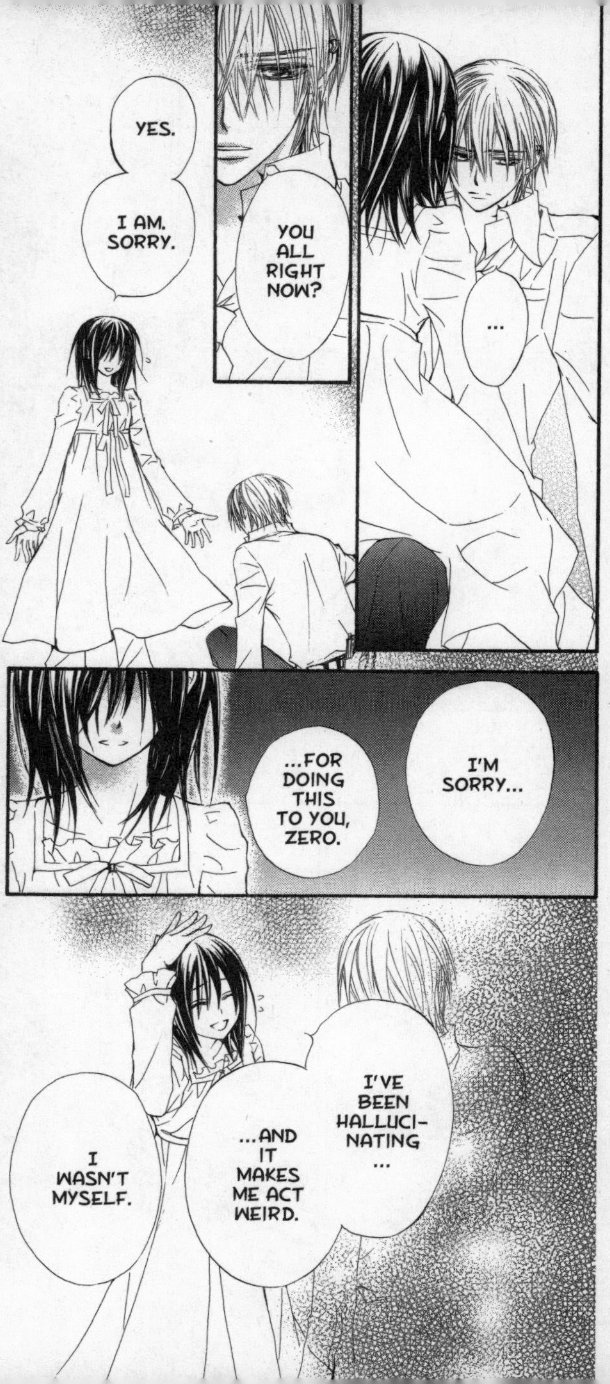
...
YOU ALL RIGHT NOW?
YES.
I AM. SORRY.
I'M SORRY...
...FOR DOING THIS TO YOU, ZERO.
I'VE BEEN HALLUCINATING...
...AND IT MAKES ME ACT WEIRD.
I WASN'T MYSELF.

In my case, this is what I did when I wanted to improve my drawing:

- I did pencil sketches of people who exist, who I thought were handsome and beautiful. I drew people of all ages, both men and women, and people who stand out. I paid attention to bone structure.
- Find someone you call your "master" and use their techniques as a reference. The trick is to depend on your memory. (This way you can free yourself from copying quickly! I think...)

◆
◆
◆

Before I knew it, I've come to the last sidebar.

I think the Shizuka side story can be included in the next volume or two.

Please look forward to volume 8!!

樋野まつり

Matsuri Hino

◆

Thank you so much!!
T.A.-sama!!
O. Mio-sama!
K. Midori-sama!
I. Asami-sama!
My editor and everyone involved.
My family and friends!!

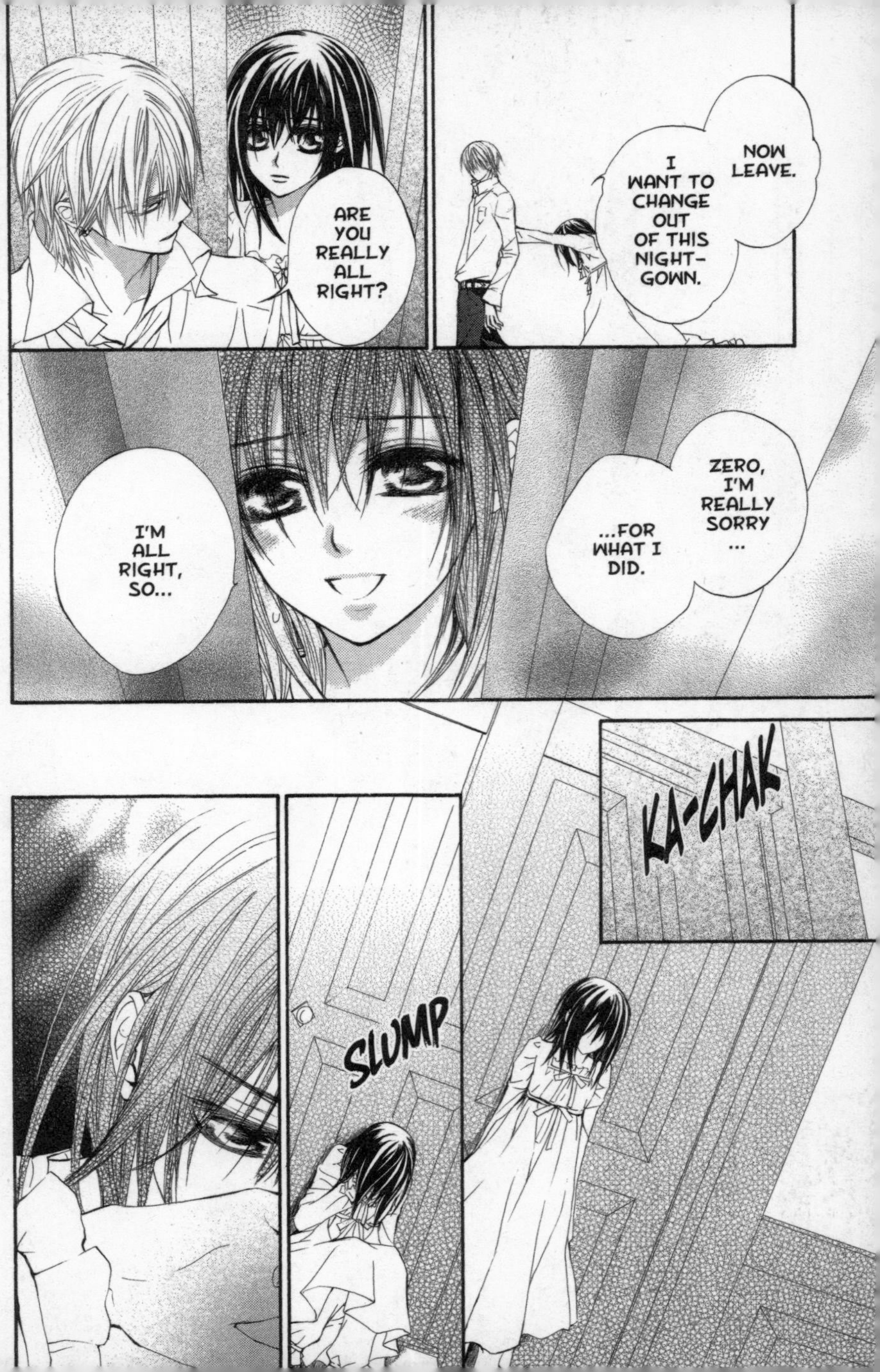
NOW LEAVE.
I WANT TO CHANGE OUT OF THIS NIGHT-GOWN.
ARE YOU REALLY ALL RIGHT?
ZERO, I'M REALLY SORRY...
...FOR WHAT I DID.
I'M ALL RIGHT, SO...
KA-CHAK
SLUMP

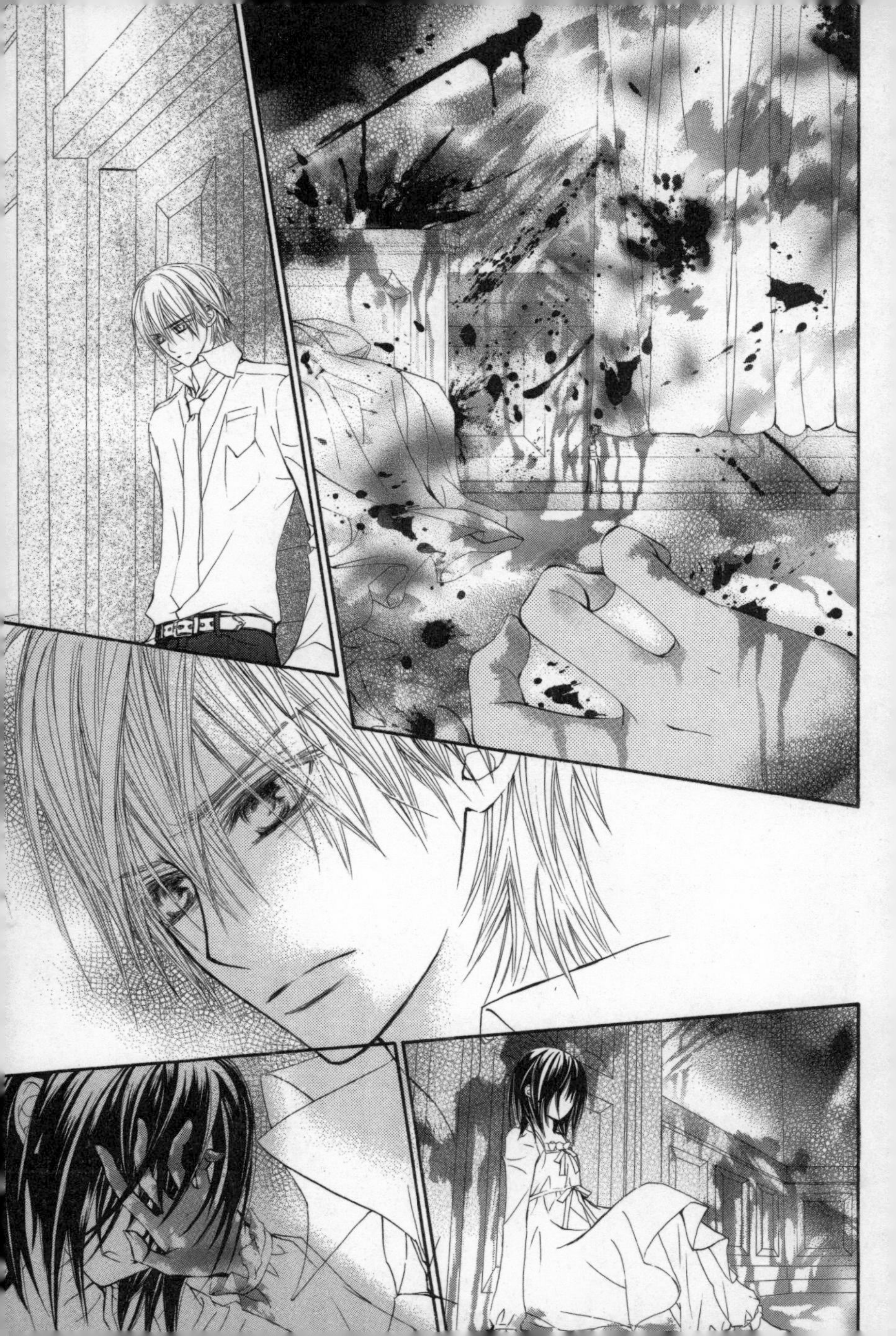

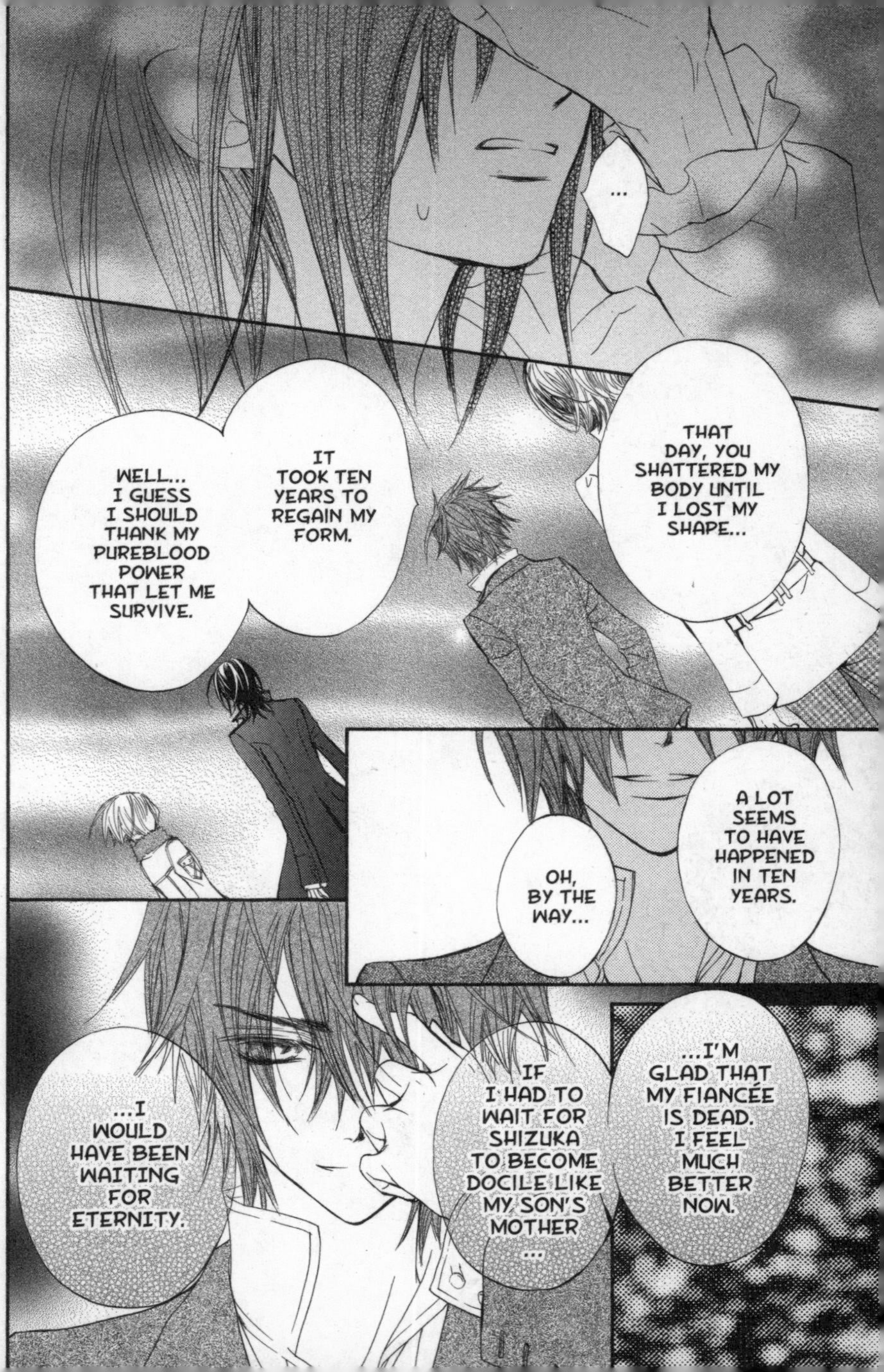
...
THAT DAY, YOU SHATTERED MY BODY UNTIL I LOST MY SHAPE...
IT TOOK TEN YEARS TO REGAIN MY FORM.
WELL... I GUESS I SHOULD THANK MY PUREBLOOD POWER THAT LET ME SURVIVE.
A LOT SEEMS TO HAVE HAPPENED IN TEN YEARS.
OH, BY THE WAY...
...I'M GLAD THAT MY FIANCÉE IS DEAD. I FEEL MUCH BETTER NOW.
IF I HAD TO WAIT FOR SHIZUKA TO BECOME DOCILE LIKE MY SON'S MOTHER...
...I WOULD HAVE BEEN WAITING FOR ETERNITY.

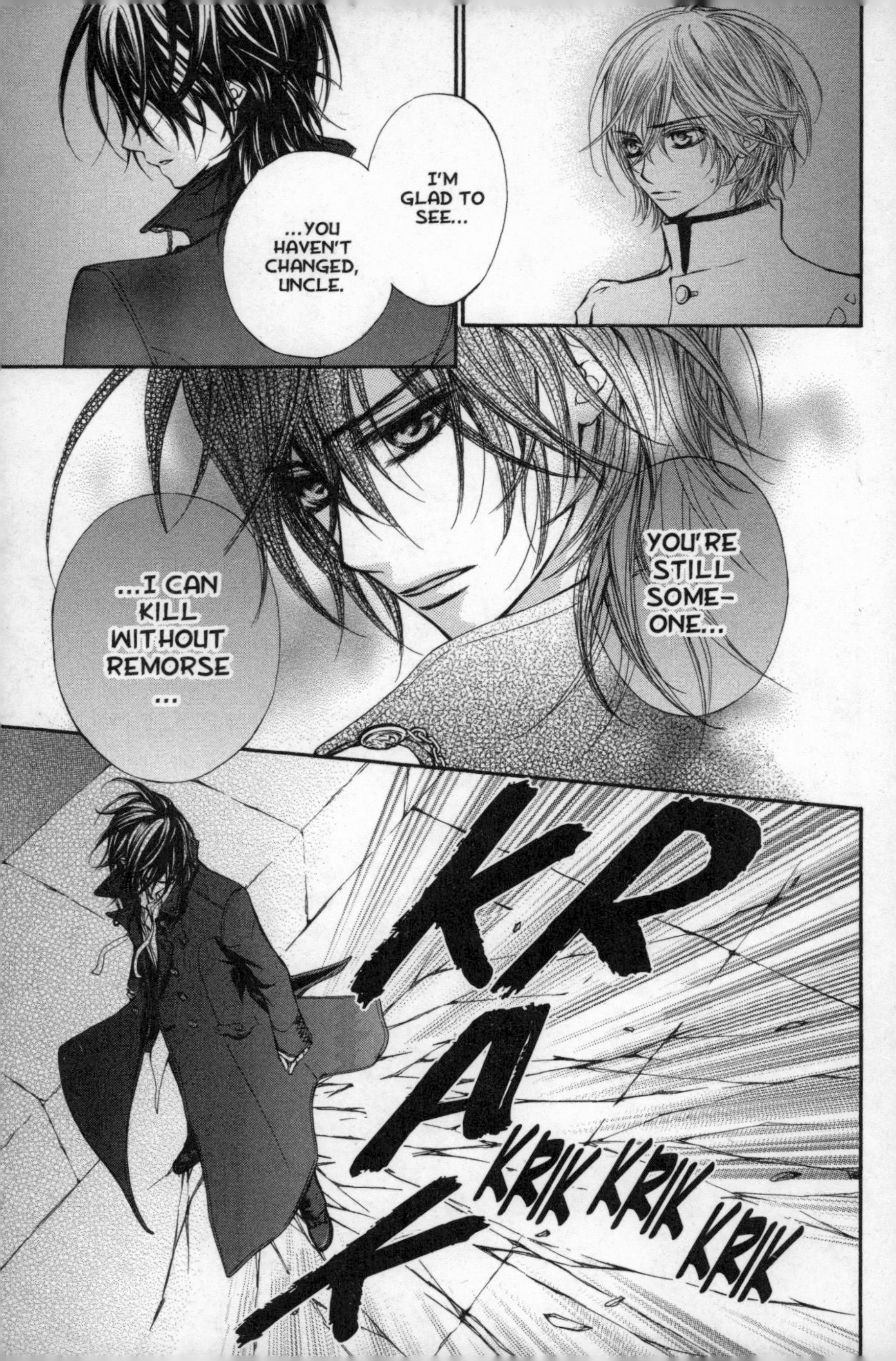
I'M GLAD TO SEE...
...YOU HAVEN'T CHANGED, UNCLE.
YOU'RE STILL SOME-ONE...
...I CAN KILL WITHOUT REMORSE ...
KRAK
KRIK KRIK KRIK KRIK

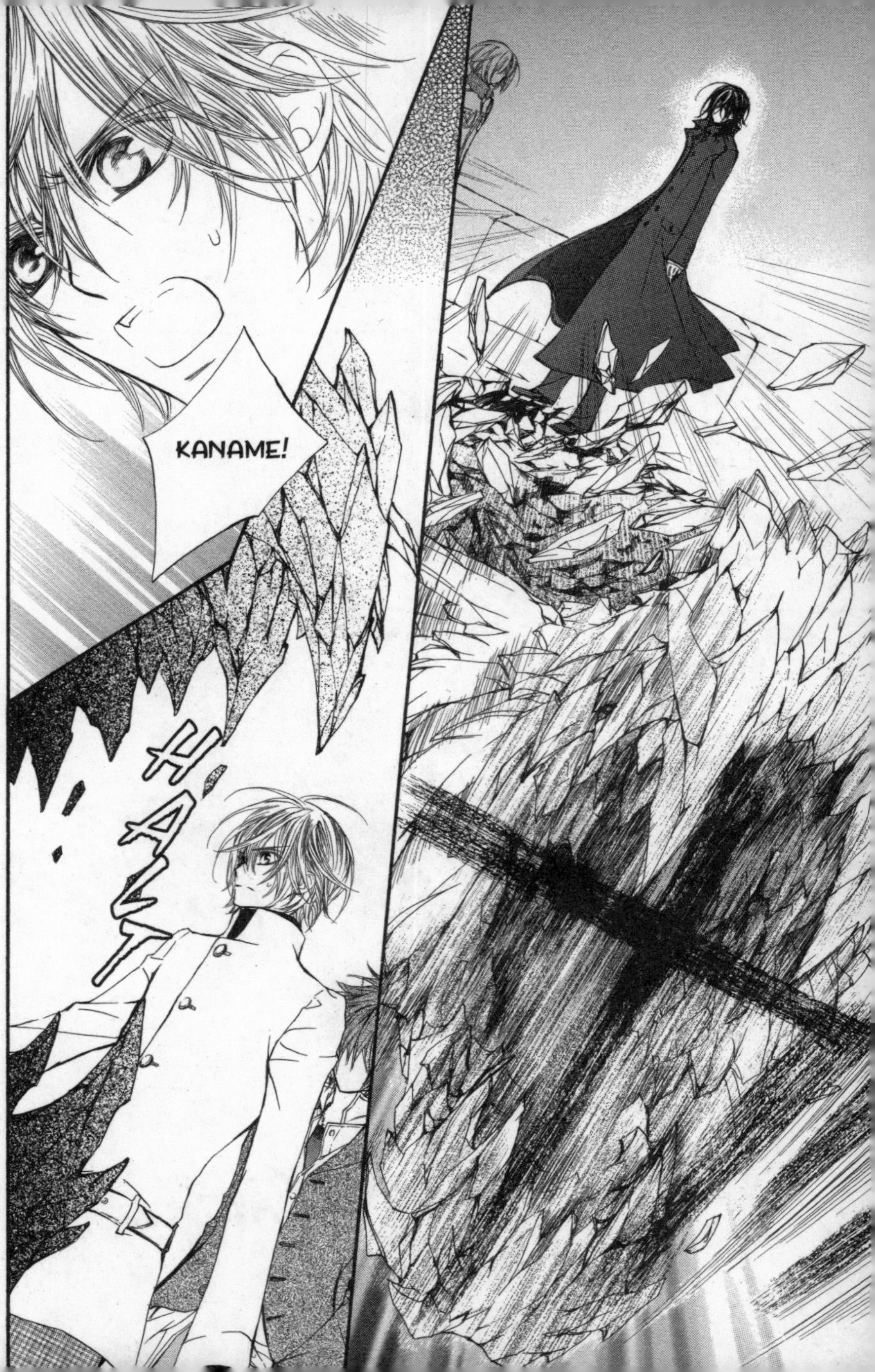
KANAME!
HALT!

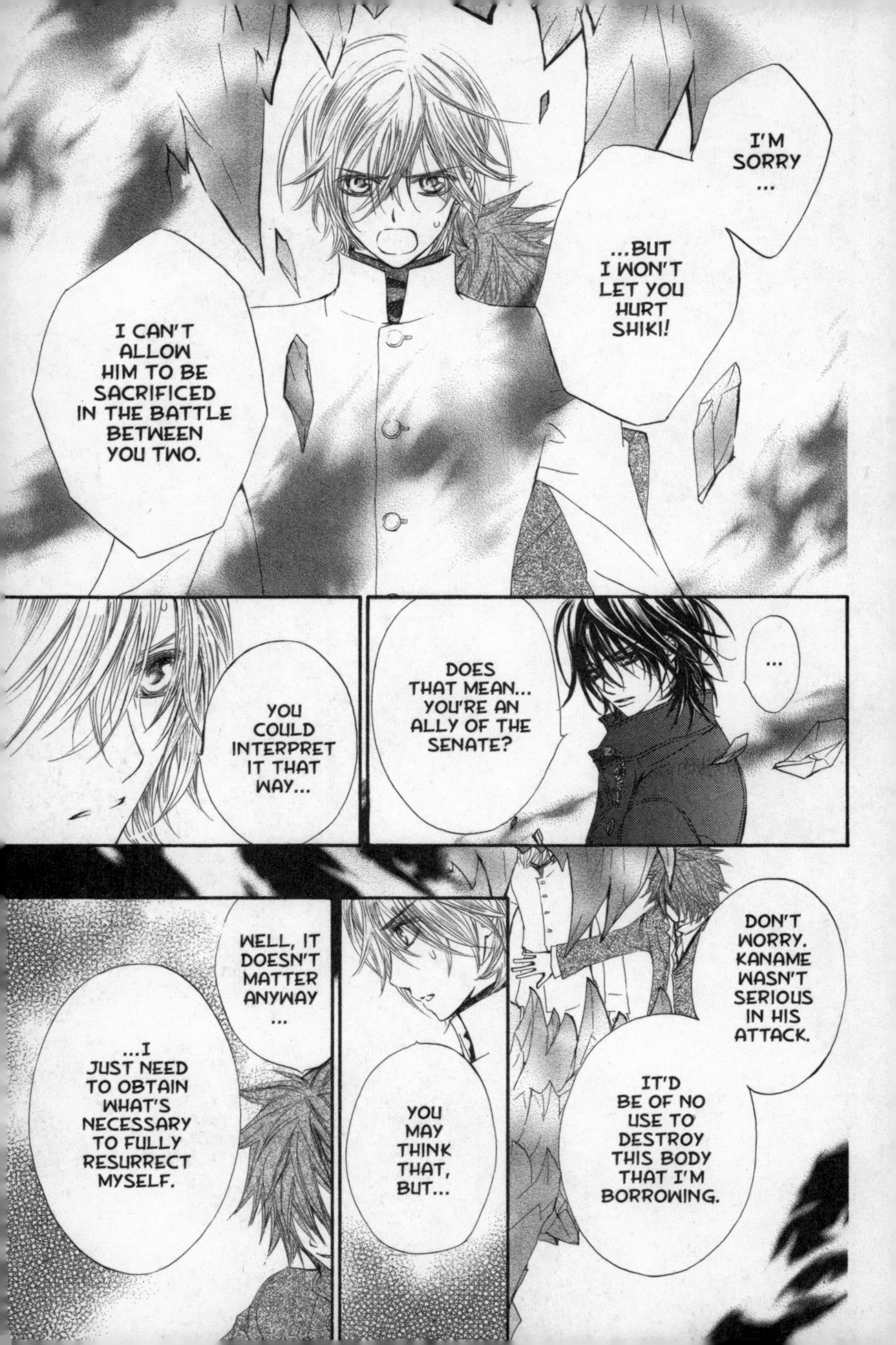
I'M SORRY ...
...BUT I WON'T LET YOU HURT SHIKI!
I CAN'T ALLOW HIM TO BE SACRIFICED IN THE BATTLE BETWEEN YOU TWO.
...
DOES THAT MEAN... YOU'RE AN ALLY OF THE SENATE?
YOU COULD INTERPRET IT THAT WAY...
DON'T WORRY. KANAME WASN'T SERIOUS IN HIS ATTACK.
IT'D BE OF NO USE TO DESTROY THIS BODY THAT I'M BORROWING.
YOU MAY THINK THAT, BUT...
WELL, IT DOESN'T MATTER ANYWAY ...
...I JUST NEED TO OBTAIN WHAT'S NECESSARY TO FULLY RESURRECT MYSELF.

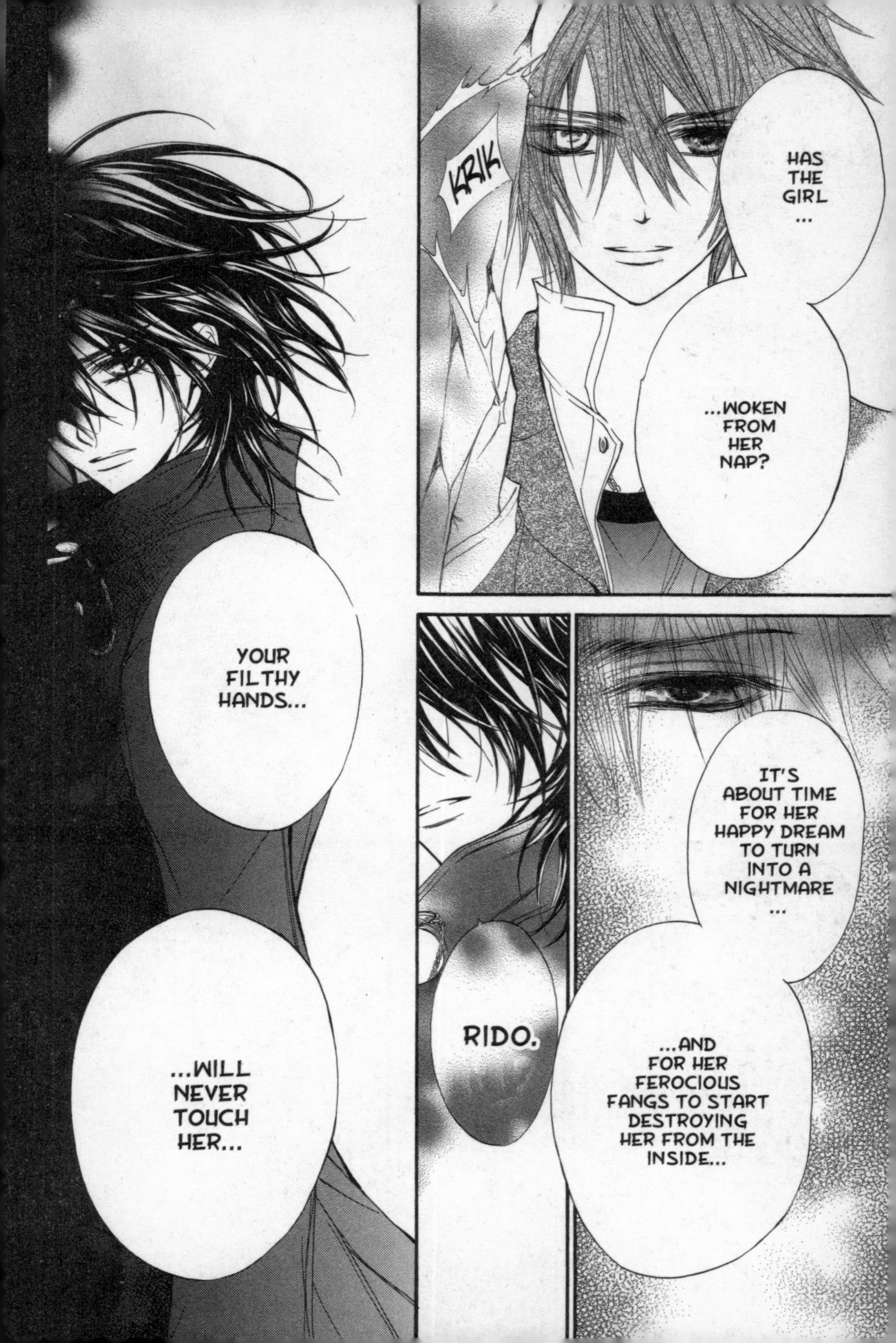
KRIK
HAS THE GIRL ...
...WOKEN FROM HER NAP?
IT'S ABOUT TIME FOR HER HAPPY DREAM TO TURN INTO A NIGHTMARE ...
...AND FOR HER FEROCIOUS FANGS TO START DESTROYING HER FROM THE INSIDE...
RIDO.
YOUR FILTHY HANDS...
...WILL NEVER TOUCH HER...

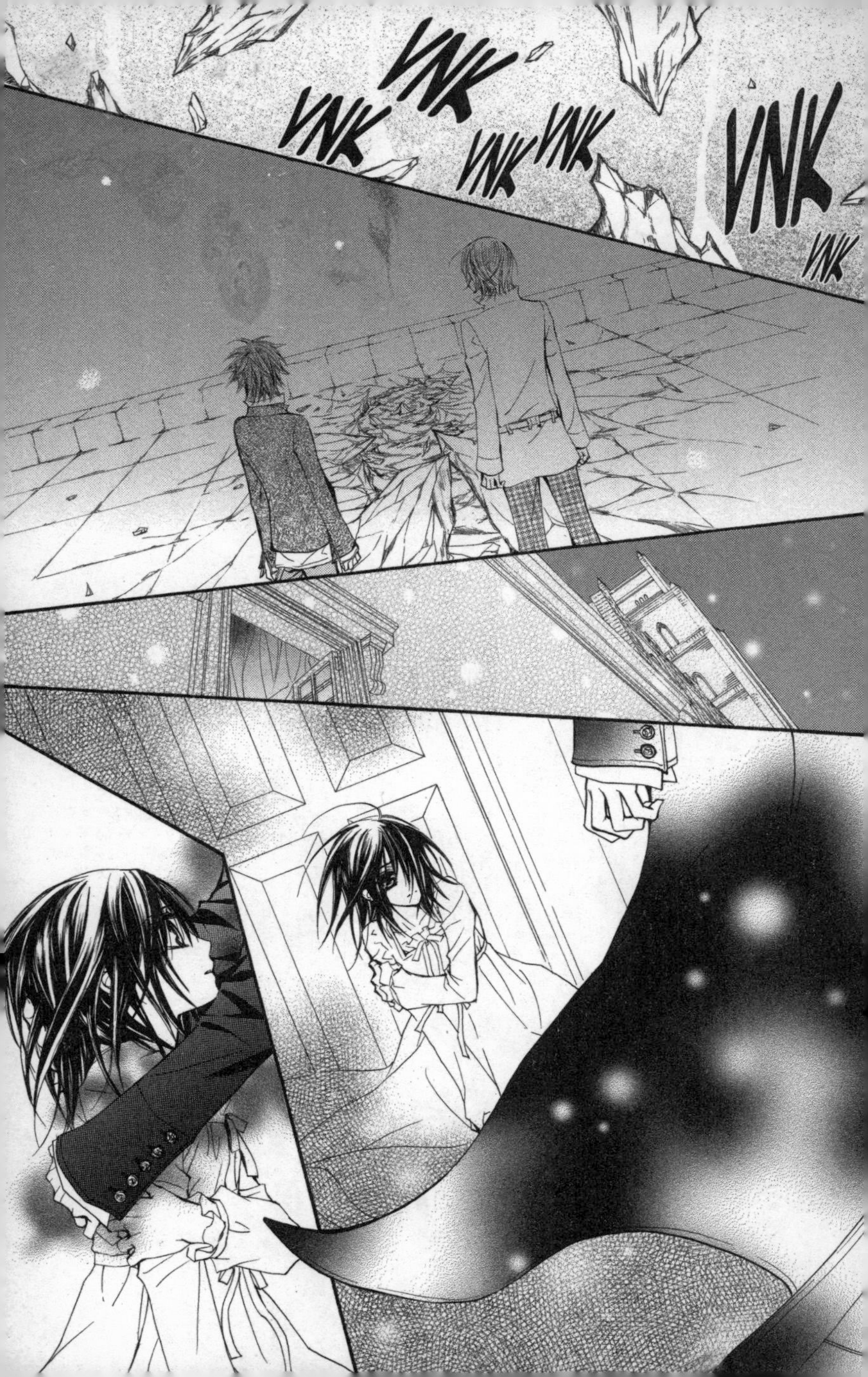
VNK
VNK
VNK
VNK
VNK
VNK

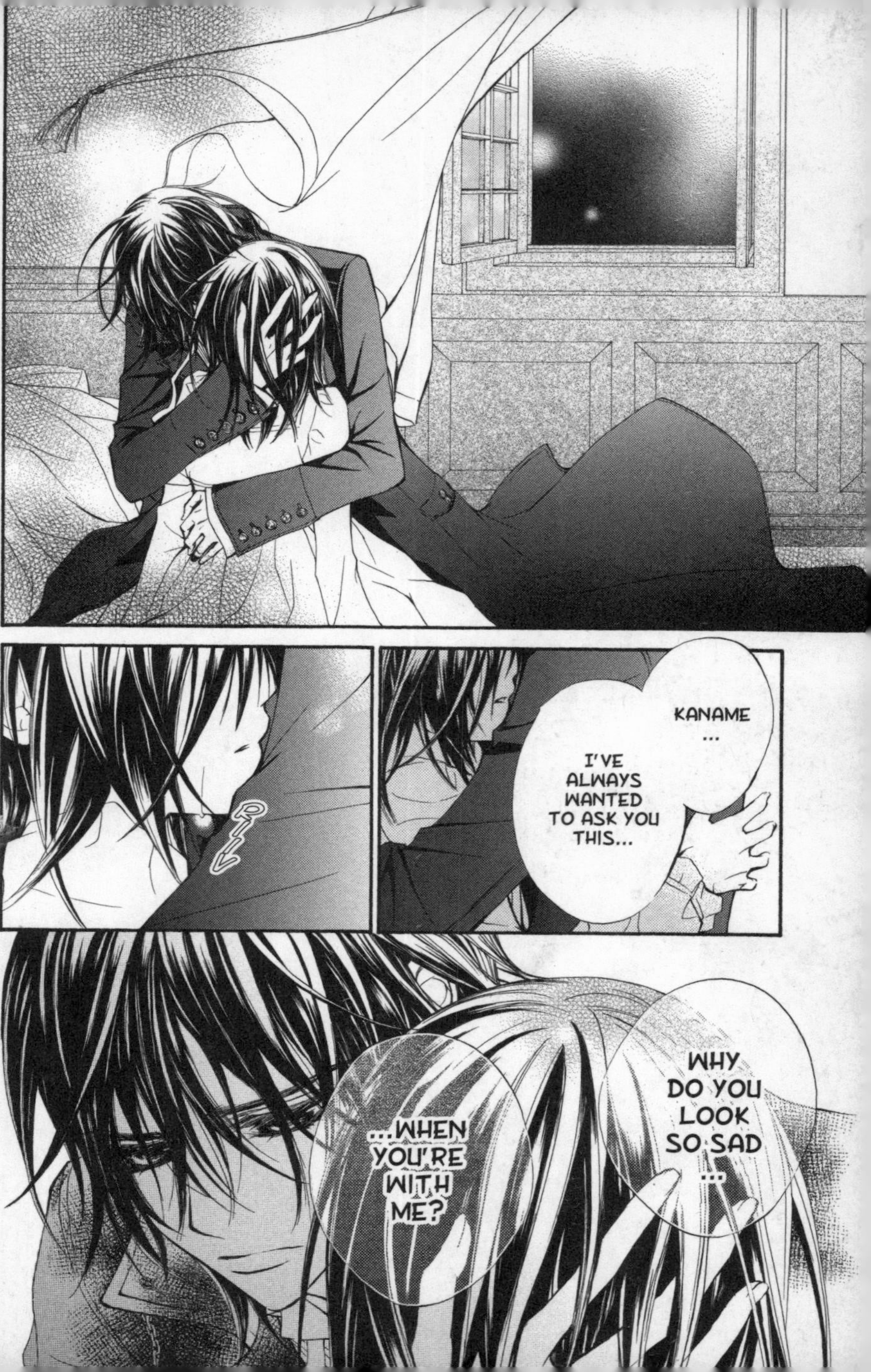
KANAME ...
I'VE ALWAYS WANTED TO ASK YOU THIS...
WHY DO YOU LOOK SO SAD ...
...WHEN YOU'RE WITH ME?

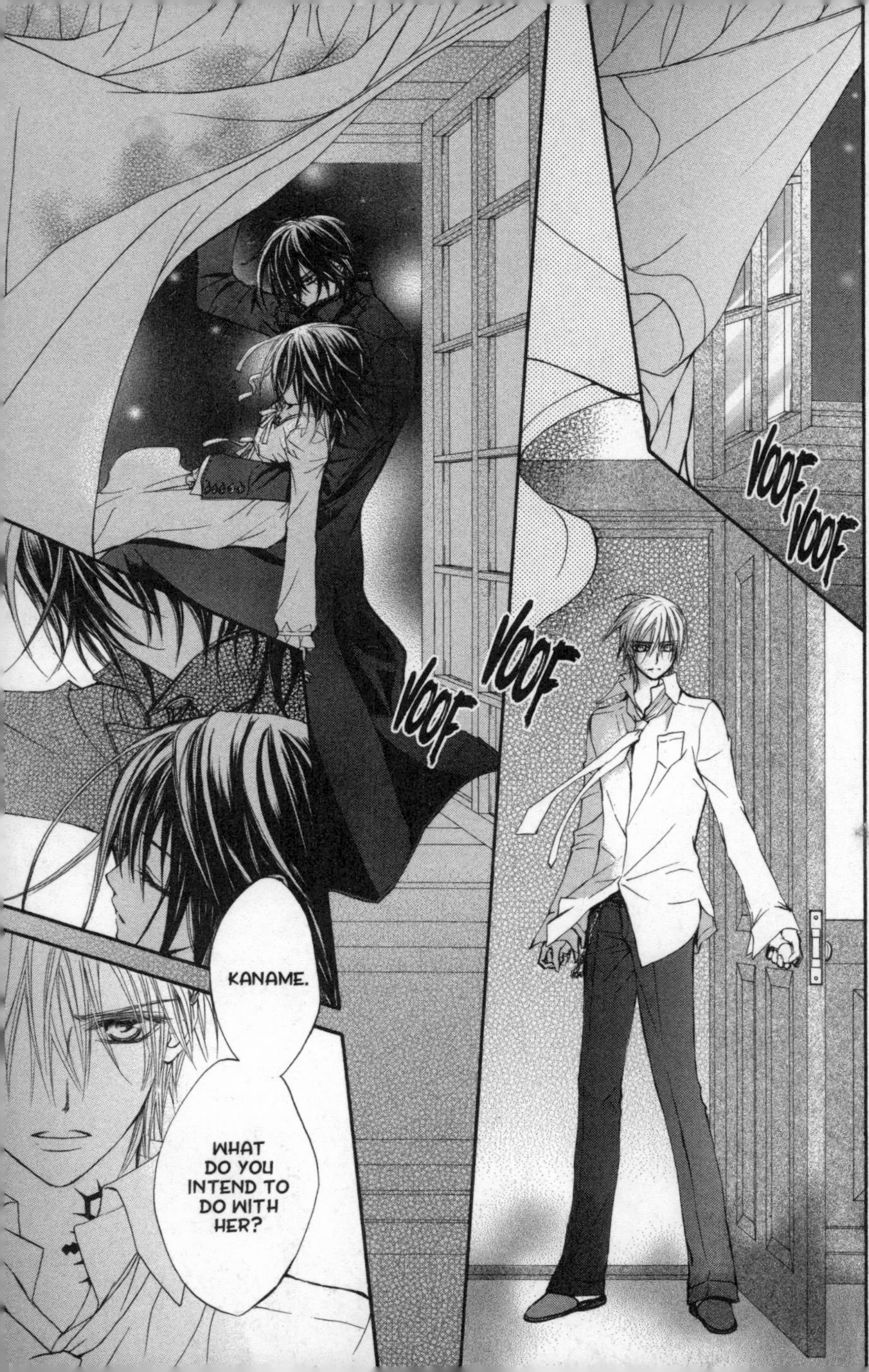
VOOF VOOF
VOOF
VOOF
KANAME.
WHAT DO YOU INTEND TO DO WITH HER?

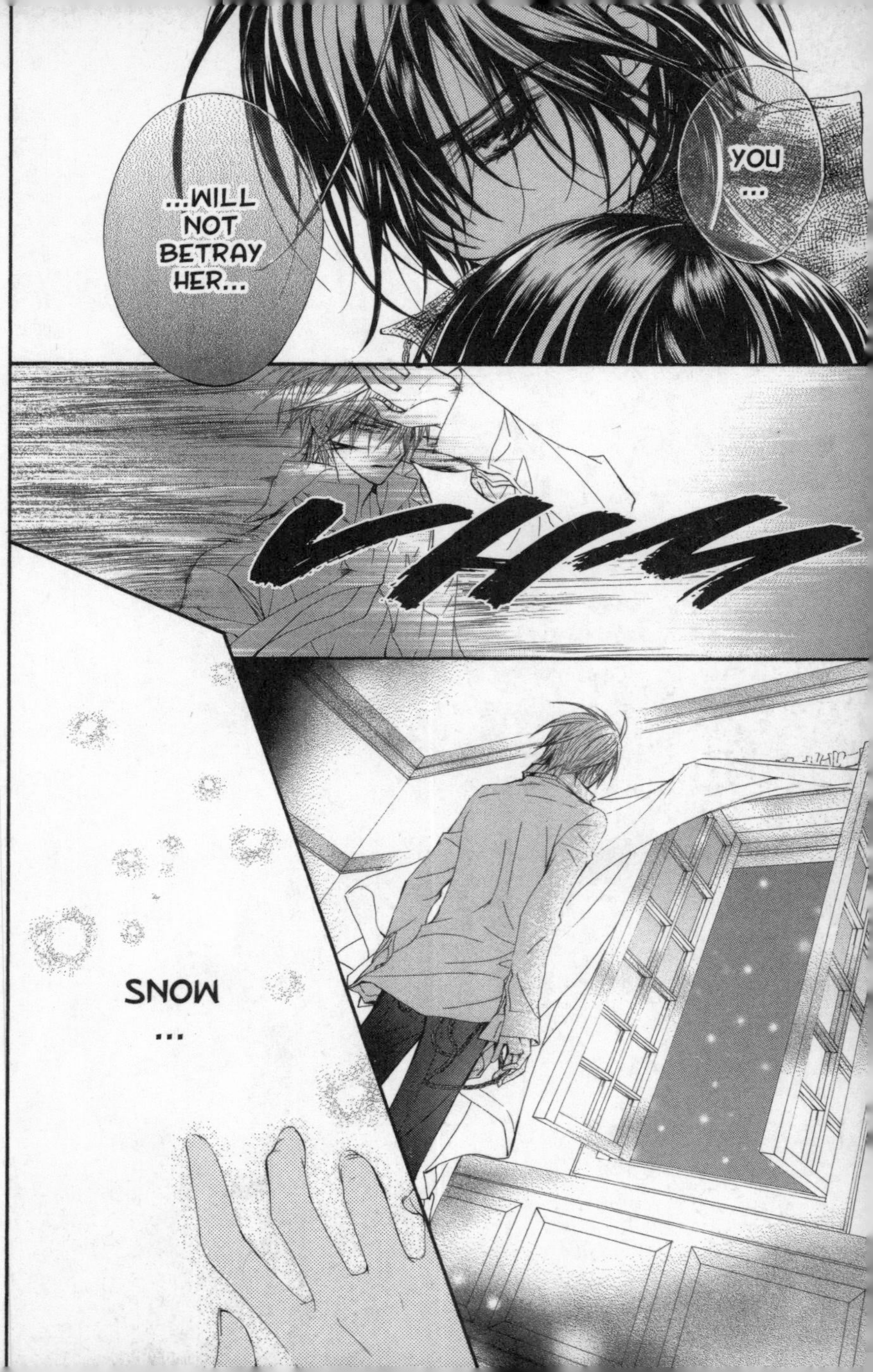
YOU ...
...WILL NOT BETRAY HER...
VHM
SNOW ...

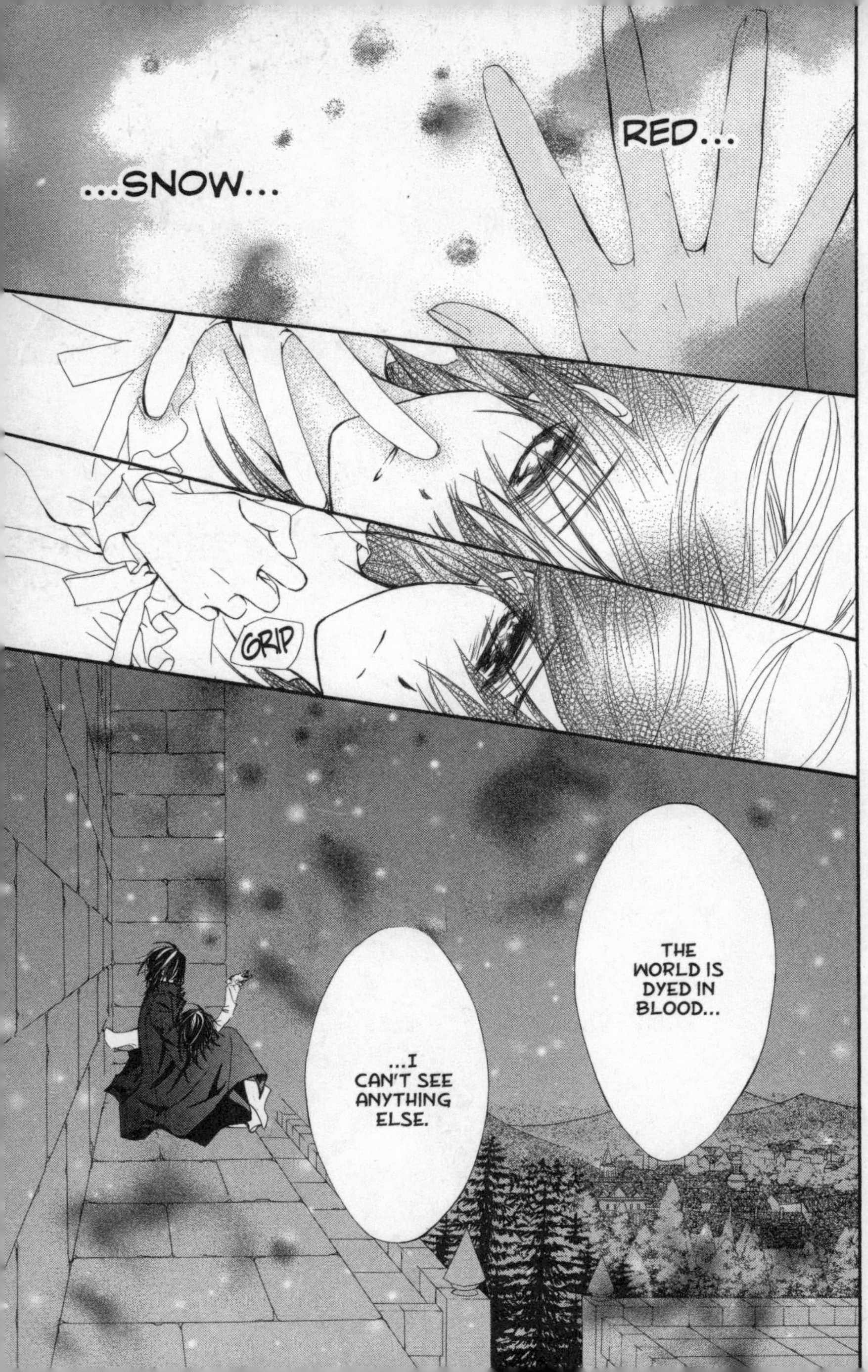
RED...
...SNOW...
GRIP
THE WORLD IS DYED IN BLOOD...
...I CAN'T SEE ANYTHING ELSE.

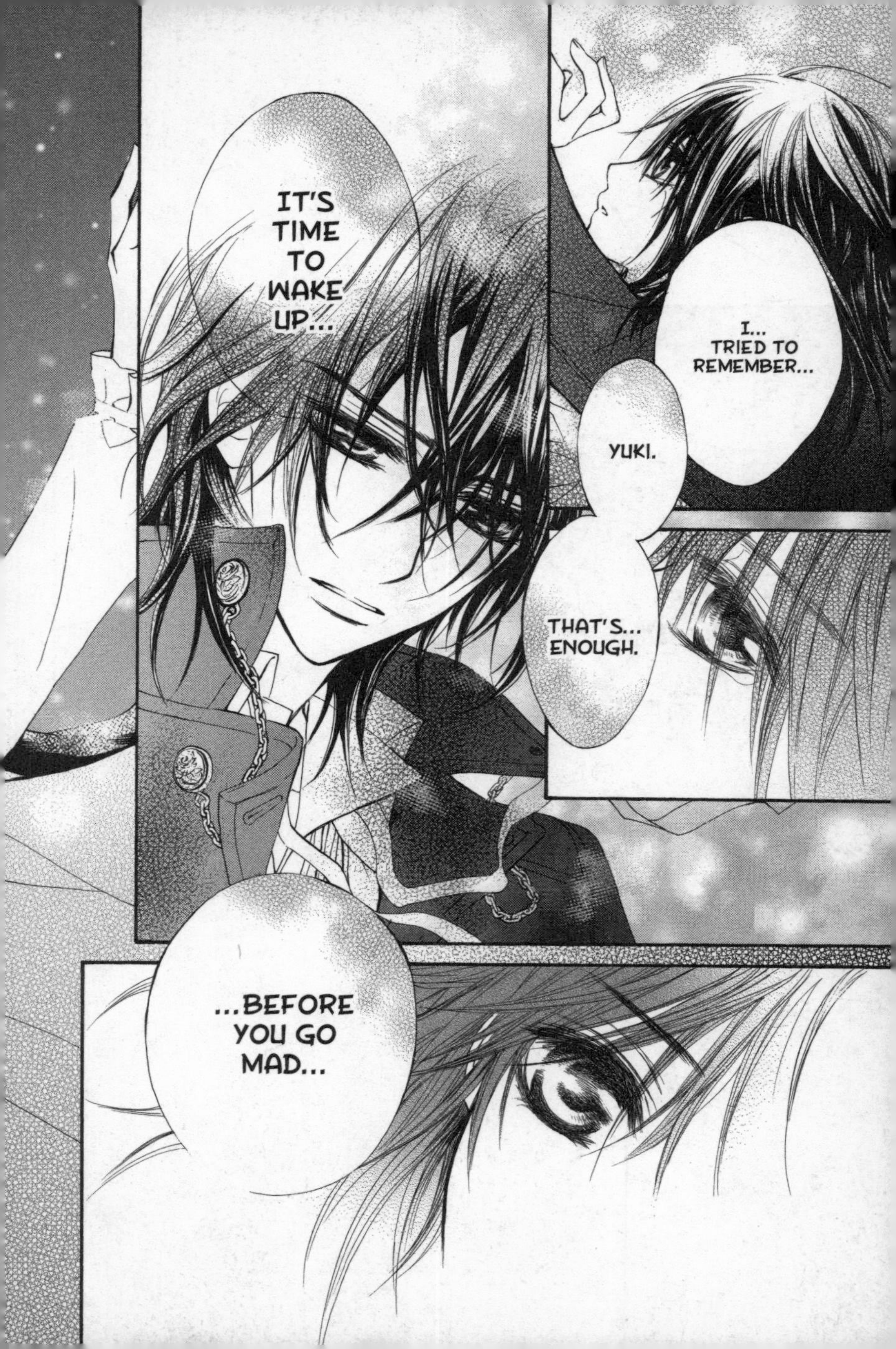
I... TRIED TO REMEMBER...
YUKI.
THAT'S... ENOUGH.
IT'S TIME TO WAKE UP...
...BEFORE YOU GO MAD...

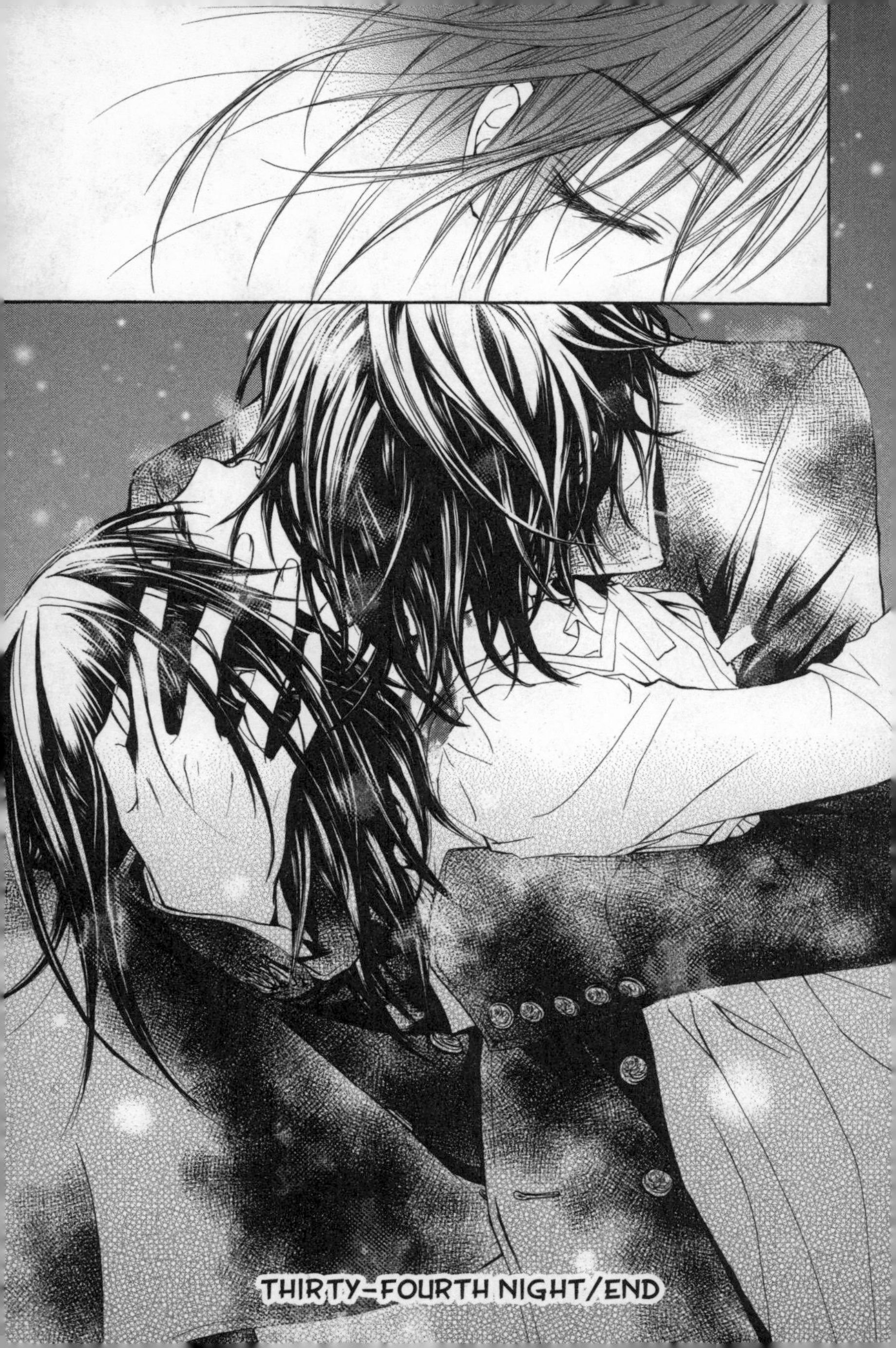
THIRTY-FOURTH NIGHT/END

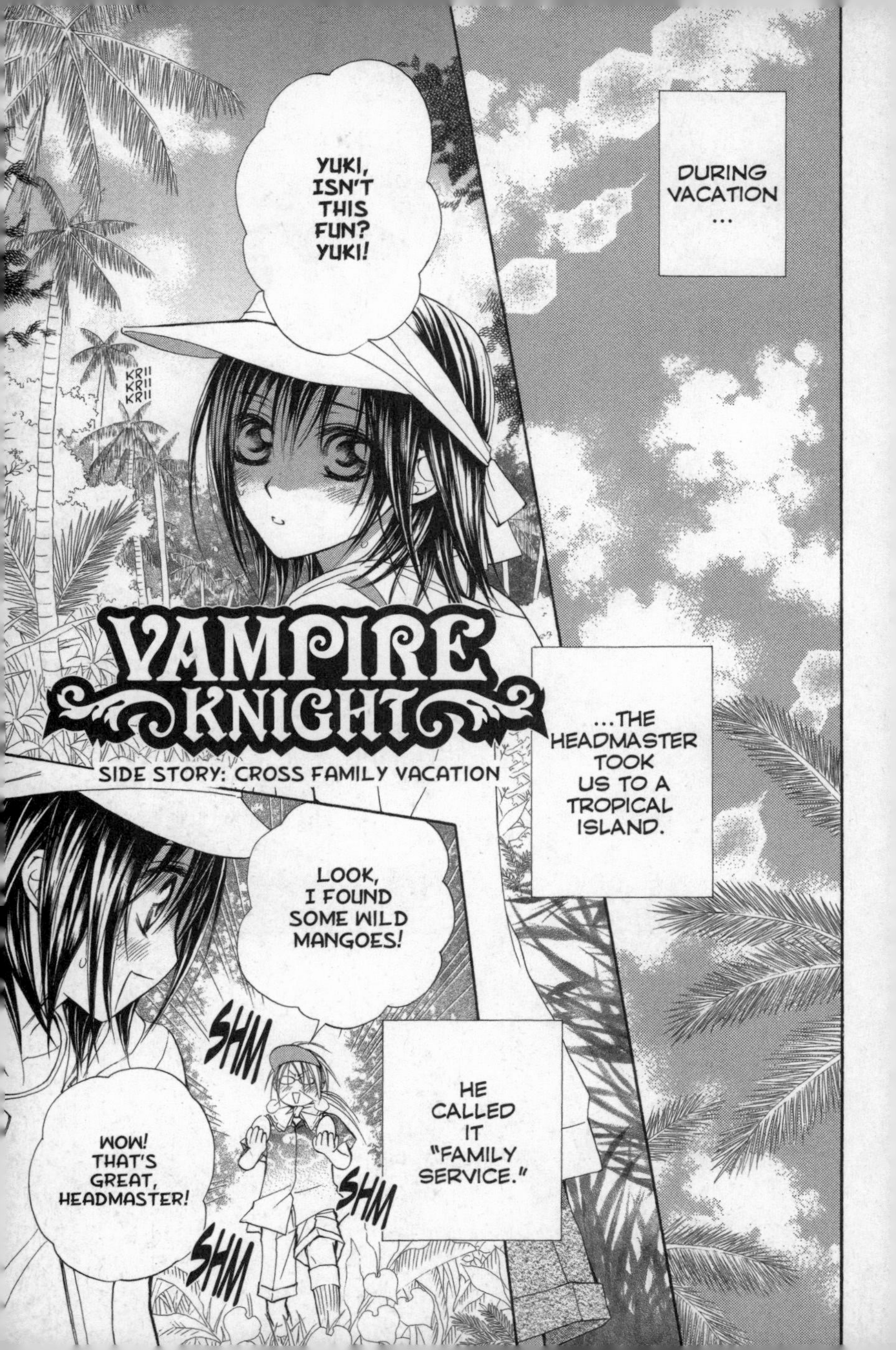
DURING VACATION ...
...THE HEADMASTER TOOK US TO A TROPICAL ISLAND.
YUKI, ISN'T THIS FUN? YUKI!
KRII KRII KRII
VAMPIRE KNIGHT
SIDE STORY: CROSS FAMILY VACATION
HE CALLED IT "FAMILY SERVICE."
LOOK, I FOUND SOME WILD MANGOES!
SHM
SHM
SHM
WOW! THAT'S GREAT, HEADMASTER!

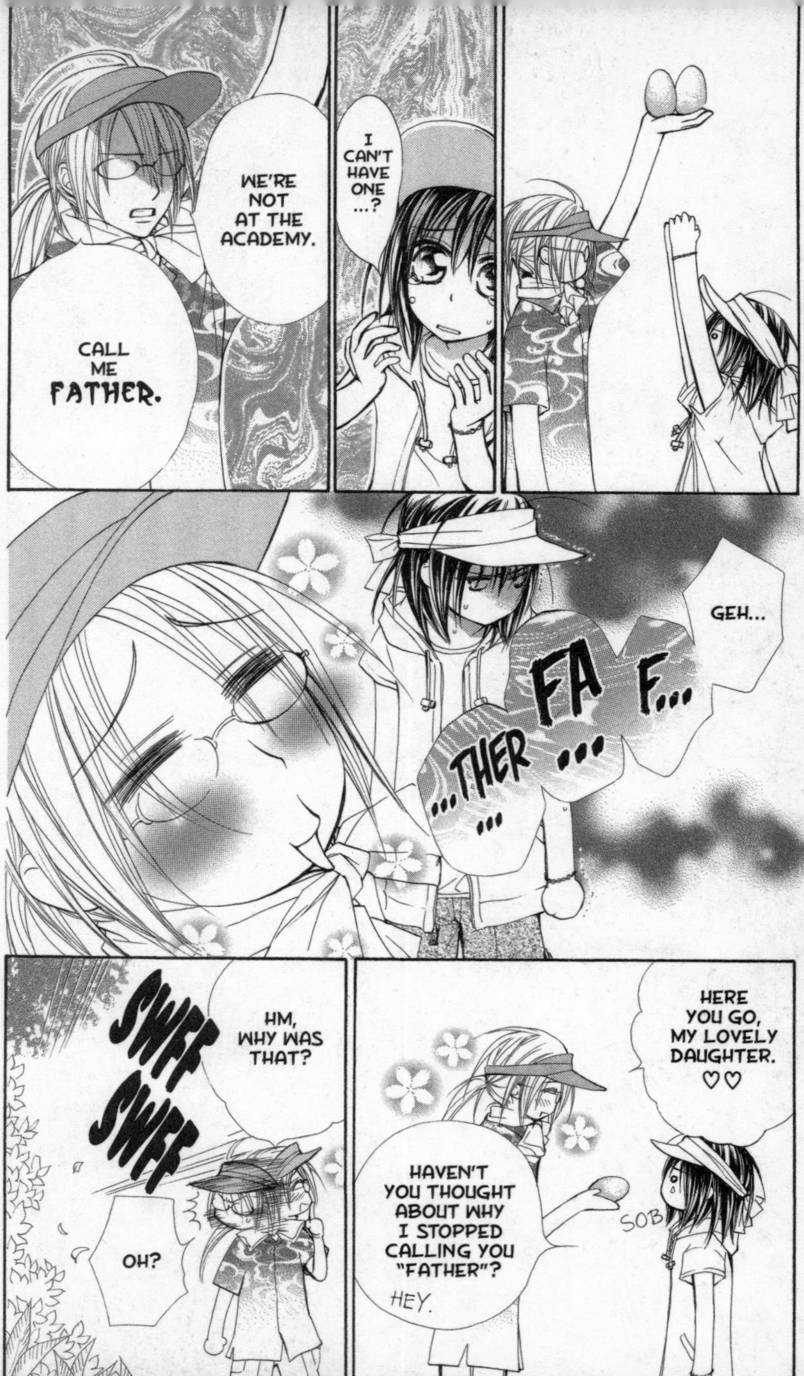
I CAN'T HAVE ONE ...?
WE'RE NOT AT THE ACADEMY.
CALL ME FATHER.
GEH...
FA F...
...THER ... ...
HERE YOU GO, MY LOVELY DAUGHTER. ♡♡
SOB
HAVEN'T YOU THOUGHT ABOUT WHY I STOPPED CALLING YOU "FATHER"?
HEY.
HM, WHY WAS THAT?
SWFF SWFF
OH?

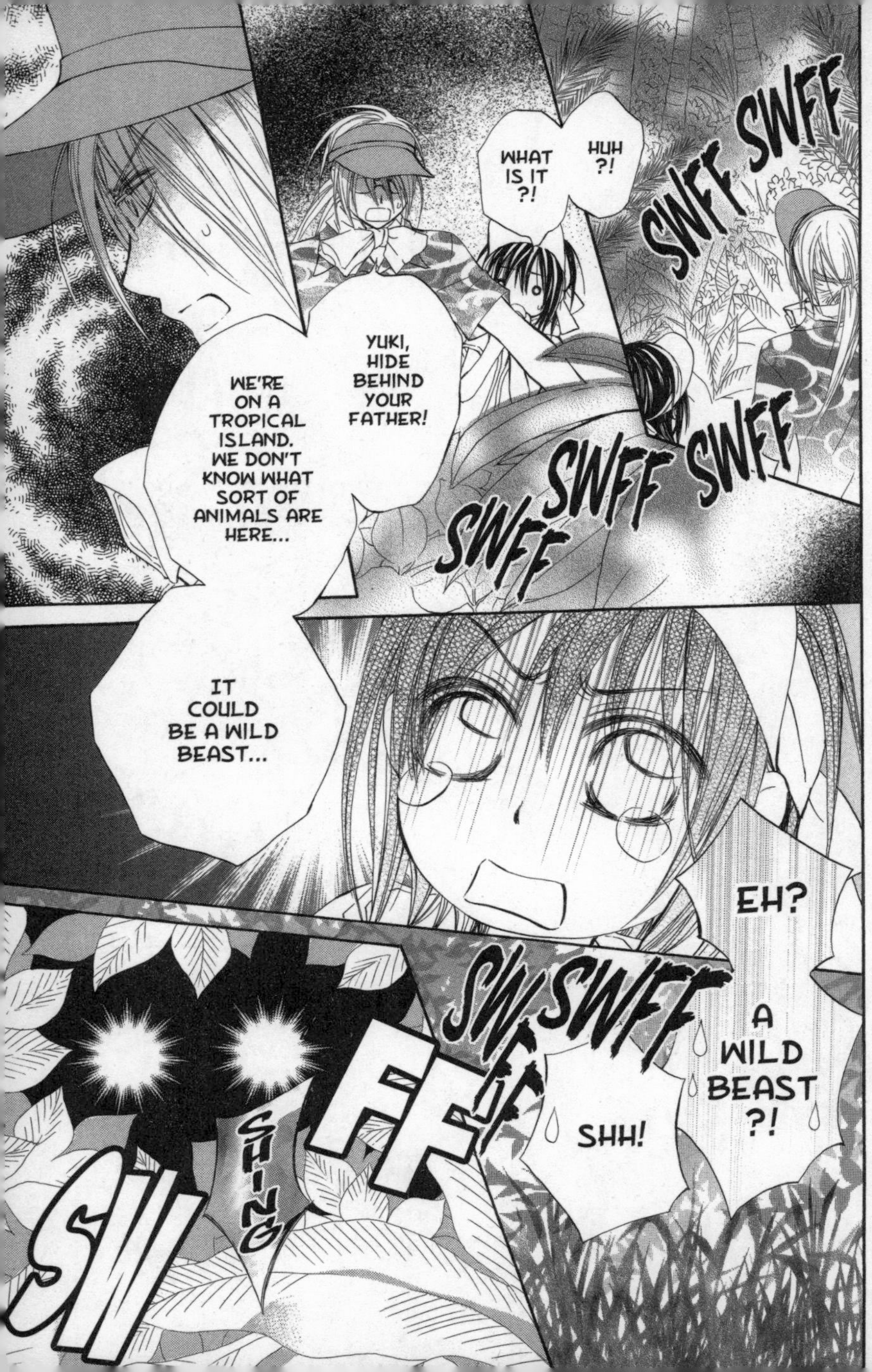

SWFF SWFF
HUH ?!
WHAT IS IT ?!
SWFF SWFF
YUKI, HIDE BEHIND YOUR FATHER!
WE'RE ON A TROPICAL ISLAND. WE DON'T KNOW WHAT SORT OF ANIMALS ARE HERE...
SWFF SWFF
IT COULD BE A WILD BEAST...
EH?
A WILD BEAST ?!
SHH!
SW SWFF
FF
SHING
SHH

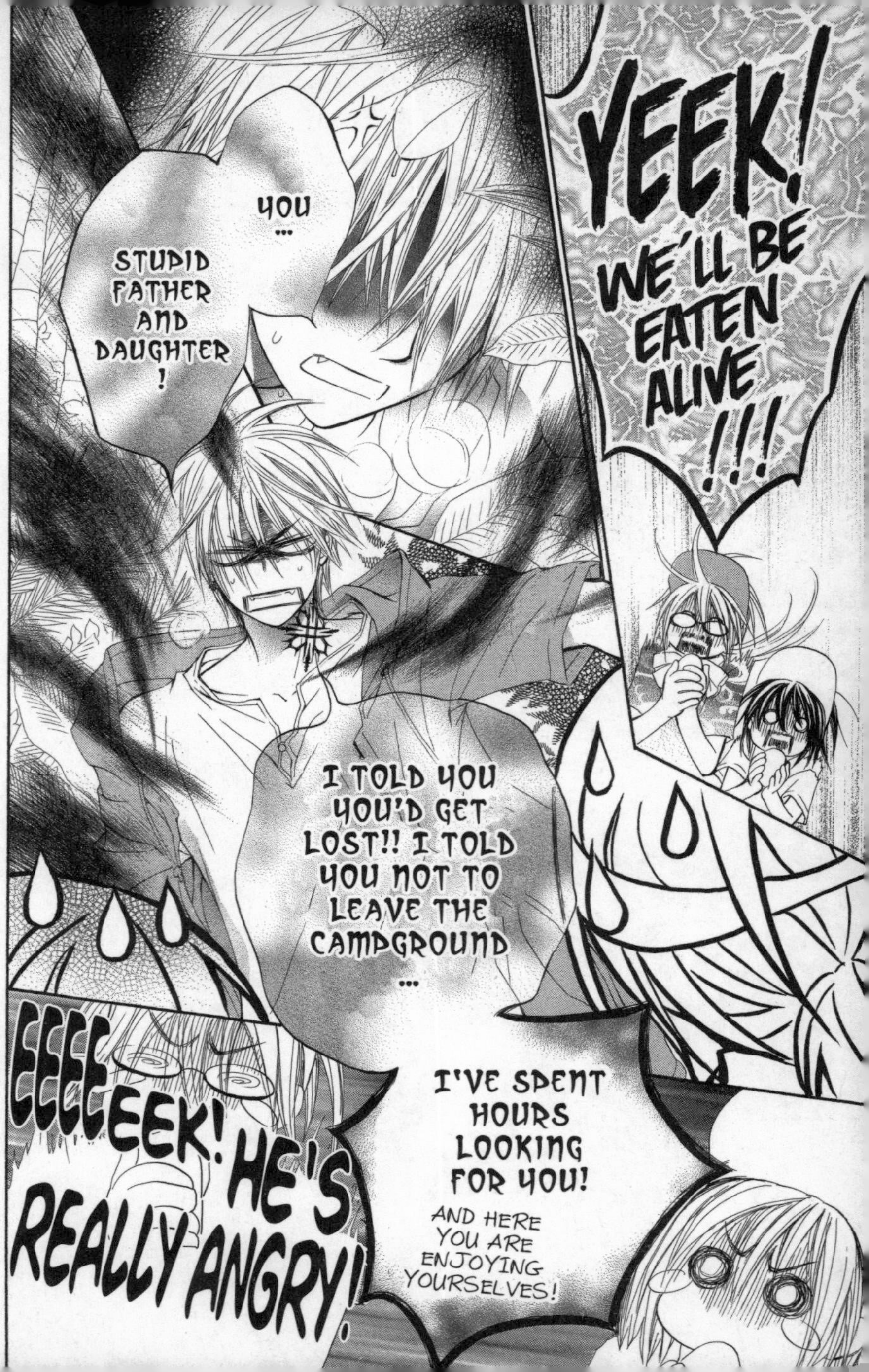

YEEK! WE'LL BE EATEN ALIVE!!!
YOU...
STUPID FATHER AND DAUGHTER!
I TOLD YOU YOU'D GET LOST!! I TOLD YOU NOT TO LEAVE THE CAMPGROUND...
I'VE SPENT HOURS LOOKING FOR YOU!
AND HERE YOU ARE ENJOYING YOURSELVES!
EEEEEEEEK! HE'S REALLY ANGRY!

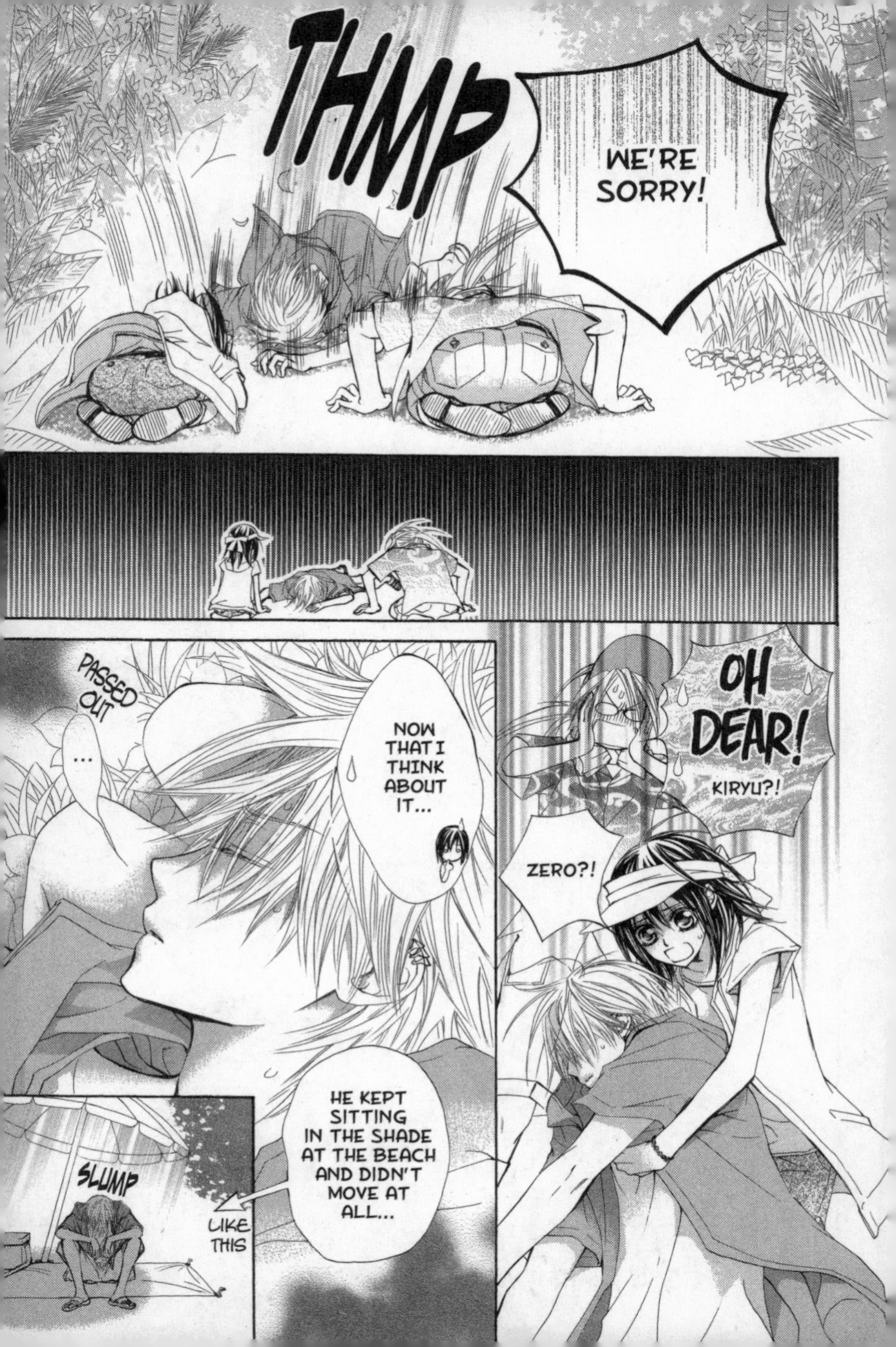
THMP
WE'RE SORRY!
OH DEAR!
KIRYU?!
ZERO?!
NOW THAT I THINK ABOUT IT...
PASSED OUT
...
HE KEPT SITTING IN THE SHADE AT THE BEACH AND DIDN'T MOVE AT ALL...
LIKE THIS
SLUMP

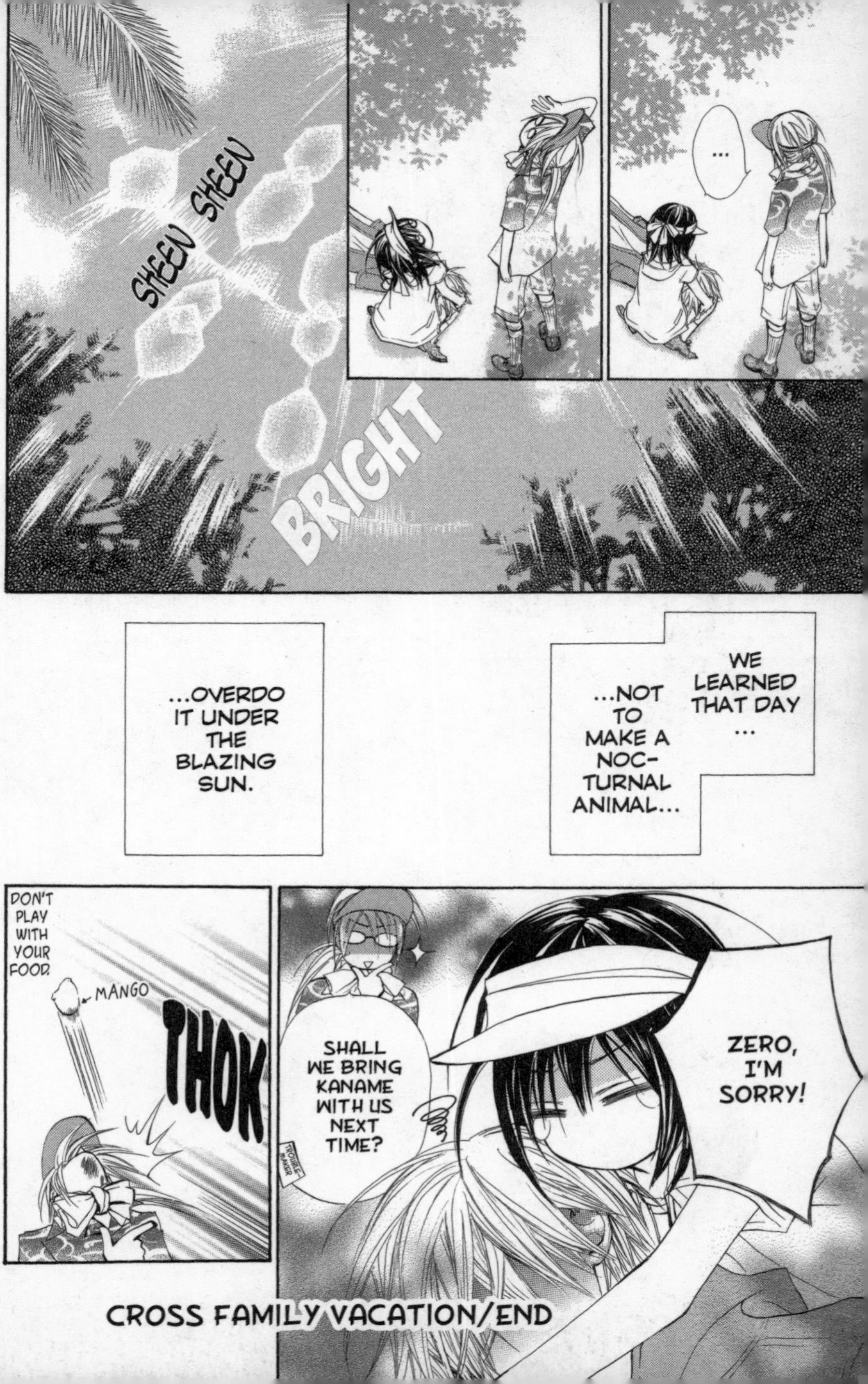
...
SHEEN SHEEN
BRIGHT
WE LEARNED THAT DAY ...
...NOT TO MAKE A NOC-TURNAL ANIMAL...
...OVERDO IT UNDER THE BLAZING SUN.
ZERO, I'M SORRY!
SHALL WE BRING KANAME WITH US NEXT TIME?
TROUBLE-MAKER
DON'T PLAY WITH YOUR FOOD.
MANGO
THOK

CROSS FAMILY VACATION/END

EDITOR'S NOTES

Characters

Matsuri Hino puts careful thought into the names of her characters in *Vampire Knight*. Below is the collection of characters through volume 7. Each character's name is presented family name first, per the kanji reading.

黒主優姫

Cross Yuki

Yuki's last name, *Kurosu*, is the Japanese pronunciation of the English word "cross." However, the kanji has a different meaning—*kuro* means "black" and *su* means "master." Her first name is a combination of *yuu*, meaning "tender" or "kind," and *ki*, meaning "princess."

錐生零

Kiryu Zero

Zero's first name is the kanji for *rei*, meaning "zero." In his last name, *Kiryu*, the *ki* means "auger" or "drill," and the *ryu* means "life."

玖蘭枢

Kuran Kaname

Kaname means "hinge" or "door." The kanji for his last name is a combination of the old-fashioned way of writing *ku*, meaning "nine," and *ran*, meaning "orchid": "nine orchids."

藍堂英

Aido Hanabusa

Hanabusa means "petals of a flower." *Aido* means "indigo temple." In Japanese, the pronunciation of *Aido* is very close to the pronunciation of the English word *idol*.

架院暁

Kain Akatsuki

Akatsuki means "dawn" or "daybreak." In *Kain*, *ka* is a base or support, while *in* denotes a building that has high fences around it, such as a temple or school.

早園瑠佳

Souen Ruka

In *Ruka*, the *ru* means "lapis lazuli" while the *ka* means "good-looking" or "beautiful." The *sou* in Ruka's surname, *Souen*, means "early," but this kanji also has an obscure meaning of "strong fragrance." The *en* means "garden."

一条拓麻

Ichijo Takuma

Ichijo can mean a "ray" or "streak." The kanji for *Takuma* is a combination of *taku*, meaning "to cultivate" and *ma*, which is the kanji for *asa*, meaning "hemp" or "flax," a plant with blue flowers.

支葵千里

Shiki Senri

Shiki's last name is a combination of *shi*, meaning "to support," and *ki*, meaning "mallow"—a flowering plant with pink or white blossoms. The *ri* in *Senri* is a traditional Japanese unit of measure for distance, and one *ri* is about 2.44 miles. *Senri* means "1,000 *ri*."

夜刈十牙
Yagari Toga

Yagari is a combination of *ya*, meaning "night," and *gari*, meaning "to harvest." *Toga* means "ten fangs."

一条麻遠，一翁
Ichijo Asato, aka "Ichio"

Ichijo can mean a "ray" or "streak." Asato's first name is comprised of *asa*, meaning "hemp" or "flax," and *tou*, meaning "far off." His nickname is *ichi*, or "one," combined with *ou*, which can be used as an honorific when referring to an older man.

若葉沙頼
Wakaba Sayori

Yori's full name is Sayori Wakaba. *Wakaba* means "young leaves." Her given name, *Sayori*, is a combination of *sa*, meaning "sand," and *yori*, meaning "trust."

星煉

Seiren

Sei means "star" and *ren* means
"to smelt" or "refine." *Ren* is also
the same kanji used in *rengoku*, or
"purgatory."

遠矢莉磨

Toya Rima

Toya means a "far-reaching arrow."
Rima's first name is a combination
of *ri*, or "jasmine," and *ma*, which
signifies enhancement by wearing
away, such as by polishing or
scouring.

紅まり亜

Kurenai Maria

Kurenai means "crimson." The kanji
for the last *a* in Maria's first name is
the same that is used in "Asia."

錐生壱縷
Kiryu Ichiru
Ichi is the old-fashioned way of writing "one," and *ru* means "thread."

緋桜閑, 狂咲姫
Hio Shizuka, Kuruizaki-hime
Shizuka means "calm and quiet." In Shizuka's family name, *hi* is "scarlet," and *ou* is "cherry blossoms." Shizuka Hio is also referred to as the "Kuruizaki-hime." *Kuruizaki* means "flowers blooming out of season," and *hime* means "princess."

藍堂月子
Aido Tsukiko
Aido means "indigo temple." *Tsukiko* means "moon child."

白蔍更
Shirabuki Sara

Shira is "white," and *buki* is "butterbur," a plant with white flowers. *Sara* means "renew."

黒主灰閻
Cross Kaien

Cross, or *Kurosu*, means "black master." Kaien is a combination of *kai*, meaning "ashes," and *en*, meaning "village gate." The kanji for *en* is also used for Enma, the ruler of the Underworld in Buddhist mythology.

玖蘭李土
Kuran Rido

Kuran means "nine orchids." In *Rido*, *ri* means "plum" and *do* means "earth."

Terms

-sama: The suffix *sama* is used in formal address for someone who ranks higher in the social hierarchy. The vampires call their leader "Kaname-sama" only when they are among their own kind.

Family service: *Kazoku service*, or "family service," is a common term that parents use when doing weekend or vacation activities with their family.

Matsuri Hino burst onto the manga scene with her series *Kono Yume ga Sametara* (When This Dream Is Over), which was published in *LaLa DX* magazine. Hino was a manga artist a mere nine months after she decided to become one.

With the success of her popular series *Captive Hearts* and *MeruPuri*, Hino has established herself as a major player in the world of shojo manga. *Vampire Knight* is currently serialized in *LaLa* and *Shojo Beat* magazines.

Hino enjoys creative activities and has commented that she would have been either an architect or an apprentice to traditional Japanese craft masters if she had not become a manga artist.

VAMPIRE KNIGHT
Vol. 7
The Shojo Beat Manga Edition

This manga contains material that was originally published in English in *Shojo Beat* magazine, December 2008–April 2009 issues. Artwork in the magazine may have been slightly altered from that presented here.

STORY AND ART BY
MATSURI HINO

Translation & English Adaptation/Tomo Kimura
Touch-up Art & Lettering/Rina Mapa
Graphic Design/Amy Martin
Editor/Nancy Thistlethwaite

VP, Production/Alvin Lu
VP, Publishing Licensing/Rika Inouye
VP, Sales & Product Marketing/Gonzalo Ferreyra
VP, Creative/Linda Espinosa
Publisher/Hyoe Narita

Printed in Canada

Published by VIZ Media, LLC
P.O. Box 77010
San Francisco, CA 94107

Shojo Beat Manga Edition
10 9 8 7 6 5 4 3 2 1
First printing, August 2009

store.viz.com

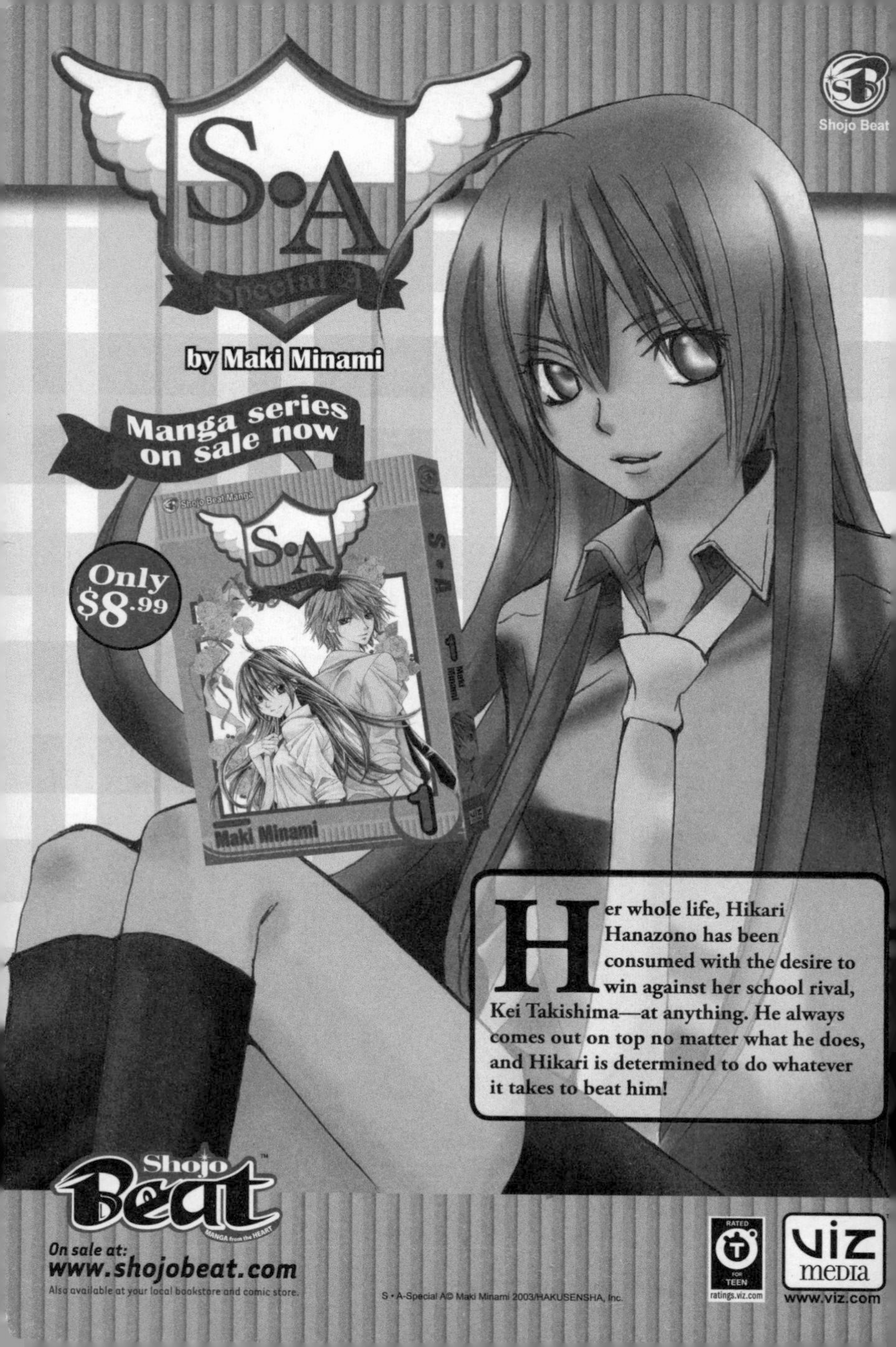
Shojo Beat
S•A
Special A
by Maki Minami
Manga series on sale now
Only $8.99
Shojo Beat Manga
S•A
Maki Minami
Her whole life, Hikari Hanazono has been consumed with the desire to win against her school rival, Kei Takishima—at anything. He always comes out on top no matter what he does, and Hikari is determined to do whatever it takes to beat him!
Shojo Beat
MANGA from the HEART
On sale at:
www.shojobeat.com
Also available at your local bookstore and comic store.
RATED T FOR TEEN
ratings.viz.com
VIZ media
www.viz.com

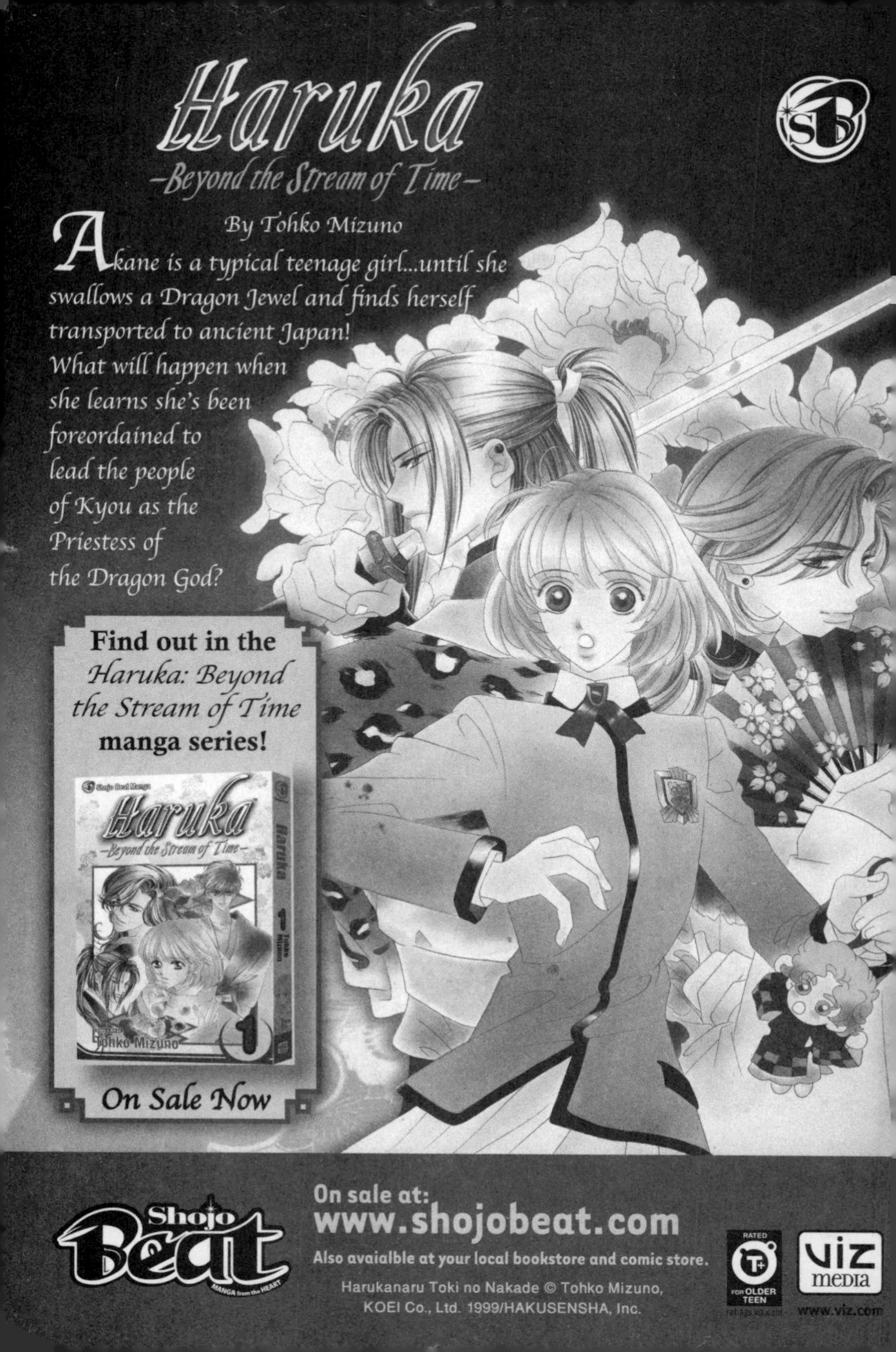
Haruka
-Beyond the Stream of Time-
By Tohko Mizuno
Akane is a typical teenage girl...until she swallows a Dragon Jewel and finds herself transported to ancient Japan! What will happen when she learns she's been foreordained to lead the people of Kyou as the Priestess of the Dragon God?
Find out in the Haruka: Beyond the Stream of Time manga series!
On Sale Now
On sale at:
www.shojobeat.com
Also avaialble at your local bookstore and comic store.
Harukanaru Toki no Nakade © Tohko Mizuno, KOEI Co., Ltd. 1999/HAKUSENSHA, Inc.
RATED T+ FOR OLDER TEEN
www.viz.com

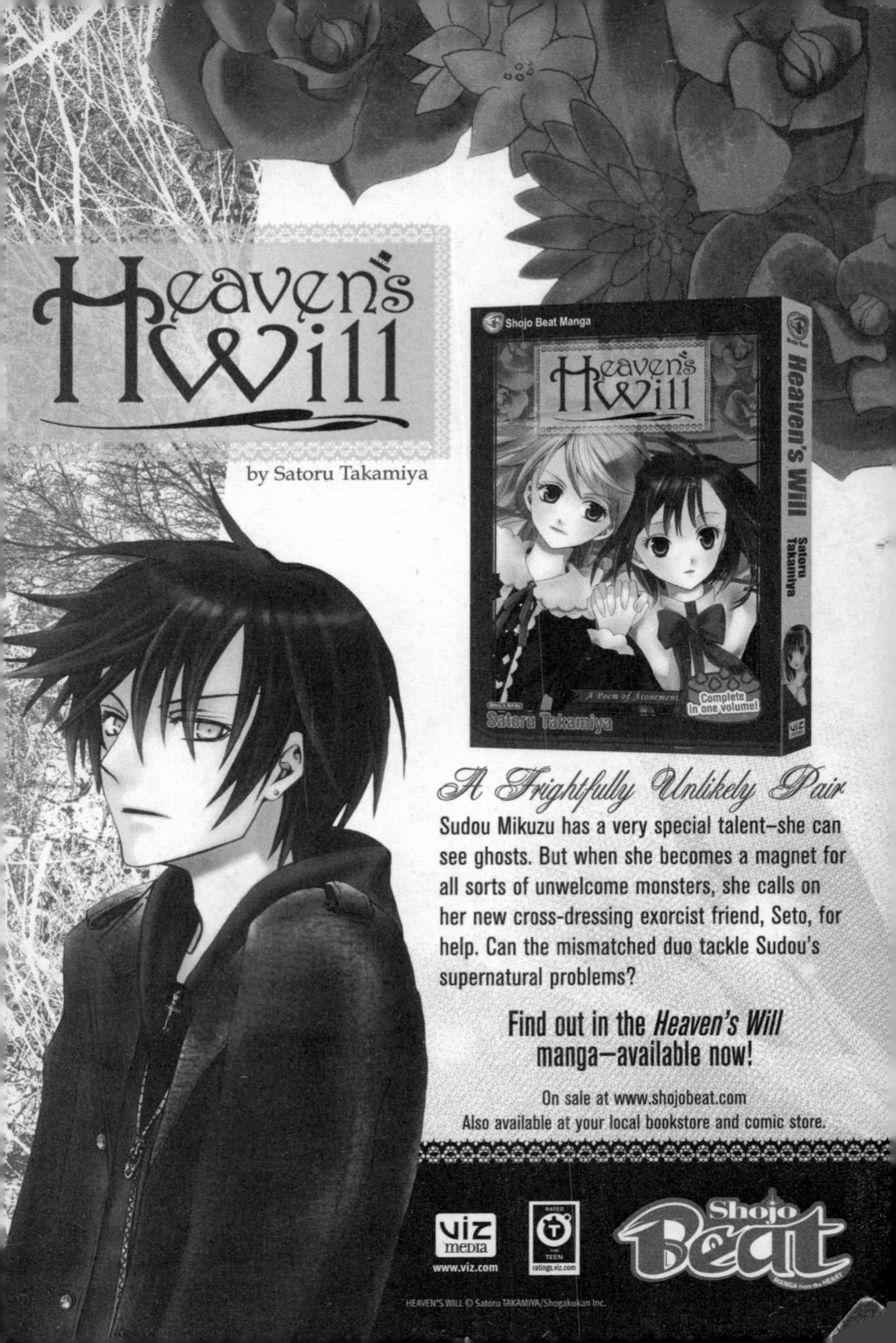
Heaven's Will
by Satoru Takamiya
Shojo Beat Manga
Heaven's Will
A Poem of Atonement
Complete in one volume!
Satoru Takamiya
Heaven's Will
Satoru Takamiya
A Frightfully Unlikely Pair
Sudou Mikuzu has a very special talent–she can see ghosts. But when she becomes a magnet for all sorts of unwelcome monsters, she calls on her new cross-dressing exorcist friend, Seto, for help. Can the mismatched duo tackle Sudou's supernatural problems?
Find out in the Heaven's Will manga—available now!
On sale at www.shojobeat.com
Also available at your local bookstore and comic store.
VIZ MEDIA
www.viz.com
RATED T FOR TEEN
ratings.viz.com
Shojo Beat
MANGA from the HEART
HEAVEN'S WILL © Satoru TAKAMIYA/Shogakukan Inc.

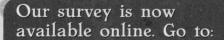